# SHEIKH ABDULLAH

INDIAN LIVES

A series edited and curated by Ramachandra Guha

*Ashoka: Portrait of a Philosopher King* by Patrick Olivelle

Forthcoming volumes:
Nico Slate on Kamaladevi Chattopadhyay
Akshaya Mukul on Jayaprakash Narayan
Aparna Kapadia on Kasturba Gandhi
Richard Jaffe on the Buddha
Srinath Raghavan on Subramanyan Chandrasekhar
Abhishek Kaicker on Anand Ram 'Mukhlis'
Harish Damodaran on Ramkrishna Dalmia
Prashant Kidambi on Bal Gangadhar Tilak
Richard Davis on Rajaraja Chola

Indian Lives has been made possible through the generous support of
Bajaj Auto Ltd and the late Rahul Bajaj
Forbes Marshall
R.G. Manudhane Foundation for Excellence

INDIAN LIVES

# SHEIKH ABDULLAH

## *The* Caged Lion *of* Kashmir

CHITRALEKHA ZUTSHI

4th
*An Imprint of* HarperCollins *Publishers*

First published in India by Fourth Estate 2024
An imprint of HarperCollins *Publishers*
4th Floor, Tower A, Building No. 10, DLF Cyber City,
DLF Phase II, Gurugram, Haryana – 122002
www.harpercollins.co.in

2 4 6 8 10 9 7 5 3 1



P-ISBN: 978-93-5699-604-5
E-ISBN: 978-93-5699-605-2



Typeset in 11.5/15.2 Crimson Text at
Manipal Technologies Limited, Manipal

Printed and bound at
Thomson Press (India) Ltd

MIX
Paper from responsible sources
FSC® C010615

This book is produced from independently certified FSC® paper to ensure responsible forest management.

*In memory of*
*Dr R.K. Zutshi*
*(1932–2021)*
*and*
*for my sons,*
*Nikhil & Jahan*

# Contents


*Series Editor's Foreword* ix

*Timeline of Major Events* xv

*Introduction: The Lion of Kashmir* xxv

1. First among Equals, 1905–1934 1
2. Defining the Leader and the Movement, 1935–1946 40
3. From Revolutionary to Prime Minister, 1946–1951 71
4. The Turning Point, 1952–1953 105
5. Reprising the Role of Revolutionary, 1953–1958 136
6. On Trial, 1958–1965 164
7. Coming to Terms, 1965–1974 193
8. The Final Stand, 1975–1982 228

*Epilogue: The Legacy* 255

*Acknowledgements* 265

*Notes* 269

*Bibliography* 309

*Index* 321

# Series Editor's Foreword

*Ramachandra Guha*

I HAVE LONG BELIEVED THAT EVERY HISTORIAN MUST, AT SOME STAGE of her career, try her hand at writing a biography. It provides different, and in some respects more exciting, challenges than crafting works of social or political history. I was, therefore, greatly interested to learn, about a decade ago, that the pre-eminent historian of modern Kashmir, Chitralekha Zutshi, was researching the life of Sheikh Abdullah. Zutshi had already published major works of political, cultural and religious history relating to Kashmir. I looked forward to reading her analysis of the life and legacy of the most influential and controversial Kashmiri of his time.

Now the final manuscript is with us, and it lives up to the high standards set by its author. Zutshi's biography of Sheikh Abdullah draws on many years of rigorous research. The range of sources is deeply impressive—they include Abdullah's speeches, his published and unpublished writings, the correspondence and writings of his colleagues and contemporaries, press reports, state records, material in private hands and focused interviews. These sources are in several different languages too. This vast array of primary materials is brought together in a finely crafted work of scholarship that provides an authoritative and richly readable account of Sheikh Abdullah's life and legacy. While focusing on Abdullah, Zutshi brings to bear her training as a social and political historian, such that through this story of a singular individual we learn an enormous amount about the contested histories of Kashmir, India and Pakistan.

Sheikh Abdullah was born in 1905 into a family of modest means. His early life in the Valley of Kashmir was a struggle, made more difficult by the absence of his father, who had passed away before his birth. College education in Lahore and Aligarh expanded his intellectual and political horizons—as, albeit in different ways, travel and education overseas had done for his older contemporaries B.R. Ambedkar and Jawaharlal Nehru. In Lahore, Abdullah could talk freely about politics with members of the Kashmiri diaspora—such open discussion was not, at that time, feasible within the stifling autocratic atmosphere of the princely state itself. At Aligarh Muslim University he took a master's degree in science, and also had the opportunity of hearing nationalist leaders who came to speak there, including Mahatma Gandhi.

Abdullah's public life extended for more than fifty years, from the early 1930s until his death in 1982. It went through many twists and turns, and was never without incident or controversy. Zutshi captures the various phases of his political career with deftness and authority. Of the first phase, when he was a mass leader, she writes that his being in and out of jail served to increase his popularity—thus, 'each turn in prison endowed him with greater political power and an almost messianic status, as people came to pay obeisance at his home much like they did in the shrines of Kashmir's saints'.

Zutshi's biography next takes us through the tumultuous years of Independence and Partition, when an armed conflict broke out between India and Pakistan over who would possess the princely state of Jammu and Kashmir. She closely examines the period from 1948 to 1953, when Abdullah served at the head of the administration of Jammu and Kashmir. She speaks of his achievements, such as a programme of land reform which 'ended tenancy and debt bondage among the peasantry and instantly made them landholders', and, on the other side, of his arbitrary, capricious and intensely personalized style of administration. As she writes, in words that apply to much more than the Kashmir of the early

1950s, 'Abdullah's regime came to embody that vision of democracy in which a supreme authoritarian leader gives voice to the popular will without the intercession of institutions such as political parties, unions, and the press.'

During this period he began to harbour dreams—or fantasies—of bringing about an independent Kashmir with the possible assistance of Western powers. This, coupled with the growing discontenment with and within his administration, led to an internal coup supported by the Indian government that removed him from office and placed him under arrest in August 1953. Abdullah spent much of the next two decades in prison, under house arrest, or in forced exile from his homeland. Zutshi shows how the incarceration once more made him a popular hero; thus, 'to the younger generation coming of age in the late 1950s and 1960s Kashmir, the figure of an incarcerated Abdullah was to take on a powerful symbolism'.

The narrative arc of the biography culminates in the last stage of Abdullah's life, when advancing age and the realization that the Indian state would never allow for a plebiscite that could go in favour of Pakistan or an autonomous Kashmir led to his forging a rapprochement with Prime Minister Indira Gandhi. In 1975, he took charge for a last spell as Chief Minister of Jammu and Kashmir. By now, Abdullah had lost a great deal of credibility among his fellow Kashmiris. All his old political associates had either died or broken ties with him, and he was 'left surrounded by sycophants and family members, most of whom had solely their own interests at heart'. As Zutshi remarks, 'by the end of his life Abdullah was in an uneasy truce with the centre, but at the cost of burning all bridges with his own people'.

Abdullah was already in his early forties when India and Pakistan were created; and he was to live another thirty-five years. His life's trajectory, thus, neatly bridges the colonial and the postcolonial; princely India and British India; the province and the nation; the periphery and the centre.

Reading Zutshi's book, one sees Abdullah's life as both distinctive and representative. His political career began with hope, idealism and courage. As a young man, his energy, ambition and oratorical prowess captured the zeitgeist, the yearning of the young Kashmiri for political and personal freedom and for an end to poverty and discrimination. The beginning promised much, yet the career ended in careerism, nepotism and perhaps failure. Like so many other politicians, past and present, Abdullah was more effective and appealing as an agitator mobilizing a popular movement than as an administrator seeking to steer the ship of state.

Zutshi adroitly illuminates the paradoxes and contradictions that Abdullah's politics exemplified and which he could never fully resolve. She writes that Abdullah 'wanted to be both a Muslim leader as well a secular, nationalist one, but succeeded in being neither'. She further observes that 'in Abdullah's nationalist discourse, the Kashmiri nation was synonymous with the Valley'. His political rhetoric and political choices willy-nilly led to a growing rift between the Valley and the Jammu region, with repercussions that linger till this day.

Among the most admirable aspects of Zutshi's book is her treatment of the secondary characters who made and unmade Sheikh Abdullah. Indian biographers tend to focus narrowly and obsessively on one individual, whom they have usually come to praise (or, much more rarely, to condemn). Zutshi, on the other hand, understands that a life is lived in relation to other lives. She provides portraits of those individuals with whom Abdullah had important dealings, inside and outside Kashmir—colleagues like Mirza Afzal Beg, rivals like Ghulam Abbas, colleagues-turned-critics like P.N. Bazaz, national leaders such as Nehru, Indira and Jayaprakash Narayan. Through her depiction of his relationships with these individuals, Abdullah himself comes vividly alive.

Zutshi also skilfully uses Abdullah's life to illuminate the history of twentieth-century Kashmir as a whole. As she remarks, for the historian, Abdullah's personal journey is 'a critical prism through which to understand the intertwined histories of twentieth-century Kashmir and India, along with the ambiguities and inconsistencies in their national projects'.

In her introduction, Zutshi writes of how 'the scholarship on late colonial and postcolonial India ... shies away from biographies in general—other than of figures such as Nehru, Gandhi, Subhas Bose, and more recently, B.R. Ambedkar—with little regard for regional leaders such as Abdullah, who played an outsized role in influencing the course of centre–region relations in the subcontinent.' Her own work superbly addresses this lacuna with regard to Sheikh Abdullah. Perhaps it will inspire similarly rigorously researched biographies of figures such as Master Tara Singh, A.Z. Phizo and E.S. Namboodiripad, often mistakenly seen as merely 'regional' leaders, but who, like Abdullah himself, had a deep and enduring influence on the course of modern Indian history as a whole.

# Timeline of Major Events

1846: Creation of the princely state of Jammu and Kashmir (J&K) through the Treaty of Amritsar between the British East India Company and Dogra Raja Gulab Singh, who becomes the first Maharaja of the state.

1857: Maharaja Ranbir Singh ascends the throne of J&K.

1885: Maharaja Pratap Singh ascends the throne of J&K; Indian National Congress founded in British India.

1905: Birth of Sheikh Muhammad Abdullah in Soura.

1906: All India Muslim League founded in British India.

1920–1922: M.K. Gandhi leads Non-Cooperation Movement against British rule.

1919–1924: Indian Muslims organize Khilafat Movement against British imperialism.

1923: Chaudhuri Ghulam Abbas establishes Youngmen's Muslim Association in Jammu.

1924: Srinagar Silk Factory workers strike; Kashmiri Muslims present memorial to Viceroy Lord Reading; Sheikh Abdullah leaves for Lahore.

1925: Maharaja Hari Singh ascends the throne of J&K; Communist Party of India founded in British India.

1929: Albion Banerjee, ex-prime minister of J&K, issues statement regarding condition of Kashmiri Muslims in the state; Congress passes Purna Swaraj resolution in its Lahore session.

1930: Gandhi launches the Civil Disobedience Movement; Sheikh Abdullah returns to Kashmir from Aligarh.

1931: Beginning of Muslim agitation against Dogra rule and the appointment of the B.J. Glancy Commission by the Maharaja to address the people's concerns and demands.

1932: Founding of the All Jammu and Kashmir Muslim Conference (MC) under the presidentship of Sheikh Abdullah.

1934: First elections in J&K and the founding of the Praja Sabha (People's Assembly).

1937: First provincial elections in British India and the establishment of provincial governments led by Indians.

1939: Outbreak of the Second World War and the resignation of provincial governments; MC converted to the All Jammu and Kashmir National Conference (NC) under Sheikh Abdullah's leadership.

1940: Muslim League adopts the Lahore Resolution, or declaration of the independence of Pakistan.

1941: Revival of MC under leadership of Chaudhuri Ghulam Abbas.

1942: Indian National Congress launches the Quit India Movement.

1944: NC adopts the Naya Kashmir Manifesto at its annual session.

1945: Second World War ends; second provincial elections in British India.

1946: Sheikh Abdullah elected vice-president of the All India States' People's Conference; Cabinet Mission visits India to discuss its constitutional future; Sheikh Abdullah launches the Quit Kashmir agitation, is arrested and imprisoned; Constituent Assembly of India founded to draft the Indian constitution.

1947: **June**—Partition plan announced; **August**—Punjab and Bengal partitioned to create the dominions of India and Pakistan; **September**—Sheikh Abdullah released; **September–October**—rebellion in Poonch and Gilgit against Maharaja Hari Singh gathers force; **October–November**—Pukhtoon tribesmen invade J&K's territory; Hari Singh signs document of accession to India leading to the arrival of the Indian Army into J&K and the Maharaja's departure from the state; first Indo-Pak war over the state commences; Sheikh Abdullah assumes role of the head of the emergency administration; All Jammu and Kashmir Praja Parishad (PP) founded by Balraj Madhok.

1948: India refers Pakistan's actions in J&K to the United Nations (UN); Sheikh Abdullah sworn in as prime minister of the state; he defends India's claim over Kashmir at the UN meeting on Kashmir at Lake Success, NY, as part of the Indian delegation; United Nations Commission on India and Pakistan (UNCIP) visits India and Pakistan on a fact-finding mission, submits ceasefire and truce proposals to both countries.

1949: India and Pakistan ratify the Ceasefire Line but reject the UNCIP's truce proposals; Indo-Pak ceasefire comes into effect on 1 January; Hari Singh relinquishes throne of J&K, and his son, Karan Singh, is appointed regent.

1950: Indian constituent assembly disbanded and the Indian constitution, which includes Article 370 that grants J&K special status, adopted; UN continues deliberations on the Kashmir issue and appoints Owen Dixon as mediator; Dixon submits his proposal, which is accepted by Pakistan and rejected by India; Sheikh Abdullah's government passes the Big Landed Estates Abolition Act.

1951: Constituent assembly elections in J&K; boycotted by the PP, 72 NC members elected unopposed; assembly convenes in October and sets about framing the state's constitution.

1952: Congress emerges victorious in the first Indian general elections, and Jawaharlal Nehru formally assumes the office of India's first elected prime minister; J&K constituent assembly elects Karan Singh as Sadar-i-Riyasat of the state; Delhi Agreement between the Indian centre and J&K state leadership announced; Jamaat-i-Islami Jammu and Kashmir founded; PP, with the support of the Jan Sangh, begins agitation against Sheikh Abdullah's government.

1953: Kashmir Political Conference founded by G.M. Karra; Jan Sangh leader S.P. Mookerjee dies in Srinagar while in custody of the J&K government; PP agitation continues; Sheikh Abdullah removed from power and placed under arrest; Bakshi Ghulam Muhammad sworn in as prime minister of J&K.

1954: Abdullah continues his incarceration at Kud sub-jail, Jammu; J&K constituent assembly adopts the provisions of the Delhi Agreement; the president of India issues order extending Indian citizenship to all residents of the state as well as inserting Article 35A into the Indian constitution granting special rights to state residents; Pakistan signs mutual defence treaty with the United States of America.

1955: Russian leaders Nikita Khrushchev and Nikolai Bulganin visit India and affirm J&K's status as an integral part of India; J&K Plebiscite Front (PF) founded under the leadership of Mirza Afzal Beg.

1956: J&K constituent assembly adopts a constitution for the state that accepts J&K as an integral part of the Indian Union, and passes a motion to dissolve itself.

1957: First state assembly elections; NC wins and Bakshi elected prime minister of J&K; Leftists within NC defect to form the Democratic National Conference (DNC); second Indian general elections held; Congress wins and Nehru begins his second term as prime minister.

1958: Sheikh Abdullah released in January, re-arrested in April; J&K government and the Government of India lodge Conspiracy Case against Sheikh Abdullah, Mirza Afzal Beg and twenty-five others; accused moved to special jail in Jammu; Indian parliament passes Armed Forces Special Powers Act, which is made applicable to the Naga Hills.

1960: NC and DNC reunite; the Conspiracy Case continues as Abdullah and Beg present their statements to the court.

1962: Third Indian general elections held; Nehru re-elected as India's prime minister; second J&K legislative assembly elections take place and Bakshi re-elected as prime minister of J&K; Sino-Indian War breaks out and India loses Aksai Chin to China; India and Pakistan begin six rounds of bilateral talks on Kashmir; Conspiracy Case drags on.

1963: Bilateral talks end in failure; Bakshi Ghulam Muhammad resigns under Kamaraj Plan and Shamsuddin becomes prime minister of J&K; Kashmir Valley rises up in protest as holy relic (hair of the Prophet Muhammad) disappears from Hazratbal shrine.

1964: Holy relic returns to Hazratbal; Awami Action Committee founded under Mirwaiz Farooq's leadership; G.M. Sadiq becomes prime minister of J&K; conspiracy charges against Abdullah, Afzal Beg and others dropped, leading to their release; Sheikh Abdullah meets with Nehru and visits Pakistan; Nehru passes away and Lal Bahadur Shastri takes over as prime minister of India; Sadiq merges NC with Congress, forming the Pradesh Congress; Abdullah issues call for boycott of Pradesh Congress and its members.

1965: Sheikh Abdullah leaves India to perform hajj and travel, meets Chinese premier; returns and is arrested and transferred to Ootacamund, followed by Kodaikanal; offices of prime minister and Sadar-i-Riyasat of J&K changed to chief minister (assumed by Sadiq) and governor (assumed by Karan Singh) respectively; Pakistan sends infiltrators into J&K, leading to second Indo-Pak war; status quo continues after ceasefire signed in late September.

1966: India and Pakistan sign a peace treaty known as the Tashkent Declaration; Shastri passes away in Tashkent; Indira Gandhi assumes office of prime minister of India; Abdullah continues his externment in Kodaikanal.

1967: Fourth Indian general elections held; Congress wins and Mrs Gandhi continues as prime minister; third legislative assembly elections held in J&K; Pradesh Congress wins and Sadiq continues as chief minister; Sheikh Abdullah moved to bungalow in Delhi to continue house arrest, where he meets with T.N. Kaul to discuss options for J&K.

1968: Sheikh Abdullah released from house arrest in January, free to travel in India; returns to Srinagar in March and organizes the State People's Convention, held in October.

1969: PF announces its intent to contest bye-elections and panchayati elections in J&K as well as the next general elections.

1970: Second State People's Convention held in Srinagar; Congress party splits into two, with Indira Gandhi forming her own Congress organization.

1971: PF banned and Sheikh Abdullah externed from the state; fifth general elections held in India, won in a landslide by Indira Gandhi's wing of the Congress; insurgency in East Pakistan and Indo-Pak war leads to the creation of Bangladesh; G.M. Sadiq dies and is succeeded by Mir Qasim as chief minister of J&K.

1972: Indira Gandhi arrives at an understanding with Sheikh Abdullah and he returns to Srinagar; Beg–Parthasarathy talks begin; India and Pakistan sign Shimla Agreement.

1974: Beg–Parthasarathy talks continue; Sheikh Abdullah inaugurates third State People's Convention in Srinagar.

1975: Indira–Sheikh (Kashmir) Accord signed; Mir Qasim steps down and Sheikh Abdullah assumes office of chief minister of J&K; PF dissolved and NC revived under Sheikh Abdullah's leadership; Indira Gandhi declares a state of Emergency.

1977: Sixth Indian general elections hand the Janata Party a resounding victory at the polls and Morarji Desai assumes office of prime minister; Sheikh Abdullah's government dissolved and fresh assembly elections held in J&K, handing victory to the NC and Sheikh Abdullah against the Janata alliance; the Jammu Kashmir Liberation Front (JKLF) founded in Britain.

1978: Afzal Beg forced to resign from the NC and his position as deputy chief minister; Sheikh Abdullah's government passes the Jammu and Kashmir Public Safety Act.

1979: Janata government falls and fresh elections are called; new structure of Hazratbal shrine inaugurated on the banks of the Dal Lake, Srinagar.

1980: Seventh general elections held in India, returning the Congress and Indira Gandhi to power; Sheikh Abdullah introduces J&K Resettlement Bill to the assembly.

1981: Sheikh Abdullah anoints his son Farooq Abdullah as successor and president of the NC.

1982: J&K Resettlement Bill is passed by the assembly; Sheikh Abdullah passes away in Srinagar; Farooq Abdullah takes over as chief minister.

1983: J&K assembly elections lead to victory of NC; Farooq Abdullah retains position as chief minister.

1984: Faction of NC led by G.M. Shah breaks away; Farooq government dismissed by Governor Jagmohan at the centre's behest; G.M. Shah assumes office of chief minister; Operation Blue Star launched against Punjab insurgency; Indira Gandhi assassinated by her Sikh bodyguards; Rajiv Gandhi assumes office of prime minister.

1986: Rajiv–Farooq Accord signed, under which G.M. Shah's government dismissed and Farooq assumes office of chief minister as part of a Congress–NC coalition government.

1987: Legislative assembly elections in J&K; Muslim United Front (MUF) formed to contest the elections against NC; NC declared winner amidst widespread allegations of vote-rigging; MUF poll agents and candidates arrested.

1988: Kashmiri protests against vote-rigging and other issues are suppressed by Farooq government; young Kashmiri Muslim men begin to cross over to Pakistan to get arms training and many join the JKLF, which declares armed revolt against India.

1989: JKLF begins campaign of high-profile assassinations and kidnappings; Jamaat-i-Islami activist founds the pro-Pakistan Hizbul Mujahideen, which joins the insurgency; Kashmiri protests intensify.

1990: Indian centre dismisses Farooq government and institutes president's rule, led by Governor Jagmohan; Indian military crackdown begins; Armed Forces Special Powers Act imposed on J&K, renewed every year since. The Kashmir insurgency gathers force.

# Introduction
# The Lion of Kashmir

IT RESEMBLED THE DAY OF ASHURA, A DEEP FOG OF MOURNING shrouding the mountains and valleys of Kashmir. As the funeral cortege wound its way through the streets of Srinagar, hundreds of thousands of Kashmiris from across the Valley poured into the city streets desperate to catch a glimpse of their departed leader, Sheikh Muhammad Abdullah, and pay final homage to him. Hearths remained unlit throughout the Valley, food uncooked and uneaten, and windows shuttered as the sound of tearful wailing rent the air. Their beloved Sher-i-Kashmir (Lion of Kashmir), Baba-i-Quom (Father of the Nation), the symbol of their emancipation, had passed away the day before and was on his last journey to Hazratbal; there he was buried at a serene spot on the banks of the Nageen Lake on 9 September 1982.[1] In death, as in life, he seemed caught between India and Kashmir, his body wrapped in the Indian flag and carried by and lowered into its final resting place by Indian Army soldiers. Today, his gravesite, surrounded by spools of concertina wire, is guarded by soldiers from the same army to protect it from defilement by the Kashmiri people.

As a scholar of Kashmir, it is impossible to escape Sheikh Muhammad Abdullah. His life has become synonymous with the modern history of Kashmir, and often, his name is invoked even for time periods long before he was a historical character. He himself likened his autobiography, *Aatish-i-Chinar: Ek Aap Biti*, to an extension of *Rajatarangini*, the twelfth-century history of Kashmir by Kalhana, with his own life as its main driving force.[2] In contemporary Kashmir, no matter how much his legacy is contested, it is within its parameters that Kashmiris continue their struggle to define themselves. As Muhammad Maroof Shah put it in a review of a recent English translation of the autobiography, Abdullah's life embodies 'Kashmir's tragic story—its divided self', as Kashmiris grapple with the 'predicament of living in a place that others call paradise but its inhabitants have felt as hell' and of trying to understand 'why in this big and beautiful world of God, Kashmiris feel homeless, voiceless and directionless'.[3]

But as much as it was and continues to be a Kashmiri story, Sheikh Abdullah's was also a deeply twentieth-century Indian public life. His political ideas were forged in the fire of competing Indian anti-colonial nationalist currents against British rule in Indian provinces and indirectly ruled princely states. He came to nationalism from the perspective of his homeland Kashmir, daring to dream of a free India within which Kashmir and its people could also be free—from authoritarianism and economic exploitation—and maintain their own political and cultural identity. He was hardly alone in these aspirations, which were held by other regional leaders in twentieth-century India, but unlike many of them, he could not resolve the essential differences between his vision for his region-nation and the demands of Indian nationalism, in part because the process of decolonization made it an uphill task. He sincerely believed that there had to be a way to bridge the divides created by the Partition of British India and worked tirelessly towards this possibility. But ultimately, like many others in the subcontinent, he was overwhelmed by the political order dominated by two antagonistic nation states and their nationalist imperatives.

This might also explain why Abdullah, perhaps more than most leaders, evokes such widely divergent reactions—from being adored as a prophet, a guide and a harbinger of freedom, to being condemned as a traitor, a demagogue and an opportunist like no other. Some elderly

Kashmiris born prior to 1947 continue to revere him as a pious, peerless individual and visit his gravesite as they do the shrines of other saints who made Kashmir their home. However, most members of the generation born after 1947—who came of age when he was in prison and were young adults at the time of the 1975 Kashmir Accord—are particularly embittered by what they see as his betrayal of their political dreams, dreams that he himself had fostered. Younger Kashmiris in general have little time for him, in part because they know him only through the region's rancorous public discourse that holds him responsible for all that plagues Kashmir today. Interestingly, their memory of him is intermeshed with three moments: 1947, when the Indian Army entered Kashmir and began what they see as Kashmir's long enslavement to India; the 1950 Land Reforms, which they are willing to admit brought some relief from economic exploitation for peasants and to an extent transformed the Kashmiri countryside for the better; and the 1975 Indira–Sheikh Accord, which foreclosed any possibility of Kashmiris being able to exercise the right to self-determination.

In Pakistan, Abdullah continues to be remembered as a leader who dared to take on India on behalf of Kashmiris, although the Kashmiri diaspora has more complicated feelings towards him. For the families who left voluntarily during the tumult of 1947, his memory is frozen in time prior to this moment, as a champion of the rights of the downtrodden Kashmiris. Those who were forced to flee during his first regime due to his repressive policies, on the other hand, hold a deep-seated animosity towards him and remember him as an Indian collaborator despite his later dismissal from office and founding of the plebiscite movement. In India, his memory seems to have faded, and even those who do choose to remember him focus merely on his secular credentials, holding him forward as an exemplary Muslim leader who dared to challenge the two-nation theory.

I was drawn to Abdullah to explore these dissonances in the way that he is remembered compared to his actual political life as a leader of unparalleled stature, but also because his path to leadership and power was unique in many ways. Although he rubbed shoulders with stalwarts such as Muhammad Iqbal, Jawaharlal Nehru and Mahatma Gandhi, he did not have the family antecedents that they did. He was from a fatherless *sarhadi* family—from the border between the city and country—considered crude in Kashmir because they were neither cultured and urbane like city folk (*shahri*) nor simple and honest like the country folk (*greez*). Nor—unlike Iqbal, Nehru and Gandhi—did his circumstances afford him the opportunity of travelling abroad for an education that would allow him to develop his ideological leanings and political vision. Even when compared to leaders who had a purely vernacular education such as he did, his was not one of immersion in the classics of history, literature and art since he was a science graduate. For all these reasons, Abdullah suffered from a deep sense of insecurity and inferiority throughout his life.

But he had an instinct for people and gravitated towards those with ideas, to whom he listened and from whom he learned. These individuals—Iqbal, Nehru, Ghulam Ahmad Ashai, Prem Nath Bazaz, B.P.L. Bedi, Mirza Afzal Beg, Bakshi Ghulam Muhammad, Ghulam Muhammad Sadiq, Chaudhuri Ghulam Abbas, Muhammad Sayyed Masoodi, Mridula Sarabhai and Jayaprakash Narayan, to name a few—became critical to his political education, and in a sense, defined his political persona. Gradually, with their help, he became a professional politician adept at drawing on multiple ideologies to shape a narrative around himself, one that he honed and jealously guarded. He also instinctively understood Kashmir, Kashmiris and what he thought they needed, and that became the singular ideology that directed him throughout the vagaries of his political life. He had enormous courage, which made him stand up for Kashmiris and stand out among an entire generation of Kashmiri youths who aspired to leadership. He was a regional leader who made a profound impact on the national stage, determined as he was to negotiate with the centre on behalf of Kashmir.

## NATIONALISM, SOVEREIGNTY AND SECULARISM

Abdullah's life compels us to understand Kashmir not simply through the lens of the territorial sovereignties of India and Pakistan, both of which claimed the region for the accomplishment of their respective nationalist projects. This is because he asserted an independent sovereignty for

Kashmir, expressed through its own individual nationalist narrative that might have been linked to India's but was at the same time distinct from it. The relationship he envisioned between Kashmir and India was akin to the relationship that existed between the princely states and the British Indian Empire, but he did not fully recognize that the type of personalized sovereignty that was vested in the person of the princely ruler had gone the way of the empire itself. For India and Pakistan, sovereignty was indivisible and based on consolidating territorial control over disparate provinces and states while also—and this was especially the case with India—establishing a centrist federation. Regional aspirations expressed through leaders such as Abdullah, in particular because he represented the country's only Muslim-majority state, were seen as a threat to this scheme. As a signatory to the Indian constitution, but not to the one of Jammu and Kashmir (J&K)—since he was a prisoner by then—Abdullah became an embodiment of the contradictions of Indian federalism and the failure of Indian policies of integration.

He was at the forefront of India's tussle with its identity as a republic in yet another significant way. When the future of Kashmir hung in the balance as India and Pakistan fought their first war over the region, Mahatma Gandhi often said that Kashmir would be the touchstone of Indian secularism. This was, of course, the basis of India's claim over Kashmir, a Muslim-majority state, and its self-identification as a secular nation state in opposition to Pakistan, which identified as a Muslim state and claimed Kashmir on that basis. But the idea of India as a secular state was severely tested as Nehru's Kashmir policy came under fire from the Hindu right, with Abdullah as its main target. As they played out throughout India's body politic, the larger repercussions of the tussle between these competing visions of India—one secular, the other Hindu majoritarian as well as the one federal and the other centrist—were in large part responsible for Abdullah's dismissal and arrest in 1953. And they continued to define both his relationship and that of Kashmir to India in subsequent decades.

Abdullah was also a casualty of the emergent global world order that would render Kashmir into a pawn in a much larger game. This was most visible at the United Nations (UN), where rather than recognizing the aspirations of the people of the different parts of the state, the Security Council turned Kashmir into a bilateral dispute between India and Pakistan. Abdullah watched in disbelief as the Council focused on the religious affiliation of the majority of the people of the state of J&K in favouring Pakistan's claim over the region. It quickly dawned on him that not only did the Anglo-American bloc have no interest in supporting India's claim, it also did not think much of an independent Kashmir. A bit later, as Cold War rivalries intensified, the Union of Soviet Socialist Republics (USSR) officially came out in support of India's stance on Kashmir.

Despite these many obstacles, Abdullah genuinely believed, and convinced many Kashmiris too, that he could and would get a better deal for Kashmir than had befallen so many other political entities in the aftermath of World War II and decolonization. He would not allow Kashmir to be merged into and fall to the tyranny of the postcolonial state after delivering it from the authoritarianism of princely rule. And yet, in one of the central contradictions of his political career, at certain times when he was in power, he himself became the postcolonial state's most trusted agent and repressor of his own people's rights. However, unlike princely rulers, who did not necessarily have to seek legitimacy through material munificence or cultural patronage, he was answerable to the people and had to live up to the narrative that he had created about himself and Kashmir's special destiny. Maintaining his stature as Kashmir's foremost leader despite obviously failing, time and again, in his stated mission became the sine qua non of his political career.

Ultimately, Abdullah's skills lay in mobilizing the Kashmiri masses for the cause of regional freedom; he was far less effective as a head of state. This was in part because he came of political age at a time when it was possible to reconcile regional aspirations within a nationalist framework. But the nationalism of the nation state demanded unquestioning fealty and left no room for accommodating demands for regional autonomy of the kind sought by Abdullah. The political organization that he founded, the National Conference (NC), likewise, did not transition well into the postcolonial period as it went from being an insurgent, anti-establishment political entity to becoming the party in power. When in power, Abdullah was no different than many postcolonial subcontinental leaders whose regimes were defined by corruption, repression and nepotism. In the case of his government, which became synonymous with the NC, these ills were amplified because J&K was the centre of an international dispute.

Abdullah's enduring popularity as the most significant leader of Kashmiris through a large part of the twentieth century is understood best through the lens of two themes that defined his political career: prison and sacred spaces. In a literal sense, prison punctuated his political life multiple times: He spent a total of 16 years, 6 months and 22 days as a prisoner either of the princely Dogra state or the J&K state within independent India that followed it. In the early years of his entry into politics, prison catapulted him to fame among the masses as a fearless opponent of a tyrannical regime, eventually earning him the mantle of the leader of the Kashmiri Muslims. He made prison-going into a political act, an act of self-sacrifice to gain freedom for the people, until he himself became head of J&K and began to place his own opponents behind bars. His plummeting popularity was instantly restored as soon as he was dismissed in 1953 and made a political prisoner again, allowing him to reprise his role as revolutionary leader of the movement for Kashmiri self-determination.

During these years, he was not a typical prisoner living out his sentences in a jail cell, but placed either in a special jail constructed for the purpose of housing him or under house arrest in bungalows with a fair bit of freedom of movement. But he was not allowed to express his views on Kashmir or, in later years when he was housed outside J&K, visit his homeland, making him an exile in a country he refused to acknowledge as his own. Despite several opportunities to take on leadership positions within India and of Indian Muslims, he did not widen his field of vision beyond Kashmir, thus remaining, in a sense, a prisoner of the Valley and his own ambitions for and within it. Kashmir was his political capital, which he expended throughout his career. He refused to recognize any equals in Kashmir, eliminating anyone who stood in his path, even if that meant turning on people and, in the process, losing countless friends, colleagues and advisors along the way. He was the sole leader of Kashmiris and a Kashmiri Muslim himself, nothing more, nothing less.

While prison allowed Abdullah to gain a following, Kashmir's shrines and mosques provided the opportunity to cement his position as leader. Abdullah had a keen sense of Kashmiri politics and the practice of Islam in Kashmir, both of which he knew were connected and rooted in its sacred spaces. He could not hope to challenge the more established religious leadership and become the unrivalled leader of Kashmiri Muslims unless he gained control over these spaces, and by extension the localities surrounding them. He accomplished this systematically, by deftly exploiting the late nineteenth-century schism over the definition of Islam between the families of the two head preachers of the city. Through his fiery and melodious multilingual oratory, he expressed his support for shrine worship, combining it with rhetoric on justice and freedom from oppression and exploitation for the masses. In a matter of a few years, his popularity had reached such heights that not many dared challenge him. For Kashmiris, he was far more than a mere political leader—he was their saviour, a messiah, an image that he, too, at some level identified with. So intertwined did his image become with shrines that he had the audacity to rebuild in marble the wooden structure of Hazratbal—the holiest of Kashmir's shrines—when his popularity was at a low ebb in the 1970s, rendering it into an indestructible symbol of Kashmiri identity and sovereignty.

Kashmir's distinctive identity and sovereignty could only truly be preserved, Abdullah believed, in the idea of the Kashmir nation, of which he became a faithful proponent. His narrative of Kashmiri nationalism carefully threaded together elements from Kashmir's narrative culture, such as its focus on Kashmir as sacred space, with elements from Indian nationalism that emphasized transcending religious and sectarian divides in the name of united nationalism. From the pulpits of Kashmir's shrines, Abdullah exhorted Kashmiris to think beyond religious community and envision the nation as a form of community that included multiple religious groups, all of which were suffering equally under authoritarian rule and economic exploitation. The only way to free the nation was for all groups to embrace secularism and join hands under the umbrella of the nationalist movement.

The multiple contradictions within this narrative haunted Abdullah's career and Kashmir's political trajectory in the twentieth century. Although he claimed to speak for the entire state of J&K, Abdullah's vision for the Kashmiri nation did not go beyond the Kashmir Valley. Key parts of the state—Jammu and Ladakh—were left out of its ambit, with their people never quite getting over their belief that Abdullah's nationalism came at their expense. And while Kashmir's minorities joined the movement, they were never quite convinced that Abdullah's turn towards nationalism and secularism was genuine, since he always presented himself as a devoted Muslim who believed in Islam as the sole means of spiritual salvation. But it was also Islam that, as he noted in a speech in 1933, taught him to fight for the rights of all his countrymen, regardless of their religious affiliation, and to protect the honour of his Hindu mothers and sisters just as he would the honour of his Muslim mothers and sisters. 'I am Muslim,' he said, 'but I see Hindus and Muslims with the same eye in worldly affairs and want them to live and work together happily.'[4] His secularism, thus, was drawn from Islam.

At the same time, while he genuinely believed that Kashmir would prosper only if all communities were included in the task of building a free society, at some level, Abdullah continued to feel that Muslims deserved special treatment because of the discrimination and abuse that they suffered in the past at the hands of the state and its officialdom. After all, his Kashmiri Muslim base felt the same way too; his supporters were willing to accept secularism to the extent of protecting and including minorities but not necessarily by sacrificing their own interests—for instance, by sharing government employment with Hindus or, indeed later, by supporting India.

As a result, Abdullah's relationship to secularism and particularly the minority community of Kashmiri Pandits remained fraught. At a personal level, he worked closely with several Pandits, many of whom were a critical part of the movement itself and then part of his administration.

But the community as a whole, he always thought, could be more amenable to thinking beyond its own interests to those of the nation as a whole. And since for most Pandits there could be no compromise on Kashmir as an integral part of India, Abdullah came to believe that they had played a key role in his dismissal from office in 1953. One of his Pandit compatriots, Kashyap Bandhu, described Abdullah years later as a man whose 'conscience was Muslim, his heart was Kashmiri, and his brain was secular'.[5]

Abdullah's life story is thus a thoroughly Kashmiri, quintessentially Indian and essentially global one that illuminates the struggles of one regional leader to balance the demands of his region with those of the nation state, the demands of his faith with those of nationalism, and the demands of his personal convictions with those of his critics.

## WRITING A LIFE

Writing a life history is a delicate and complicated task, made especially so in Abdullah's case because his legacy is so contested in the present. But that is also what makes his individual life such a critical prism through which to understand the intertwined histories of twentieth-century Kashmir and India, along with the ambiguities and inconsistencies in their national projects. As Daniel R. Meister has suggested, historical biography has the ability to 'strike a balance' between larger historical processes and 'the reality of people's complex, contradictory, and messy lives',[6] foregrounding neither and thus making a deeper contribution to sociopolitical and cultural history.

This biography, accordingly, probes the ways in which Abdullah's life—along with the lives of many other individuals who surrounded him—interacted with, was influenced by and in turn shaped historical events, processes and ideologies in the twentieth century. It is as much a biography of Abdullah as that of a generation, of national ideas and of the two states, in particular India, that emerged from the debris of the British Empire in South Asia. At the same time, it addresses a gaping lacuna in the scholarship on late colonial and postcolonial India, which shies away from biographies in general—other than of figures such as Nehru,

Gandhi, Subhas Bose and more recently, B.R. Ambedkar—with little regard for regional leaders such as Abdullah, who played an outsized role in influencing the course of centre–region relations in the subcontinent.

Being Abdullah's biographer has been challenging for another reason, namely that he has left behind such a sparse written record. He was not a particularly introspective man, as evident in his autobiography, and did not write very much, even in prison, where he preferred to spend much of his time gardening and raising poultry. He did, however, write letters, many of which I was able to access through the private collections of the individuals, including Nehru, to whom they were addressed. Most of his own papers, including the letters he received, have been lost along the way, especially during moments of his arrest and transfer from one prison to another, when all documents on his person would be seized by the authorities, never to be seen again. Even his own family has little in the way of a personal archive that would help reconstruct his complicated and controversial life. The recent collection, *Sheikh Mohammad Abdullah's Reflections on Kashmir*, edited by his granddaughter Nyla Ali Khan, is a compilation of Abdullah's speeches and some writings from previously published sources.[7]

The only significant document that he left behind for posterity is his autobiography, *Aatish-i-Chinar*, published a few years after his death in 1986; as a result, it has become the single most important source of information about his life. I would argue that the book is useful not so much as a repository of facts, but as a political document that he narrated at the end of his life, his final attempt at controlling the narrative around himself and his political choices. In its prologue, he notes that this was no ordinary narrative, because since he had been the architect and standard-bearer of the revolutionary movement, the story of his life *was* history, and 'a part of our glorious saga'.[8] For him, Kashmir's history, magnificent in the early period and then steeped in injustice, dishonour and slavery, began its new glorious phase with the emergence of the nationalist movement under his guidance. The inclusions and omissions in the narrative thus offer clear insights into how he wanted his life story and Kashmir's modern history to be told. They also offer a window into his state of mind at the end of his life.

The narrative's translations and reprintings too have appeared at critical moments to rehabilitate Abdullah's political image, and along with it that of his party, the NC. Khushwant Singh's abridged English translation, *Flames of the Chinar: An Autobiography*, was published in 1993, at the height of the Kashmir insurgency against the Indian state.[9] The second official edition in Urdu was published in 2007, as the NC prepared to take on its rival, the People's Democratic Party (PDP), in the 2008 state assembly elections. A complete English translation by Mohammad Amin, entitled *The Blazing Chinar: Autobiography*, appeared in 2013, when the J&K government headed by Abdullah's grandson, Omar Abdullah, was facing angry street protests led by Kashmiri Muslim youth at its handling of a series of misdemeanours by the Indian Army in the Valley.

Abdullah was not an intellectual or an ideologue, but he surrounded himself with individuals who were deeply committed to particular ideologies. Hence, I was able to make up for the paucity of his writings by sifting through the private collections and interview transcripts of the individuals who had a profound impact on shaping his political career. This allowed me to write his life not simply through his own lens, but through the eyes of his close colleagues and friends. In the process, it revealed hitherto unknown facets of the personalities and political lives of these individuals as well. The documents of Bazaz, Munshi Ishaq, Balraj Puri, Nehru, Jayaprakash Narayan, T.N. Kaul, Y.D. Gundevia, N.N. Raina, and Mridula Sarabhai proved particularly useful in this regard. The post-1947 Jawaharlal Nehru papers, housed at the Nehru Memorial Museum and Library—that had remained closed for decades and which I was fortunate enough to be given permission to access—were a revelation in terms of Abdullah's relationships with a number of key individuals, especially at sensitive moments of his political life, and their role in shaping the history of Kashmir and India.

Since Abdullah was in politics for decades and so closely identified with the Kashmiri people, there were many others whose lives he touched, including his staff, lower-level NC functionaries who formed the backbone of the party and ordinary Kashmiris who had been caught up in the fervour of the movement. I was able to interview many of these people who had come of age during Abdullah's time, or their descendants, all of whom were quite willing to share, along with a cup of tea, their memories of their own and their elders' relationships and interactions with Abdullah. Many had collections of documents that, along with their reminiscences, proved invaluable in constructing a multifaceted picture of his life. These conversations took me across the Valley, and to Jammu, Delhi, Mumbai and Lahore.

Abdullah was keenly sensitive at all times to his public image, particularly as presented in the press. The Urdu-language press in the Punjab had played a key role in promoting the Kashmiri movement and him as its sole leader in the 1930s. Throughout the 1940s, the British Indian press kept tabs on the ups and downs of the Kashmir movement and its leader. In the immediate post-Independence period, he became engaged in a battle with the Pakistani press, which took it upon itself to malign his name because of his support for J&K's accession to India. But his longest-running feud was with the Indian press, which lasted through most of his career in the post-1947 period, in many ways shaping Abdullah's relationship to the Indian public and the government. These press reports, as well as Abdullah's attempts at regaining control over the narrative at key moments, are a rich source for understanding multiple aspects of his relationships with a cross section of individuals, institutions and political entities during his career.

Most regional leaders from the subcontinent could not boast the extent of international coverage—both from the press and government agencies—that Abdullah was subject to for the obvious reason that Kashmir was a disputed region. These detailed reports and dispatches in newspapers, magazines and from the US Department of State and intelligence agencies such as the CIA were critical in providing fresh insights into Abdullah and his associates, and others such as Prime Minister Nehru, from an external perspective. They highlighted how Abdullah and those around him were perceived in the global arena at critical moments, particularly in the context of developing Indo-US/US-Pakistani relations and the Cold War. Abdullah's interactions with the foreign journalists, diplomats, political operatives and visitors who generated these reports add yet another layer to the complex mix that fashioned his political personality.

I also had access to the voluminous secondary literature on Kashmir generated mostly after the beginning of the insurgency in J&K, which at some level deals with Abdullah and his legacy. But the books I found most helpful were published in Pakistan in the 1960s and '70s by individuals who had themselves been involved in Kashmir's political scene prior to Independence and Partition and continued to play a significant role in the politics of the part of Kashmir in Pakistan. Sardar Ibrahim Khan's *The Kashmir Saga* and Muhammad Yusuf Saraf's *Kashmiris Fight—For Freedom*,[10] although far from scholarly, provide a textured picture of Abdullah's personality and his interactions with his peers and the masses, especially during the early years of his political life. These books give us a sense of Abdullah before he became a towering political personality, and the tumultuous political climate teeming with jostling ideas and individuals through which he emerged as one. When read alongside his own autobiography, these works as well as the autobiographies of his peers, such as Ghulam Abbas's *Kashmakash*,[11] were instrumental in providing a multidimensional view of Abdullah's political temperament.

As noted earlier, there are far fewer biographies written of Abdullah, both in English and Urdu, than one would expect, given how important he was to the twentieth-century history of Kashmir and the subcontinent. Those that do exist are unidimensional and mostly brief studies of his political career, usually with a particular partisan objective in mind; many are based almost entirely on previously published sources, most often on an indiscriminating reading of his autobiography. Few delve deeply into Abdullah's political mind or the minds of the individuals who were the driving forces in his life. As a result, these biographies are more helpful in terms of understanding how certain groups perceived Abdullah and created a narrative around him at specific moments than in gleaning any significant information about his life. The Urdu biographies, published in Pakistan and dating mostly from the 1960s, are concerned with keeping Abdullah's memory alive during the years of his long incarceration.[12] The more recent biographies, both in Urdu and English, published mainly in

India, are attempts at making sense of the situation in contemporary J&K in the context of Abdullah's legacy.[13]

Ajit Bhattacharjea's *Sheikh Mohammad Abdullah: Tragic Hero of Kashmir,* for instance, as the title indicates, is an attempt to rehabilitate Abdullah's image in the Indian context by presenting him as a heroic, misunderstood champion of secularism.[14] It is told entirely from Abdullah's own perspective, with his critics—even those of the secular bent—painted with the broad brush of communalism. Bhattacharjea makes no attempt to engage with the complicated politics behind Abdullah's emergence as a leader, uncritically accepting the NC line that he was dedicated to social and economic justice because he put forward the Naya Kashmir Manifesto, the context for the adoption of which remains unexamined as well. Other important aspects of Abdullah's political life also get a cursory treatment, including the reasons behind his dismissal in 1953 and the long-term context of the Kashmir Accord. The more recent biography by Altaf Hussain Para, *The Making of Modern Kashmir,* is an attempt to address these issues, but again as the title suggests, reads more like a history of modern Kashmir than a biography of Abdullah per se.[15]

In the case of this biographical narrative, Abdullah is its driving force, but it is told not from his perspective alone. It is as much about the events, individuals and ideas that shaped Sheikh Abdullah's life as it is about the narrative surrounding them, fashioned in part by Abdullah himself, his colleagues and friends, as well as his interlocutors and critics. It is organized into an introduction, eight chapters—with chapter four serving as a hinge—and an epilogue. Each chapter is framed around a moment that was crucial in Abdullah's life and political career, with most of the discussion in the chapter leading up to the moment. The discussion places the moment in its longer historical and broader local, regional and international contexts. And it attempts to understand its internal logic from Abdullah's perspective: how it was shaped by while at the same time shaping Abdullah's character, and from the vantage of those around him. Each chapter highlights the role of one or more individuals and ideas in defining the moment for Abdullah.

However fallible Sheikh Abdullah might have been through his political life, he was the bridge that connected Kashmir and India, and in some ways also kept the idea of Indo-Pakistani reconciliation on the table. His death began the process of sundering these relationships, in part due to his own actions during his lifetime, thus beginning an era of confrontation and insurgency. Abdullah, therefore, continues to cast a long shadow over the subcontinent. After all, his was a thoroughly South Asian political life in the global twentieth century, which while singular in many ways, was by no means unique in its vision, contradictions and compromises.

# 1

# First among Equals, 1905–1934

SRINAGAR WAS BUSTLING WITH POLITICAL ACTIVITY IN AUGUST 1934 as campaigning for the elections to the newly constituted legislative assembly, the Praja Sabha, gathered momentum. The candidates made fiery speeches amidst fluttering banners representing their political organizations. People attended these events in droves, driven by the fervour of electing their own political representatives for the first time in the history of Kashmir. To them, it did not matter that Sheikh Muhammad Abdullah was not one of the candidates running for a seat in the legislative assembly, for he was already Sher-i-Kashmir, the one who had made it all possible. They enthusiastically supported his organization, the Muslim Conference (MC), and on the day of polling—3 September 1934—voted overwhelmingly for its candidates against that of the Azad Muslim Conference, the party of his opponent, the Mirwaiz Kashmir, Yusuf Shah.[1]

An unknown figure a mere few years earlier, when he was one of the many keen, educated aspirants for a government position, Abdullah now appeared to be the undisputed leader of the Kashmiri Muslims and their movement against government autocracy and authoritarianism. But the road on which he had travelled to emerge victorious was littered with rocks, the cracks on its surface already visible and lingering on long after and deep into his political career. Not only had the elections been fought against the wishes of the Jammu members of the MC—many of whom preferred to boycott the Praja Sabha altogether for being not representative enough—but they had also seen the institutionalization of the main rift within the movement in the Kashmir Valley itself. Yet, the trajectory of Abdullah's rise from relative obscurity to the position of leader and symbol of freedom for Kashmiri Muslims—a position he maintained for some four decades—was intermeshed with his ability to unify a community while at the same time skilfully creating and exacerbating pre-existing divisions within it to consolidate his own position as leader from among a field of several equally qualified candidates.

It was these very people who hoisted Abdullah on their shoulders to make him leader, because the story of his political emergence is very much the story of an entire generation of Kashmiris. Members of this generation might have been divided in ordinary times along lines of class, caste and religion, but in these extraordinary times, they came together with the primary objective of demanding their political and economic rights from a regime under whose repressive rule they had come of age. They all faced wanton discrimination because of their religious affiliation and regional identity, they were stifled due to the lack of freedom of expression, and many struggled under the yoke of poverty and economic exploitation. Even those who did not directly come in contact with the currents of anti-colonial nationalism, communism, socialism and Islamic reform movements—as many of this generation did in British India—had enough personal experience of oppression to recognize the need for change. Abdullah, with his boldness and manifest sincerity to the cause, came to embody the possibility of that change.

Abdullah's early political life, thus, represents this Kashmiri generation as its members grappled with being subjects of a princely state within the larger British Indian Empire. Beyond his outrage at the condition of Kashmiri Muslims and fearless outspokenness against it, Abdullah had little familial, educational or ideological capital on which he could draw, particularly in the early years. He was almost entirely dependent on the support of his Kashmiri and Punjabi patrons to navigate the thicket of Kashmir's politics. The more established Kashmiri Muslim leadership put him forward as the fresh, modern face of Kashmiri revolt against Dogra rule. Punjabi Muslims, many with Kashmiri ancestry, who had been organizing against the atrocities of the Dogra regime since the early twentieth century, provided critical moral, material and ideological support for the burgeoning movement.

Indeed, the schisms within the movement emerged in the context of its association with Punjabi movements and organizations, and Abdullah's attempts at making it—as well as himself—independent of them and of the earlier Kashmiri leadership. Even as he asserted himself as leader of a movement for Kashmiris by Kashmiris, the influence of Indian anti-colonial movements would continue to cast a long shadow on Abdullah's political life. Nevertheless, once in the fray, he rose to the top by skilfully exploiting the larger political and economic context that had generated fury among ordinary Kashmiris and by surrounding himself with individuals possessing specific organizational abilities and ideological leanings who helped him to channel this anger into an organized political movement.

## A GENERATION OF REBELS

A few miles to the north of Srinagar, on the road to Ganderbal, was a small village named Soura. Located on a beautiful spot on the banks of the Lake Anchar, it was a resting place for Hindu pilgrims before they crossed the lake by boat to their holy place, Tulmul. A village of mostly Muslim labourers and shawl workers, Soura was neither quite in the city nor part of the countryside. As the entry point into the city, it was the location of an octroi post where villagers seeking to enter Srinagar to sell their goods had to suffer daily indignities at the hands of the petty tax collectors manning the post. It was in this village that on a chilly morning in early December 1905, the third wife of Sheikh Muhammad Ibrahim—a trader in pashmina wool who had passed away a fortnight earlier—gave birth to a baby boy. She named him Muhammad Abdullah. The family's ancestor, a Kashmiri Brahman, had converted to Islam in the late eighteenth century[2] and, like other such converts, adopted the title Sheikh (or Shaikh).

The turn of the twentieth century was a grim moment to enter the world as a subject—particularly a Muslim subject—of the princely state of Jammu and Kashmir (J&K). Founded in 1846 through the Treaty of Amritsar—signed between Gulab Singh, the Dogra chieftain from the hills of the Punjab, and the British East India Company—the state brought together the territories of Jammu, Ladakh and the Kashmir Valley under one political umbrella. Gulab Singh, who ascended its throne, and his successors set about defining their dynasty and the territories it now controlled in terms of their Aryan, Hindu heritage by patronizing Hinduism, its holy places and its texts. These structures of legitimacy effectively excluded the Muslim population, which, at 76 per cent, formed an overall majority in the state.[3]

By the late nineteenth century, the combined impact of the Dogra state's policies—including importing non-Kashmiri Hindus to run the expanding state bureaucracy; British colonial interventions, such as the land settlement; and global trends, including the decline of the shawl trade—had upended social and political structures within the state's provinces. The traditional Muslim landholding and commercial elites were under considerable pressure, while middle and lower classes of Muslims bore the brunt of the state's neglect of the community, particularly in the Kashmir Valley. The turn of the century saw the emergence of political organization among Kashmiri—as well as Jammu—Muslims, led largely by religious leaders, to better define the contours of the community and provide educational and other opportunities for its members.

Abdullah would ultimately become a beneficiary of these early organizational attempts, but his childhood and young adulthood were plagued by the privation and discrimination that surrounded him. Because of her husband's passing, Abdullah's mother was entirely dependent on her older stepsons, who now took over the household, for financial support to raise her four children, of whom Abdullah was the youngest. As a child, Abdullah was acutely aware of his mother's plight as he saw her struggling to maintain her dignity amidst the taunts of her stepsons. She increasingly found solace in her faith, a deep attachment to which she instilled in the young Abdullah.

Growing up without a father in straitened circumstances made him sensitive to the troubles of the crushingly poor shawl artisans and labourers who lived in the village and of the peasants in the surrounding countryside. In his own telling, losing to hunger a young friend—the son of oil-pressers—left a lasting impression, as did witnessing the thrashing of a villager by an official at the octroi post. This was because the villager, on his way to the city to sell bundles of wood that he had gathered from the surrounding forests, had refused to pay him extra beyond the octroi. The young Abdullah was livid and intervened on the villager's behalf. The official backed down but reported Abdullah to the Office of the Inspector of Customs, from where he received a summons. Upon explaining himself, he was given a warning and asked to leave.[4] This was his first taste of trouble at the hands of the authorities.

In another incident, he was a silent, fuming witness to the ignominy suffered by his oldest brother, Sheikh Muhammad Khalil, when he was slapped by a visiting state official. The official's visit was in response to a petition sent by their locality to the government asking to be included in the rationing system that would allow them access to cheap food grain. When the official arrived to make his assessment, he asked who the head of the locality was and the people identified Sheikh Khalil; upon hearing this, the official slapped him before continuing his assessment. A stunned Abdullah struggled to understand the reason for such treatment; his mother's response that God ruled the world did not explain the existence of such stark injustice, particularly when Muslims were so clearly the target.[5]

It became clear to Abdullah early on that the Dogra regime had little regard for its Muslim subjects, since it appeared in the lives of ordinary Kashmiris only in the form of ever-present petty officials, extracting from them and providing little else but abuse in return. State-run schools were few and far between, most of the education being provided by makhtabs and pathshalas connected to local mosques and temples. Abdullah too was enrolled in a makhtab near his home at an early age, where he learned to recite the Quran, a skill that he excelled at and that would stand him in good stead later as a speaker and organizer. By the time Abdullah was ready to go to school, he was able to benefit from the efforts of the early generation of Muslim leaders to build educational institutions through organizations such as the Anjuman Nusrat-ul-Islam as well as from the belated efforts of the state to provide education to its subjects. He walked several miles to primary and later secondary school in Srinagar despite the protestations of his stepbrothers, who wanted him to work and contribute to the family's income.

Abdullah dreamed of becoming a doctor, but he was an indifferent student, at least in part due to family pressures and the hardships of travelling long distances to get an education, which took a toll on his mental and physical health. He hoped for a government scholarship to study medicine, but none was forthcoming. This was a particularly difficult time in his life, as his mother, to whom he was close, passed away suddenly, leaving him bereft. After completing the last two years of high school at Sri Pratap College in Srinagar, Abdullah sought admission into Prince of Wales College in Jammu for a BSc but was denied admission in favour of the son of an official who was not himself a native of Kashmir. This was his first personal encounter with discrimination, not only because he was Muslim but also because he had no family connections. Instead, after receiving a scholarship from the All India Kashmiri Muslim Conference—an organization founded in 1920, headquartered in British-ruled Punjab—to study at Islamia College, Lahore, he left the Kashmir Valley in 1924, a move that would alter the course of his life.[6]

Since there were few options in Kashmir for those interested in pursuing an education, a diverse group of students from a variety of social and religious backgrounds attended the same institution as Abdullah—the Government High School, Bagh-i-Dilawar Khan, Srinagar. Although they did not connect at the time, Prem Nath Bazaz, born to a middle-class Pandit family from Srinagar a few months before Abdullah in July 1905, was one of his classmates. The Kashmiri Pandit minority had fared much better than Kashmiri Muslims during Dogra rule, particularly in Srinagar, where many Pandits were employed as low-level bureaucrats (Bazaz's father was a police officer). But they too struggled under systemic discrimination and corruption that kept them mired in poverty and backwardness. Early on, Bazaz came under the influence of Pandit social reformers who were focused on social issues facing the Pandit community, such as child marriage, dowry, female illiteracy and so on. On entering Sri Pratap College in 1923, Bazaz began writing for newspapers in the Punjab, including *Akhbar-i-Am* in Lahore, on matters of interest to Kashmiris, such as the inefficiencies of the Dogra administration, mismanagement of public funds and a variety of miscarriages of justice.[7]

At the same time, in the neighbouring province of Jammu, another young man, whose life circumstances were quite different from that of Abdullah, had already begun organizing the Jammu Muslims. Born to a petition writer named Chaudhury Nawab Khan a year before Abdullah and Bazaz, Ghulam Abbas was raised by his maternal uncle, who was a lawyer in the Jammu courts. Abbas had the benefit of not one, but two fathers, under whose care he grew up wanting for nothing. He too, of his own admission, was an indifferent student, in this case not because he had too many cares, but because he had so few.[8]

In 1923, while a student at Prince of Wales College, he and a few other college friends became involved in reviving the Jammu Muslim association known as the Anjuman-i-Islamia, renaming it the Youngmen's Muslim Association (YMA). It worked to unite the severely divided Muslims of the Jammu province and to prevent the spread of Hindu conversion campaigns from the Punjab, such as Shuddhi, among them. The organization had strong ties with Punjabi Muslim organizations, including the Anjuman-i-Tabligh-i-Islam, and although it was concerned with the social and educational welfare of Jammu's Muslims, the organization's primary objective was to organize them to preserve their Islamic religious and political identity. After serving as president of the YMA for a few years, Abbas too left for Lahore to pursue an LLB.[9]

British India had beckoned others of this generation of Kashmiris for further studies, several of whom had already returned to Kashmir to take up positions in the administration by the time Abdullah and Abbas were preparing to leave for Lahore. Ghulam Ahmad Ashai, born in 1895 into an affluent shawl-trading family from Srinagar, became the first Kashmiri Muslim to earn an MA, in his case in Oriental Languages from the University of Calcutta in 1918. Back in Kashmir, he started as a teacher, was promoted to lecturer and finally rose to the position of assistant inspector of schools. He was deeply concerned with the level of benightedness among Kashmiri Muslims and had begun to discuss these and related issues with others of like mind—such as Moulvi Abdullah Vakil, a prominent Kashmiri of the Ahmadi sect—before formally establishing reading rooms to educate Muslim youth in the 1920s.[10]

Hailing from a family of traders, farmers and pirs, Muhammad Sayyed Masoodi was born in 1901 in the district Muzaffarabad; the family later moved to Ganderbal, some 40 miles north of Srinagar. Masoodi graduated from Oriental College, Lahore, with an honours degree in Arabic, Persian and Urdu; upon his return to Kashmir in 1926 he was appointed lecturer in Persian at Prince of Wales College, Jammu, and then transferred to Sri Pratap College, Srinagar. Much like Bazaz, he too wrote for newspapers in the Punjab, such as *Zamindar,* and like Ashai, being concerned with the level of illiteracy among Kashmiri Muslims, established a reading room to educate Muslim boys that was patronized by the managers of two of Srinagar's important shrines.[11]

Other religious figures were also concerned with the elevation of the status of Kashmiri Muslims. The Mirwaiz (head preacher) family of Srinagar had already established a number of schools for the education of Kashmiri Muslims when their scion—Yusuf Shah, born in 1895—went on to study at the Deoband Theological Seminary in the mid-1920s. There he came into contact with the wider Indian nationalist movement, particularly the Khilafat Movement, as well as with other reform-minded Kashmiri Muslims. Upon his return to Kashmir, he too turned his attention to ways of uplifting the community and their political education by, among other things, establishing a Khilafat Committee.[12]

Another notable figure, Tara Chand Koul, who later took the name Kashyap Bandhu, was a rebel from an early age. Born in 1899 in Traal into a poor Kashmiri Pandit family, he was fired from his first job as a scribe in the Revenue Department, which he had joined soon after graduation, for arguing for better treatment of peasants. He then went on to Lahore, where he joined an Arya Samaj institution, eventually becoming the editor of the *Arya Gazette*. He wrote extensively on social reform issues within Hindu society as a whole as well as his own community, dedicating himself to its social and political uplift once he returned to Kashmir in 1931 as founding president of the Sanatan Dharma Youngmen's Association.[13]

Not all members of this generation had the luxury of travelling to British India for an education. Munshi Mohammad Ishaq, for instance, born in 1901 into a Shia family, attended the Tyndale-Biscoe Mission School in Srinagar because his father was the Arabic and Persian teacher there. But he could not complete his education due to his father's illness, instead taking up a position in a transport company in Rawalpindi. By 1927, Ishaq had been promoted to manager of this company, which owned trucks that connected Kashmir to the Punjab by plying the Srinagar–Rawalpindi route. He later started his own transport business that became critical to the movement of people, ideas and funds between Kashmir and the Punjab.[14]

Born to a midwife and an unemployed labourer in downtown Srinagar in 1907, Bakshi Ghulam Muhammad likewise did not have the family means that would allow him to pursue a higher education. He too attended the Biscoe Mission School until middle pass (eighth grade), and left for Skardu and Leh soon thereafter to work in mission schools located there. A resourceful and energetic young man, Bakshi displayed leadership abilities that far exceeded his age and educational attainments, and was soon managing the schools. Concerned that their son might convert to Christianity, his parents asked him to return home to Srinagar, where—having come into contact with Gandhian and Congress ideologies in Leh—he began work at the local branch of the All India Spinners Association, later moving to the Khadi Store as salesman.[15]

Mirza Afzal Beg, born a year after Bakshi in 1908, hailed from a far more affluent family in Anantnag, situated 35 miles southeast of Srinagar. The family, which had been granted the title of Mirza for service to the Mughals, were well-established jagirdars (landlords) of Anantnag. After completing his schooling in Anantnag, Beg graduated from Sri Pratap College in Srinagar and went on to acquire an LLB from Aligarh Muslim University (AMU). He attended AMU a few years ahead of Ghulam Muhammad Sadiq and Ghulam Mohiuddin Karra, both born in 1912 into the same family of affluent traders of pashmina wool with vast interests in Bengal (their fathers were brothers). After an idyllic childhood in Srinagar, where they attended school, they became involved in organizing youth protests against Dogra rule in college. In the early 1930s, they studied law at AMU, where they were further exposed to ideologies such as communism.

Hailing from the city, the countryside and somewhere in between; from affluent to middle-class to poor families; and from a range of religious, sectarian and educational backgrounds, this generation of individuals, born in various parts of the princely state of J&K at the turn of the twentieth century, would be brought together partly by circumstances and partly by design around the figure of Sheikh Abdullah to ignite one of the most significant anti-autocratic movements in princely India.

## COMING OF AGE

The year 1924 was a significant one. It was the year that Abdullah left Kashmir for the first time to attend Islamia College in Lahore. It was also the year when Kashmiris' discontent spilled over into ferment. In the almost thirty years since Maharaja Pratap Singh had ascended the throne in 1885, the princely state had seen far-reaching transformations in its political economy, in part due to British colonial intervention. The older nobility and trading class were in decline, being rapidly replaced by a new class of landholders, who were usually high-level, non-Kashmiri administrators within the Dogra bureaucracy. The late nineteenth-century revenue settlement spearheaded by the British Residency had created a more readily identifiable class of peasants as well as spawned a class of revenue officials now ubiquitous throughout the countryside. New modes of revenue collection led to a series of grain shortages that culminated in a major grain crisis in 1921, in which the poorest suffered the most. Rural–urban migration, urban sprawl and congestion, and poor working conditions in shawl, silk and other factories, coupled with mounting unemployment, made the situation even worse.[16]

Finally tiring of the situation, workers of the Silk Factory in Srinagar struck work in 1924. The Dogra state took swift measures to suppress the protests by force, refusing to give in to what they saw as the Muslim community's attempt at pressuring them into making concessions. This spurred the prominent members of the Muslim community into action, and when the viceroy, Lord Reading, visited the princely state in October that year, they were ready to present him with a memorandum of demands on behalf of Kashmiri Muslims. These included the grant of proprietary rights to Muslim peasants whose land had been snatched from them, greater inclusion of Muslims in the state administration, abolition of forced labour and the appointment of a European commission to consider the grievances of Muslims. Signatories included Saad-ud-Din Shaal and Khwaja Hassan Shah Naqshbandi, both from prominent trading and landed families of Srinagar, as well as the Mirwaiz Kashmir and Mirwaiz Hamadani, the city's two head preachers. Again, the response of the administration was swift, and the signatories were either exiled from Kashmir or removed from government service. This did not have the desired effect, as several of these individuals became the driving force behind the campaign against the Dogra state from their exile in the Punjab.[17]

Abdullah, like many others of his generation, watched these events with a mixture of anticipation and confusion, not quite sure what to make of them. Lahore, where he went soon thereafter to pursue his higher education, provided him with the opportunity to understand the broader context that had shaped these events and how he felt about them. In general, Lahore was a revelation. It was a city abuzz with the 'most magnificent' social life, as B.P.L. Bedi, a student at the city's Government College in the late 1920s, recounted. Bedi, born in 1909 to a well-to-do landed Sikh family from Dera Baba Nanak, was to later become a dedicated communist and deeply involved in Kashmir's politics. Wrestling matches, fairs, cinemas, all-night eating shops and *mandavas* (theatres) kept everyone, from the elites to the middle and poorer classes from all religious communities, entertained. *Punjabiyat*, rather than Hindu, Muslim or Sikh religious affiliations, defined people's social interactions.[18]

Added to the social life was the nationalist fervour that permeated the air in Lahore. Personalities such as the poet and philosopher Muhammad Iqbal, the political stalwart Lala Lajpat Rai and the newspaper editor Maulana Zafar Ali Khan moulded public opinion through their speeches, participation in mushairas (poetry gatherings) and editorializing in newspapers such as *Zamindar*, *Milap* and *The Tribune*. Leaders from other parts of India, such as Sarojini Naidu, were frequent visitors. Students at Islamia College, Oriental College and Punjab University were avid consumers of their speeches and editorials in newspapers. They had the opportunity to meet with these leaders, who kept their doors open to anyone interested in discussing relevant social and political issues. The students organized meetings and processions, where a gamut of ideas were debated with much ardour. Abdullah, who lived in Wilson Hostel on Beadon Road, was also swept up in the currents of this social scene, watching a silent film at the cinema for the first time, listening to Sarojini Naidu's beautiful elocution and meeting students and leaders from different regional, religious, class and ideological backgrounds, while figuring out his own political stance on various issues.[19]

It is difficult to overstate the impact this scenario must have had on the young, parochial Abdullah. Freed from the demands of his family and the Valley's stifling environment, he could thrive here, not merely in academic terms but in terms of his political education as well. In that respect, what most shaped Abdullah was the fact that Lahore, and the Punjab in general, was home to an expatriate community of Muslims from Kashmir that had since the beginning of the century been the centre of movements to redress the grievances of Kashmiri Muslims living under the repressive rule of the Dogra maharajas. He came into contact with organizations such as the All India Kashmir Committee, the Anjuman-i-Himayat-ul-Islam and the Anjuman-i-Kashmiri Musalman, the latter two patronized by Muhammad Iqbal, who himself belonged to a Kashmiri family that had migrated to the Punjab a couple of generations earlier. These organizations were especially active in the mid- to late 1920s following the tumult in J&K and the recent influx of members such as Shaal. Their members contributed articles on matters related to Kashmir to the cacophonous Punjabi press, including newspapers such as *Zamindar* and *Inquilab*. Abdullah followed these voices, which reached a crescendo with the ascension of Hari Singh to the throne of J&K in 1925, with pro- and anti-Maharaja newspapers battling it out in their pages.[20]

At the same time as he encountered the prosperous Kashmiri families who had been settled in the Punjab, some for several generations, he was also confronted with another group of Kashmiri Muslims who made the Punjab their home during the winter months. These seasonal migrants, who came to labour in the Punjab after a hazardous journey across the mountains of Banihal and Murree, were dirt poor, wandering around Punjabi cities in tatters in search of any kind of work. As Lahore glittered around them, they could barely fill their stomachs and suffered untold abuse and scorn at the hands of Punjabis. Their bodies could sometimes be found in the streets of the city, unclaimed and unsung. Abdullah was mortified by these sights and infuriated by the situation that allowed these men to suffer to this extent. All he could think about was the Maharaja and his administration enjoying the beauties of Kashmir and living in luxury while Kashmiri Muslims could barely eke out a living in their own homeland. He could also feel Punjabis treating him differently because he was a Kashmiri.[21] It left a lasting mark. Surely, he felt, something could be done that would prevent this level of insult to Kashmiris' self-respect.

At a meeting of the Anjuman-i-Himayat-ul-Islam, Abdullah had occasion to watch Iqbal in action for the first time. Iqbal's recitation of one of his poems moved Abdullah to tears and made him recognize the power of the spoken word. He would later emulate Iqbal's delivery and quote his poetry freely in his own speeches to rouse Kashmiris and bring them into the fold of the movement. Iqbal kept his home on Mayo Road in Lahore open to students, and one day Abdullah and a few friends ventured out to meet him. Iqbal sat on a white sheet and asked his servant to bring them salty Kashmiri tea, which they eagerly sipped while listening to Iqbal speak of Kashmir and its woes. In awe of the poet, Abdullah did not say much at this and several subsequent meetings.[22] But gradually he began to open up and Iqbal could see something special in this quiet and serious young man, so moved by the plight of his fellow Kashmiris and so eager to do something about it. Iqbal became one of Abdullah's most enduring inspirations, almost a father figure, and remained so long after his death in 1938.

At Islamia College, Abdullah became close to Professor Ilmuddin Salik, who was friends with Iqbal as well as with Muhammad Din Fauq, a journalist and author from another Kashmiri Muslim family settled in the Punjab, who would later publish a history of the people of Kashmir. Since Fauq and Salik spent their summers in Kashmir, Abdullah was able to stay connected to his mentors, with Salik in particular gently grooming him for leadership. It was on his suggestion that Abdullah went on to AMU for an MSc in Chemistry, where his political education continued.[23] He lived in Mumtaz Hostel, which was a hotbed of student political activity. Sadiq and Karra would also be residents of this hostel, whose warden at the time was a dedicated communist committed to economic justice.[24] Fired with the passion of nationalism, the faculty at Aligarh encouraged their students to become part of political movements and to not back down in the face of repression. Abdullah had occasion to watch many nationalist luminaries who passed through AMU during his time there, including Mahatma Gandhi, whose magnetic personality and genuineness impressed him.[25]

The most significant event during his time at Aligarh, which would ignite Kashmiri Muslim students and other well-wishers of Kashmiris, was the publication of Sir Albion Banerjee's statement on the condition of Kashmiri Muslims within the princely state of J&K. Banerjee issued this statement upon his resignation as J&K's prime minister in March 1929 after being thwarted by the Maharaja and his inner circle from implementing reforms that he had felt were necessary to address some of the ills he saw in the state. In his searing statement, he described the Muslims of Kashmir as 'dumb-driven cattle', who were 'utterly illiterate' and leading lives of destitution. Further, they had no recourse for a redress of their grievances since any attempt to do so was swiftly repressed and also because the Maharaja suppressed the growth of any kind of public opinion by denying press freedom. The statement caused a furore in colonial and nationalist circles. For Abdullah, it felt like a vindication: Finally, someone from within the administration was giving voice to the suffering of the Kashmiri people. As the Dogra administration attempted to stem the damage by issuing counter-statements defending its record, Abdullah decided he could no longer be a bystander and wrote a letter to the *Muslim Outlook* exposing the administration's sinister designs. He was overjoyed when it was published.[26] This was his first public foray into politics.

Lahore and Aligarh were political training grounds for not just Abdullah but also an entire generation of young Kashmiri men. The mid-1920s to mid-1930s was a heady time to be a student in the Punjab and United Provinces, where the rancorous nature of nationalist politics was particularly visible. The non-cooperation and Khilafat movements had tapered off, exposing the fault lines within the nationalist movement. Rifts along religious lines opened up—as evident in the stances towards the Maharaja of J&K—as did the divisions within Muslim, Hindu and Sikh politics. The revolutionary Hindustan Socialist Republican Army (HSRA) emerged as a counter to Gandhi's non-violent philosophy, and carried out violent attacks on colonial institutions and individuals. Muslim sects such as the Ahrars and Ahmadis battled it out to define the past and present of the ideal Muslim community and its place within Indian nationalist politics.[27] The Communist Party of India, founded in 1925, spread its influence through workers' and peasants' organizations throughout India. At the national level, as the Indian National Congress and the All India Muslim League began defining their positions on the future of India, especially in terms of the power balance between the centre and regions, and power-sharing among religious communities, the differences in their visions became apparent. An independent India seemed like a possibility, even if its final form continued to be a matter of debate.

Being a part of these momentous debates, if only from the sidelines, had a profound impact on these men. It gave them a language through which they could begin to place the princely state, and their own position as Kashmiri Muslims, within a much broader context. Freedom, which had been an abstraction until this point, now became a concrete political ideal.

## ASCENSION TO LEADERSHIP

The embers of the 13 July 1931 events outside the Central Jail, Srinagar, were still warm on the early morning of 14 July when Abdullah was arrested for the first of what would be multiple times during his political career. In 1931, Abdullah was still a political novice, but imprisonment would cement his role as leader of Kashmiri Muslims while also allowing him to spend time with like-minded members of his generation behind bars to chart their future course of action. Indeed, the incidents of 1931 would unite his generation of educated Kashmiri men into a movement against the Dogra regime, with him as their chosen spokesperson. Between his return to Kashmir in 1930 after completing his higher education at Aligarh and the incidents of July 1931, Abdullah managed to secure an important place for himself within educated Kashmiri Muslim society through, in part, the support of significant individuals within it. He was yet to be recognized by the authorities as a major troublemaker and had relative freedom to find his own niche. He stood out due to his boldness during and subsequent to the events in 1931, steadily rising in the people's estimation to eventually take over the reins of the movement by founding Kashmir's first political organization.

When he returned to Kashmir, Abdullah was one of many young men filled with bluster against the regime, even as they held out hope of acquiring government positions. It was spring 1930 and Kashmiri society was ready for revolt; while the working poor continued to toil under conditions that were worsening due to the Great Depression, the educated were smarting under new rules instituted by the regime to recruit young men into administrative positions. These rules—such as replacing Urdu, Persian and Arabic with Hindi and Sanskrit as elective languages for the civil service entry test—were designed to make it difficult for Muslims to qualify for the civil service in the state. By this time, Ashai had been dismissed from his position as assistant inspector of schools allegedly on corruption charges—but the more likely reason was that he had been leading a reading room where interested individuals discussed issues facing the Kashmiri Muslim community. It was apparent early on to men such as him and Masoodi, who had also organized a reading room, that without a coherent movement and an individual to represent it, they would achieve little.[28]

After casting around for some time, with his family putting pressure on him to get a job, Abdullah was appointed science teacher in the same State High School in Srinagar that he had attended, at a monthly salary of Rs 60. He also became involved in another reading room at the house of Mufti Ziauddin in downtown Srinagar. Every day, he would make the long trek from Soura to teach and then attend meetings of the Reading Room Party, as it came to be called. These loosely organized parties would smuggle in newspapers from the Punjab into Kashmir for discussion and distribution by stuffing them into the spare tires of trucks belonging to Munshi Ishaq's trucking company. Many of the articles in these newspapers were written by Kashmiri Muslim expatriates and sought to highlight the conditions facing Muslims in Kashmir.[29] Men far more connected to Kashmir's social and political scene, some from well-known families, surrounded Abdullah at these gatherings. He was from an unknown family with few means but was drawn to important figures who could guide him and bring him into the limelight.

One of the first of these was Ashai, regarded as the most educated Kashmiri Muslim at the time. Abdullah had occasion to meet Ashai when, along with some other members of the Reading Room Party, he went to seek his help in drafting a memorandum to submit to the government against the new civil service recruitment rules. Ashai agreed to help, and as he got to know more about Abdullah's situation, offered him a room in his house in Srinagar to cut down his daily commute to work. Abdullah stayed with Ashai for a few months, learning from him the workings of the administration and the ways of politics while impressing Ashai with his zeal in the process.[30] When the memorandum received a response from the government, which asked the signatories to send two representatives to discuss the matter with the Council of Ministers, Ashai suggested Abdullah as one of the names.[31]

During the meeting, Abdullah fearlessly spoke out against the rules, terming them unfair towards Muslims. Why, he asked, were there so many poorly qualified non-Muslims in official positions while highly educated Muslim men remained unemployed? While nothing concrete came out of this encounter, since the government dismissed it as the rantings of a disgruntled youth, it emboldened Abdullah and gave him the experience of speaking on behalf of Kashmiri Muslims. It also brought the Reading Room Party to the notice of the Jammu YMA, which sent a deputation to Srinagar in the winter of 1930, and during the meeting, the two organizations decided to join forces.[32]

Abdullah had started to get noticed by the well-connected members of the Muslim community. One such supporter, Ghulam Ahmed Jeweller, offered Abdullah a free room in Fateh Kadal, to which he moved, not wanting to overstay his welcome at Ashai's home. This room became the centre of feverish political activity with discussions that went on into the night. Many of the young men who came to see Abdullah also frequented the home of Moulvi Vakil, a respected religious scholar of Ahmadi persuasion who gave passionate religious sermons that were replete with patriotic fervour, seeking to educate youth about their duties as Kashmiri Muslims. Abdullah too attended these sessions and was deeply moved, imbibing at the same time the valuable skill of combining religious sentiment with political messaging.[33] Vakil was taken by this shy, inexperienced young man who clearly suffered from an inferiority complex, becoming one of his early supporters, and might even have suggested a match between his daughter and Abdullah.[34]

Early 1931 presented Abdullah with another opportunity to make his mark on the impending occasion of the Maharaja's return from Europe with his newborn son, Karan Singh. The loyalists, who included many Muslim jagirdars and government officials, were organizing a welcome committee to pay their respects to the Maharaja and congratulate him on the birth of his son. Wanting to subvert the loyalties of these Muslims, the Reading Room Party persuaded a young jagirdar to call a meeting in his house to discuss the event. About 200 Muslim elites, including the young Moulvi Yusuf Shah, fresh from Deoband, attended. Abdullah stood up and made an impassioned speech, this his first public address, exhorting Muslims to shake off their servility and regain their self-respect by resigning from the welcome committee. He was prepared to do the same, he said, and ready to go to prison for it. He was greeted with thunderous silence before the room erupted into cries of disapproval. But Abdullah had made his presence known. The news of this man, who was willing to sacrifice his freedom for the quom (community/nation), spread quickly through Kashmiri society.[35]

In the coming weeks, he continued to be present at important events within the Muslim community where he would be noticed not just by prominent individuals but also the masses. He led the funeral procession of the Mirwaiz Ahmadullah, giving a speech at the assembly organized to announce his successor. And in yet another speech at the Mirwaiz's memorial at Islamia High School, a scuffle between a heckling detractor and his young supporters in the crowd was portentous of the growing popularity of Master Abdullah, as he was by then known.[36] In the meantime, the government increased its repression of political activities, and Hindu-owned newspapers in the Punjab began a virulent anti-Muslim campaign. Hatred of the government ran so high in Kashmir that even the religious heads of the Muslim community, the Mirwaiz Kashmir Yusuf Shah and the Mirwaiz Hamadani, bitter opponents who had usually stayed aloof from politics, joined the meetings of the Reading Room Party. At one of these meetings, Mirwaiz Yusuf Shah gave voice to what was on the minds of all the members—that it was time to elect a leader.[37]

Abdullah seemed like the obvious choice, for a number of reasons. His sheer physical stature set him apart at first glance—he was six feet four inches tall and literally towered over a crowd. He was fearless, sincere, charismatic and modern, a perfect figure to lead Kashmir out of medieval servitude and into the new age of freedom and rights. He was a devout Muslim without being fanatical about his faith. His melodious recitations of the Quran stirred the very soul of those listening, while his Urdu recitations of Iqbal's poetry and his speeches in Kashmiri could persuade them to follow him to the ends of the earth. He was not from a prominent family with a political history that could hold him back in any way; he was a fresh face with little to lose. The party unanimously elected him the leader.

Soon thereafter, a series of incidents in Jammu and Srinagar would become Abdullah's training ground as he continued to cement his position as leader, especially among ordinary Kashmiris. The insult of a copy of the Quran in the Jammu Central Jail by a sub-inspector, followed by the discovery of some leaves of the holy book in a public latrine in Srinagar, both in June 1931, caused an uproar among Muslims as news of the incidents spread. This was mainly due to the efforts of the YMA in Jammu—with Ghulam Abbas at its helm—which smuggled in posters printed in the Punjab detailing the incidents and, with the help of the Reading Room Party, distributed them across the Valley. Abbas had returned to the state from Lahore in the wake of Banerjee's report and had been organizing the Jammu Muslims.[38]

The arrest of a volunteer for pasting a poster in Srinagar provided Abdullah with the pretext to call a protest meeting at Jama Masjid, Srinagar. His prowess as a speaker was on display at this meeting, which was attended by 30,000 people, most of whom began wailing loudly as he recited the Quran. Abdullah followed up with an impassioned speech in Kashmiri against the insult of Islam and the need for Muslims to rise up against the injustices they suffered every day. Several resolutions were passed at the meeting, demanding that the Maharaja bring those who had insulted Islam to justice. The crowd was so mesmerized that it refused to disperse after the meeting, following Abdullah to his room, chanting slogans of 'Islam Zindabad' and 'Sheikh Abdullah Zindabad'.[39]

This was Abdullah's first taste of adulation, and he was riding high on it when he heard the news that the government had banned public meetings and was considering his arrest. This is what he had been waiting for, because it gave him the opportunity for rule-breaking and to demonstrate that he was unafraid of going to prison for the cause. He called another meeting in protest, which was attended by thousands of people eager to hear him speak. The government decided to transfer him from his position in Srinagar to a school in Muzaffarabad, which gave him a reason to resign from his job. He announced his resignation at a large meeting at Khanqah-i-Mualla shrine in downtown Srinagar, electrifying the crowd once again by declaring that he was no longer prepared to serve a repressive regime and that the time had come for him to serve his quom. Zafar Ali Khan, the founder and editor of *Zamindar*, who was visiting Srinagar at that time and was reportedly present at the meeting, watched Abdullah in action and, awed at his oratory, exclaimed, 'Sher-i-Kashmir.'[40] The lion had arisen.

From henceforward, Abdullah became part of the field of professional politics and came to embody the movement in Kashmir. For a brief moment, he was even able to persuade Muslims from across the state to overcome their sectarian, class and regional differences to unite against the Maharaja's rule. He organized a large event at the Khanqah-i-Mualla shrine to greet the representatives of the Jammu Muslims, including Abbas, who visited Srinagar to discuss future steps with the Valley leadership and present a joint memorial to the Maharaja. Men, women, young, old and the two Mirwaizes stood shoulder to shoulder as Abdullah gave a rousing welcome address that emphasized the need for unity in the face of repression. It had become customary for him to begin with verses from the Quran, followed by a few lines of poetry, and this time it was the verse: 'God, Grant us the strength of Haider / So that we can defeat the infidel troops and enter the gate of Khyber'.[41] The two Mirwaizes shook hands to bury the hatchet and the entire congregation took an oath on the Quran to be unwavering in its struggle for the quom. Then Abdullah read out the names of the seven representatives who would speak on behalf of the community, including Mirwaiz Yusuf Shah, Mirwaiz Hamadani, Shaal, Ashai, Abbas and himself.[42]

July provided Abdullah with further opportunities to demonstrate his mettle as an organizer of rallies and a speaker who could arouse the masses into action. The arrest of Abdul Qadir, a butler to an Englishman who was visiting Kashmir, on the charge of making incendiary speeches against the Maharaja turned into a significant event that would end in

Abdullah's own arrest. He spoke out against Qadir's arrest at meetings around the city, but asked the people to desist from marching on the Central Jail on 13 July, the day of Qadir's hearing. The people disregarded him as throngs gathered outside the prison, chanting slogans for Qadir. The crowd pelted rocks at the armed policemen who had been brought in to restore order, which led them to fire into the crowd. Several people died in the ensuing melee, and the frenzied crowd began moving towards the city carrying the bodies of the dead. On hearing the news, Abdullah rushed towards Jama Masjid, where the crowd was headed, horrified at the carnage, but also recognizing that the spark that this incident had lit would not be easily put out. He was in prison the next day, along with Abbas and a few others.[43]

While the prisoners languished in Hari Parbat Fort, awaiting their fate, the regime imposed martial law across the state as the Valley and the districts of Poonch, Mirpur and Rajouri rose up in revolt. The situation was untenable from the perspective of the government, while for the prisoners too it was important to be on the ground, directing the emergent movement. Ashai, Mirwaiz Yusuf Shah and some others, such as Vakil, brokered an agreement between the government and the prisoners that led to their release in a few weeks. This brief spell in prison was enough to elevate Abdullah even higher in the estimation of the masses, who were convinced that the government had buckled under the sheer force of his spiritual prowess and thus had no choice but to release him.[44]

What made Abdullah the perfect leader for this moment in Kashmir was that he was masterful at speaking the language of justice in the Islamic religious idiom. No other leader, religious or otherwise, had done this before him in Kashmir. Rather than haranguing people with moral injunctions and threats of heaven or hell in the next life, like Kashmir's preachers had done for centuries, he told anecdotes from the Quran and his own life about the lives of the poor and the downtrodden. He thus convinced his audience that they had the power, if they arose from their slumber, to take on an authoritarian state and change the direction of their lives in the present. And in so doing, they would be following in the footsteps of the Prophet Muhammad himself.

In a way, he was also cast as a messianic figure by the elders within Kashmiri society, who were critical in promoting him as their leader. As Muhammad Yusuf Saraf, himself Abdullah's follower who later joined the MC, notes in his history of the Kashmir movement, Kashmir's respected people:

> Treated him, in the glare of watchful congregations, as a Saviour who possessed the powers of spiritualism and was capable of miracles. For instance, they would bow before him; someone would take out his shoes; another one would kiss his hands; yet another would touch his clothes and then raise his hands in prayer; while retreating from him, they would not turn their backs towards him. All this created a deep impression on the thousands of spectators and gave him an aura of holiness.[45]

And outside of Kashmir, it was the Punjab press, particularly *Inquilab* and *Zamindar*, that played a large role in bringing and keeping Abdullah in the limelight.

Abdullah knew that momentum was on their side, and it was time to take the movement, and introduce himself as its leader, to the countryside. Malik, his professor from Lahore, while summering in Kashmir, helped Abdullah tailor his speeches to appeal to the people of rural Kashmir. K.N. Pandita, who grew up in Baramulla, described how Abdullah spoke in a different tenor to rural folk, dwelling at length on the land and the reasons why it yielded so little for those who toiled on it, the natural disasters that brought with them famine and the bureaucrats who fleeced the suffering peasants.[46] In a speech in 1933, he noted that the Quran taught that the purpose of human existence was to help others and he had done and was doing what God demanded of him. He continued:

> It is not that your motherland cannot provide you with *roti* [bread]; its every corner is filled with treasures, but what can we do if our hands and feet are tied and those who control our fate have no pity on us? What kind of *aazadi* [freedom] is this, that 90 per cent of the people of Kashmir, which was once the centre of knowledge and talent, cannot

> recognize the alphabet? What happened to that industry and craft that filled our hearts with pride? What happened to the shawl that made us famous in foreign lands? Oh poor compatriots, this is a painful tale, but as long as God and your love is with me, we will continue to work towards our goal together.[47]

The aftermath of 1931 also brought others—such as Bakshi and Beg, who had been on the sidelines until this point—more squarely into the movement, thus establishing and bringing together a coterie of leaders who would form Abdullah's inner circle for years to come. Abdullah deputed Beg, with his roots in the countryside, to help spread the message among the peasants. At the same time he suggested Beg's name, due to his legal background, as a translator for the investigative commissions set up by the Maharaja to look into the incidents of 13 July and their aftermath.[48] Bakshi came to the forefront as leader of the war councils that were set up to manage the crowds as they battled the police and the army.[49] The movement was small-scale and disorganized at this time, but there was a camaraderie among those who were involved. The small shop owners on the third bridge in Srinagar would smuggle Abdullah from one shop to another to keep him hidden from the authorities. They even deputed a tailor to sew a burqa for him so that he could get around without detection, but his height gave him away.[50]

By the end of 1931, Abdullah had come to the notice of the British Resident as the 'strongest local champion of Muslim demands', who had a 'following greater than any other local leader'.[51] By this time, the fire of rebellion had engulfed the entire state, with no-revenue campaigns springing up in various parts of Jammu without the consent of the leadership. The situation was further complicated by the involvement of Punjabi Muslim organizations and groups, some of whom stormed the state in support of their Kashmiri brethren. While the Kashmir Committee, formed under the guidance of Iqbal with several Ahmadi members, was in favour of taking a less extreme position, the Majlis-e-Ahrar, which was responsible for sending bands of volunteers into the state to support Kashmiri protesters, wanted Kashmiri Muslims to demand fully responsible government.[52]

Abdullah was caught in the middle, attempting to bring about a consensus so that a memorial could be presented to the Maharaja. He himself did not take a stand on either side, although it was clear that he was more inclined towards the Kashmir Committee due to his relationship with Iqbal. Ultimately, the Kashmir's Committee's version of the memorial won the day—this demanded that the Maharaja constitute an assembly to allow people's representatives a voice in governance. But this rift would come back to haunt the movement. As Abbas wrote years later, he and Abdullah were naive enough in the early days to expect justice from the Maharaja.[53]

Under pressure on all fronts, the Maharaja relented enough to appoint a commission led by B.J. Glancy, an official lent by the colonial state to J&K, to consider Muslim and non-Muslim demands and make recommendations for their redress. Muslim memorials to the Glancy Commission mainly focused on two issues: the affront to Muslim religious sensibilities as a result of the state occupation of their sacred spaces, such as Pathar Masjid in Srinagar, and the lack of adequate educational opportunities for Muslims of the state. In his memorial, Abdullah focused on the latter, writing, 'I have never heard of any truly useful steps having been taken by the Government, to strike at the root causes, that play a prominent part, in alienating the Musalman from Educational Institutions.'[54] After all, he argued, the teaching staff of all the government schools was Hindu and did not inspire much confidence in the Muslim boys, who dropped out of primary schools in large numbers as a result. In spite of these hardships, he continued, the Muslims who succeeded in passing the higher examinations were not given their share in the state services: 'The successful Muslim student rots and vegetates on a meagre salary while the misbehaved pandit, returns home a qualified hand, thanks to his Hindu patrons. If under these circumstances the muslims [*sic.*] remains in the same rut into which he was forced by the (unfortunate?) fact of his being muslim, is he to blame?'[55]

Abdullah was also one of the Muslims who gave oral evidence during the commission's hearings, focusing on providing numerical proof of Muslim educational backwardness and lack of representation in government service. At this stage, for him and the others involved in the movement, what mattered most was securing the religious rights of the Muslim community by ensuring the return of their sacred spaces to the community from the state, which was in control of a number of mosques, and the economic rights of educated Muslims. In the latter, Abdullah was willing to single out the Kashmiri Pandit community and point to its role in keeping Muslims backward. Kashmiri Pandits retaliated in kind, refusing to acknowledge their culpability, instead focusing on their own inability to gain entry into government services. Communal tensions ran at an all-time high, especially since Hindu and Muslim organizations from outside the state loudly defended the claims of their respective communities. This was not yet a movement that spoke the language of the nation, of transcending religious and class differences to fight autocracy.

In the short term, the movement was successful in securing recommendations from the Glancy Commission that addressed the major Muslim concerns. But it also brought out the divisions within the community and between Kashmiri Muslims and Pandits. Some Muslims felt that the commission rushed its report and that it was not revolutionary enough.[56] Although he signed the report, Abbas felt compelled to write a lengthy note of dissent, in which he proposed drastic measures to ensure fair representation for Muslims in civil services and the administration of the state.[57] From Abbas's perspective, what began in 1931 was an Islamic movement to address the demands of the Muslims, because it was the Muslims of the state that had been suffering under the rule of Hindus.

Kashmiri Pandits, for their part, were bitterly opposed to the commission's proposals because they felt that their implementation would threaten their foothold in government service. Prem Nath Bazaz, on the other hand, went against his community in endorsing the proposals, drawing such wrath that he had to leave the Sanatan Dharma Youngmen's Association, the Pandit organization of which he was a member.[58] Kashyap Bandhu, another prominent Kashmiri Pandit, also saw the legitimacy of Muslim grievances and approved of the commission's recommendations to redress them. Ashai arranged a meeting between him and Abdullah in 1932, and the two men had a long, frank discussion about the possibility of forming a joint front between Muslims and Pandits to end autocratic rule. During moments of communal tension, Bandhu often took the stage with Abdullah, exhorting the audience to maintain peace and brotherhood.[59]

Most importantly, the events of 1931 and the Glancy Commission helped catapult Abdullah into the public eye. By the time the dust settled on the commission's deliberations, Abdullah had done a few more rounds in prison and emerged as the leader to contend with. Not unlike Gandhi in the case of British India as a whole, Abdullah legitimized and politicized the act of being imprisoned. Indeed, prison would become the defining theme of his political life. Each turn in prison endowed him with greater political power and an almost messianic status, as people came to pay obeisance at his home much like they did at the shrines of Kashmir's saints. Ladishah, Kashmir's travelling poets, began spreading the news about the events of 1931 and Abdullah's miraculous abilities around the state; their renditions would usually begin with the words, 'Keep your ears peeled; I'm about to relate the story of Sher-i-Kashmir.' One such story was that Abdullah had emerged unhurt from a cauldron of burning oil into which he had been thrown while in prison.[60]

A Kashmiri *masnavi* published in 1932 entitled *Safinaye Nooh, almaroof Sach Aawaaz* (Noah's Ark, or the True Voice), hailed the voice of truth and justice that had descended on Kashmir through Abdullah. The poem likened the 1931 incidents to the martyrdom of Hassan and Hussain in Karbala:

> Look at the light of faith, the greatness of Allah
> Who are the real Muslims?
> Only they became famous who died for their rights,
> And embraced the way of the royal jails.
> Those faithfuls were shot in the chests
> And sacrificed their lives, look at the greatness of Allah.[61]

Other pamphlets, all written and published in the Punjab, declared that the exalted Abdullah arrived on the scene to 'lift the burden of oppression off the shoulders of Muslims'. Although he was terrorized by the government and incarcerated, he continued to work for the Muslims and said, 'I am a Muslim, devoted to my community … If the ruler puts me to death, another Muslim will succeed me and will never turn back; we are several thousand in number. But even then I shall feel that my coreligionists are being oppressed.'[62] Another part of the same pamphlet entitled 'Well done, Lion of Kashmir' stated that Abdullah 'bore the standard of the faith'. He 'came boldly into the field. He suffered jail three times for our sakes, and denied himself the necessaries of life, saying that his brethren in Islam were being persecuted.'[63]

While he did not actually perform miraculous feats in prison, Abdullah insisted that the jail authorities make a distinction between common criminals and him and his fellow rebels by demanding their rights as political prisoners. In a February 1932 report, a frustrated jailor noted that Abdullah refused to be searched by the warder, throwing away all his clothes and bedding in protest. This was because the prisoners received regular news in the form of newspaper cuttings and letters from the outside world, smuggled in through prison workers and visitors. And in turn, Abdullah sent instructions to the workers outside jail to send emissaries to specific places to spread the message of the movement. Some weeks later, the jailor had to contend with a hunger strike led by Abdullah and other prisoners in protest against poor prison conditions and the allegation that Kashmiri Pandit prisoners were being given better treatment.[64] This was strikingly similar to the hunger strikes in the late 1920s led by jailed members of the HSRA, including Bhagat Singh, to draw attention to their movement from behind bars. In a sense, prison became a training ground for Abdullah, both in terms of trying out the techniques of civil disobedience as well as sharing ideas and planning the course of the movement with individuals who held similar beliefs.

But his mass appeal at this moment belied the fact that Abdullah faced an uphill task: He had been pushed to the top by the support of prominent Kashmiris and now he had to maintain this position in the face of rising schisms within the community on the future of the movement. He was acutely aware that what made him popular and a good choice as leader—that he was a fearless orator with no family connections—also made him both a threat to some and more vulnerable in general. While most of the young men who were involved in the movement—with the exception perhaps of Bakshi—could turn to their families for financial and other kinds of support, he could not. The time had come to parry the challenges to his authority and secure his position as paramount leader of Kashmiri Muslims.

## CONSOLIDATING POWER

Abdullah was gradually coming to believe in his own powers. The leap from being an unknown man from a modest family background with few prospects to having his hem kissed by people as he walked by them and having strands of his hair snatched as souvenirs was overwhelming; as he noted later, 'I was but an average man and felt crushed under their expectations.'[65] But it must also have been deeply appealing to his sense of self and assuaged somewhat the sense of inferiority that had hounded him all his life. At this time, he also came to recognize that he would never become the sole leader of Kashmiri Muslims unless he superseded the position of the head preacher of Kashmir. While Mirwaiz Hamadani, with his base in Khanqah-i-Mualla, remained Abdullah's supporter, the Mirwaiz Kashmir Yusuf Shah, with his base in the Jama Masjid, had come to regard Abdullah as a threat to his position and begun to challenge him publicly by questioning his faith.

But as the Mirwaiz would soon find out, Abdullah could be a deadly opponent. He effectively utilized the decades-old schism between the two Mirwaizes to carve up the city and take control of its shrines. Since the return by the state of the Muslim community's sacred spaces was one of the basic demands of the movement, having control over the most significant of these shrines and mosques ensured Abdullah's supremacy in any political contest. It was a masterstroke, because it allowed Abdullah, throughout his career, to claim Kashmiri Muslim sovereignty over Kashmir, and his own leadership, through these sacred spaces.

At a basic level, the contest between Abdullah and Mirwaiz Yusuf Shah had a significant class dimension. The Mirwaiz and his supporters were the old-guard landed elites as well as government servants who had much to lose by taking on the Maharaja and his administration. From the beginning, they had been uncomfortable with Abdullah's tactics and what his rise meant for their own economic position in Kashmiri society. Although the Mirwaiz had initially been drawn to the revolutionary fervour of the movement, he was now concerned about the challenge the movement and Abdullah's emergence as a serious rival posed to his and his family's comfortable position as the state-recognized head preachers of the city of Srinagar, and the mass following that it brought with it. This position gave him economic security as well as protected him politically, for instance, by keeping him from being imprisoned.

On the other hand was Abdullah, who represented the newly educated professional classes that were chafing at the bit to revolt against the regime on behalf of Kashmiri Muslims, and willing to risk prison for it. They spoke the language of justice and rights, not of loyalty and forbearance. Theirs was a powerful rhetoric that made sense to the urban proletariat that was struggling under the yoke of economic exploitation. In fact, Abdullah, with the help of Bakshi, became especially skilled at deploying the 'Jumakher' (Friday ruffians), as they were known—young men who worked as unskilled labour in shops and factories and 'physically dominated' the streets, especially around shrines, on Fridays when their workplaces were closed—as 'storm troopers with iron bars' of the movement. They were the ones who would gather for a demonstration at short notice or a protest outside a prison or courthouse or other administrative offices, even rioting if the need arose. Abdullah retained their support until the mid-1940s.[66]

It was these men whose loyalty to Abdullah the Mirwaiz tried to subvert by labelling him an Ahmadi, and thus not a true Muslim. In this, he was harking back to the rhetoric of the late nineteenth-century dispute between the then Mirwaiz Kashmir and the Mirwaiz Hamadani. This battle had also been about gaining control over the city's shrines and mosques and was fought on the terrain of defining and defending what was held to be 'true' Islam. The Mirwaiz Kashmir's forebear had labelled his opponent a *mushrik*, or sacrilegious saint-worshipper, while he himself was charged with being a Wahhabi who was against Kashmiri Islam, of which saint-worship was a key component.

Mirwaiz Yusuf Shah's attempts at maligning Abdullah with the title of *kafir* (infidel) and Ahmadi held a similar purpose and also took aim at his close relationship to the Kashmir Committee. But they had the consequence of turning his rival, Mirwaiz Hamadani, as well as other shrine managers against him and bringing them over to Abdullah's side along with their substantial followings. More effectively still, Abdullah levelled a much more damaging charge against the Mirwaiz and his family; they were no longer labelled Wahhabis, but something far worse: loyalists of the Maharaja and the Dogra state. That Yusuf Shah never seemed to be in prison provided proof enough for this charge to be credible.[67]

Thus, by the time Abdullah gave his welcome address in October 1932 as president of the newly formed organization named the All Jammu and Kashmir Muslim Conference—that heralded a new phase in the history of Muslim politics in the state—the movement had already frayed. This organization was the brainchild of the Kashmir Committee in Lahore and the efforts of Kashmiris such as Masoodi, who was closely allied with the committee. Masoodi had occasion to meet Abdullah for the first time in Central Jail in Srinagar in January 1932; he had been arrested after resigning from his position at S.P. College and making a speech at Khanqah-i-Mualla declaring his sympathy with the movement. After spending some time with Abdullah, during which they became close, Masoodi felt that Abdullah was the right man to lead the movement because he was larger than life and had the ability to mobilize people. Masoodi proposed the idea of a political party that would become the representative of the movement and suggested the name Muslim Conference. Abdullah readily accepted.[68]

After their release in June 1932, a committee was convened that worked on the organization's constitution and adopted its name. Abdullah had become the chief spokesperson for the movement by this time; as he stated in an interview to the *Civil and Military Gazette* in July 1932, 'I am fully in favor of giving them [the regime] a chance of overhauling the administration and redressing our genuine grievances. I shall, as far as possible, try to co-operate with the administration and help it in reconstructing the State. This, however, depends on ... the future policy of the administration itself.'[69] Not surprisingly, he was unanimously elected as the organization's first president. Ghulam Abbas was elected as the first general secretary.

October 14, 15 and 16, 1932, were historic days for the movement and Abdullah as its leader. Two hundred representatives and 300,000 people gathered around the stage that had been constructed at the site of Pathar Masjid, one of the sacred spaces that had been handed over to the Muslim community by the state under the recommendations of the Glancy Commission. The flag of the MC was hoisted and Ashai read the welcome address. Abdullah then gave his presidential address, calling on Kashmiri Muslims to unite, gain an education and be prepared to serve notice to the government as well as to participate in assembly elections as soon as they were called. He recalled the past glory of the Kashmiris, which was lost when they became the slaves of non-Kashmiri rulers. Emphasizing that the Kashmiri Muslim movement was non-communal, he went on to accuse the administration of holding communal views, which had led them to insult the Quran and injure the religious feelings of Kashmiri Muslims. He assured the minorities that the movement was not directed against them and that 'we shall always try to redress their grievances but they must also respect our just rights'.[70]

Late 1932 to 1933 was a busy time for Abdullah as he took to his new role as an elected leader of a political organization with alacrity. Recognizing that it depended to a large extent on support from Punjabi organizations and the Punjabi press, a fact that he had acknowledged in his presidential address, he shuttled back and forth between Lahore and Kashmir during this time, accompanied by Ashai, among others, meeting with Muslim leaders and attempting to determine how to pressure the Dogra regime to implement the Glancy Commission's recommendations. But he was also confronted with the challenge of representing a community wracked by internal discord, for which he was himself partially responsible. Although the Mirwaiz had participated in the first session of the MC, he now took the opportunity provided by Abdullah's frequent absences from Kashmir to ratchet up the rhetoric against him.

But Abdullah was not one to back down. He deputed Bakshi, who had an ear to the street and was a master organizer, to raise a volunteer corps—a regiment of which consisted of lorry drivers from the locality of Maisuma in Srinagar—to enforce their control over the city's sacred spaces. Masons, embroiderers, carpet weavers soon joined in. By mid-1933, the city was divided between Abdullah and the Mirwaiz, with the former claiming the right to make speeches from most of the city's shrines, including Hazratbal, while the latter was restricted to the area around Jama Masjid in the old city of Srinagar. Violent clashes between the supporters of the two sides—now known as Shers (Abdullah's supporters) and Bakras (the Mirwaiz's supporters)—became commonplace.[71]

Individuals belonging to one group were often attacked while making their way through the city by the other side's supporters. Bakshi's 'Maisuma Regiment', as it was called, frequently harassed and often assaulted the Bakras, pulling off their dussas (shawls) as a mark of depriving them of their wealth. Abdullah himself was often seen moving around the city with these men, hockey stick in hand, engaging in pitched battles with the other side.[72] In time, Bakshi became his right-hand man, keeping Abdullah anchored to the practicalities on the ground of running a movement, an organization and, later, an administration. For instance, he was in charge of the construction of the headquarters of the MC, Mujahid Manzil, on the land adjacent to Pathar Masjid, a project begun in 1933 and completed in 1935. He also organized and monitored the neighbourhood (mohalla) committees that were the sinews of the MC organization.[73]

Soon enough, the Sher–Bakra schism had spread throughout the Valley and into towns and the countryside beyond Srinagar. Everyone within the movement felt forced to take sides, so strongly entrenched was this division. Abbas, for instance, clearly recognized that Abdullah was the future, but at the same time, he was uncomfortable about speaking out against the Mirwaiz or questioning his personal integrity.[74] A new generation of Kashmiris, who were born in the late 1910s/early 1920s, grew up politically aware of the movement and the nature of the schism between Abdullah and the Mirwaiz, which had also found its way into educational institutions. Syed Mir Qasim, who was born in 1919 and raised in Anantnag, noted in his autobiography that the town was divided between the opponents and supporters of Abdullah and the Mirwaiz. He himself attended the high school patronized by the Mirwaiz Hamadani that promoted Abdullah's progressive politics, which prompted him to organize a protest against a local landlord when he was in the eleventh grade. The other high school in the town, patronized by the Mirwaiz Yusuf Shah, espoused his more conservative views.[75]

By 1933, Abdullah was already well-established politically as he approached the age of twenty-eight. But his deep involvement in political affairs had left him little time to attend to his personal life. He continued to operate from a rented room with hardly any support from his family. And questions had begun to be raised about his relationships to the women who visited him. It was apparent to his supporters, and not least to himself, that the time was nigh to settle down, get married and start a family. This would not only anchor him, but also dampen his detractors, who were looking for any reason to besmirch his name. It was a difficult task to find a bride for a leader who had dedicated his life to the cause, and had few financial prospects and an uncertain future, especially since the union had to benefit the movement as much as Abdullah himself. But his colleagues, such as Shaal, were determined to find a suitable match.[76]

They chose Akbar Jehan, the daughter of Michael Henry Nedou—an Austro-Hungarian convert to Islam, whose father had built hotels in Lahore, Gulmarg and Srinagar at the turn of the twentieth century—and Mir Jan, a Gujjar woman. This was a canny choice that would ensure Abdullah's financial and political security, since the Nedou family was wealthy without displaying any overt political leanings. It was financially beneficial in other ways too because it led many of Abdullah's wealthier supporters to raise money for him to make him financially independent of his father-in-law. The couple, whose marriage was solemnized by the Mirwaiz Hamadani in October 1933, moved into a small house behind the Nedou Hotel in Srinagar. Akbar Jehan would spend winters with her parents in Lahore, where Abdullah would sometimes join her.[77]

Eventually, Abdullah would build a house, known as Sher-i-Kashmir Manzil, near his ancestral home in Soura with help from his brothers, where his growing family would settle down. His wife was primarily responsible for raising the children, since until 1947, if he was not serving a sentence, Abdullah was on the road for much of the time. Personal financial worries dogged Abdullah throughout his life. He himself admitted in his autobiography that his wife's family helped her out during lean times.[78] Akbar Jehan would also come to play a significant political role in the movement after Abdullah's arrest in 1946, during the crucial period preceding Indian Independence and Partition as well as during Abdullah's long years of incarceration after 1947.

His personal life more settled, Abdullah turned to confront the gathering storm on the political horizon. The Mirwaiz had broken away from the MC and launched his own political organization, the Azad Muslim Party Conference, in late 1933. In his presidential address on the founding of the Azad Party, the Mirwaiz drew attention to the role played by his family in the Kashmiri Muslims' struggle for their rights, and his own activities in 1931 as the logical continuation of this role. But he struck out on his own as soon as he realized that the Ahmadis controlled this movement and would not let the Ahrars help the Kashmiri people, realizing that 'to stay out of politics would be a crime against Islam'.[79] Around this time, the Mirwaiz also began to sidle up to the regime: In a letter to the Maharaja asking for a reconsideration of the order banning religious sermons, the Mirwaiz expressed his sincere loyalty to the government. He claimed that he had dissociated from the 1931 movement so that he could preach religious sermons exhorting people to remain peaceful. Additionally, when he realized that Sheikh Abdullah and his party wanted to launch an agitation against the government, and 'thereby plunge the country in the depths of destruction', he opposed their mission. He asked them to stop the agitation immediately and dispense with 'Mirzaies [Ahmadis] and such revolutionary men'.[80]

The Mirwaiz was echoing the increasing Ahmadi–Ahrar rift that had opened up in Punjabi Muslim politics and spread to the Kashmir Committee, with Ahrars demanding the resignation of its Ahmadi members. In 1933, they had pressured the Ahmadi Khalifa Mirza Bashiruddin to resign as head of the committee and replaced him with Iqbal. Although he decried this move, Abdullah increasingly felt that the movement in Kashmir, and he himself on a personal level, needed to steer clear of this acrimony and began to separate the MC from Punjabi Muslim politics. He made it clear that he did not want to be identified with the Ahmadi movement. This led to the resignation of several prominent Kashmiri Ahmadi members, including Vakil, from the MC.[81]

In the meantime, the movement within Kashmir had taken on a life of its own, much to Abdullah's discomfort. Local leaders had emerged in various towns across the Valley and were organizing protests and demonstrations, leading to police retaliation and bloodshed. These gathered steam after the Maharaja's announcement in early 1934 of the foundation of a state assembly, which was to be known as the Praja Sabha. The assembly was to have no more than the power of interpellation, passing resolutions and discussing the budget, with the Maharaja retaining the ultimate political power in that the executive was responsible to him and not to the assembly. Its thirty-three elected members would be elected through a limited franchise.[82] At the MC's working committee meeting, Abdullah expressed his disappointment at this announcement, but also felt that the agitation had to be called off because it was setting a dangerous precedent by allowing anyone to organize a protest without consulting with the MC.[83] Abdullah's concern with threats to his own authority both within and outside the organization was apparent early on in his career.

And on the matter of the Praja Sabha, which Abdullah did not want to boycott outright, he seemed to be on a different wavelength with the majority of the other members of the working committee. For him, the idea of being able to field candidates in the assembly elections and win the twenty-one seats allocated to Muslims in the Praja Sabha, thus establishing the predominance of the MC over Muslim politics in the state, was too attractive a prize to ignore. There were so many promising young men that had recently joined the MC and could be fielded as candidates, such as Sadiq, a fervent communist recently returned from

Aligarh with a degree in law, as well as Sadiq's cousin Karra, also an Aligarh graduate. This led to one of the early disagreements between him and Abbas, who was an uncompromising proponent of the boycott. Abbas was in prison for his views when Abdullah visited to persuade him to support the MC's participation in the elections. He refused and was shocked to find out that Abdullah was going ahead with it despite his strong reservations, and had hand-picked the candidates, including Beg and Sadiq, to represent the constituencies.[84]

Although the MC won sixteen seats unopposed and beat the Azad Party candidates in five others, MC workers were disillusioned with Abdullah and the movement, according to Abbas, for playing into the hands of the regime.[85] But from Abdullah's perspective, this was a triumph. He had achieved his goal of putting the Mirwaiz in his place and demonstrating to the Maharaja and the national leadership outside Kashmir that he was not simply an unemployed agitator, but was to be reckoned with as the sole leader of Kashmiri Muslims.

## THE LIFE OF A LEADER

Abdullah had indeed achieved something quite remarkable in a short period of time. He had made a leap from a life of obscurity to life in the limelight. And he had established a political organization that in a matter of years was running a parallel administration in most neighbourhoods of Srinagar and other cities, mediating and settling small property disputes and family conflicts while collecting funds and rice for financing the movement.

Most remarkably, he had done this despite or perhaps because he came from a humble background, with no claim to any political connections or even descent from the illustrious line of the Prophet. Yet, it was Abdullah, a descendant of a Hindu convert to Islam, who stirred the very souls of Kashmiri Muslims with his prophetic call to fight injustice. Iqbal's verse, which he often recited during his speeches, was his call to arms, 'Love's duty was to raise a cry: that is done / Now hold your heart and wait to see the effect of that cry!'[86] Since he was a science graduate and had not received an education in the literary classics or the classics of historical and political literature, he was self-educated and developed a political instinct through pure experience. His route to leadership was sui generis, in a sense. And his achievement, for which he had to surmount his own feelings of inferiority, was a testament to his mental and physical toughness, and his keen ability to utilize the larger context and the people around him to his fullest advantage.

Abdullah's political education in Lahore and Aligarh gave him a vocabulary for his feelings towards the exploitation, repression and penury he saw around him while growing up in Kashmir. In this, he was no different from the generation of Kashmiris from a variety of walks of life who were chafing at the authoritarianism of the Dogra regime and were angered and embarrassed in turn at the suffering of Kashmiri Muslims both within and outside Kashmir. Much like him, they sensed that the time was ripe to organize the restive Kashmiri population into a movement, but many were constrained by family and employment situations. What set Abdullah apart was that he had few such constraints and an impassioned personality that gave him the courage to speak out. The older members of the generation groomed him to take on the role of leader and put him forward to the people as a spiritual figure with a political message. He took to the role with dedication and enthusiasm, drawing the masses into the fold with his towering personality and progressive politics that interwove Islamic rhetoric with Iqbal's poetic vision of sacrifice, defiance and justice.

Although he emerged on top, 1931 gave rise to a crop of leaders—Kashyap Bandhu would later refer to this moment as having generated a 'leader industry'—some of whom Abdullah gradually cultivated as his circle of advisors.[87] Foremost among them were Bakshi, Beg and Sadiq, with whom he would have indispensable yet rocky relationships into the future. Other early supporters, such as Abbas, came to disagree with his politics and tactics and gradually distanced themselves from him. And yet others became lifelong adversaries, particularly the Mirwaiz, as Abdullah simultaneously united the Muslims of Kashmir in the fight against injustice while also dividing them to cement his position as their leader.

He wrested control of a large portion of the shrines and mosques of the Valley from the religious leadership, and at the same time demanded that the government return those under its control to the community, thereby appropriating these sacred spaces as political symbols of Kashmiri sovereignty and freedom. He set himself and the movement apart by presenting both as belonging to the people. But at this stage, Abdullah was not beyond labelling Hindus as the other and responsible for the plight of Kashmiri Muslims. These early moves cast him as the undisputed leader of the Valley's Muslims, leaving unresolved the issue of representing all the inhabitants of the princely state regardless of their religious affiliation or region, a tension that would define his political career.

For all the adulation he received, Abdullah cut a strikingly solitary figure in these years. He had many colleagues and multitudes of supporters, but almost no close friends. He was not particularly close to anyone in his immediate family, and even after his marriage, he remained aloof from domestic life due to his immersion in political work. In a way, this was the moment when he chose Kashmiris, perhaps unconsciously, as his family, and came to believe that he was the father of them all.

# 2

# Defining the Leader and the Movement, 1935–1946

Well done, O braveheart, shepherd of the watan!
Well done, O guide of the youth.
The hearts of the young and old are in the palm of your hand,
You are the Sher of our homeland, Jammu and Kashmir!

—Epigraph, P.N. Bazaz, *Kashmir ka Gandhi* (1935)

THE YEAR 1935 PROVED CRUCIAL IN WHAT WAS AT THAT TIME SHEIKH Abdullah's nascent political career. He had managed to prove his mettle as the representative of Kashmiri Muslim interests since the incidents of 1931, the subsequent establishment of the Muslim Conference (MC) and the victory of its candidates in the first Praja Sabha elections. But what exactly he and the movement stood for was still unclear. His leadership of the Kashmiri Muslim community as a whole continued to be challenged by the Mirwaiz. He faced a barrage of rumours that he was an Ahmadi, and hence a Muslim apostate, along with charges that he was a communal Muslim who was working against Hindu interests, all of which poisoned the atmosphere against him. So Abdullah decided to take charge of his own image and that of the movement, placing the task in the hands of his new friend, P.N. Bazaz. In 1935, Bazaz published a biography of Sheikh Abdullah that cemented his persona as Sher-i-Kashmir, as evident in the above-mentioned epigraph to the book, and created a specific image of Abdullah as a secular Muslim that has endured through the decades.[1] Also in the same year, the two joined hands to found the newspaper *Hamdard* to serve as the mouthpiece of the emergent movement.

Bazaz's *Kashmir ka Gandhi* was a profound intervention into Abdullah's image, designed to counter the propaganda against him and, in a sense, present him to the wider world of Indian nationalist politics. Yet, the biography's representation of Abdullah as a secular warrior against injustice for the entire Kashmiri nation rather than merely a warrior for Islam and Kashmiri Muslims—in the tradition of the Frontier Gandhi, Khan Abdul Ghaffar Khan, for the Pashtun nation, or indeed Gandhi himself for the Indian nation as a whole—ran somewhat counter to his image on the ground in Kashmir. The constant negotiation between this image and reality defined Abdullah's entire political life, but especially the years when he was attempting to establish himself as the leader of the movement in Kashmir. The nature of the movement became intertwined with the increasingly unresolved tension between these two facets of Abdullah's persona as leader: a committed Muslim devoted to Islam and Kashmiri Muslims, and a secular nationalist devoted to securing political and economic rights for all Kashmiris. This was further complicated by the fact that Abdullah the secular nationalist defined the Kashmiri nation as the Kashmir Valley, even though he claimed to speak on behalf of the entire state. These tensions were heightened in the context of ideologies such as communism, socialism and nationalism, along with their proponents, that filtered into Kashmir through British India, influencing Abdullah and nudging him to take a stand regarding the movement's alignments and direction.

The year 1946 proved to be yet more decisive in Abdullah's political career. It began with his triumphant participation in the All India States' People's Conference (AISPC), held in January in Udaipur, where he was elected vice-president of the organization (with Jawaharlal Nehru as its president). He had finally attained the wider recognition that he so craved; he now represented the aspirations of not only the people of some backwater that could be easily dismissed, but all the Indian princely states. He took to his new role with alacrity, making speeches during his travels through Rajasthan demanding the recognition of the rights of the people of the states and questioning the All India Muslim League's policy on states' rights. Despite his new-found status, however, when he paid an impromptu visit to Maharaja Hari Singh in Bombay, he was told to make an appointment with the ruler's prime minister. That slight stung and stayed with him.[2] By the middle of the year, he was the Maharaja's prisoner, having given the call for the Quit Kashmir agitation, which demanded an abrogation of the Treaty of Amritsar and an end to the Maharaja's rule.

The period between 1935 and 1946, during which Abdullah emerged as a leader of national stature and in prison for his views and activities, is most illustrative if examined from the perspective of the deep divides within Abdullah's political personality. These divides—between being a Muslim versus nationalist leader; between crusading for employment opportunities for educated Muslims versus economic rights for the poor; between representing the interests of the Kashmir Valley versus those of the people of the entire state—are crucial to understanding the course of not just Abdullah's political career, but quite as much the political fate of the princely state of Jammu and Kashmir (J&K). Ultimately, many of the choices Abdullah made in these years between these facets of his personality played an enduring role in rendering J&K into a battleground between the newly independent states of India and Pakistan.

Nonetheless, his singular contribution during these years—the age of nationalism—was to conjure up the Kashmir nation by deftly weaving together existent ideas about Kashmir in its own narrative tradition as exceptional space, region and watan with ideas borrowed from Indian nationalism. In a sense, the narrative of Abdullah's life and the Kashmir nation were written together, melding into each other and becoming one.

## THE ABDULLAH–BAZAZ PARTNERSHIP

Abdullah and his supporters, led by Bakshi, had succeeded in establishing his leadership in the city of Srinagar by the mid-1930s. The city's sacred spaces were effectively divvied up between the Shers and the Bakras, with the larger portion coming under Abdullah's sphere of influence. The two sides continued to trade vicious verbal attacks in the public domain and physical clashes sporadically broke out on the city streets between their followers. The working poor were the shock troops that helped Abdullah, and the MC, maintain control over the city. But the organization—which was founded to address the demands of the educated unemployed and facilitate their access to government positions—had little to say about the welfare of the poor who toiled in miserable conditions. At the same time, the educated themselves seemed to be turning away from the organization, since the Glancy Commission's recommendations had opened up new avenues for them within the administration.

Bazaz, meanwhile, had been wrestling with the position of his own community, Kashmiri Pandits, in the emergent movement. He was aware that Pandits disliked the Dogra state's autocratic form of government but were also terrified of what they thought of as the communal agitation of Kashmiri Muslims. He attempted to draw the attention of Congress leaders to the movement in Kashmir, asking them for advice on its future direction. In a detailed letter to Mahatma Gandhi in 1934, he described the conditions in the state that led to the birth of the movement, seeking his counsel regarding whether Kashmiri Pandits should continue to oppose it because they feared that Muslim demands would lead to their annihilation, or if they should participate in the movement and thereby realign it along national lines. Bazaz felt strongly that Kashmiri Pandits should take the latter path. Although Gandhi's dismissive response, 'Seeing that Kashmir is predominantly Mussalman it is bound one day to become a Mussalman State,'[3] puzzled Bazaz, it did not deter him from joining hands with the up-and-coming Abdullah to recalibrate the movement and draw in minorities.

For his part, Abdullah saw in Bazaz an individual who could give the movement some heft and counter the charges that it was merely a predictably communal movement of Muslims against a Hindu Maharaja. Bazaz had proven his credentials when as a member of the Grievances Enquiry Commission and Constitutional Reforms Conference he genuinely attempted to redress Muslim grievances and voted for a representative assembly on a national basis. Thus, during one of their meetings in the beautiful environs of the Chashma Shahi Garden overlooking Dal Lake, when Bazaz presented the idea of adopting a more national programme for the movement that cut across class, sectarian and religious lines, Abdullah was instantly convinced.[4] He recognized that this would draw the working poor and peasantry, along with minorities, into the movement. It also had the added benefit of creating a new image for himself as a leader of the masses, thereby countering lingering ideas that he was a pawn of Punjabi Muslim organizations and that the movement in Kashmir was being directed by them for their own purposes. This was his opportunity to wrest control of the narrative.

The choice of *Kashmir ka Gandhi* as the title for Abdullah's biography, thus, was not accidental. As noted earlier, the book presented Abdullah as occupying the same stature in Kashmir as Gandhi did in British India, while also conjuring up regional Muslim, pro-Congress leaders such as Khan Abdul Ghaffar Khan of the Northwest Frontier Province (NWFP), himself known as Frontier Gandhi. Bazaz pointed out in the preface to the book that the credit for waking up a dormant quom went entirely to Sheikh Abdullah, who had not yet turned thirty and had already managed to become the ideal of Kashmir's youth. Much like Gandhi in India, the real political strings in Kashmir were pulled by Abdullah, who had been an unknown figure until a few years ago and could now command young men to sacrifice themselves for their mulk. Most significantly, Abdullah resembled Gandhi because he had always been a follower of the Congress path and now wanted to run the movement officially along Congress lines. Bazaz hoped that the book would neutralize the propaganda against him and gain Abdullah the recognition as Kashmir's Gandhi.[5]

The biography followed Abdullah's evolution from a young boy who was moved by instances of injustice around him to a young man who could not bear to see the ill-treatment meted out to Kashmiri labourers in the Punjab. Most of the book meticulously recorded the years since Abdullah's return to Kashmir in 1930 after completing his higher education, as he rose to become the undisputed leader of the movement through various stints in prison. Explaining why the movement had focused solely on Muslim grievances thus far, the book argued that Abdullah had always been non-communal by orientation and knew that Kashmiris were being oppressed regardless of their religious affiliation. But he realized that the political status of Muslims had not reached the stage that would allow non-Muslims to accept a Muslim as leader, and Muslims would not be drawn to the movement unless it was under the rallying cry of 'Islam in Danger'. Hence, in the early stages, he focused on working for the advancement of Muslims so that they could realize their potential as the majority community. Once this had been achieved, he felt that it would become easier to persuade minorities to join the movement.[6] Throughout this early period, according to the book, Abdullah attempted to calm down the rising tensions between Kashmiri Muslims and Hindus by appealing to Kashmiris to maintain peace in the name of their motherland.[7]

The book also addressed the issue of the acrimony between Abdullah and Mirwaiz Yusuf Shah, and their respective followers, by attributing it to the Mirwaiz's jealousy at Abdullah's rise as leader of Kashmiri Muslims, a position that he claimed as rightfully his. According to Bazaz, the Mirwaiz, who was driven by love for his quom as well and wanted to participate in the movement, could not abide the adoration that Kashmiri Muslims were showering on Abdullah, and began to accept money from the Dogra regime to defame Abdullah among Muslims. He started a propaganda campaign accusing Abdullah of not being a true Muslim by suggesting, incorrectly, that he was a follower of the Ahmadi sect and had married a Christian woman. But people saw through these ploys as Abdullah went to prison multiple times in service of his quom and overwhelmingly supported him and his party.[8]

By late 1934, according to the book, Abdullah was convinced that the time was ripe to take the movement in a national direction. After spending a few months in Punjab and Delhi with Congress workers, whose honesty and dedication impressed him, Abdullah declared that he would found an organization in Kashmir that would operate on Congress principles. He asked Punjabi Muslim organizations to stay out of

Kashmir's internal affairs and blamed the recent communal disturbances in the state on their machinations.[9] The book ends with extracts from Abdullah's speeches that proved that he was secular, not anti-Maharaja and dedicated to the service of all Kashmiris regardless of class and religion.

This biography established a basic narrative about Abdullah's rise and his political proclivities that Abdullah himself held on to in his public persona, especially in political circles, and continued to do so until the end of his life, as evident in his autobiographical narration, *Aatish-i-Chinar*. The newspaper *Hamdard*, with Muhammad Sayyed Masoodi as its first editor, served as the public voice of the movement and its founder. In the speech declaring his intention to found the newspaper, Abdullah noted that it was designed to spread the virtues of '*sahi quomparasti*' (correct patriotism) that would enable Kashmiris to continue their struggle along nationalistic lines. It was time, he said, for Muslims to earn the trust and goodwill of minorities and bring them into the movement so that it did not face the same accusation as was being levelled by Muslims against the Congress in India.[10]

While at some level the attempts by the biography and the *Hamdard* to link Abdullah's image to Gandhi, and hence the burgeoning movement to the Congress, can be viewed as propaganda, one also has to recognize the striking similarities between the two leaders. Much like Gandhi, Abdullah was deeply committed to his religion, but drew on it to imagine a plural nation. He thus spoke the language of justice and rights in the idiom of his faith, also like Gandhi. And again, much as in the case of Gandhi, this evoked mistrust among minorities regarding his true intentions.

In an exchange of letters with Nehru in 1936, Bazaz attempted to apprise him of the challenges facing the movement in Kashmir and draw the Congress more actively into supporting it. This exchange, published in an issue of the *Hamdard* later the same year, illustrated that Nehru thought of the Kashmir movement as a 'local struggle' bound up with the larger struggle for Indian independence. And in that light, he agreed with the need for taking the Kashmir movement in a national direction, because the issues facing the people, not just in Kashmir but everywhere in the world, were national and economic, not communal. 'All talk of Pan-Islam and Pakistan', according to Nehru, 'is the veriest nonsense' and 'a passing phenomenon'. He advised Kashmiri Pandits, as the educated minority, to give up their narrow communal outlook and 'think of their own welfare in terms of the welfare of Kashmir as a whole'.[11] Nehru's 'Advice to the Youth of Kashmir', also published in the *Hamdard* the same year, quite bluntly stated:

> Kashmir's destiny is intertwined with that of Hindustan because if Hindustan gains independence then Kashmir will definitely ask for its share ... The fate of the 8 crore people of the princely states cannot be separated from that of the people of British India. In fact, both peoples are riding in the same boat. If Kashmiris would only recognize that their education, economy and culture was in the hands of an irresponsible government, then nothing could stop them from attaining their rights.[12]

Nehru's words demonstrated his personal interest in and views on Kashmir, but also reflected the increasingly interventionist stance of the Congress towards the internal affairs of princely states, starting in the mid-1930s and gathering steam after Congress victories in the 1937 provincial elections held in British India. The 1938 Haripura Resolution officially declared princely states to be an integral part of India and pledged to engage in activities to bring about political, economic and social freedoms in these states along the lines of British India.

This had far-reaching consequences in a state such as J&K, particularly for Abdullah's leadership. Linking the movement, and hence Abdullah himself, with the Congress and its 'nationalism' in so public a manner created two kinds of rifts. The first was a dissonance in Abdullah's own political persona—while he might have been cultivating his image as a secular leader for Pandits, select educated Muslims and outsiders, he continued to present himself as a spiritual leader to Kashmiri Muslim masses and speak to them in an Islamic idiom. Indeed, his popularity with the people of Kashmir was deeply intertwined with the shrines and mosques that they regularly visited. From their pulpits, Abdullah's melodious recitations of the Quran interspersed with fiery rhetoric against autocracy drew people to him in droves. For them, Abdullah was a messiah who had been sent down by Allah to lift them out of their oppression and degradation. Thus, it seemed that he spoke in a different language to Kashmiris than he did to outsiders. As Abdullah himself argued, there was no necessary contradiction between being secular and Muslim; indeed, it was Islam that had set him on the path of secularism, but in the context of Indian politics, he could never quite shake off the doubts about his primary loyalty that arose as a result.

Questions about Abdullah's Muslim versus nationalist allegiances also defined the second, equally significant, rift in J&K politics as a whole that eventually created the conditions for its partition between India and Pakistan. The rhetoric of nationalism did not appeal to educated Muslims, who had joined the movement to advance their own interests and not those of Kashmiri Hindus or their more oppressed brethren. To them it looked like Abdullah had traded one master, Punjabi Muslim organizations, for another less appealing one, the Congress. That many of these Muslims were from the Jammu province meant that this was the decisive moment for Abdullah's leadership when he began to lose Jammu's support, thereby increasingly confining his leadership to the Kashmir Valley.

Fiery broadsides appeared accusing Abdullah of selling out Islam in the name of nationalism. The authors of a one-page proclamation published in the summer of 1937, for instance, appealed to Muslims to rise up against the movement because it was designed to wipe out any trace of Islam from Kashmir's politics under the guise of *wataniyat* and *quomiyat* (nationalism). The purpose of the MC, they argued, had originally been not only to bring about political progress, but also to preserve Kashmir's Islamic identity. Abdullah had fallen under the influence of individuals such as Bazaz, who had elevated him to the position of Kashmir's Gandhi, and was steering the movement in a catastrophic direction. Launching a strident critique of the *Hamdard*, the proclamation noted that the objective of Abdullah and his co-conspirator, Bazaz, was to convince Muslim youth that an Islamic administration would be communal and murderous, and to establish a dictatorship under Abdullah. The authors declared that Abdullah had hammered the final nail in the organization's coffin by adopting nationalism as the credo of the MC in its 1937 annual session in Poonch.[13]

Meanwhile, it was clear that the Hindus of Jammu were not interested in the nationalist turn either, nor in joining a Muslim-majority organization, evident from the agitation they launched against the proposed changes to the cow slaughter laws of the state as demanded by the MC. Abdullah issued a lengthy statement to the press in response to this agitation, noting that the MC had not demanded the complete abrogation of the law, but rather a reduction in the sentence for cow slaughter, especially of old and diseased animals. They had also requested that the government be responsible for providing for the upkeep of such animals. He ended by saying that although the MC was approaching this from the perspective of nationalism, such laws, which imposed harsh sentences for acts that were considered lawful by Muslims, were simply unacceptable in a state that was 80 per cent Muslim. J&K could not, he noted, be called a Hindu state.[14]

These were heady times for Abdullah. He had spent time with Nehru earlier that year and was drawn to his handsome and innocent demeanour as well as his love and concern for Kashmir. He had not intended to accompany Nehru to the NWFP from Lahore, but they got so lost in conversation in the railway compartment at the Lahore station—'as if we had been friends for years'—that before they knew it, the train had reached Shahdara. Nehru then insisted that Abdullah accompany him all the way to the NWFP, where Abdullah met the charismatic Pathan leader Khan Abdul Ghaffar Khan, and likely witnessed the Khudai Khidmatgar movement's close association with the Congress. He was deeply affected by these meetings, and no doubt also impressed by the Congress's performance in the 1937 provincial elections, leaving him more convinced than ever that the movement in Kashmir needed to change direction and open itself up to people of all religious backgrounds, especially to garner the powerful support of Indian nationalist leaders.[15]

He became a frequent visitor at Congress gatherings in Lahore, which were attended by prominent nationalist Muslims such as Maulana Abul Kalam Azad and Mian Muhammad Iftikharuddin (he would later, in 1945, join the Muslim League). Not having a similar social or educational pedigree as most political leaders in British India, or even in Kashmir, Abdullah always craved recognition. Aligning with the Congress movement and rubbing shoulders with leaders of high standing offered him both the personal satisfaction as well as the political opportunity of being elevated from a mere provincial leader to one of national stature.

Nevertheless, his close association with the Congress cost him dearly, and charges that he was a stooge of the party dogged his entire political career. He was responding to these charges even at the end of his life, saying that Muhammad Iqbal, in the same year as he met Nehru, had also advised him to open the membership of the Conference to all Kashmiris to more successfully form a united front against autocracy.[16] But at that time, Abdullah's enthusiasm for the nationalist turn knew no bounds as he attempted to convince other Kashmiri leaders of its necessity. They all, including those who had nationalist leanings, such as G.M. Sadiq, had deep misgivings about tying the Kashmir movement to the Indian nationalist movement so closely, because they were unsure about what it would mean for its image within Kashmir itself. It was also clear to them that the Congress had its own reasons for cultivating a leader such as Abdullah at this juncture, especially in the wake of its poor showing amongst Muslims in the 1937 provincial elections: to bring a Muslim-majority princely state into its sphere of influence through its recently launched Muslim mass-contact campaign. After all, it was K.M. Ashraf, the Congress socialist in charge of the campaign, who had visited Kashmir in 1937 to meet Kashmiri leaders and then organized the Lahore train station meeting between Abdullah and Nehru.[17]

To Chaudhuri Ghulam Abbas from Jammu, it appeared that Abdullah—who, in Abbas's view, was incapable of holding independent opinions and would change ideologies depending on the person that had his ear at any given moment—had fallen victim to the views of his most recent advisor. He had drunk so deeply of the draught of nationalism that he was unwilling to see any reason during the intense discussions between the two men, which eventually descended into a bitter argument, right before the 1937 annual session.[18] Abbas told Abdullah that the Muslims of Jammu had been fighting to preserve their own interests in the face of Hindu opposition and narrow-mindedness since the 1920s, and would never accept their entry into the organization, nor would Hindus want to work with Muslims. Kashmiri Muslims were in a different position because they were a majority in the Valley, and Hindus were so small in number that they had little choice but to go along with the majority.[19]

Abdullah was quite aware that he was leading Kashmiri Muslims towards the Congress when Indian Muslims were decoupling from it. But for him, the situation of Indian Muslims as a minority community seeking to safeguard its interests from Hindus was completely different from the situation of the Muslims of Kashmir, who were in a confident majority and for whom it made political sense to align with an organization that supported the rights of the people of the states.[20] Throughout his political career, he sympathized with the predicament of Indian Muslims, but did not consider their interests to be similar to those of Kashmiri Muslims.

And he possessed a degree of doggedness once he had made up his mind about something that made it impossible to convince him otherwise. The strident opposition only made him more determined to push through his agenda of nationalizing the MC, and he brought the matter to a vote in the 1938 annual session in Jammu. This was a particularly inimical place to do so because the Jammu Muslim delegates were dead set against the move, as a result of which a resolution to change the name of the organization to the National Conference (NC) was passed, but with a crucial amendment. This amendment, tabled by the Jammu leader Allah Rakha Sagar, proposed a postponement of the decision until the next session to give delegates more time to canvass the views of their constituents.[21] For the next year, Abdullah kept up a steady drumbeat of speeches and Bazaz followed up with a campaign in the *Hamdard* to push for a national organization with the slogan of responsible government.

## NATIONALISM, COMMUNISM AND ISLAM

In a statement to the press on 16 June 1938, Abdullah argued that the time was nigh to change the constitution of the MC to include non-Muslims into its ranks and adopt all progressive elements into the new organization's agenda. Only then would Kashmir play an 'honourable part in the comity of federated units of India'.[22] Article after article in the 31 July 1938 issue of the *Hamdard*, entitled the 'Responsible Government Number', noted the importance of changing the platform of the movement from a demand for government jobs to addressing the economic exploitation of peasants and labour, and Kashmiris in general regardless of their religious affiliation, as well as demanding responsible government. For instance, one of the articles, penned by 'a liberal Muslim graduate', argued that '*naukri* politics' (employment politics) was responsible for the creation of a communal divide between Hindus and Muslims, and the objectives of the movement had to change to make it more palatable to minorities. Kashmiris wanted the government to run on democratic lines and be answerable to the people so that their economic concerns could be addressed.[23]

In his message to the people in this issue, Abdullah focused almost entirely on the problems of poverty and economic exploitation, which he said were economic, not religious, issues. The plight of the poor was attributable not to religion, but to capitalism and capitalists. The state treasury, he said, was a pond that had been filled through the work of peasants and labouring classes, but the right to distribute the water had been given to a select few who were not answerable in any way to those who filled the pond. 'Demand your just right to the water from the pond by uniting against the exploiters,' he exhorted.[24] In another speech, he noted that just like Muslims, Hindus and Sikhs too were struggling under an irresponsible and unfeeling government; they too had to pay high taxes; they too were starving and indebted. And as a result, they needed to be brought into the organization to fight the common enemy. He added that the downtrodden peasants in the countryside and struggling labourers in cities had to be organized and brought under the flag of this united movement.[25]

This shift in Abdullah's rhetoric towards issues of social and economic uplift has to be attributed at least in part to leftist, in particular communist, influence. By 1938, prominent literati associated with the Communist Party of India and the Progressive Writers' Association—including Muhammad Din Taseer, Faiz Ahmed Faiz, Mulk Raj Anand and Balraj Sahni—had begun to summer in Kashmir and socialize with Kashmiri leaders. In 1941, Taseer accepted the position of principal of Sri Pratap College, Srinagar. They were soon followed by other leftists such as B.P.L. Bedi and his British wife, Freda Bedi, both of whom became especially close to Sheikh Abdullah. Several Kashmiris themselves, including Bazaz, N.N. Raina and Sadiq, had been impacted by leftist ideologies while studying in British India and introduced them to the MC, eventually bringing other Kashmiris into the fold.[26] Sadiq organized the Kashmir Mazdoor Sabha, along with Bazaz, to represent the interests of peasants and labour.[27]

Abdullah's nationalist and socialist tilt also brought an influx of new blood into the organization, including seasoned Kashmiri Pandit leaders such as Kashyap Bandhu, who joined the NC in 1938, and younger Kashmiri Pandits and Hindus from Jammu. This new generation of Kashmiris and Jammuites, such as D.P. Dhar, P.N. Jalali, Om Saraf, Krishna Dev Sethi and Balraj Puri, among others, were born in the 1920s at the very eve of the launch of the movement and had grown up in the midst of the political changes ushered in by it. Most were educated in British India and many were dedicated communists. They were impressed by Abdullah's progressive politics and believed in the potential of the organization to usher in real changes by ending economic exploitation, particularly in the Jammu province, which was riddled with landlordism.[28]

Although Bakshi did not officially proclaim his communist credentials, he was most responsible for organizing the working classes—that had helped Abdullah's side gain and maintain control over the city—into trade associations. With a keen political instinct, he recognized that the movement had to keep happy the volunteers on the ground who controlled the street. This in turn meant that the demands of the economically depressed but enterprising classes, such as silk factory workers, tongawallahs, motor drivers and carpet weavers, had to be addressed. For instance, Bakshi brought together motor drivers, who had emerged as a distinct group that plied the hazardous route on the Jhelum Valley Road connecting Srinagar to Rawalpindi, to form the powerful Motor Drivers Association. The members of this association would play a critical role in maintaining lines of communication between the imprisoned and underground leaders of the Quit Kashmir agitation in Kashmir and those in the Punjab in 1946–7.[29] In 1937–8, such organizations submitted a series of memorials listing their demands to the J&K government and organized a spate of strikes, which endowed the new rhetoric of the movement with credibility on the ground.[30]

This provided the larger political-economic context for the conversion of the Muslim Conference to the National Conference, which officially took place at the 1939 annual session in Srinagar under the chairmanship, significantly, of Sadiq. Abdullah, fresh out of a six-month prison term for his political activities, chose him to lead this historic session because he felt that Sadiq was firmly secular and 'represented a forward-looking generation'.[31] As the delegates made speeches at the site of the historic Shahi Masjid, Abdullah basked in the glory of being celebrated as the primary agent of this momentous change that was about to take place. He was especially satisfied with Abbas's speech, which endorsed his views and called on Muslims to accept the change and welcome minorities into the organization.[32] But this moment of triumph was short-lived. Although the vote to change the organization's name and direction won with an overwhelming majority, rumblings of dissent could already be heard during this session. And despite his speech, Abbas himself remained unconvinced of the merits of this change, as was amply clear in the spirited discussions among the leaders prior to the official session. This was the beginning of the break that would rent asunder the politics of the state and take Abdullah down with it.

Almost immediately after this session, educated Kashmiri Muslims, especially those in government service, began to drift away from the movement. Others who wanted government positions felt caught in a bind between the movement and their ambitions. Agitated, Abdullah went to Lahore to meet with prominent Congress leaders and attempted to persuade them to visit Kashmir so as to stem this tide. Saifuddin Kitchlew and Gopi Chand assured him that they would explain the situation to Nehru and, on receiving a favourable response, organize a Congress conference in Srinagar.[33] On his return, Abdullah either denounced the individuals who were leaving the NC as careerists or ignored them, both of which he could afford to do because the educated middle class among Kashmiri Muslims was small compared to Jammu Muslims.[34]

Even though their delegates voted for the resolution, Jammu Muslims were entirely against the conversion and felt that the organization was no longer representative of their interests. There were several reasons for their alienation, a basic one being that although it was never openly stated, in Abdullah's nationalist discourse, the Kashmiri nation was synonymous with the Valley. It evoked its exceptionality, its beauty and its status as paradise on earth. In the definition and past of this nation, Jammu appeared as an afterthought. The Jammu Muslims were also far more tied to Punjabi Muslim politics, which was not particularly enamoured of the Congress version of nationalism. The Muslim League's Lahore Resolution of 1940 made them partial to the Pakistan idea and wary of an organization that was not linked to the Muslim League, but its rival, the Congress.

Abbas and his coterie had agreed to vote for the resolution on certain conditions, including that the organization would continue to represent the special interests of Muslims, Abdullah would not follow the direction of the Congress working committee, and there would be no opposition to the Muslim League's agenda. But it became apparent to them quickly that Abdullah had no intention of sticking to these conditions. When he visited Lahore to meet Nehru and wrote articles for *The Tribune* praising the Congress vision while criticizing the Muslim League and Jinnah, Abbas was convinced that Abdullah had accepted Nehru as his guru, even perhaps his spiritual leader. Abdullah's sudden love of nationalism, he felt, was simply a ploy to acquire international fame and fortune and held no consideration for the future of his quom.[35]

These ideas were cemented in the context of Nehru's visit to Kashmir with Khan Abdul Ghaffar Khan in the summer of 1940—clearly to counter the impact of the Lahore Resolution—which was celebrated with much fanfare by the NC. In his speeches in Srinagar, Nehru successfully linked the future of Kashmir with that of India and the native states as a whole, making veiled criticisms of 'communal organizations' that 'are opposing the Congress at every stage and on every question', including in the states. Addressing the Kashmiri Pandit demand for separate electorates, he noted that 'safeguards and weightages', which also 'the enemies of India's freedom attach great importance to', would not assuage their fears or rid them of their minority status. Their only choice was to join the NC organization and become part of a movement with a far greater goal. For Abdullah, he reserved special praise, describing him as a 'brave and far-seeing leader' who 'has made Kashmir a bulwark of our national movement'.[36]

These actions, coupled with Abdullah's refusal to protest government measures seen as inimical to Muslim interests, led many supporters to cut ties with him. M.A. Sabir, Moulvi Abdullah Vakil's son, who had been one of his earliest backers, noted, 'The Congress aimed at the annihilation of Islam, and India and Nehru had come to Kashmir to make Kashmiri Muslims the slaves of this organization.'[37] By 1941, prominent Jammu Muslims, led by Abbas, had defected from the NC to revive the MC. As Abbas noted, this was a sad day for the Kashmir movement because it was now divided and its leadership at odds.[38] This division fell firmly along regional lines, with the MC (based in Jammu) allying itself with the Muslim League, while the NC (based in the Valley) allied itself with the Congress. To add to the mix, the Mirwaiz immediately jumped onto the MC bandwagon to cut his opponent down to size, and several prominent Kashmiri Pandits were lured away from the NC by the regime.[39]

The NC thus lost powerful and wealthy backers, leaving Abdullah himself in financially straitened circumstances. His family life was suffering as a result and also because of his frequent absences from home. His wife, Akbar Jehan, wrote to P.N. Bazaz in 1940, after the birth of their baby daughter, that her father had recently passed away and her mother and brothers were helping to financially support the family, while Abdullah seemed too busy to pay attention to them.[40] By 1943, Abdullah was father to five children, none of whom saw much of him. Farooq Abdullah, born in 1937, stated that Abdullah was mostly absent during his childhood, and he and his siblings were raised by their mother and the extended family in the house built by Abdullah's brothers for his family in Soura, their birthplace.[41] Besides his own and his wife's family, several individuals, including Bazaz and Munshi Ishaq, made financial contributions for the upkeep of Abdullah's family and the organization.[42]

Faced with defections, divisions, financial worries and the revival of an organization that he had fought so hard to convert into something entirely new, Abdullah busied himself with what he did best, especially during troubled times—he appealed to his base. And he did this almost always by returning to the sacred sites that had allowed him to establish political control over the city. In a brilliant move that linked Kashmiris' religious aspirations with their political and economic rights, the NC established the All Jammu and Kashmir Auqaf Trust in 1940 for the development, maintenance and control of religious places, including Hazratbal shrine and the religious sites that the state had returned to the Muslim community in the 1930s. Abdullah was named its founder president.[43]

The trust was designed to address several issues at once. It allowed Abdullah, through the NC, to control major religious sites and the lands associated with them across the Kashmir Valley. These lands were converted into orchards in some cases and rented out to shopkeepers in others, thus yielding major financial benefits for Abdullah's family as well as the organization. Other areas near the famous Pathar or Shahi Masjid were reclaimed by the trust to build the headquarters of the NC, Mujahid Manzil, from where the daily activities of the organization were carried out and its newspapers printed.[44]

The control of the religious sites also renewed the political support of the local shrine managers and their substantial followings; these, significantly, included workers' associations that visited shrines to make supplications on behalf of the group.[45] Further still, it became a means to nudge Abdullah's political rival, the Mirwaiz, out of his sphere of influence, most significantly Hazratbal shrine, under numerous pretexts, such as the need for an orderly exhibition of the holy relic that was housed in the shrine and the general lack of cleanliness around it.[46] The most important function served by the trust was to assure Kashmiri Muslims on the ground that Abdullah remained their spiritual leader.

Abdullah's appeal to his base through organizations such as the Auqaf brought him in conflict with the secular wing within the party, especially Bazaz, who felt that such practices smacked of sectarianism and should be carefully avoided. In long discussions, the two debated the merits of using such tactics, with Bazaz attempting to persuade Abdullah not to give up on the nationalist creed. But Abdullah, and others within the party, such as Masoodi and Afzal Beg, were not prepared to cede ground to the revived MC. The NC's public meetings, as earlier, began with recitations of the Quran, and some of its members continued to attack non-Muslims for dominating the administration. In 1941, the NC members within the legislature loudly protested the Educational Reforms Commission's recommendation on the medium of instruction, which was to be simple Urdu that could be written both in the Devanagari and Persian scripts. They labelled this an attempt to eradicate Urdu from the state. All Hindu members of the NC working committee resigned on this issue and Bazaz walked out of the meeting in which Abdullah was delivering a fiery speech against this measure.

Bazaz was dismayed especially because the NC had approved a similar measure at its meeting in Mirpur and recommended it to the commission, but in public opposed it in order to assuage Muslim sentiments. This was neither democratic, nor secular, in Bazaz's view. He grew increasingly disillusioned with Abdullah and doubted his capacity to stick to a truly nationalist agenda. In November 1941, he resigned from the NC and in 1942 founded the Kashmir Socialist Party. Over the next decade, he became the NC's, and Abdullah's, staunchest critic.[47]

Other Kashmiri Pandits too were disillusioned with what they perceived to be Abdullah's increasing turn towards the politics of religion to solidify his base as well as his dictatorial tendencies. Kashyap Bandhu, who had worked with Abdullah to reconcile Muslims and Hindus long before he officially joined the NC, was upset on two counts, both of which he outlined to Abdullah before resigning from the NC in 1941. First, he felt that the NC working committee, of which he was a member, should have been consulted before issuing Nehru an invitation, since the implications of such a visit would be far-reaching and needed to be considered. Instead, on 26 May, he was informed that Nehru would be arriving in Srinagar on 30 May. When he brought this up with Abdullah, the latter was livid and said that he did not care if this was a contravention of democratic norms within the organization.[48]

Second, Bandhu had all along observed that Abdullah wanted to be both a nationalist leader as well as a leader of Muslims, roles that were irreconcilable in his opinion. Both he and Bazaz took umbrage at Abdullah's speech on the Prophet's birthday, describing him as the last messenger of God and the Quran revealed through him as being so perfect that there was no longer any need for divine guidance. Abdullah's retort—that he had spoken purely as a Muslim, and that he was a nationalist in much the same way as was Maulana Azad, who also shared the same beliefs as a Muslim—did little to convince them. They did not share his view that 'religion is the progenitor of national consciousness'.[49] Bandhu repeatedly requested Abdullah to hand over the leadership of the Auqaf Trust to another individual because it cast doubt on his nationalist credentials, but Abdullah refused. He told Bandhu in a conversation that he was a Muslim first and last, and had chosen the path of nationalism because the Quran instructed him to do so.[50] What Bandhu did not seem to recognize was that besides his personal faith in Islam, Abdullah was very mindful of the fact that devoid of his political identity as a Muslim that was so tied to his control over shrines, he would not have much of a mass base at all.

Nevertheless, his attempts to reconcile the two facets of his political personality—as a Muslim and a nationalist—were failing. By 1942, he had alienated, among many others, two of his closest allies, both of whom separated themselves from the movement, hence leaving it ideologically bereft, in a sense. Each man had very different ideas on the direction of the movement: While Abbas believed that the movement should be focused on promoting the interests of the Muslims of the state, Bazaz believed that it should follow secular principles that uplifted all communities of the state. Abdullah's actions convinced neither of them that he was committed to their cause. He wanted to be both a Muslim leader as well as a secular, nationalist one, but succeeded in being neither. At the same time, he became much more self-confident as a leader and began to think of himself as a national figure who required the outward trappings that such a role afforded him, including a house, a car and an expensive shawl on his shoulders. He bore little resemblance to the diffident man who had been pushed to the forefront of the movement by the earlier leadership in 1931–2. N.N. Raina, an active communist in the party, described him as a 'patriotic person with elementary nationalistic feelings and sympathy for the poor'.[51]

It was at this delicate juncture that the space left by individuals such as Bazaz and Abbas, both in Abdullah's life as well as the life of the organization, was taken over by communists. This was not without its own problems. Abdullah had to walk a precarious line between communists and their detractors within the NC, as divisions between the two sides began to come to the fore. Sadiq led the communist camp while Masoodi led the anti-communist camp, with some others flitting in between the two depending on personal animus and political contingencies. As a result, although he seemed to be following the leftist line, Abdullah never declared an allegiance to the Communist Party of India (CPI) or communism, since that would not have resonated well with his image as a devout Muslim. Moreover, it would not be conducive to continued Congress support, since the Congress right-wing was already suspicious of the strong communist presence within the NC.[52]

Abdullah's response was to stay silent, although he did tacitly give his blessings to the formation of the Kashmir Youth Congress, an anti-Communist organization led by Muhammad Yusuf Saraf and K.N. Bamzai.[53] But overtly, he did not take sides on any major issue such as of self-determination for all nationalities, which was the CPI's official stand but not that of the Congress. At the same time, the NC did not openly support the Congress's 1942 Quit India resolution, which was against the CPI's official pro-Allies policy during the war, instead passing a resolution for the overthrow of fascism.[54] As long as the communists within the NC did not form their own coterie that would challenge his leadership, Abdullah was willing to give them a wide berth. Indeed, the squabbles amongst the top leadership might have ultimately worked in his favour, allowing him to play patron to both as well as mediator between them, and prevent the formation of a front against him. But most importantly, Abdullah needed the communists to provide the organization with a viable ideology and much-needed programme for action to keep it relevant during those trying times.

## NAYA KASHMIR

It was 1943, and ordinary Kashmiris were suffering the economic impact of the war. This was made worse by a drought that sent the prices of food grains skyrocketing. Abdullah in the meantime had decided to work with the regime, in the hope of turning it against the resurgent MC. The regime was more than happy to oblige, and appointed NC members to the boards that issued rice ration tickets and fuel permits as well as allowing them wide licence to suppress MC activities in the Valley.[55] As its activities descended into violence, favouritism and corruption, the NC drew harsh criticism in the MC press as well as papers such as the *Hamdard*, which threatened to erode the organization's position and Abdullah's own image among common Kashmiris. The result was that the MC started making inroads even into NC strongholds in the Kashmir Valley, such as Baramulla and Anantnag.[56]

At this moment, the Maharaja convened a Constitutional Reforms Commission that was charged with the task of making recommendations to bring about a progressive system of governance in the state, and nominated Beg and Sadiq to join it. This commission, Abdullah realized, would amount to not much more than window dressing, and the participation of the NC in it would give credence to his critics' charges that he had turned into a loyalist of the regime. In addition, the middle tier of NC leaders, who had emerged as a result of union organizing in the late 1930s and maintained the NC's popular support, were itching for the declaration of a radical policy platform that would represent the rights of the common working people. This group found the communist message linking the struggle of the Kashmiris with workers around the world highly attractive.

So when B.P.L. Bedi—the prominent Punjabi communist who had by this time become Abdullah's close friend and confidant having taken Bazaz's place in the inner circle—suggested to him that the moment was ripe to present the commission with an alternate constitution and to make the membership of the NC leaders on the commission contingent on its acceptance, Abdullah seized the opportunity.[57] The communist members of the NC, such as Sadiq and Raina, along with non-Kashmiris such as Bedi, Freda Bedi, Taseer, K.M. Ashraf and Ehsan Danish, had already been at work on this document and made the final push to complete it for presentation to the Maharaja.[58] This was the genesis of the Naya Kashmir Manifesto, which was meant to consolidate and re-energize support for the NC. And it did draw back in leaders such as Bandhu, who rejoined the NC in 1943 and was appointed a member of its working committee.

The need to unveil this new people's constitution for J&K became even more pressing after Jinnah's visit to Kashmir in July 1944, which was organized by the MC. Although Abdullah attempted to woo Jinnah by inviting him to attend a meeting of the NC, it was clear from the start that Jinnah had no intention of endorsing Abdullah as the undisputed leader of Kashmiris. In fact, he politely turned down Abdullah's offer of hospitality by saying that he had made his own 'arrangements and secured accommodation' for his stay in Kashmir.[59] He did attempt to broker a peace between Abbas and Abdullah, which came to naught since they held widely divergent ideas about the future of the state. And Jinnah ended his visit by making a public speech in which he declared the MC as the representative organization of 99 per cent of the Muslims of the state and Abbas its leader. He even asked Abdullah to disband the NC and bring his followers into the MC fold under Abbas's leadership.[60]

Abdullah could not take this lying down, and in private asked Jinnah to stop meddling in the politics of J&K; he might be the leader of Muslims in India, but beyond Kohala, Jinnah was seen as the Maharaja's puppet.[61] In public, Abdullah poured vitriol on Jinnah for bringing the 'evil germs of British India politics here' and criticized the Muslim League's policy of supporting the princes, declaring, 'Even if lakhs of Jinnahs come to Kashmir they cannot effect any change in the local politics.'[62] His supporters went so far as to mob the Quaid's motorcade in Srinagar. For Abbas, this was evidence that Abdullah was neither a nationalist nor a communalist, but rather a rank opportunist.[63] An editorial in the *Hamdard*, now an anti-NC paper, declared that Abdullah's overtures to Jinnah had proven to be politically suicidal for him, and if he wanted Jinnah's support, he would either have to give up his nationalism or end his political career.[64]

This did not prevent Abdullah from calling on nationalist Muslims to 'liquidate the leadership of Mr. Jinnah' in his speech to the Frontier Province Political Conference, which he attended in Peshawar in April 1945. But as he himself noted in this speech, while 'judged by any standard Mr. Jinnah was far inferior to the Congress President, Maulana Azad, the League President swayed the hearts of Muslim masses',[65] including, he well knew, even many of his own supporters. Therefore, Abdullah did not push the envelope on Jinnah too far within Kashmir itself. He also recognized the need for drastic action to resurrect himself as the true flag-bearer of the Kashmiri people's struggle against the ruling elites.

The Naya Kashmir Manifesto did just that. In fact, in the minds of the people at that time, and for posterity, Abdullah and its revolutionary objectives became synonymous. No matter how disillusioned Kashmiris grew of him as a leader in later decades, they would not deny that he had brought about an awakening among Kashmiri Muslims along the principles of Naya Kashmir. Released in pamphlet form, with the stirring image of a woman unfurling the NC flag (white plough on a red background) on its cover, this iconic document was adopted at the September 1944 session of the NC held in Srinagar, and presented in person to the Maharaja. Since the Maharaja rejected it as the blueprint for a constitution, the NC members on the Constitutional Reforms Commission resigned, and the organization dedicated itself to spreading the message of Naya Kashmir to the people.

In his introduction to the manifesto—written, much as the manifesto itself, by his communist comrades—Abdullah noted that the commission was simply another hurdle on the long road paved with thorns that Kashmiris had travelled on their way to Naya Kashmir. While the introduction recognized that the issue of Kashmir's independence during this time of war was linked to India's independence in particular, it explicitly brought the Kashmir struggle in line with communist movements around the world, especially Russia. As it pointed out, the Russian Republic had proven, as evident in part in its refusal to submit to Nazi Germany, that real freedom could only arise out of economic freedom; the NC's jihad had always been of the poor and downtrodden against the exploitative tyrants who remained unaware of the plight of the working people. The NC had been in search of a model state, Abdullah declared, and the blueprint it had come up with recognized that establishing a programme for the economic betterment of the people was the real foundation of democracy.[66]

Andrew Whitehead has shown that the text of the manifesto was lifted in large part from Stalin's 1936 constitution for the Soviet Union.[67] Its chapters on women, workers and peasants included revolutionary ideas such as equal wages and paid maternity leave, and the abolition of landlordism and the return of land to those who worked on it. Further, the manifesto propagated economic planning and state control of industries. It also advocated freedom of speech, press and assembly as well as equal rights irrespective of race, religion, nationality, birth or gender. And, it provided for universal suffrage for those aged eighteen and over to participate in the election of a national assembly that would exist as part of a constitutional monarchy subject to the authority of the Maharaja.[68]

Freda Bedi—described by Abdullah in *Aatish* as 'Bedi's sharp-minded, elegant wife' who had 'typed the manuscript'—had a far more substantial impact on the document than Abdullah let on.[69] She was at least in part the inspiration behind the cover as well as the passages that placed women on an equal footing.[70] The Bedis were also responsible for persuading Abdullah not to get Kashmir involved in the Congress's Quit India campaign and were active participants in the NC's annual sessions: In the 1943 meeting in Mirpur, Freda led a group of activist women in discussing the issues faced by women in Kashmir. She also described how poor Kashmiri women on the journey to Mirpur received Abdullah with songs of praise: 'Beggars at the door of history, they were singing for the only ray of light they knew. For one who fought for the poor and would see them ruling in the land of their poverty.'[71]

Abdullah, and the NC as a whole, had not considered the practicability of the manifesto, but once published and adopted, it became a powerful rhetorical device to attract the masses. The influential Kashmir Mazdoor Union began to popularize it among its members, even as feudal elements launched sharp attacks. There were others too who criticized it because they saw it as a ploy on Abdullah's part that hid his true intentions. Mohammad Amin Chugtai, a poet from Jammu, summed up their feelings:

> It is Sheikhji's fervent wish that New Kashmir emerges,
> And this New Kashmir is his own *jagir* [fiefdom].
> Even the tongawallahs in this New Kashmir should be ready for the
> battlefield,
> Everyone in this realm should become politically aware.
> If anyone dares to raise their voice against him,
> Bakshi's stick will transform into a sword in one moment.[72]

These criticisms notwithstanding, Naya Kashmir established Abdullah as a man of the people, a saintly figure guiding them out of poverty and deprivation.

But it was much more than that for Abdullah; for him, Naya Kashmir was a means to enter the Indian national stage and be taken seriously on it. The NC's August 1945 session in Sopore was the high-water mark of this moment for Abdullah. An influential group of non-Kashmiris attended this session, including Nehru, Maulana Azad, Indira Gandhi,

Khan Abdul Ghaffar Khan, the Baluchi leader Abdul Samad Khan Achakzai, the Gandhian activist Mridula Sarabhai, and B.P.L. and Freda Bedi. *The Civil and Military Gazette* gushed:

> How six years of systematic and vigorous spade-work among the backward and ignorant masses of Kashmir has made them a politically conscious, disciplined and progressive people was demonstrated on Friday when Sher-Kashmir Sheikh Mahomed Abdullah, President-elect of the All-Jammu and Kashmir National Conference was taken in a three-mile long procession. Men, women and children in their thousands marched like a disciplined army, shouting slogans of 'Inquilab Zindabad' and 'New Kashmir Zindabad'. Peasant women turned out in their thousands and lent colour to the procession. The procession passed through 100 tastefully decorated gates. In the evening, before a crowd of one lakh, Sheikh Abdullah delivered his presidential address.[73]

In this fiery address, Abdullah described the NC as a child of the war, because both began in the same year and because the organization had matured through the course of the global conflict. It had become more democratic and responsive to the needs of the people, as workers on the ground gained experience in distributing food and other essentials to the people. This experience would come in handy in the implementation of Naya Kashmir's goals, towards which the NC would move in peacetime. Naya Kashmir was a local document, he noted, yet one that could be applied to address national problems of Hindustan as a whole.[74]

Abdullah assailed the critics of the manifesto, labelling them as communal elements who were being directed by exploitative capitalists, and appealed to the workers of the NC to work hard to gain new members and spread Naya Kashmir's ideas to every corner of the mulk. Although criticizing the government, he requested the Maharaja to accept Naya Kashmir and help in its implementation, beginning with reforming the outdated and inefficient assembly.[75] To the Indian leadership of the Congress and the Muslim League, his message was simple: Resolve your differences and come to an agreement, because you are keeping Hindustan from progressing towards freedom. This was especially significant to the people of Kashmir because the question of its freedom was tied to the freedom of Hindustan.[76]

While he was appealing to the major Indian political organizations to mend their differences, Abdullah's own differences with Abbas were heating up within Kashmir itself. Indeed, his invitation to Nehru to attend the NC session was in response to Abbas's earlier invitation to Jinnah, which had not ended so well for Abdullah. Nehru's acceptance of the invitation was meant to bolster Abdullah's credentials and keep J&K firmly within the Congress fold. In his speeches at the session and in Srinagar, Nehru praised the NC as a mass, non-communal organization and its leader as a visionary. He called upon Kashmiri Pandits to give up on sectarian demands and join the organization, which welcomed all with open arms.[77]

The rancour of national politics, however, had made its way into Kashmir. It was on full display when MC workers assailed the river procession in Srinagar that had been organized for Congress leaders by the NC with violent protests. Sounding somewhat disingenuous in his statement to the press regarding the incident, Nehru said that he had 'tried to avoid ... incursions into the domestic politics of Kashmir', but had to express his 'sorrow at the regrettable incident', because he was shocked at the 'utter vulgarity and the absolute obscenity of the people's behaviour'.[78] Khan Abdul Ghaffar Khan also condemned the incidents in his speech at the annual session, noting, 'Such actions do not bring prestige and honour to the people's leaders; they only degrade those who commit such unseemly things.'[79] It was easy for Nehru, Ghaffar Khan and Abdullah to label such incidents as the work of 'communal' organizations from the morally righteous place of inclusive nationalism, but the fact remained that the NC had done the same to disrupt Jinnah's visit the previous year. Abdullah was certainly not past encouraging his followers to engage in violent sparring with his opponents if the occasion demanded it.

By the end of the summer of 1945, Abdullah was nationally recognized as a 'Nationalist Muslim', huddling in Srinagar with the likes of pro-Congress regional Muslim leaders such as Ghaffar Khan and Abdul

Samad Khan for long hours after the conclusion of the NC annual session to discuss matters of national importance.[80] He was also financially much more stable. Indira Gandhi, a frequent summer visitor to Kashmir in the 1940s, wrote to her father on 3 June 1945, 'I have seen Sheikh Sahib only once or twice. He seems to be very busy, making money, amongst other things. He takes contracts to supply things ... [and] is increasingly being influenced by the Communists.'[81] But at the same time, and precisely because he had embraced his status as 'Nationalist Muslim' and pushed the nationalist agenda with such alacrity, Abdullah was staring in the face of the profound divide that had emerged in the state's politics. Even within his own organization, he had to manoeuvre around the anti-communists and those with League sympathies who were not happy with the direction of the movement.

Some of Abdullah's personal relationships with NC members were also strained; he had a falling out with G.M. Karra, Sadiq's cousin and a prominent pro-communist member, because Abdullah turned down his offer of marriage between Karra's younger brother and Abdullah's eldest daughter.[82] Abdullah considered Karra a threat because he had an independent basis of support among silk factory and other workers; this feeling would become more pronounced in the next few years as he continued to undercut Karra and build Bakshi up in his stead. Other, younger members of the organization, such as Muhammad Yusuf Saraf, chose to leave the NC to join the MC at this moment.[83] In addition, Abdullah was at a loss on how to respond to the appointment of a local Kashmiri Pandit, R.C. Kak, as the prime minister of the state. He did not want to appear communal by criticizing him, but at the same time was frustrated at Kak's anti-NC, pro-MC attitude.[84] By 1946, the situation had come to a head, and Afzal Beg had to resign as member of the assembly since Kak was making it impossible for him to function within the body.

## A MOMENT OF TRIUMPH?

Abdullah had just turned forty when he was elected vice-president of the AISPC in January 1946. This was a remarkable achievement for a regional leader from a princely state who had been virtually unknown, even in Kashmir, a decade ago. Although their friendship did not survive the decade, he and Bazaz had achieved what they set out to do with the publication of *Kashmir ka Gandhi*. Abdullah became not just popular in his own state but also a well-known leader in India who regularly rubbed shoulders with none other than Nehru as well as other prominent Indian leaders. He was feted for redirecting the movement in J&K to bring it in line with the ideas and objectives of the wider Indian nationalist movement. This would have been difficult to imagine for a schoolteacher from Kashmir with an MA in Chemistry from Aligarh Muslim University. Abdullah's achievement rested in his ability to ally at strategic moments with particular individuals who would introduce him to global ideologies that provided him with the intellectual ammunition to shape the movement.

Bazaz brought to him the possibility of broadening the scope of the Kashmir movement by framing it in terms of nationalism, secularism and economic justice. As Abdullah came to recognize the benefits of this redirection, he worked closely with Bazaz to reshape his image as a secular leader more concerned with the economic well-being of all Kashmiris and not just educated Muslims. This was an image more for the outside world than for Kashmir itself, where he continued to be a spiritual leader of the Kashmiri Muslim masses, who could now also rely on him to address their concerns as they toiled and lived in miserable conditions with no recourse. But for educated Muslims, what appeared as Abdullah's wholesale embrace of a secular ideology in line with an organization such as the Congress was a threat to their interests. The fact that more Muslims from Jammu were educated meant that the rupture within the movement took on a regional character.

Abdullah was caught in a bind; politics in J&K and British India seldom allowed a leader or an organization to be both Muslim and secular, so he straddled the line. These attempts at being both did not convince educated Muslims and ended up alienating the minorities. Abdullah responded by broadening and cultivating his base by forming the Auqaf Trust to bring shrines under the organization's control, while at the same time promoting the political freedom and economic uplift of all Kashmiris regardless of religious affiliation. But these moves only heightened the tension between the two identities. Bedi, Raina and Sadiq, among others, introduced him to the ideology of communism, convincing him of the applicability of its ideas and practical dictates to Kashmir's problems and the organization's larger agenda. Although he never openly embraced it as he did nationalism and secularism, communism and the CPI's line dictated many of his political stances in these years.

Abdullah's actions ensured that the Kashmir movement became far more than a parochial movement of educated Muslims, instead becoming intermeshed with the wider trends of Indian nationalism and global communism. But by bringing it into the limelight and making himself subject to the dictates of these movements, he sowed the seeds of his own demise. This would become especially clear in the context of the Quit Kashmir agitation, followed by the partition of British India into India and Pakistan, which led to Abdullah's rise to the premiership of the Indian state of J&K.

# 3

# From Revolutionary to Prime Minister, 1946–1951

IN HIS SPEECH ON 5 NOVEMBER 1951 AT THE JAMMU AND KASHMIR (J&K) constituent assembly soon after its inauguration in October of the same year, Abdullah hailed it as 'the harbour of our freedom, a freedom which, for the first time in history, will enable the people of Jammu and Kashmir, whose duly elected representatives are gathered here, to shape the future of their country ... No person and no power can stand between them and the fulfillment of this—their historic task.'[1] For Abdullah, the constitution of this body, composed entirely of members of the National Conference (NC), was in many ways a triumph. But, in reality, it encapsulated the derailment of the Kashmiri nationalist movement, the multiple ills of Abdullah's first tenure as head of state, and the state's worsening relationship with the Indian centre.

The Quit Kashmir agitation, which Abdullah unilaterally launched in 1946 with similar bluster as he called on the Maharaja to quit Kashmir, also belied the reality on the ground. In both cases, Abdullah was struggling to bring about some cohesion in a movement that was flagging and fraying. Much had changed between the launch of the Quit Kashmir agitation in 1946 and the inauguration of J&K's constituent assembly five years later. The princely state of J&K no longer existed; the Maharaja did have to quit Kashmir after he had signed a document of the state's accession to India, but not without some struggle; India and Pakistan fought their first war over the state, leaving it truncated, with Abdullah ascending to the position of prime minister of the part that became the Indian state of Jammu and Kashmir; and perhaps most importantly, Kashmir was now the centre of a United Nations (UN)-meditated dispute.

Since he was in prison during the crucial period between May 1946 and September 1947, Abdullah had remarkably little involvement in the course of the momentous events that took place during these months. Even after his release in September, events took on a life of their own, forcing him to modulate his responses accordingly even as he tried to shape their course. This continued once he officially took over as head of state in 1948, a period that saw him attempting to seize the initiative on multiple fronts—locally, domestically, regionally and internationally—so that he could continue to remain salient as his popularity within J&K and beyond steadily dwindled. National and global events between 1946 and 1951 shaped Abdullah's transition from being a rebel fighting a despotic regime to the prime minister of a state that, while instituting some of the most progressive economic measures in the subcontinent's recent past, became despotic in its own right.

## QUIT KASHMIR AND ACCESSION

Abdullah was facing a crisis in mid-1946. The NC was beginning to look weak and the movement that Naya Kashmir had jumpstarted seemed to have peaked. The All India Muslim League had performed much better in the 1946 provincial elections than expected, winning over 80 per cent of Muslim seats in the provinces. Bakshi's suggestion that the NC revert to its Muslim roots was untenable, because Abdullah had been elected vice-president of the All India States' People's Conference (AISPC) and was sworn to uphold the principles of nationalism. His personal animus towards the Maharaja had deepened after the Maharaja refused to see him in Bombay and later accepted Mirza Afzal Beg's resignation from his council, appointing Mian Ahmad Yar Khan of the Muslim Conference (MC) in his place. It was clear to Abdullah that a stand needed to be taken against the regime that would galvanize Kashmiris and draw national attention to the NC and its cause. The occasion to do so was provided by the Cabinet Mission.

Besides its more lengthy proposals on the future of the provinces of British India, the Cabinet Mission briefly addressed the question of the princely states. It held that decolonization would result in the lapse of paramountcy, with all the rights that had been yielded by the states to the paramount power—Britain—reverting back to them. At this point, the states would have to enter into '"a federal relationship" or "particular political arrangements" with the successor government or governments'.[2] This raised the question of who ultimately had the right to decide the future of the states—the rulers or the people; the Congress came out in support of the latter under the aegis of their rulers, while the Muslim League supported the rights of the rulers with little regard for the people's movements in the states. Amidst this debate, Abdullah saw an opportunity to assert the rights of the people of J&K, and his own organization as their representative, to be the sole arbiter of the state's future by penning a memorandum to the mission.

This document defined the Valley as not only 'our homeland', but also the 'cradle of the Kashmiri nation, which by virtue of the homogeneity of its language, culture and tradition and its common history of suffering is today one of the rare places in India where all communities are backing up a united national demand'.[3] It then demanded the abrogation of the Treaty of Amritsar, thereby ending Dogra sovereignty over J&K and the establishment of a responsible government of and by the people. In effect, it asked the Dogra ruler to quit Kashmir. The primary dissonance within the movement and Abdullah's rhetoric was visible in this document: It defined the nation as the Kashmir Valley but demanded sovereignty on behalf of the entire princely state. Nevertheless, it set off the Quit Kashmir agitation.

To an extent, Abdullah did achieve his intended purpose, although at high cost to himself and the NC. Shortly after the memorandum became public, he was arrested on his way to Delhi for consultation with Congress leaders in mid-May of 1946. Other leaders too, including Afzal Beg and Kashyap Bandhu, were arrested soon thereafter, and N.N. Raina and Maulana Masoodi ended up in prison for offering *satyagraha* (sit-ins) on behalf of the arrested leaders. Some others, such as G.M. Karra, went underground in Kashmir, while G.M. Sadiq and Bakshi Ghulam Muhammad escaped to Lahore. And, in no uncertain terms meaning to crush the movement before it could gain momentum, the Dogra regime let loose a wave of repression against ordinary Kashmiris, adding to their already miserable plight.

But the movement, with Abdullah as its initiator, garnered national attention, in large part due to Nehru's willingness to take up cudgels on its and Abdullah's behalf. In his statement to the press regarding the incidents, Nehru was livid about the J&K government's tactics that had forced Abdullah and the NC to launch the movement. He acknowledged that the goal of the movement went against Congress and AISPC policy, which remained the attainment of responsible government under the aegis of the rulers, and that it was unfortunate that these bodies had not been consulted before this policy was adopted by the NC. 'But I recognise,' he noted, 'the feeling which gave rise to this policy in Kashmir and the total ineptitude of the State authorities which gave rise to that feeling.' As to the response of the J&K authorities to the agitation, it was simply unacceptable, according to Nehru, for which the Maharaja would 'have to suffer'.[4]

Although many Congress leaders were unhappy with his undiluted support of Abdullah and the agitation, Nehru continued to give statements to the press and offered to organize a defence for Abdullah when the regime announced that he would be tried on charges of sedition. At the same time, he wrote to the Maharaja about his impending visit to Kashmir and also requested him to suspend the trial and release all prisoners. Not only did the Maharaja not suspend the trial, but he also advised Nehru not to visit Kashmir. And when he attempted to do so in June, J&K authorities detained him, thus not allowing him to enter the state.[5] Nehru did finally make it into Kashmir in late July, met with Abdullah and persuaded him to not challenge the Maharaja's right to rule and instead to place Quit Kashmir in the context of the transfer of power to India in his statement.

In this long statement, Abdullah made clear that the agitation was not aimed at the person of the Maharaja or the Dogra dynasty, but was rather a recognition of the policy of the AISPC, which had laid down that 'the old treaties between the States and the British Government or its representatives are obsolete, and must end. That applies to all treaties including the Treaty of Amritsar, which has some special and unhappy features which make it a kind of sale deed of the territory and people of Kashmir.' This was further endorsed, he added, by the Cabinet Mission's declaration of the end of paramountcy, which would, in effect, lead to the termination of the treaties between British India and the states as well. The Maharaja rarely comes up in the statement; instead, Prime Minister R.C. Kak and his policies emerge very clearly as the focal point both for the agitation as well as for the ferocity of the response to it.[6] Despite the strident defence mounted by Asaf Ali, Nehru's close friend, on his behalf, and the other powerful attendees at the trial, including the British communist Rajani Palme Dutt (who had described Abdullah as 'one of the most honest, courageous and able political leaders'[7]), Abdullah was convicted of treason and sentenced to three and a half years in prison.

While in prison, Abdullah seemed to become disconnected from the agitation itself, as well as the momentous happenings outside, at least for the first year of his incarceration. For the first time in their marriage, Begum Abdullah came out of purdah, literally and figuratively, to take on a political role and became Abdullah's only trustworthy link to the NC machinery on the outside as well as a benevolent face of the movement for the suffering masses. She organized food committees to relieve hunger and deprivation among Kashmiris and travelled tirelessly across the Valley giving speeches to raise morale and keep the movement from waning. In summer 1947, she represented the NC in welcoming Gandhi to Srinagar and led a prayer meeting with him.[8] For these efforts, she would come to be known as Madar-e-Meherbaan (benevolent mother), thus claiming the status of mother to her husband's status as father of the Kashmiri nation. G.M. Shah, who would later marry Abdullah's eldest daughter, Khalida, joined the movement as a party worker at this time.[9]

These family members would have a profound impact on Abdullah's future political trajectory and that of the movement as a whole.

For the NC leadership, the declaration of Quit Kashmir came as a surprise, since Abdullah seemed to have taken the step without consulting them. According to N.N. Raina, the leaders and workers of the party were taken aback by the gravity of this announcement and the enormity of the undertaking before them. The party did not have the organization or funding necessary to carry out this kind of a movement without any preparation, especially given the severity of the response from the Dogra state.[10] As more of the leaders ended up in prison, they began to bicker over who was responsible for this arbitrary decision. The divide within the party among communists and non-communists became more pronounced as the former were blamed for encouraging Abdullah towards this 'mad adventure'.[11]

From the letters that were circulating among NC leaders during the agitation, both within and outside prison, it is clear that Karra led the actual movement on the ground from his hideout in Srinagar; Bakshi and Sadiq coordinated its propaganda from Lahore; and Munshi Ishaq, based in Rawalpindi, the headquarters of his own trucking company, managed the communication and financial aspects of the movement. Karra's letters careen between gloomy descriptions of a poorly organized movement with interest in it waning amongst the people, and upbeat missives about the certain victory of NC candidates in the upcoming assembly elections, announced by the regime to take place in the winter of 1946–7. Bakshi's and Sadiq's letters too are concerned with how to prepare for these elections, since Nehru had advised that the NC should participate in them. Abdullah's letters from prison, in contrast, are consumed with poor prison conditions, organizing a hunger strike to protest them and making sure that word of the strike was disseminated to the world outside.[12] In his October 1946 letter from Reasi sub-jail to Freda Bedi, who was doing her part for the movement by smuggling messages between leaders, Abdullah wrote:

> I will force these devils to treat me as a decent human being & not as an ordinary criminal. These devils have put me in a place where even

> ordinary necessaries of life are not available. It is cut-off & therefore very difficult for my friends to interview me. However, I asked these devils to put me in some better place & provide me with necessary amenities of life. If they don't do it by the 6th Oct: I will start hunger-strike.[13]

In the meantime, even as political and economic conditions on the ground in Kashmir were worsening, politics in British India was rapidly moving away from a federal consensus towards Partition. In his statements and speeches since the late 1930s through 1946, Abdullah had made clear that the NC stood for the freedom of India and Kashmir as an autonomous unit within it: 'The slavery of the states is linked to the slavery of Hindustan. Once Hindustan is independent, so will the states. The right to self-determination is the only political solution.'[14] But the possibility of a free India composed of units organized along cultural and linguistic lines with the right to self-determination died alongside the possibility of a united India, a fact that Abdullah did not quite grasp.

In part this was because he was imprisoned at the height of the federal moment, which subsequently disintegrated once it became clear that the Congress was unwilling to concede to the confederal idea of India if it meant dismantling the centre. This made Partition inevitable, and on the same day (3 June 1947) as the Partition Plan was formally announced by Viceroy Louis Mountbatten, Bakshi wrote to Abdullah in prison, asking for advice on how to respond to this new situation that had placed the NC leadership and Kashmir in a very complicated position.[15]

In the absence of access to Abdullah's response, it is difficult to say what exactly was going through his mind at this moment. But those who were close to him in prison said that his hair turned grey in a matter of a couple of weeks on hearing the news of the Partition; he could not eat or concentrate on anything for quite some time.[16] His worst nightmare had come to pass: There were now two dominions on the subcontinent, both of which coveted J&K. Rather than coming out on one side, he instead focused his attention on ridding Kashmir of the Maharaja's rule so that it could be free to decide its own fate. The choice of whether to join India or Pakistan would depend in large part on which dominion was willing to give the state maximum autonomy to carry out its Naya Kashmir agenda. Abdullah's close relationship with Nehru and the Congress, and its support of the NC and its objectives, in contrast to the Muslim League's support for a 'capitalist feudal ideology' meant that accession to India was for him a more attractive option.[17]

What he perhaps did not appreciate was that the question of J&K's accession was intermeshed with India's broader state-building project: It involved the integration of princely states into India's body politic as soon as possible by ensuring that the rulers of these states ceded their sovereignty over their territories to India. Its newly constituted States Department (later known as the States Ministry), headed by Sardar Vallabhbhai Patel, had begun this organized and protracted process and secured the accession of many states by a variety of methods even before India officially came into existence. In this scenario, the independence of the states was simply not acceptable; as Nehru declared to the All India Congress Committee Meeting on 15 June 1947, 'We will not recognize independence of any State in India. Further, any recognition of such independence by any foreign power will be considered as an unfriendly act.'[18]

J&K was significant to India in ideological and strategic terms, but what made it an especially complicated case in the summer of 1947 and thus worthy of attention was that its ruler was dithering on making a decision about accession. As a Hindu ruler, Maharaja Hari Singh could not quite come to terms with acceding to Pakistan, but his poor relationship with the Congress due to its support of the Quit Kashmir agitation made accession to India an unattractive option. Meanwhile, he dreamed of an independent Kashmir. He was also refusing to release the leaders of the NC who would support India's cause. Mahatma Gandhi's visit to Srinagar in late July was designed to put pressure on the Maharaja to do just that. Nehru, in particular, was anxious for Abdullah's release, since he had cultivated Abdullah to shape the NC into a pro-India organization for exactly this moment. As he wrote to Patel on 27 September 1947, he wanted Abdullah to work with the Maharaja to bring about the state's accession to India.[19]

Other Congress leaders, such as Acharya Kripalani, also visited Kashmir to assure the Maharaja that the Congress supported the rulers' right to decide on accession. That too was designed to ensure the merger of J&K into India. In addition, Viceroy Mountbatten visited Kashmir in June 1947 with the intention of persuading the Maharaja to release Abdullah. There were no parallel attempts to bring about the release of MC prisoners; Abbas, for instance, remained in prison until Abdullah released him in late 1948 after becoming prime minister of J&K as part of the transfer of prisoners, which was one of the terms of the UN-mediated Ceasefire Agreement that ended the first Indo-Pak war over J&K. Therefore, the semblance of choice that was being offered to the people of the princely state through Abdullah was chimerical at best.

By the time Abdullah was released on 29 September 1947, he was a despondent and weary man; not only had he been forced to present a *thali* (tray) of gold coins to the Maharaja at being set free as a conciliatory measure, making it almost impossible for him to work together with the ruler to smooth the process of accession, but also the creation of Pakistan had been a serious blow. He and the other Kashmir leaders knew that Pakistan would spell 'Dakistan' (ruin) for Kashmir.[20] He insisted in speeches that once the state was free from Dogra rule, its people would decide on accession. In a speech on the day of his release, he declared that Jinnah had been the enemy of Kashmiris and Nehru their friend, but if joining Pakistan would best serve the interests of the people of Kashmir, then their relationships with Jinnah and Nehru would be put aside.[21] But these very relationships, in part, made it difficult to negotiate with Pakistan, which Abdullah attempted without much success.

Besides, Jinnah appeared to be in no mood to negotiate. Pakistan sent a delegation that included Abdullah's old comrades M.D. Taseer and Faiz Ahmed Faiz to Srinagar on 1 October 1947 in the hopes of persuading him to join the dominion. On 3 October, they returned to Lahore with Sadiq, who was to serve as Abdullah's emissary in discussions with Jinnah. One of the demands of the NC was that if the state acceded to Pakistan, it would be administered on the basis of the Naya Kashmir programme. Not only did Jinnah not agree to meet Sadiq, but he also sent a message that there was nothing to discuss because Kashmir had to join Pakistan unconditionally.[22] Sadiq returned disillusioned from the trip, confirming for Abdullah what he already knew—that he had burned all bridges with Jinnah and would not be accepted as the leader of the state if it acceded to Pakistan. On the other hand, India would surely acknowledge him as the sole spokesman of the state and its people. His personal friendship with Nehru was testament to this fact. Abdullah did not seem to be taking the independence option for the state as a whole too seriously at this point, although that was always a hope that he entertained, knowing full well that it was not possible until guaranteed by both India and Pakistan.[23]

As Abdullah travelled around making speeches in late September and early October demanding freedom from autocratic rule, he faced a precarious political situation. International opinion seemed to favour J&K's accession to Pakistan based on its Muslim majority; the US Embassy in Delhi, for instance, supported a settlement between the two governments that would resolve not just the issue of J&K, but also that of the other two princely states that were contested, with J&K going to Pakistan and Junagadh and Hyderabad to India.[24] This was based on conversations in mid-October with V.P. Menon, secretary of the States Ministry, who seemed resigned to J&K eventually joining Pakistan.[25] Although Abdullah did not acknowledge the presence of the MC, the organization—despite being in disarray, with Abbas still languishing in prison—had its own ideas about the future of the state. A small group within its leadership was in favour of independence, but the large majority of its leaders supported accession to Pakistan.

It was also clear that troops were amassing on the border for an incursion into the state's territory as the theatre of action had shifted to Poonch, where rebels were in the process of freeing large parts of the state from the Maharaja's rule.[26] Abdullah's Kashmiri critics at this time, such as Bazaz, labelled him an opportunist and a political novice who did not have the right to call himself the representative of the entire population of the state. Articles in the *Hamdard* accused Abdullah of stalling on the issue of accession even though he had decided that J&K would join India:

> Why keep parroting the idea of responsible government as the main issue when what is most critical is to choose a dominion, after which responsible government will follow? Abdullah calls himself a lover of freedom, but all he cares about is his own leadership, which he wants to secure in the new setup before he announces his position on accession. His indecision is not in any way linked to the welfare of the people of the state, most of whom he does not represent.[27]

Although the Congress presented him as speaking for the entire state, Abdullah's leadership remained confined to the Kashmir Valley at this critical moment. The Congress leadership in general was not interested in understanding the intricacies of politics on the ground in various parts of J&K. Nehru viewed Abdullah solely through the prism of securing (and later maintaining) the state's accession to India, which was essential to establish India's secular credentials and to secure its frontier. Thus, Abdullah's image as a secular nationalist in a sea of communalism and as the most popular leader in the state became more important than the actual political reality in Kashmir, which included other leaders of equal import.

Articles in Indian magazines and journals presented Abdullah as synonymous with the recent political history of the state: 'the hero, as well as the author, of the political drama that has been enacted in the state', someone who was in 'personal touch with the lowliest of his people', while declaring that it was the 'good fortune of both Kashmir and India that such a man leads the Kashmiri people at this critical juncture'.[28] They repeated the familiar narrative of his rise from humble roots to becoming a leader of Muslims until his transformation into the 'greatest protagonist of communal harmony'.[29]

The reality was that even among those Kashmiris who supported Abdullah and what he stood for, many were not happy about the possibility of joining India and quite a few had an affinity for Pakistan. The violence against Muslims in the Punjab in the lead up to the partition of the province had shaken the conviction of many a secular Muslim and hardened the attitudes of many others. A deputation of Kashmiri

Muslims, including Mufti Jalaluddin and Ghulam Ahmad Ashai, who had been the earliest founders and supporters of the movement against the Maharaja but had since distanced themselves from it, visited Abdullah after his release to warn him against allying with India. They advised him that if he felt that he had no other choice but to do so, then to make sure that the Indian Army was not allowed to enter Kashmir, or else it would never leave. Abdullah told them that allying with India was better than being raped and pillaged by Afghans, and he trusted Nehru to withdraw Indian forces when the time came.[30] Others, such as Masoodi, were in favour of an independent state under the auspices of the Maharaja.[31] This, too, was unacceptable to Abdullah. Nevertheless, recognizing the anti-India bent of Kashmiri public opinion, Abdullah did not attempt to steer Kashmiris unequivocally towards accession to India until it became absolutely necessary to repel the raiders.

In part, this was also because he wanted to negotiate a better deal with the Indian leadership. He presented himself to them as the bulwark against militant Muslim communalism, pointing out that the accession to India and the transfer of power to the NC had to be simultaneous so that the regime could counter Muslim League propaganda effectively. Nehru's secretary, Dwarkanath Kachru, wrote to him in early October from Srinagar, where he was working closely with Abdullah, that if the Congress did not force the Maharaja to come to terms with Abdullah on accession, the state would be overrun by Pakistan's armies.[32]

And the course of events was, indeed, moving in that direction. The Poonchi rebels—by now calling themselves the Azad Army—having freed large parts of Mirpur and Poonch from Dogra rule, were joined by the Pukhtoon tribesmen on 22 October 1947. And two days later, the Army had declared the formation of the Provisional Azad Government.[33] The tribal raiders, consisting of a loose band of fighters from the tribal areas bordering Afghanistan, who had entered the state to help their Muslim brethren and ensure that the state acceded to Pakistan, took control of Muzaffarabad, Domel and Uri soon after coming into the state. But they were also interested in booty, and resorted to looting, raping, pillaging and murdering, in Baramulla in particular, which delayed their advance to Srinagar.[34] Later, this would help Abdullah and India to tarnish any opposition to Abdullah's regime from the Azad government by labelling them as a marauding, external force supported by Pakistan.[35]

Most importantly, it allowed time for J&K's prime minister, Mehr Chand Mahajan, to seek Indian military help, and ultimately led to the Maharaja's agreement to the state's accession to India on 26 October. A frantic Abdullah, who was present at the meeting of the Defence Committee in Delhi in which the matter was decided, saw the writing on the wall, gave his consent to the accession and pressed Nehru—ever-reluctant to use the military option—on the immediate need to send troops to J&K to secure the capital. In his letter accepting the accession, Lord Louis Mountbatten, now India's governor general, noted that since the accession had taken place in 'special circumstances', 'as soon as law and order have been restored in Kashmir and her soil cleared of the invader, the question of the State's accession should be settled by a reference to the people'.[36]

This sentence would, of course, become the basis of the UN recommendation of plebiscite as a solution to the Kashmir issue, while also providing the moral and legal grounds for the later plebiscite movement led by Abdullah. And at that time, it allowed Abdullah to claim to his followers and Kashmiri Muslims in general that he had not accepted the accession of the state to either India or Pakistan, but merely ensured India's military assistance in repelling the raiders; the permanent status of the state remained to be decided. From the Indian perspective, the addition of this proviso has to be seen in the context of its policy towards Junagadh, a tiny princely state in western India, which was under Indian military blockade after its ruler had declared his intention to accede to Pakistan. In early October, Nehru had assured the Pakistani prime minister, Liaquat Ali Khan, that India would not send its troops into Junagadh until a plebiscite had been held to determine the will of the population. This, Mountbatten had added, was India's policy towards all princely states where the accession was contested in any way.[37]

On 27 October, the day after Mountbatten accepted J&K's accession, Indian forces landed at Srinagar Airport to successfully prevent the

Kashmir Valley from falling into the hands of the opposing army. In the meantime, the Maharaja's accession to India prompted another part of the state—Gilgit—to revolt against his authority on 1 November 1947 and declare for accession to Pakistan.[38]

The locus of events now shifted to Srinagar with the Maharaja's appointment of Abdullah as the head of the emergency administration and his own hasty departure from the state. Once Abdullah took over, he actively suppressed Kashmiris' pro-Pakistan sentiments to uphold his Indian nationalist credentials. But before long, as his relationship with India soured, he reverted to his roots as the leader of Kashmiri Muslims and a representative of their aspirations.

## ABDULLAH AS PRIME MINISTER

As B.P.L. Bedi—now the director of communications and correspondence for the new regime—remembered many years later, after the Maharaja's desertion, with 'not a drop of petrol anywhere to run transport and not a pie in the treasury to run the State ... the National Conference came and just picked up the government ... Power was assumed first and Sheikh's appointment followed later.'[39] Abdullah thus became the head of the government of J&K almost by default. It was an open question as to how well he would transition from being a revolutionary political leader to being a head of state. But finally, after years spent battling the Dogra regime, many from behind bars, it was his time to shine: to show Kashmiris, India and the world that he was the true and only leader of Kashmiris.

What complicated matters was that he had inherited a particularly ugly and complex situation in the state, which was already a shadow of its former self. Not only had large parts of it broken away, but it was also under full-scale attack. Its administrative apparatus had collapsed; towns such as Baramulla lay in ruins; Hindu and Sikh refugees escaping violence in the Punjab were flooding into Jammu, even as Jammu Muslims flooded out in the face of large-scale reprisals against the Muslim population, in many cases aided and abetted by the Dogra forces;[40] and acute shortages of food and essential commodities were causing great misery for the people.

India, to which the state had officially acceded, was in no position to help, other than by providing troops to push back the raiders. Kashmiris felt deeply vulnerable, caught between the assurances of India and the lure of Pakistan, even possibly of independence. What is more, by 1948, Kashmir had been internationalized and become an 'issue'—a dispute between India and Pakistan. Even a more seasoned politician would have found it difficult to navigate these waters and it is no surprise that Abdullah foundered.

The NC itself was in shambles in the wake of the Quit Kashmir agitation and the large-scale imprisonments of its leadership. It was beset by infighting over the state's accession to India and between communists and those that staunchly opposed communist influence. Political personalities within the NC, such as Bakshi, Beg, Karra, Sadiq and Masoodi, many with their own bases of support, had to be either accommodated or marginalized. All NC workers, from the lowest functionary to the highest leader, were chafing at the bit to get their due and exercise some power after operating in the shadows for years.

A tall order indeed, but Abdullah rose to the occasion in the early days. His ability to rally people was visible at this moment perhaps more than any other. A noticeably greying and shaken man, he stood resolute at Pathar Masjid, itself a symbol of the movement, and began softly, his voice rising to a crescendo. He reminded the crowd of the sacrifices they had made during the movement, of his desire to give both India and Pakistan an equal chance in terms of accession, and Pakistan's perfidy in sending raiders to enslave them. But Kashmiris would not allow this to happen; so he asked every man, woman and child to pick up sticks, stones and axes to fight the enemy and defend the homeland from this 'forcible slavery'. Raina, in the crowd at this speech, felt instantly electrified, and by the end of the day, the entire city was galvanized. Sheikh Abdullah, Raina recalled, 'soared to the skies ... Whenever he felt desperate, he had the capacity to soar, if only for a few hours, to the highest level of audacity.'[41]

Under Abdullah's direction, the emergency administration went into high gear, mobilizing young men and women to enter the newly formed National Militia—that even had a women's wing, the Women's Self-

Defence Corps (WSDC)—and patrol the streets of Srinagar to protect residents from attack. The militia and its women's wing resonated deeply with Kashmiris, who felt empowered by taking upon themselves the responsibility of their own defence after centuries of being oppressed by outsiders. Meanwhile, the party's Cultural Front, to which the WSDC was critical, set the tone by promoting a vision of secular Kashmiri nationalism that endorsed the state's accession to India. Begum Abdullah continued her political involvement by busying herself in organizing relief and rehabilitation for refugees displaced by the conflict.[42]

In fiery speeches, Abdullah lambasted Pakistan and celebrated India, emphasizing Kashmir's tradition of communal harmony. He exhorted Muslims to maintain peace and protect minorities, with their lives if necessary. 'Those who attacked us in the name of Islam gravely insulted Islam. We have to protect the mulk at all cost… they should come and see how the people stood up to them,' he declared in one of these speeches in November 1947.[43] Gradually, from its base in the Palladium Cinema, the NC took control of the entire administrative apparatus; Bedi described it as 'a seizure of power', albeit a peaceful one.[44] While to Abdullah's supporters, such as Krishna Misri, a member of the WSDC, this was a beginning of a momentous new era, to horrified members of the MC and supporters of Pakistan, it looked as though Abdullah had pulled off a coup d'état.[45]

To the outside world, Abdullah remained a firm secularist and champion of the rights of the downtrodden. In late December 1947, he took a tour of northern India, addressing a number of public meetings in which he exhorted his audiences to give up the cry of 'religion in danger' and unite Hindus, Muslims and Sikhs under 'one national organization, as they had done in Kashmir, to achieve real freedom'.[46] Bedi and his wife, Freda, penned a short biography of him in this period, describing him as 'not just a clever politician' but rather 'one of the vital minds of our generation', and Kashmir as not just a 'corner of the subcontinent' but rather the very 'birthplace of a new social order'.[47] Abdullah the 'lion-hearted', the biography pointed out, was a devout Muslim and Mahatma Gandhi's spiritual heir; in his fight against fanaticism in Kashmir, he was the 'guiding star of the India that is to be'.[48] There was no space for the MC in these narratives, while the Muslim League and Pakistan appeared as the usual villains that had sponsored the raids on the state.[49]

Abdullah's regime came to embody that vision of democracy in which a supreme, authoritarian leader gives voice to the popular will without the intercession of institutions such as political parties, unions and the press.[50] Abdullah's autocratic tendencies were already on display in the very early days. He in turn energized, cajoled and threatened the people to toe the line. 'Today we are free,' he proclaimed in another speech in November 1947, adding ominously, 'and we will protect our freedom at any cost. Traitors will be punished and martyrs will be celebrated.'[51] Freedom certainly did not include the freedom of expression. Abdullah brooked no dissent. As Andrew Whitehead points out, one of the tasks of the members of the National Militia was to 'root out' sympathizers of Pakistan, leading to 'a tradition of vigilantism which persisted in the Kashmir Valley long after the military threat abated'.[52] Anyone who dared to challenge Abdullah on any grounds, especially the state's accession to India, he labelled as a traitor and had forcibly removed to the other side of the border. Many, including Mirwaiz Yusuf Shah, chose to go into voluntary exile to Pakistan. Others he silenced by invoking their patriotic duty to not question the leader during a time of war.[53]

Jai Lal Tamiri, a member of the NC from Srinagar, wrote to the editor of the *Janata*, asking him to pass his letter on to J.P. Narayan, describing the endemic corruption that suffused the NC regime, made worse by the fact that any criticism was simply not tolerated. According to Tamiri, Abdullah had called a meeting of NC workers and 'threatened those workers who criticized his Ministers with dire consequences'. When Tamiri argued against this, Abdullah told him in no uncertain terms: 'I warn you to keep quiet or step aside for the time being. I need workers like you but I cannot tolerate your criticism.' When Masoodi spoke up in Tamiri's defence, Abdullah changed tack and said that he was not against Tamiri, but that his criticism was 'discouraging my Ministers and our enemies are laughing at us'.[54]

Prior to 1947, the interests of the trade unions and the party had been aligned—both were against the Dogra state. Once the NC took over the government, communists and union leaders were now potentially arrayed against it. Government administrators had little time for workers' demands. Abdullah thus oversaw either the cooptation of their leaders by handing out favours and local positions to them, or the political destruction of those who were not amenable. Communists, meanwhile, were denounced as atheists and their organizations appropriated for cultural activities that bolstered the regime's mantra of progressivism and secular democracy. Even Bedi, who had played such an important role in the Kashmiri nationalist movement—a 1948 US Embassy Report described him as the 'real brains behind Sheikh Abdullah', who 'appeared to be a tool in [his] hands'—had been sidelined by the early 1950s. In part, this was done to appease the Indian government, which was battling an armed insurrection launched in early 1948 by the Communist Party of India (CPI) against the Indian state, and was, as a result, increasingly concerned about communist influence in Kashmir. Whatever the reason, these moves in effect dismantled the NC's own bases of support.[55]

The party was thus reorganized to become an arm of the government. Indeed, the party *was* the state during Abdullah's tenure as prime minister, which officially began in March 1948. D.D. Thakur, a young delegate to the district convention of the NC in Doda in 1950 and later a member of Abdullah's cabinet after his return to power in 1975, observes in his autobiography, 'In those days there was no difference between a National Conference worker and a government servant.'[56] While he himself headed the departments of education, legislation and broadcasting, Abdullah installed his inner circle of party leaders in other important cabinet positions: Bakshi as deputy prime minister, Beg as revenue minister and Sadiq as minister of development. G.L. Dogra and Shyam Lal Saraf were appointed finance minister and health minister respectively. At the same time, he sidelined other leaders such as Karra—who was immensely popular after directing the Quit Kashmir agitation from underground and hence a threat—by playing them off against leaders such as Bakshi. Not only did this elevate Bakshi, but it also immediately led Karra to court the sympathies of Muslim bureaucrats who had always been uncomfortable with the secular outlook of the NC.[57]

The NC's pyramidal structure, with mohalla (neighbourhood), halqa (district) and tehsil (township) committees, allowed its mid- to low-level functionaries to implement the writ of the state at all levels. As Josef Korbel, who visited Kashmir as a member of the United Nations Commission on India and Pakistan (UNCIP), wrote in 1948, the NC, which existed even in the smallest villages, 'decide[d] everything: who is going to be elected to what office, who will get a job, who will receive the supplies which it alone distributes'.[58] Munshi Ishaq, who had played such an important role in the NC through the 1940s, noted bitterly in his history of the movement that the halqa committees acted as dictators that decided who would get government positions for which all educated people clamoured. These local committees also acted as Abdullah's eyes and ears, ensuring that everyone toed the regime's political line. Meanwhile, the poor continued to toil in terrible conditions of deprivation.[59] Already by late 1948, disillusionment with the NC government ran deep and the only reason, according to one NC member, that the people were not in open revolt was because of 'Sheikh Sahib's old magic influence'.[60]

Abdullah's consolidation of control over the state looked complete, but for the Maharaja. The Maharaja's presence was a constant reminder to Abdullah that he, as representative of Kashmiris, did not exercise complete sovereignty over Kashmir. As Pakistani propaganda against him gathered force, so did his attacks on the Maharaja. The Maharaja's son, Karan Singh, writes at length in his autobiography about 'the old bitterness between the Dogras and Kashmiris' that resurfaced in the now reversed circumstances of Abdullah's executive control over the state administration.[61] In a private meeting with the Maharaja in June 1948, Abdullah demanded that the state military forces be placed under the control of the state government. These forces, he said, had carried out atrocities against Muslims in the Jammu province in 1947, resulting in the massacre of thousands of Muslims.[62] When the Maharaja resisted by suggesting that the forces should be under the control of the Government of India's States Ministry, Abdullah flared up in anger. He declared that he would not allow the States Ministry to direct affairs in J&K, and threatened to resign, leaving the people to decide whether to go to India or Pakistan.[63]

In a December 1948 meeting in Srinagar with Tilak Raj Chadha, a member of the Kashmir Committee of the Socialist Party, Abdullah outright rejected the idea of a link office of the party being established in the state. But he also took the opportunity to complain bitterly about the States Ministry's support of the Maharaja, whose hands were smeared with the blood of Muslims and whose 'Hindu fascist henchmen' in India were spreading misinformation about the Muslims of Kashmir. He also accused the Maharaja of obstructing his proposed land reforms and of secretly working for a partitioning of the state, while he, Abdullah, had relentlessly crusaded against the two-nation theory.[64] In public too he began to openly accuse the Maharaja of directing the massacre of Muslims in the Jammu province.[65]

This bickering put a great strain on the relations between Abdullah and the Indian government, in particular the States Ministry, as well as between Abdullah's regime and Jammu. Nehru was clearly sympathetic to Abdullah in this tussle of wills, although he asked him to take a more diplomatic approach and wished he would stop making 'foolish statements'.[66] The Maharaja, from Nehru's perspective, was a vestige of the past, a man who did not realize that India was now a democracy. As for Abdullah, Nehru regarded him as a bastion against Pakistan and truly believed that he was the only man who could deliver the Kashmir Valley to India. Nehru thus defended Abdullah to Patel, noting that he was a 'straight and frank man' who was 'not a very clear thinker and sometimes goes astray in his speech as many of our politicians do', but he had the best interests of Kashmir in mind. And the reason that Abdullah was against the Maharaja was because his continued presence gave Pakistan a powerful tool for propaganda against his regime.[67]

Abdullah, who was convinced that the States Ministry was against him because he was Muslim—as he told Indira Gandhi in the summer of 1948 during her visit to Kashmir[68]—would not let up, giving vent to his feelings towards the States Ministry and the Maharaja in a long, defiant letter to Sardar Patel. The letter detailed the Maharaja's many crimes, including keeping the state forces under his control to ensure that no Muslims would be able to enter them. Abdullah warned Patel that if he were not given leeway to run the state the way he wanted, Muslims would grow alienated from India and become more sympathetic towards Pakistan.[69] Patel's exhaustion with Abdullah is palpable in his slightly patronizing response, in which he tried to persuade Abdullah to be more tactful because the Maharaja had no actual power, while noting, 'In politics, a one-track mind does not ultimately gain.'[70] But as Karan Singh points out, 'Plebiscite being the watchword at that time, this became the trump card in the hands of Sheikh Abdullah. As the man who was supposed to win the plebiscite for India, he could virtually demand his pound of flesh. And this he did repeatedly, not only by assuming power, but by pursuing my father relentlessly.'[71]

Ultimately, the Maharaja had to go, because Nehru and Patel felt that the atmosphere in Kashmir was becoming too toxic. Patel persuaded him to relinquish the throne, with the eighteen-year-old Karan Singh appointed regent in 1949, later elected the first head of state or Sadar-i-Riyasat, in 1952. The Maharaja's departure not only alienated the Dogra population of Jammu but also led the Pakistani propaganda machine to tout Karan Singh's regency appointment as a victory for Abdullah's opponents.[72] To Karan Singh at that time—as he tried to 'steer a middle path between appearing subservient to the Sheikh on the one hand and offending him and Jawaharlal on the other'—Abdullah appeared as 'physically an impressive man', 'at that time at the height of his powers'.[73] Abdullah may have won this particular battle, but the war was just beginning. What's more, the war was to involve the entire world.

## THE INTERNATIONAL AND THE DOMESTIC

The Indian government's referral of Pakistan's actions in Kashmir to the UN at the very beginning of 1948 ensured the internationalization of the Kashmir issue. Abdullah was thrust into this scenario without much warning, and he was never quite able to figure out his place, or that of J&K, in the international arena. Initially, he enthusiastically defended India's claim over the state given Pakistan's perfidious attack, but soon he soured on that position. It became clear to him very quickly that the Security Council did not recognize India's claim and was more sympathetic to Pakistan. And he realized that he was seen as an Indian lackey on the world stage. This drove him to take steps to prove that he was indeed the chosen representative of Kashmiris and legitimate leader of the state. The repercussions of these steps ultimately cascaded into his political demise.

Abdullah was part of the Indian delegation to the UN at Lake Success, New York, in February 1948. D.P. Dhar, J&K's deputy home minister, was his assistant and had been deputed by the Indian government to ensure that Abdullah did not meet with members of the Pakistani delegation, many of whom, such as M.D. Taseer, were his old friends. But this did not prevent communication between Abdullah and the Pakistani delegation, which Dhar then reported to the other members of the Indian delegation.[74] Abdullah had thought, most likely much like the rest of the Indian delegation, that India's case would be quickly accepted and the matter settled in India's favour. Pakistan would be chastised for its actions and forced to withdraw its forces from Kashmir. He had not counted on the interests of the powerful Anglo-American bloc in the context of the looming Cold War. Neither had he counted on the power of the Pakistani delegation, led by Zafarullah Khan, to make an eloquent case for Pakistan's position. Khan pointed to, among other things, the Government of India's hypocrisy and perfidy in its acceptance of J&K's accession to India on the one hand while rejecting the Nawab of Junagadh's accession to Pakistan on the other, instead following it up with a 'direct act of hostility' by entering and annexing its territory and later conducting a farcical plebiscite to validate its actions.[75]

Abdullah could see that instead of running the show as the complainant, the Indian delegation was on the defensive. He was stunned as he watched Gopalaswami Ayyangar, the head of the Indian delegation, beseeching the Western powers to recognize India's claim over Kashmir while the Pakistani delegation's (what to Abdullah were) 'lies, threats, and impudent behavior' were taken at face value. The 'timid, ingratiating Indian delegation' gave the impression that India had no clout on the world stage.[76] And Pakistan, rather than facing censure and opprobrium, now had an equal seat at the table.

This realization coloured Abdullah's actions from henceforward. His worst nightmare had come to pass—Kashmir was caught between India and Pakistan, and he might have chosen the losing side. Doubts began to set in about whether he had made the right decision by allying with India. The last straw was the Security Council's suggestion that his government would have to resign for a free and fair plebiscite to take place in the state. He did not support a plebiscite not just for this reason but also because he feared that given the dire economic situation, Pakistan would win it, even in the Valley. So, he defended India's claim, and by extension his own right to rule Kashmir, in an impassioned speech that was 'blunt, direct, and devoid of diplomatic language': 'There is no power on earth which can displace me from the position which I have there [in Kashmir]. As long as the people are behind me I will remain there ... The dispute arises when it is suggested that, in order to have the free vote, the administration must be changed ... To that suggestion we say "No".'[77] He even rebuked the British representative, Philip Noel-Baker, for supporting Pakistan's mendacious claims.[78]

Abdullah returned from Lake Success feeling gloomy and helpless, convinced that the UN was not going to resolve the Kashmir problem. And if it did, it would not be in India's favour. He felt vulnerable and confused, his faith in the Nehru government's ability to defend the state's accession to India deeply shaken. It did not help that the thorny question of J&K's constitutional relationship to India came up soon after his return, and that Nehru appointed Ayyangar to work with Abdullah, now a member of the Indian constituent assembly, to draft Article 370 of the Indian constitution. Ayyangar and Abdullah did not see eye to eye, returning from meetings with different understandings of what had been discussed. The situation deteriorated to the point where the two were no longer on speaking terms, with Abdullah threatening to resign from the assembly; Maulana Azad had to intervene with Abdullah to bring them back to the table.[79]

This significantly increased the tension in the already complex negotiations that led up to the adoption of the article, during which Abdullah was insistent that the article preserve J&K's autonomy vis-à-vis India by acknowledging that the state had acceded to India only in the three subjects of defence, foreign affairs and communications. Accession in any further subjects, as well as which portions of the Fundamental Rights and Directive Principles of the Indian constitution would be applicable to J&K, should be left up to the state's constituent assembly, when convened. The final draft of the article that was passed by the Indian constituent assembly did not meet with Abdullah's approval. He felt that it brought Kashmir under India's purview to a much greater extent than he had envisioned or had agreed to with Nehru, thus violating 'the discharge of his duty to his own people'.[80]

Upon learning of this from Ayyangar, Patel replied testily, 'Whenever Sheikh Sahib wishes to back out, he always confronts us with his duty to the people. Of course, he owes no duty to India or to the Indian Government, or even on a personal basis, to you and the Prime Minister who have gone all out to accommodate him.'[81] This wrangling over the Indian constitution reveals that from very early on, Abdullah's vision for Kashmir within India did not fit within India's constitutional vision of itself as a centralized union of states with a uniform set of laws applicable to all states.

Around this time, Abdullah began to chart his own course by undertaking domestic policies to shore up his support among Kashmiris. And, he began to seriously consider the idea of some sort of independence for Kashmir. This was not an elaborate plot to betray India, since he suggested this quite openly, but simply a possibility to be explored. To be sure, it would make him ultimate master of his domain, free of the Indian government, but it would also extricate the state from the India–Pakistan tangle. As early as the summer of 1948, Abdullah had suggested the possibility of independence when he met with Korbel, member of the UNCIP, to discuss options for Kashmir. He felt that a truly comprehensive plebiscite would be difficult to carry out because of the dislocation of the population. It also raised the question of whether India and Pakistan would accept the verdict. He suggested independence of the state under the joint guarantee of India, Pakistan, China, the Soviet Union and Afghanistan as another option. Abdullah was even willing to meet with Ghulam Abbas, MC leader in the Pakistani part of Kashmir and his colleague in the not-too-distant past, to discuss this possibility further. He recognized, he said, that even if this were to come to pass, the entity would not last for long. The final possibility mooted by Abdullah was a partition of the state, with some parts going to Pakistan and others to India. This, for him, was an option of last resort because he wanted to maintain the unity of the state.[82]

By April 1949, Abdullah was giving interviews to foreign correspondents, including to *The Scotsman*, suggesting that Kashmir might be better off not connected to either India or Pakistan, but maintaining friendly relations with both.[83] He had to retract the comments at the insistence of the Indian government; Patel in particular was furious at Abdullah and told him, 'India would not permit the blood of its soldiers to be shed to defend Kashmir at a time that Kashmir's political leaders, while pretending that they wished the country to adhere to India, were scheming for independence.'[84] It was not altogether clear in these public statements whether Abdullah was speaking in terms of independence for the entire erstwhile princely state or simply the Kashmir Valley, but in many private conversations, it was fairly clear that he, his family and his colleagues were thinking in terms of independence for the Valley. According to J. Wesley Adams, advisor to the US representative on the UNCIP, during their conversations while in Kashmir, Begum Abdullah said many a time that 'she saw no reason why Kashmir should not be independent like Switzerland'. This point was elaborated on further by others close to Abdullah.[85]

When Loy Henderson, who served as US ambassador to India from 1948 to 1951, visited Kashmir in May 1949, he was taken aback by how candidly Abdullah and his close associates talked about their desire for the Valley's independence as the only solution to the Kashmir problem;

he also noted the palpable animosity between the civil administration and the Indian military.[86] In his conversation with Henderson, Major General K.S. Thimayya, commander of the Indian forces during the Kashmir operations, described Abdullah as 'a dreamer and an idealist', given to 'impracticability which caused him frequently to make rather serious errors in judgment and a political naivete which permitted him to be hoodwinked by designing persons whom he regarded as friends'. At that time, noted Thimayya, Abdullah had surrounded himself with communists, such as B.P.L. Bedi, without realizing the danger they posed by encouraging an independent Kashmir, 'a weak state at the apex of Asia'. According to Thimayya, Abdullah had given the interview to *The Scotsman* at Bedi's behest, and also seemed unaware of, or unwilling to deal with, the level of corruption and bribery within his administration.[87]

By this time, Abdullah had grown into the ways of politics and was skilful at modulating his personality to fit the occasion. Henderson was impressed by him during their meetings, describing Abdullah as an 'interesting and not unattractive person ... about six feet four inches in height, smooth shaven, his face habitually grave, although not stern; and he has a pleasant smile ... an agreeable soft voice and speaks English exceedingly well'.[88] He also came to recognize that the US had been underestimating Abdullah's role in the Kashmir problem. 'Although,' wrote Henderson, 'his long friendship with and admiration for Nehru incline him towards India he is not an Indian tool. He has quixotic intellectual independence', and, according to Henderson, would perhaps be able to persuade Nehru to hold off on a plebiscite.[89] Henderson accurately identified the difficult position Abdullah found himself in at this juncture: 'He is likely to lose a plebiscite of the kind which the United Nations would insist on being held, and he is just as likely to lose his influence over the people of the Valley in case the holding of the plebiscite is long delayed.'[90]

In 1950, the UN appointed Owen Dixon, an Australian diplomat, to act as mediator between India and Pakistan on the Kashmir dispute. Dixon shuttled back and forth between the two countries, visiting the two sides of J&K and meeting with leaders on both sides, before submitting his report. This report proposed a partitioning of the state, with Ladakh going to India, Azad Kashmir to Pakistan, Jammu divided between the two and a plebiscite being limited to the Valley to decide its future. While Pakistan reluctantly agreed to the proposal, Nehru rejected the terms under which a plebiscite would be held in the Valley, the most significant being the one that required the replacement of Abdullah's government with a neutral UN-led administration during the conduct of the plebiscite.[91] Abdullah, for his part, roundly rejected the proposal for obvious reasons—since he wanted to be at the helm when a plebiscite was held in the Valley—but as a whole, Dixon's proposal came closest to what he envisioned for the state. This would become clear in 1953, when he supported a similar proposal as the ideal solution to the dispute.

Given his dilemma and recognizing that he ultimately had little control over which, if any, of the options on the table with regard to Kashmir came to pass, Abdullah began to focus on what he could control, which was domestic policy in Kashmir. He needed to give Kashmiris something to hold on to during this time of uncertainty, something that would convince them that he was still their true leader despite the disappointments and repression. And he needed to remain in the limelight on the world stage, which just might give him some say in the future of Kashmir. He took precipitous action, as he was wont to do in such situations, and launched two projects: the process of land reforms and the constitution of the state's constituent assembly. Both policies and their impact created divides within the state and set him on a collision course with India.

## LAND REFORMS AND THE CONSTITUENT ASSEMBLY

The Big Landed Estates Abolition Act, passed in October 1950, was the brainchild of Mirza Afzal Beg, the revenue minister in Abdullah's regime. Beg had an astute legal mind, and much like Abdullah, fiercely held on to the idea of Kashmir's autonomy. Abdullah had been drawing closer to Beg as he increasingly relied on his legal advice regarding, for instance, the intricacies of Article 370, but it was in crafting and implementing the land reforms that Abdullah came to recognize in Beg a kindred spirit.

Beg—short, rotund and unassuming to Abdullah's tall, lean and imposing figure—convinced Abdullah at this moment, and would in many others in the future, to take radical measures to assert the J&K government's autonomy in internal matters.

It was on this matter that Abdullah came to loggerheads with Karan Singh and that began the 'slow evaporation of goodwill' between them, because much to Abdullah's chagrin, Karan Singh refused to put his signature on the land reforms proclamation without first referring the matter to the Government of India. According to Karan Singh, although he broadly sympathized with the measures, he was also aware of the ill effects of the measures on large populations of the state and felt that consultations with the Indian government were necessary before any steps were taken. As he noted, 'I tried to function not so much as a Dogra but as an Indian. Indeed, it would be correct to say that the basic difference between Sheikh Abdullah and me lay in the fact that while he looked upon himself as a Kashmiri who happened to find himself in India, I considered myself an Indian who happened to find himself in Kashmir.'[92]

After some reluctant negotiations with the Indian government, the Act was passed and limited the amount of land any landlord could hold to 182 *kanals* (22.75 acres), expropriating and transferring the rest of the land to the tenants, who had until that point worked as serfs on that land. In theory, the government was supposed to pay the landlords a portion of the land revenue from the expropriated lands as compensation, but this did not come to pass. This was because the peasants were unable to pay a temporary land tax to the government which would have gone towards the compensation. In effect, then, the lands were expropriated without compensation. Another provision of the Act allowed for the expropriation of the property of 'enemy agents', or those who had expressed pro-Pakistan views.[93]

The Act was revolutionary in many ways. And this one aspect of Abdullah's legacy has withstood the test of time, even among his contemporary detractors. It ended tenancy and debt bondage among the peasantry and instantly made them landholders. Yet, its implementation was left to a highly corrupt state machinery that undid many of these gains. The NC cadres in charge of the redistribution of land allowed the landed gentry to keep most of the good land, sometimes even beyond the permissible limit of 22.75 acres. For instance, the land reforms certainly did not dispossess the Beg family of Anantnag district—to which Mirza Afzal Beg belonged—of most of its land.[94] The peasants, meanwhile, received small plots of land that were often infertile and marshy. The stranglehold of the government over the distribution system of revenue, grain and goods as well as the government transport monopoly provided further opportunities for corruption and nepotism.[95]

By 1951–2, India's States Ministry was flooded with letters and representations from various individuals and organizations, especially from Jammu, complaining about the impact of the land reforms and the government's economic policies in general. These letters were particularly bitter about the policy of non-compensation for land appropriation, warning the Indian government not to be misled by the idea that they would necessarily lead to a pro-India verdict in the event of a plebiscite. They also protested the monopoly over trade, contracts and services by a few individuals within the J&K administration, leading to their enrichment while the rest of the population faced impoverishment. They usually ended with a supplication to the Indian government to impose the Indian constitution in the state.[96]

The Indian government attempted to stay out of these matters, precisely because they had been warned by Abdullah that any attempts at interference would lead to a negative verdict against India in the event of a plebiscite. The successful implementation of the reforms, on the other hand, would ensure a political victory for India. The States Ministry thus responded to these letters by saying that it had no 'locus standi' in the matter, which was the jurisdiction of the government of J&K.[97] But in private, the arbitrary manner in which the reforms were declared and implemented deepened the rift between the Indian government and Abdullah's regime. As an irritated Patel pointed out, the legislation was not representative in any way; it was 'a mere fiat of the government'.[98] And, along with Abdullah's crusade against the Maharaja, his economic policies, including the land reforms, rendered Jammu ripe for revolt.

In the meantime, the state had been in effect partitioned between India and Pakistan as the Ceasefire Line brokered by the UN came into effect on 1 January 1949, although neither country recognized it as the official border. As the Security Council continued its deliberations on Kashmir and a series of UN representatives made their way to India and Pakistan to find a resolution to the issue, Abdullah was increasingly convinced that the two countries would not be able to come to an agreement. By this time, the failure of negotiations had led to the forcible integration of the princely state of Hyderabad into the Indian Union through a military invasion, with alarming reports of atrocities against Muslims in its wake beginning to filter out.[99] Abdullah began a vociferous campaign for a constituent assembly for the state, keeping up a steady drumbeat against the UN and its power to make decisions regarding Kashmir. In a speech in March 1951, he declared:

> The fate of 40 lakhs cannot be left in the hands of an intermediary. American and British recommendations are not helpful to Kashmir; they are designed to promote their own interests. The Security Council's recommendations are a murder of justice and truth. This mulk belongs to the people, not a handful of intermediaries.[100]

His expectation was that the state's constituent assembly would give representative sanction to his policies and stances, with the ultimate objective of formulating a constitution for J&K.

But the conduct of the NC in the constituent assembly elections added fuel to the already raging fire against Abdullah's regime, particularly in Jammu. The NC had never been popular in Jammu, and after 1947, it became even less so. Abdullah made no attempt at creating a base for the party there, farming the work out to Bakshi, who in turn delegated it to lower-level NC workers. The negative attitude in Jammu towards the party in general, and Abdullah in particular, allowed for the emergence of more right-wing alternatives, such as the Praja Parishad (PP), which was the only viable opposition party in the entire state. Abdullah's response to any individual or group running for elections as independents or under another party's banner was that they were anti-India, and hence could not be allowed to run. The MC opposed the constituent assembly elections on precisely these grounds.[101]

Abdullah could not make that charge against the PP and its members, however. Instead, he labelled them anti-Muslim communal elements bent on thwarting his administration. The government authorities rejected the nomination papers of PP candidates in thirteen constituencies on technicalities and other tenuous grounds. This led the PP to boycott the elections altogether. The NC thus won all seventy-five seats to the constituent assembly unopposed, out of which Jammu had twenty-nine seats, while the Valley was represented by forty-four seats.[102] Earlier, Abdullah had refused the demand of Sikh leaders for two reserved seats in the assembly, which led the Kashmiri Sikh community, hitherto loyal NC supporters, to turn against him as well.[103] Abdullah's shortsightedness in (for all practical purposes) rigging these elections and ignoring Jammu and other constituencies would cost him dearly.

The J&K constituent assembly convened in October 1951. Abdullah saw it as a bulwark against India and the world. He asserted in private and public time and again that as a popularly elected body, it was the only sovereign authority legally capable of making a decision on Kashmir's future. In his aforementioned speech to the body in November 1951, he drew a parallel between the role played by the Indian constituent assembly in transforming India into a constitutional republic and the four major tasks that lay ahead of the J&K assembly as the sovereign body representing J&K. The first and second of these tasks were the framing of the state's constitution and making the decision on the future of the royal dynasty and its position in the state. The third was the ratification of the land reforms, and finally, perhaps the most momentous task, was to come to a 'reasoned conclusion regarding accession'.[104] He elaborated in particular on the position of the royal dynasty, noting that the institution of monarchy was 'incompatible with the spirit and needs of modern times' and should, therefore, be abolished.[105] Again, the compromise would be to accept Karan Singh—who, according to Abdullah, had impressed him and his colleagues with 'his intelligence, his broad outlook and his keen desire to serve the country'—as head of state.[106]

The speech then went into the matter of accession, with Abdullah detailing at length the pros and cons of acceding to India or Pakistan, and then raising the third alternative of 'making ourselves an Eastern Switzerland, of keeping aloof from both States but having friendly relations with them'.[107] Abdullah's speech recognized that this last alternative was a difficult one to attain, given the practicalities involved; therefore, the best course was to cooperate with India while 'safeguard[ing] our autonomy to the fullest extent possible so as to have liberty to build our country according to the past traditions and genius of our people', with Indian 'cooperation and assistance'.[108] But by raising the third option, Abdullah hoped to get India's attention, especially on the matter of preserving the state's autonomy within the Union.

All of these undertakings were problematic from the Indian government's perspective, but the final one raised potentially explosive issues. It became clear that Abdullah and Nehru had two fundamentally opposing visions for J&K's constituent assembly: while Abdullah saw it as a means of preserving Kashmir's autonomy, Nehru had hoped that it would help integrate the state into the Indian Union. This gulf widened as the months passed. The international community's increasing pressure on India to rein Abdullah in and prevent him from using the assembly to make a unilateral declaration on the status of the state added further to the mounting tension.

## THE TWO PRIME MINISTERS

There is a telling photograph of Nehru and Abdullah on a dais in front of the Palladium Cinema in Lal Chowk, Srinagar, on 11 November 1947: Both leaders are smiling, their palms intertwined in a firm handshake.[109] In his speech on that day, Nehru had declared to the people of Kashmir, 'I assure you that, as in the past, so in the future, Kashmir and India will stand together and face the enemy. This is the pledge I give here today to your leader the *Sher* of Kashmir.'[110] Hailing Kashmiris for the communal harmony that prevailed in the Valley amidst the chaos, he noted, 'You have not only saved Kashmir, you have also restored the prestige of India, your mother country. Kashmir has set an example to the whole of India.' He celebrated the bravery of the Indian troops who were resisting the invaders, but also warned them that they had been sent to Kashmir 'to help Sheikh Abdullah and his administration to drive out the invaders; you have to bear this fact in mind in your dealings with the local administration and people'.[111]

This moment was the high-water mark of the relationship between the two leaders, as well as between India and Kashmir. But the different visions they had for the relationship between their homelands was visible even then. Although Abdullah was genuinely grateful for the help offered by the Indian Army and especially reposed great faith in Nehru's friendship and support, he was continually on the guard against any attempt at curtailing his own government's autonomy in internal matters. Nehru's letters to Abdullah during this period are replete with reassurances that the latter was, in fact, the one in charge in J&K, especially vis-à-vis the Maharaja. This did little to assuage Abdullah, who continued to negotiate with India as though it was a federation of autonomous units, not a centralized polity.

Once the immediate threat posed by the raiders had passed, matters became more complicated as Nehru took the issue to the UN, which rendered India and Pakistan as equal parties to the dispute. The question of the withdrawal of Indian troops from the Valley now became intermeshed with the larger bilateral dispute and was no longer simply a matter of negotiation between the governments of J&K and India. The realization gradually dawned on Abdullah that the warnings of Ghulam Ahmad Ashai and Mufti Jalaluddin regarding the Indian Army might actually come to pass. He was thrust into the limelight, defending his support of the state's accession to India on the international stage, but just as importantly to his own people. After all, even those Kashmiris who were pro-India did not think of it as the 'mother country'.

By 1951, Abdullah was battling on multiple fronts. Within the state itself, he resorted to repressing dissenting voices and implementing some of the promises of the Naya Kashmir agenda, which in turn widened the gulf between his administration and Jammu and Ladakh, even as his popularity dwindled among his own constituency of Kashmiri Muslims.

He was beset with and chafed at the relentless Pakistani propaganda—which the international community also believed—that he was an Indian puppet and hence not a true representative of the people. To India, he presented himself as the bulwark against Pakistan's claims over the state while at the same time considering independence, largely to maintain his leverage in relations with the Indian government.

He did not seem to recognize that the postcolonial state drew a line at opposing claims to sovereignty, especially in the context of a bilateral dispute and rising domestic inter-religious tensions over the issue. The reason India had accepted J&K's special status and endowed Abdullah with the title of prime minister of the state was because the territory was disputed, not because it intended on allowing the state to go its own way. India could not have more than one prime minister. At the end of the road Abdullah was travelling on lay a precipice.

# 4

# The Turning Point, 1952–1953

IT WAS THE SUMMER OF 1953 AND KASHMIR AND DELHI SIZZLED WITH rumour and intrigue. On his travels through Asia, the American statesman Adlai Stevenson—who had been the Democratic presidential candidate in 1952—visited Kashmir in May and met with Sheikh Abdullah. The Praja Parishad (PP) movement raged in Jammu, challenging Abdullah to implement the Delhi Agreement (discussed later in this chapter) and prove his loyalty to India. One of its supporters, the Bharatiya Jan Sangh leader Syama Prasad Mookerjee, was arrested in May while crossing into the state without an official permit from state authorities and died in June while under house arrest in Srinagar. The atmosphere was further befogged by the almost daily speeches by Abdullah and other members of the National Conference (NC) that appeared to be at cross-purposes with each other in terms of the state's relationship to India.

In Delhi, Jawaharlal Nehru was beside himself with worry and confusion. Had he been wrong in supporting Abdullah and his regime since 1947 no matter the cost? Since early that year, he had been deeply concerned about Abdullah's state of mind, expressing his worries to Maulana Azad about his friend: 'Sheikh Sahab, in his present state of mind, is likely to do something or take some step, which might make things worse.'[1] The attacks on Abdullah by the Indian press had now reached a frenzy and also implicated Nehru himself, especially after Mookerjee's sudden death. Reports were flying that Abdullah no longer wished Kashmir to remain a part of India and was cavorting with foreign powers such as the United States to seek the state's independence. Abdullah's own speeches, questioning Kashmir's relationship to India, made matters worse. The situation in Kashmir was a serious distraction as Nehru prepared for the impending India–Pakistan summit in Karachi. Abdullah, it appeared, was quickly becoming a liability, especially as Nehru's repeated attempts to invite him to Delhi for talks were met with prevarication or outright rejection.

For his part, Abdullah felt under attack from all quarters. The PP agitation had shaken his faith in India and its commitment to secularism. Such bitter communalism in his own state did not bode well for Kashmiri Muslims and Kashmir's status in India. He felt aggrieved that the Indian leadership, especially Nehru, had not done enough to contain the movement and that the Indian press actually saw merit in its call for ending Kashmir's special position within India. Secularism could be deployed at cross-purposes in postcolonial India—for Indians, Abdullah was not secular enough because he promoted the interests of Kashmiri Muslims, while for Abdullah, Indians were not truly secular until they recognized the need for the protection of Kashmiri Muslim interests. Meanwhile, Kashmiri Muslims themselves were drifting away from his party, the NC, for not living up to the promise of ushering in a new Kashmir free of corruption and privation.

Pakistan kept up a steady drumbeat of propaganda against Abdullah and his regime for being corrupt Indian stooges. The international press too presented him as an Indian agent with tenuous legitimacy to rule Kashmir. The NC's leadership itself was divided on how to respond to these challenges, particularly on how to define Kashmir's relationship to India in the wake of the Delhi Agreement. What's more, some of them appeared to be actively working against him, perhaps even with Delhi. And there were rumours that Nehru was no longer on his side.

Abdullah faced a tough choice at this moment. If he pushed for the implementation of the Delhi Agreement, he risked losing his increasingly alienated base—Kashmiri Muslims—altogether. If he stood up to India and insisted on Kashmir's autonomy, even demanded plebiscite, he would be in serious trouble with the Indian government. But surely his friend Nehru would ultimately protect him, as he had done so many times in the past. On the other hand, this move would seal his position as the true representative of Kashmiris within Kashmir itself and the world at large. The ploy might even yield some concessions from India. This appears naive in retrospect, but Abdullah most likely believed that Nehru's commanding influence in Delhi and their personal relationship would surmount all other factors, despite rumours to the contrary.

But he miscalculated. He seriously misjudged the amount of power Nehru actually had or would be willing to exercise to defend him given the context. Barely a year after the first general election had endorsed his position as India's prime minister, Nehru felt that his primary responsibility was to preserve India's unity, which seemed to be under threat from various quarters, including through a wave of protests on the linguistic issue. Added to this was the Abdullah–Kashmir factor, for which he faced a barrage of criticism from within and without his own party and government. Morarji Desai, then chief minister of Bombay State, wrote an angry letter to Nehru holding him responsible for the situation in Kashmir and urging him to take action to prevent further damage: 'Your confidence in him [Abdullah] has, I'm afraid, been abused and a very difficult situation has arisen. I hope you will deal with it strongly and stop further deterioration. If he is permitted to go his own way, it will have serious repercussions on public opinion in this country.'[2]

In many ways, Abdullah failed to account for the broader canvas of the early 1950s against which his actions would be received. The Indian centre was in the process of establishing itself and included an entire bureaucratic apparatus besides Nehru. It faced numerous challenges to its centralizing, secular vision and authority as it attempted to assert sovereignty over all of India's far-flung and very diverse territories. Jammu and Kashmir (J&K), where regional and religious identities came together in a potent mix to openly defy the centre's writ, was perhaps the most significant. Although it involved many other individuals and groups, Abdullah became the face of this defiance and had to be removed from the scene. International pressure on India and Pakistan to resolve this dispute was intense as well, and Abdullah's incendiary rhetoric was complicating any possibility of its resolution.

Three members of Abdullah's own cabinet—Bakshi Ghulam Muhammad, Shyam Lal Saraf and Girdhari Lal Dogra—expressed their lack of confidence in the government in a memorandum dated 7 August 1953. The memorandum accused Abdullah of being arbitrary and dictatorial and of making 'public pronouncements' that 'arbitrarily sought to precipitate a rupture in the relationship of the State with India'. It charged him with supporting his close associate and revenue minister, Mirza Afzal Beg, who 'has persistently been following policies of narrow sectarianism and communalism which have seriously undermined the oneness of the State'. It concluded that under these conditions, the cabinet could no longer give the people a 'clean, efficient, and healthy administration'.[3] Karan Singh, the Sadar-i-Riyasat of the state since 1952, dismissed the cabinet in a letter to Abdullah.[4] Under the cover of the night of 8–9 August, Abdullah ceased to be prime minister of J&K. Not only was he dismissed, but he was also placed under arrest. Bakshi, his deputy, was installed as the new prime minister.

In August 1953, besides the support of very few individuals such as Beg, Abdullah stood alone. Most of his long-time friends and compatriots from the Kashmir nationalist movement had abandoned him. In his letters to his friend Mehmooda Ahmed Ali Shah—a Kashmiri communist and lead organizer of the Women's Self-Defence Corps in 1947—G.M. Sadiq, Abdullah's close colleague from the early days of the movement, referred to him as the 'Tall Fool' who had been overtaken by a 'strange, mad fervour' that would end in his 'political destruction'.[5] In an interview, Karan Singh wryly admitted that his opponents at this time referred to Abdullah as 'Frankenstein', an apt description, since having created the monster of Kashmiri nationalism, Abdullah now had to pay the ultimate price.[6] Karan Singh's use of the term is also a window into his own views on Abdullah, whose commitment to Kashmiri nationalism Singh admired but always found incompatible with Indian nationalism; in later years, he would be firmly behind keeping Abdullah out of the political sphere for as long as it was politically expedient.

Two related priorities drove Abdullah at all times: to maintain the position of his party, the NC, and to ensure his own position as leader of the party and sole representative of Kashmiri Muslims in the Kashmir Valley. He was willing to court extremes in service of these goals, and he often did. His colleagues overlooked his dictatorial ways so long as he remained a symbol of Kashmiri freedom. By 1953, however, his image had taken a severe beating. Ironically, his dismissal restored his position as standard-bearer of Kashmiri self-determination, but at the cost of removing him from active politics for nearly two decades.

## THE LONGER BACKDROP

Sudden as the events of August 1953 may seem, their foundation was laid long before, even before Abdullah became head of the emergency administration in late 1947, and then the prime minister of the Indian state of J&K in 1948. As we have seen, Abdullah unilaterally launched the Quit Kashmir agitation in May 1946 to infuse new life into the Kashmir movement and to push the Maharaja towards devolving power to the people's representatives. Not only did the agitation not achieve these objectives, but it also ended up sowing the seeds for many of the divisions that erupted in 1953, while also removing Abdullah from the political scene in the crucial months leading up to India's Independence and Partition.

While most of the NC leadership went along with the movement despite considering it ill-advised, it did lead them to question Abdullah's leadership abilities and brought their differences out into the open. The leadership of the Indian National Congress was not happy either with Abdullah's declaration of what amounted to war on the Maharaja. While Congress policy supported people's movements within the princely states, especially ones aligned with their goals, it did not want to alienate a princely ruler. Although Nehru came to Abdullah's defence, many leaders, such as J.B. Kripalani and Sardar Vallabhbhai Patel, were suspicious of the agitation because it challenged the right of the princes to decide the future of their states and was being directed by communists.[7] This friction between an element of the Congress leadership and Abdullah due to his stance on the Maharaja would survive into the post-1947 period.

The most lasting result of the agitation was that it created an unbridgeable rift between Abdullah and the Maharaja. Abdullah was not released by the Maharaja until late September 1947 and that too after repeated personal entreaties by Patel and Nehru on the grounds that he was needed to counter the impending Pakistani assault on the state.[8] He also had to pledge loyalty to the Maharaja before his release, which he never forgot nor forgave. Abdullah thus considered the Maharaja his nemesis—the feeling was mutual—and regarded his continued presence as the ruler while he was prime minister of J&K as a slap in the face. For him, the Maharaja also served as a convenient foil that he could challenge or even attack openly whenever he felt politically under siege. He repeatedly called for the Maharaja to be deposed during the early years of his tenure as prime minister, when Pakistani propaganda against him was at its height and he was afraid of losing his status among Kashmiri Muslims. Managing this relationship became one of the biggest headaches for Patel, the head of the States Ministry.

This was the cause of Abdullah's worsening relationship with Jammu, made even worse by some of the policies undertaken by his government, especially the Land Reforms. The blatantly rigged constituent assembly elections, followed by the inauguration of the assembly itself in the autumn of 1951, brought matters to a head not just between him and Jammu, but also with New Delhi. By mid-1952, Nehru was expressing his deep unease with the direction taken by the constituent assembly. He was particularly concerned about the impending vote in the assembly to end hereditary rulership in the state.[9] As he wrote to Abdullah on 5 June 1952, the removal of the Maharaja, who had acceded to India, would raise questions about the legality of the accession itself and hence the decision should be postponed. In response, Abdullah did postpone the decision for a month, during which time a state delegation visited Delhi for consultations.[10]

As Nehru and other Indian government officials held discussions with the delegation— comprising Afzal Beg (who represented Abdullah's views most closely), Maulana Masoodi (at the time general secretary of the NC) and D.P. Dhar (who had a pro-India bent)—the need for clarifying the position of Kashmir within the Indian Union became evident. Nehru emphasized this point to the delegation that before the state's constitution was finalized, these matters needed to be worked out. Once that was done, the question of the headship of the state would also be resolved.[11] The subsequent discussions, which included Abdullah, led to the Delhi Agreement between the Indian government and the government of J&K. Announced on 24 July 1952, the agreement reaffirmed some of the principles of Article 370 and limited the central government's authority to the three subjects. It granted state residents Indian citizenship, but allowed their rights and privileges to be determined by the state assembly based on the state's constitution. The state assembly had the right to recommend the head of state, who would be recognized by the president of India. And finally, the central government could intervene and implement emergency powers only if requested by the state's assembly.[12]

Instead of bringing the two entities closer, the Delhi Agreement became the main point of contention between Kashmir and India in the next year. In particular, it created distrust and tension between Abdullah and Nehru. Again, Abdullah viewed the agreement as a means to reassert and preserve the state's autonomy, while for Nehru it was a means of integrating the state into India. As A.G. Noorani has pointed out, the agreement 'had no legal force by itself'. It could be implemented only after the state constituent assembly approved it, which would be followed by an order under Article 370.[13]

But Abdullah's statement on the agreement to the constituent assembly on 11 August 1952 made subtle changes to the language of the agreement. The statement also reverted to the agreement that the state had arrived at with India in 1947 through the instrument of accession and celebrated its soundness, warning that 'any suggestions of altering arbitrarily this basis of our relationship with India would not only constitute a breach of the spirit and letter of the Constitution, but it may invite serious consequences for a harmonious association of our State with India'.[14] Nehru was concerned about what looked like pushback on the agreement from Abdullah. In his note to Abdullah dated 25 August 1952, Nehru outlined his views on Kashmir's relationship to India, noting that these views had not changed in four years. He was not worried about the UN or even Pakistan, but rather about Kashmir, where among the leadership, 'I have found doubt and hesitation ... and not clarity of vision or firmness of outlook.'[15] Indeed, he was so 'perplexed' about Abdullah's attitude, as he explained to Karan Singh, that he wanted him to accept the position of Sadar-i-Riyasat, so that there could be someone 'on the scene to be able to help if some problems arose in the future'.[16]

Margaret Lee Weil, an American photographer and journalist who was later accused of being a spy, attended many of the constituent assembly meetings in September 1953 and provided an outsider's view of the situation in the state at the time. She was utterly baffled by the confusing messages emanating from the NC leaders, including Abdullah. The speeches were in one breath for India, proclaiming undying fealty, in another breath asking India for money, and in the next one, declaring that they would not allow Kashmir to be dragged down to the status of an ordinary Indian state. Kashmiri leaders seemed to want the advantages of belonging to the Indian Union but none of the responsibilities, she remarked. She was not sure whether these were Abdullah's views or the views of other leaders as well. 'Yet what goes on in this strange state? Is it communalism in disguise? Is it nationalism? Is it the lust for power? Is it inflated egos because Kashmir has been put into such importance?' wrote Weil.[17]

These questions are pertinent and to arrive at the answers, one must turn to the context of politics in the state as a whole, particularly Jammu. This especially explains Abdullah's attitude to the Delhi Agreement and to India more broadly. The Jammu agitation against Abdullah's regime, as well as his dwindling popularity in the Kashmir Valley itself, ultimately undid the fragile relationship between Kashmir and India as well as between Abdullah and Nehru.

## PRAJA PARISHAD AGITATION

The All Jammu and Kashmir Praja Parishad was founded in 1947 by Balraj Madhok, a Rashtriya Swayamsevak Sangh (RSS) activist, to represent the interests of the Hindus of Jammu and to safeguard their rights from what was considered the anti-Dogra and Kashmir-centric government led by Sheikh Abdullah. Its main objectives were the entire state's complete integration into India, or barring that, its division along the Ceasefire Line with the state's integration into India, or barring that, the integration of Jammu and Ladakh into India. The situation at that time, with a divided state granted autonomy within the Indian Union and an NC regime in power, was seen as deleterious to Hindu interests and hence unacceptable.[18] Since the regime did not allow for the existence of opposition parties, the PP became a conduit through which a range of groups within the state with grievances against the NC and its policies could express themselves. The RSS, and later the Bharatiya Jana Sangh, provided support to the party and the agitation that it organized as a means to undercut the Congress government at the centre.

The PP clashed early on with the NC regime, and Abdullah externed Balraj Madhok from the state in 1948. Jammu Hindus resented this deeply, and the Dogras especially could not abide Abdullah's steady drumbeat against the Maharaja. In general, Jammu Hindus were acutely unhappy with the economic policies of the NC, which they felt were aimed specifically against them. The anger mounted as the nomination papers of the PP candidates running for the constituent assembly elections were rejected by the NC authorities in 1951.[19] The constituent assembly, which Abdullah so proudly proclaimed as the 'harbour of freedom' for the people of the state, was seen as a sham by people in Jammu, even those not affiliated with the PP. Soon thereafter, as the negotiations between India and the NC leading to the Delhi Agreement were taking place, the PP, now led by Prem Nath Dogra, organized an agitation calling for the state's integration into India. The movement demanded 'Ek Vidhan, Ek Pradhan, Ek Nishaan' (One Constitution, One Prime Minister, One Flag). The end of the Dogra dynasty with the abdication of Maharaja Hari Singh and the election of his son, Karan Singh, as Sadar-i-Riyasat added fuel to the raging fire.

From the beginning of the agitation, Abdullah was its main object and would remain persona non grata for the Indian Hindu right throughout his political career, even after he had been dismissed. He did not represent the end of autocracy for the people of Jammu; instead, he was the symbol of the transfer of power from Jammu to the Kashmir Valley, from Dogras to Kashmiris, after 200 years. According to Balraj Puri, a member of the NC from Jammu who was expelled from the party by Abdullah, Abdullah expected the people of Jammu to submit to his diktat in the same way as the people of the Valley. But the people of Jammu were too heterogeneous to accept one leader as paramount, especially an individual from the Valley. As Puri pointed out to Nehru in 1950 and 1952, the one-party state that was being run by Abdullah was simply not acceptable to the people of Jammu.[20] Karan Singh, now Sadar-i-Riyasat, was taken aback by the level of sympathy for the agitation that he observed across the province of Jammu in late 1952, and reported to Nehru that it was driven by 'deep-seated and genuine economic and psychological reasons', and could not be dismissed 'as merely the creation of a reactionary clique'.[21]

From the perspective of Jammu, Abdullah came across as at best disinterested and at worst unsympathetic towards its people's demands. It did not help that the NC did not have very deep roots in the region and the Jammu NC representatives were particularly corrupt individuals with little influence within the regime. As a result, the people of Jammu felt voiceless and unrepresented in the upper echelons of power.[22] Organizations such as the New Kashmir Committee—which was led by Balraj Puri and was against the PP as well as the conflation of the Dogra community with Jammu—were willing to support Abdullah's regime if he at least attempted to address some of the demands of Jammu and put in place a more democratic administration in the state.[23]

Abdullah's stifling of all criticism, even from sympathetic quarters, meant that there were no organizations left in Jammu that would stand up for his regime at this time. The newspaper *Ranbir* is a case in point. Founded in 1924 under the Dogra regime by Mulk Raj Saraf, the newspaper supported Abdullah's regime and its defence of secular democracy. It recognized the immense pressures faced by Abdullah as he took over the ravaged state and was highly critical of the PP agitation in its early stages. But as the newspaper began to point out the rampant corruption creeping into the various levels of government, the pressure from the regime grew so intense that the newspaper had to shutter its doors in 1950. In his autobiography, Saraf writes that he once pointed out to Abdullah that he had rid the people of one maharaja but imposed many maharajas on them instead. Abdullah grew purple with rage, shouting at Saraf about the reports he was receiving about his changed attitude, and warning him that it would land him in prison if he was not careful. According to Saraf, 'The Sheikh permitted himself to be surrounded by a set of sycophants who were always busy poisoning his ears to grind their own axe.' In this case, the *Ranbir* was a threat to their activities, and therefore, they tried their best to turn the Sheikh against the paper.[24]

Nehru wrote to Abdullah to deal with the PP agitation in both psychological terms and in terms of law and order by parsing out the mischief mongers from those who had real grievances that needed redress. By conciliating the latter group, and with 'careful handling', Nehru felt, the agitation would 'subside'.[25] Abdullah, for his part, did little to bring about any kind of reconciliation with Jammu. His letter to Nehru regarding the agitation is telling because it illustrates how he actually saw the movement, describing it as 'a violent reaction on the part of Jammu landlords and other upper classes'. He added that the problems facing Jammu were not related to its association with Kashmir or India, but were rather of 'wretchedness, poverty and degeneration of the vast masses of Jammu people'.[26]

Despite Nehru's much-publicized visit—accompanied by Maulana Azad and Abdullah himself—to Ladakh in September 1952 to consult with its leadership, by the end of that year, the head lama, Kushak Bakula, had become more vocal on behalf of Ladakh's separation from J&K and Ladakhi autonomy within the Indian Union. Here again, Nehru—perhaps without realizing that similar advice could apply to his own handling of J&K as a whole—advised Abdullah to 'create a sensation of self-rule or partnership in self-rule' in Ladakh before the problem got out of hand.[27] But on the larger issue of the lack of freedom of expression and allowing an opposition in the state that had been raised by Puri, Nehru remained silent.

Abdullah's repression of the communists came back to haunt him at this stage, as they used the situation in Jammu as an opportunity to raise their own profile at Abdullah's expense. The changing international scenario, with the USSR taking an overtly pro-India stance on Kashmir at the UN to undermine the Anglo-American bloc and the fact that the Communist Party of India (CPI) had abandoned armed insurrection against the Indian state in favour of participating in the 1951–2 general elections, further turned the communists against Abdullah. In late June 1953, the CPI passed a resolution on Kashmir that stated that it was against an independent Kashmir, supported limited accession of Kashmir to India and called on democratic forces inside and outside the NC to resolve the Kashmir issue. It also endorsed the legitimacy of the Jammu agitation, noting that it was a result of real grievances that the Abdullah government had been unable to address.[28] This deepened the wedge between Jammu and the Kashmir Valley as well as the pro-communist and anti-communist members within the NC.

Since 1951, communist treatises had been asserting that the Kashmir affair was a creation of the imperialist designs of the Anglo-American bloc in which both India and Pakistan were embroiled. By 1952–3, the communists were increasingly convinced that Abdullah was under the thrall of this bloc, which was encouraging his quest for independence. Americans such as the US ambassador Loy Henderson and his wife, both of whom frequented Kashmir in the summers and spent time with Abdullah, were seen as backing his dreams of an independent Kashmir.[29] Adlai Stevenson's visit to Kashmir in May 1953—during which he held three long talks with Abdullah, gushing afterwards about Kashmiri hospitality and pleading with India and Pakistan to resolve the dispute—added further grist to the mill. Sadiq, recognized as a noted pro-communist member of the J&K cabinet, wrote in June 1953 to Mehmooda Ali Shah that the 'Tall Fool' was 'poisoning people's minds' and 'we have decided to expose all his foreign conspiracies and thus defeat him'.[30]

The *Blitz*, a tabloid that promoted leftist, anti-imperialist ideas and had initially been supportive of Abdullah's regime, now turned against him.[31] It and other magazines published sensational articles about Abdullah's anti-national and corrupt tendencies, including his misuse of state funds to cultivate a lavish lifestyle, such as going to offer evening prayers at Nehru Park in an American-made Cadillac convertible car. An article in the 8 August 1953 issue of the *Current*, Bombay, trenchantly noted: 'The arrival of the Rs. 82,000 Cadillac has helped enrich and deepen the myth of Sher-e-Kashmir in the eyes of the under-fed and under-clothed Kashmiri Muslim. The Maharaja of Kashmir may have been liquidated, but a new Nabob was fast installing himself in his place.'[32] Speaking in his own defence during the conclusion to the defence arguments in the Kashmir Conspiracy Case in 1961, Abdullah alleged that R.K. Karanjia, the founder and editor of the *Blitz*, had been especially conscripted by Rafi Ahmed Kidwai, Nehru's close advisor, to organize a propaganda campaign against him to mould public opinion before the events of 1953.[33]

By 1953, Abdullah had lost control of his own cabinet, his party and certainly of the political messaging. The group whose unadulterated voice he claimed to represent and thus the group that mattered most to his survival as the supreme leader—Kashmiri Muslims in the Valley—had been steadily moving away from him. The corruption, nepotism, repression and misrule during his tenure as prime minister had turned even his and the NC's most ardent supporters against him and the party. For instance, individuals such as Munshi Ishaq—who had been a dedicated NC member and believed in the promise of a New Kashmir—had soured towards the regime and Abdullah as early as 1950. Ishaq's writings from this period are replete with disillusionment at the course of politics in the state.[34] The disgruntlement with the direction of politics in the state had led to the founding of the Jamaat-i-Islami Jammu and Kashmir as a separate political organization—distinct from the Jamaat-i-Islami Hind—in 1952.

Pakistan's propaganda against Abdullah's regime was remorseless, even using the PP agitation as evidence of India's communal nature and of how ineffectual Abdullah's regime actually was in stemming this tide. Karra, who had been sidelined early on by Abdullah, and had been working against him ever since, took this opportunity to found the Kashmir Political Conference, with pro-Pakistan proclivities, in June 1953. In this scenario, Abdullah felt that distancing himself from India and asserting Kashmir's independence from it was the surest way of winning his popularity back and showing to Pakistan, as well as those who were pro-Pakistan, that he was not India's puppet. Another narrative move was to distance himself from the corruption of his administration by laying the blame on others within it.

In the meantime, the RSS and Jan Sangh propaganda war against Abdullah, as well as against Nehru for supporting him and his regime, was raging continually. The Delhi Agreement itself, followed by news of Abdullah going back on parts of the agreement, helped them stoke the fires. Reports of repression of the protesters by Kashmir authorities and the maltreatment of prisoners, who were presented as *satyagrahi*s carrying out non-violent protests, kept the movement in the news. Responding to the arrests of PP agitators in Punjab, the Jan Sangh and Hindu Mahasabha passed a resolution declaring their demands 'just and fair', adding further, 'It is deplorable that the Government of India is helping Sheikh Abdullah's government in suppressing the Praja Parishad agitation by sending its police.'[35] Nehru grew increasingly vexed at the communal nature of this agitation, which he saw as aimed at undermining his government. He wrote to Abdullah in February 1953, saying that he was not afraid of the agitation, but asked him to implement the Delhi Agreement so that the agitation would be deprived of its main plank.[36]

Abdullah keenly resented that the agitation was aimed specifically at him, although it helped him present himself and Kashmiri Muslims as martyrs of a communal conspiracy. He most likely also felt that the Indian government was either directly behind the movement or at least tacitly supported it because it would lead to his removal from power. Until this point, Nehru was the only person in the Indian government that Abdullah had trusted, but now he came to believe that if Nehru had wanted, he could have stopped the agitation in its tracks, a belief he held on to until the end of his life. Nehru, for his part, was powerless to stop the agitation.

A series of letters between Nehru and Mookerjee from early 1953 illustrate that they differed fundamentally on their vision for India and Indian policy towards Kashmir. Nehru noted that the PP agitation was 'not only communal but supported by communal elements in India', and was attempting to settle a constitutional and bilateral issue by means of a war. He repeatedly called on Mookerjee and other Jan Sangh leaders to withdraw the agitation because it was playing into Pakistan's hands, damaging India's reputation in the world and hurting its position in Kashmir.[37] But they had other ideas. Although Mookerjee somewhat dampened his speeches in parliament, the Jan Sangh continued to support and encourage the movement.

For Mookerjee, J&K's accession to India could not be considered final and irrevocable until the J&K constituent assembly had passed a resolution declaring that the state had acceded to India, which would obviate the need for its special status. As he wrote to Abdullah:

> There cannot be a republic within a republic. There can be one and only sovereign Parliament and that is the Parliament of India. Consciously or unconsciously, you are creating a new sovereignty for Jammu and Kashmir state. India has been torn into two by the two-nation theory. You are now developing a three-nation theory, the third being [the] Kashmiri nation. These are dangerous symptoms and are not good for your State or for the whole of India.[38]

Abdullah defended J&K's special position within the Indian constitution, which had been arrived at after careful consideration between the two governments and could not be rewritten 'by pressure or intimidation'.[39] Their positions remained irreconcilable, and the agitation raged on.

Abdullah grew more isolated within his own party, retreating further into himself and away from India, hedging on implementing the Delhi Agreement and refusing even to meet with Nehru to discuss the situation. In February 1953, he wrote to Nehru about his 'distress at various things', calling the agitation a 'tremendous shock' for the Muslims of the state that had 'unhinged' them. He was, of course, talking about himself. He then expressed doubt at whether the wound inflicted by the agitation could ever be healed. And he continued to make excuses about why it was taking so long to implement the Delhi Agreement. He asked Nehru to visit Jammu to discuss the situation because he was too busy to meet him in Delhi.[40] Ignoring the slight, Nehru attempted to reason with Abdullah in his letter of 1 March, agreeing with him that the uncertainty of the situation was distressing, but to suggest that nothing could be done about it was not helpful. They had to keep working to resolve the issues that had arisen.[41] On the same day, he wrote to Maulana Azad, 'I fear that Sheikh Saheb's mind is so utterly confused that he does not know what to do.'[42]

By then, Nehru had begun to rely more on other figures within the J&K administration, including Karan Singh, D.P. Dhar and particularly Bakshi, for information about the situation on the ground in Kashmir, which was becoming increasingly confusing. Nehru's relationships with these men, all of whom had direct access to him and with whom he kept up a steady correspondence besides also meeting them regularly, were not new.[43] As Karan Singh notes in his autobiography, Nehru trusted him as well as Dhar, and always gave their views—which were 'able to counteract to some extent the belligerent Muslim Kashmiri chauvinism represented by the Sheikh'—'a careful hearing'.[44]

Moreover, Bakshi, as the person closest to the actual workings of the J&K administration, had always appealed to the Indian government. He gave off the impression, as he had to Ambassador Henderson during his visit in 1949, of being a man of 'great energy and of considerable forcefulness ... primarily a man of action rather than of theory'.[45] He was considered second only to Abdullah in popularity in Kashmir, where he was known as Khalid-i-Kashmir. Bakshi established good relations with the Indian Army early on once he took over the defence portfolio as deputy prime minister. Army officials began to describe Abdullah as 'stand-offish' while Bakshi was the 'grandest chap that Kashmir has'.[46] They saw Abdullah as an idealist who surrounded himself with communists, even as Bakshi was a realist who was awake to the dangers of communism, and as General Thimayya, the commander of army operations in Kashmir, noted, 'frequently saved Abdullah from the consequences of his own naivete'. Comparing Abdullah and Bakshi, Thimayya went so far as to state, 'Sheikh Abdullah might be considered as the Nehru of Kashmir and Bakshi as the Patel.'[47]

After Nehru's return from Kashmir in May 1948, where he was attending Freedom Day celebrations, he mentioned to Patel that Abdullah enjoyed great popularity in the Valley, but Bakshi was the most efficient person 'who gets things done though in doing this he does not always follow rules and regulations'.[48] As early as 1950, he wrote to Vijayalakshmi Pandit that Abdullah was behaving 'very badly' and 'poor Bakshi Ghulam Muhammad is very unhappy about it all but does not know what to do'.[49] Intelligence Bureau reports regularly described Abdullah as oscillating from one position to another, while Bakshi was seen as 'unambiguous, predictable, stable, and pro-India'.[50] Karan Singh, too, found it easier to work with Bakshi, noting that he 'was more pragmatic, a superb organizer and a man with excellent public relations with all sections of people including many in Jammu ... His whole stance vis-à-vis the Accession was also distinctly more amenable to strengthening the relationship between the State and the Centre, and less charged with the Kashmiri chauvinism so sedulously fostered by Sheikh Abdullah.'[51]

Nehru's correspondence with Bakshi steadily increased during the agitation in Jammu in early 1953, with the latter appealing to Nehru to take more interventionist steps to mitigate the upsurge.[52] Nehru's feelings towards Bakshi were probably crystallized after his visit to Kashmir from 23 to 25 May 1953 to meet with Abdullah. During this visit, Nehru insisted on addressing a meeting of NC workers at Abdullah's house, where he lambasted its leadership and pointed out all the faults with the functioning of the organization. Abdullah was livid, and later, in the privacy of his living room, told Nehru angrily that what he had done was intolerable and that he should have discussed matters with him before making his concerns public. Nehru, not to be outdone, lost his temper in return and said that he had every right to do so because Kashmir had acceded to India. Abdullah retorted that he was still the prime minister of the state and should have been consulted, to which Nehru replied that he was the prime minister of India. The meeting ended without any resolution.[53]

When they met again—in the presence of Maulana Azad and K.N. Katju, the Union home minister, who had accompanied Nehru on this visit—Abdullah declared that there was no middle ground between complete integration and complete autonomy. And since the majority of Kashmiris would not accept the first course, then the second option remained the only practical solution. Even as Nehru suggested to him that this was not the case and that intermediate possibilities did exist, he could also see that Abdullah did not command the support of the majority of the leadership of the NC.[54] At this point, Karan Singh's letters to Nehru regarding the situation in the Valley and the challenging nature of Abdullah's speeches became increasingly urgent.[55]

Abdullah himself kept pushing for alternatives to implementing the Delhi Agreement, hoping to bring the NC leadership in line with his own views. He was especially interested in one of the four proposals put forward by the subcommittee he had appointed to consider the alternatives (which presented its report on 8 June). This resembled Dixon's plan of partitioning the state between India and Pakistan with plebiscite in the Valley with an option for independence. The working committee of the NC rejected this, although Bakshi made a pretense of supporting Abdullah's wishes on the matter. The option was unacceptable to India since it amounted to the Valley's independence.[56]

What brought matters to a head was Mookerjee's death on 23 June 1953 in Srinagar under what were presented by Abdullah's opponents and the PP in particular as 'shrouded circumstances'.[57] The J&K government had arrested Mookerjee as he attempted to enter Kashmir without a permit in support of the idea that the state was an inalienable part of India, and hence a special permit should not be required to enter it. The propaganda war against Abdullah and Nehru became even shriller in the wake of his death. The speeches made by Jan Sangh volunteers on the occasion of the immersion of Mookerjee's ashes in Hardwar accused the Government of India of being in league with Abdullah to poison Mookerjee, alongside chanting slogans such as 'Sazish kiski hai—Nehru aur Abdullah ki' and 'Nehru aur Abdullah ko fansi do' (Whose conspiracy is it—Nehru's and Abdullah's; Hang Nehru and Abdullah).[58]

But Nehru continued to defend the Abdullah regime in public. He wrote to the socialist leader J.P. Narayan that the regime had provided enough evidence that they had taken good care of Mookerjee while he was in detention and that further enquiry into the matter would simply question the government's authority.[59] In private, he expressed his 'anguish' to Karan Singh, among others, at the turn of events in Kashmir and Abdullah's refusal to engage with him.[60] As Abdullah refused to meet with Nehru and his public pronouncements became more unhinged in the wake of the Mookerjee affair, Bakshi increasingly took the lead in representing the J&K government in Delhi. Always ambitious, he exploited the opportunity created by the rift between Abdullah and Nehru to scale the ladder of power. The road to Abdullah's dismissal had been paved.

## ABDULLAH'S DOWNFALL

By July, the rifts within the NC itself were out in the open. It was obvious that most members of Abdullah's own cabinet and other senior NC leaders did not agree with his stance on Kashmir's future, albeit for different reasons. Bakshi had been working closely with the Indian government for a long time and saw himself as Abdullah's successor to the prime ministership of the state. Sadiq had communist leanings and hewed closely to the stance of the CPI on the Kashmir issue, which was clearly against independence. He and the other leftists were also convinced that Abdullah was being directed by the Americans to pursue this suicidal course, and the imperialists' designs had to be thwarted. Masoodi was anti-communist, but did not agree with the idea of independence because he believed it to be impractical. Bakshi and Sadiq were pushing back publicly against Abdullah's ideas in their own speeches. Beg appeared to be the only cabinet member who saw eye to eye with him.

Abdullah began to call weekly NC workers' meetings at his own home to convince them of his position, broadcast speeches on the radio and travel around the state making speeches in an attempt to take the initiative back from those who seemed to have stolen it. In a speech on 14 July, he said that all the parties involved in the Kashmir dispute recognized the people's right to self-determination, but none were willing to create the conditions necessary for its exercise. In a speech broadcast on Radio Kashmir on 15 July, he warned people to be wary of the corrupt sycophants within the NC, 'a group of men ... who are in it just for achieving their selfish ends by all means, fair and foul'. This was clearly aimed at Bakshi, who had declared his undying loyalty to Abdullah as their 'sole and greatest leader' in a speech on 6 June: 'We may be hanged, but like Majnoon, our lips will utter just one word, "Laila, Laila".'[61] But in other speeches, he went completely against Abdullah's position in emphasizing Kashmir's accession to India and warning anti-national elements against questioning it.[62] It was obvious that he was working with Delhi behind the scenes.

In another speech, Abdullah questioned why he was called a nationalist when he condemned Pakistan but a communalist when he ran down any communal organization in India.[63] 'I am constantly being declared untrustworthy in India,' he said in a speech on 10 July at Mujahid Manzil, the headquarters of the NC, and 'a time will, therefore, come when I will bid them good bye'.[64] The PP agitation in some ways allowed him to make these kinds of charges because it proved that he was a victim of a communal war and that India was not as secular as it claimed.[65] But this was a double-edged sword because it also proved Pakistan's point that Abdullah had been wrong in agreeing to the state's accession to India. And it allowed the Indian press to argue that Abdullah was 'lay[ing] a smokescreen of wild charges of communalism against India behind which to campaign for an independent Kashmir'.[66] As it was, his speeches had begun to question the very foundation of the state's relationship to India. On 31 July, Abdullah openly challenged India by emphasizing the extraordinary circumstances leading up to the accession and stating that it was up to the Muslims of Kashmir to decide on accession since Hindus would never vote for Pakistan.[67]

His private communications with Nehru and Maulana Azad matched his public pronouncements during this time. He sounded irate, almost petulant, at the pressure being put on him to meet with Indian leaders and take steps to implement the Delhi Agreement. In his lengthy letter of 4 July to Nehru, he noted that Kashmir wanted to steer a middle course between full integration and full autonomy, which had resulted in Article 370. But it was under siege because of the Jammu agitation, which began as soon as hereditary rulership was abolished in the state. The implementation of the Delhi Agreement required 'a calm atmosphere, free from conflict and coercion ... and this is precisely what is being denied to us'. And the bigger problem—the lack of resolution of the dispute between India and Pakistan—remained.[68]

He continued that the majority community in Kashmir did not feel secure within India any longer and did not wish to be swamped by the majority community in India. He argued that Muslims were not being recruited into the armed forces or the civil services in India and conceding union with India in all subjects would curtail employment opportunities for Kashmir's Muslims. 'The educated Muslims here are on the whole feeling somewhat bottled up in the matter of service and enterprise. They see their horizons shrinking in this direction,' he wrote.[69] He also insisted that there were no disagreements among the leadership of the NC on Kashmir's future and that he continued to believe in the principles of secular democracy. His honour was linked to Nehru's honour, and he hoped that Nehru would understand his position.[70]

Nehru responded briefly in what would be his last letter to Abdullah before his dismissal. He noted that Abdullah's charges against India were unfair, but that Kashmir and India needed to move forward by implementing the Delhi Agreement, which had been arrived at after full consideration of all factors. As for resolving the dispute with Pakistan, he was prepared to go the distance, as long as it did not compromise India's basic principles, especially its commitment to secularism. He requested Abdullah once again to visit Delhi for a meeting, so that all the issues between Kashmir and India could be thrashed out.[71]

Azad, who had received a copy of Abdullah's 4 July letter to Nehru, wrote to Abdullah that he was perplexed and confused about what Abdullah really wanted. Did he want the independence option, as he seemed to be declaring in his speeches, because that would simply hand the Valley over to Pakistan, wrote Azad. He had suggested to Abdullah in their meeting in May that year, he stated, that the middle course was the best course and India was prepared to stand by it, but at that time, too, Abdullah had rejected it. He ended the letter with the words:

> My dear Abdullah, I have a two-fold relationship with you—public and private. And now I'm telling you this as a friend—there is only one way of safeguarding the future well-being of the people of Kashmir and that is the way we laid down in 1949 and which you then accepted. Hold steadfastly to this way and be assured that you will never have to regret it.[72]

Abdullah refused to give ground. In his response to Nehru on 15 July, he wrote, why make a 'fetish of such agreements', especially given that the people of Kashmir had accepted the Delhi Agreement, but not the people of India. Could the agreement, he asked, become the basis of the state's relationship with India given this fact? He then insisted that India live up to its promise to the people of Kashmir by creating conditions for the exercise of their 'fundamental and democratic right'. Refusing to meet Nehru yet again, he noted that 'it can serve no purpose to continue endless discussions on issues that have been thrashed out a number of times'.[73]

Abdullah's failure to appear in Delhi for talks could not but come to the notice of the Indian press. Attempting to probe Abdullah's reasons, *The Times of India*'s political correspondent suggested that walking the tightrope between swearing loyalty to India while at the same time rejecting merger or integration with it was Abdullah's means of bargaining with the Indian government. He was set to lose his bargaining power if India and Pakistan came to an amicable agreement on Kashmir—as appeared likely if the impending talks on the issue between Nehru and his Pakistani counterpart, Mohammad Ali Bogra, were successful—and had thus concluded that 'the time for persuading India into more concessions is before the Nehru–Ali talks get well under way'.[74]

Abdullah's place in Delhi was filled by Beg and Bakshi as representatives of the J&K government. Upon his return from Delhi, Bakshi wrote in detail to Nehru on 17 July regarding Abdullah's position, giving his assessment of why Abdullah continued to act the way he did.

He told Nehru that many people, including Dhar and Masoodi, had met with Abdullah to persuade him to desist from his 'campaign of bitterness' against India, but he continued to make incendiary speeches. According to Bakshi, Beg was partially responsible because he was encouraging Abdullah's stance. He had reached Abdullah before Bakshi had had a chance to convey Nehru's concerns and position to Abdullah (which he later did), and had given him the impression that if he continued to insist, Nehru would eventually give in to his position.

Also, Abdullah had hoped that his continued insistence on taking India on would yield results that did not seem to have materialized. For instance, he had hoped that Pakistan would agree to his solution and that India too would be forced to agree given its internal situation and international position. He had banked on the Kashmiri masses coming out in support of his plan, but they appeared confused and in no mood to revolt. He had also expected the Indian press to be far more hysterical than it had been with his speeches and course of action, which would have vindicated his stance.[75]

Bakshi continued that since Abdullah's hopes had not panned out, he was thinking afresh and along the lines of a plebiscite. He had begun to characterize as unreasonable India's conditions for holding a plebiscite. Bakshi suggested that Abdullah was capable of demanding a withdrawal of Indian and Pakistani forces, the formation of a coalition between the NC in J&K and the MC in Azad Kashmir, and the conduct of an overall plebiscite in the state. This, Bakshi warned, would create fear and confusion in the minds of the people of Jammu and Ladakh, who would revive their demands for a separation of these two divisions from the state. The UN would likely step in, and under these conditions, Abdullah hoped, India would be forced to concede his demand for independence for the Valley. Various Americans were not helping by discussing the possibility of independence with Kashmiris. Abdullah's disruptive tactics, noted Bakshi, 'has got to be arrested somewhere and that too very quickly'.[76]

In her reports to Nehru in July 1953, Mridula Sarabhai, a prominent Gandhian who had worked closely with Gandhi himself and been close to

Abdullah since the mid-1940s, noted that rumours were rife in Kashmir that there had been a falling out between Nehru and Abdullah, and that Bakshi was now Delhi's point man. These were being spread by the Intelligence Bureau and the Ministry of Kashmir Affairs and needed to come to an end because they were impacting Abdullah negatively, making him ever more reluctant to meet Nehru to discuss matters.[77] Nehru became increasingly cross with her defence of Abdullah and her assessment of the situation in Kashmir, which he felt had the effect of encouraging 'recalcitrant elements' (most likely meaning Abdullah himself). He wrote to her that her appraisal of the situation ran counter to his own views on the matter and that she needed to stop her meddling.[78]

By this time, Nehru had already given up on Abdullah, and Bakshi's assessment must have cleared any misgivings he might have had. He had ceased to include Abdullah in his fortnightly letters to the chief ministers of Indian states, since many of these letters included information regarding Abdullah's position and the situation in Kashmir. Nehru's close advisors, such as Rafi Ahmed Kidwai—who had himself unsuccessfully attempted to bring Abdullah in line—were telling him that he should not hesitate to withdraw support from Abdullah. His recalcitrance on meeting with Nehru, who had built him up as a national leader and backed him and his regime despite deep shortcomings, was seen as a testament to Abdullah's disloyalty.[79] According to Ajit Bhattacharjea, 'Sensitive to signs of a backlash among Indian Muslims in reaction to Abdullah's campaign for *azaadi*, Kidwai was keen to have him removed.'[80] Many political leaders, including Morarji Desai, were putting pressure on Nehru to do something about the situation.[81]

International press coverage of what appeared to be Abdullah's open revolt against India was reaching uncomfortable levels, with there being reports of an alleged agreement between India and Pakistan to partition the state and grant independence to the Valley. As Robert Trumbull wrote in *The New York Times* on 4 July 1953, although Sheikh Abdullah was not among them, several Kashmiri leaders 'of a strong group now said to favour independence' were in New Delhi for talks with the Indian government.[82]

Nehru was particularly concerned about the message that the confusing reports would send to the Pakistani prime minister as both sides prepared for the talks on Kashmir. He wrote to Bakshi on 24 July that he needed a clear picture on where the J&K government stood so that he could convey that to the Pakistani prime minister, but if it was not forthcoming, then he would act according to what he felt was right during the talks.[83] After his return from Karachi, Nehru again wrote to Bakshi informing him about the gist of his talks with Bogra. The Pakistani prime minister and other leaders were eager to resolve the issue and had casually mentioned that independence was not a feasible option, to which Nehru had agreed. The two prime ministers had also agreed that the status quo might be the best solution, but Bogra might not be able to get support for that in Pakistan. They decided to meet again in September to continue the talks, before which Nehru said that he wanted to have a talk with Bakshi to sort out various issues, since he did not wish to 'ignore the wishes of the people of Kashmir'. He noted at the end of the letter that he wanted to discuss these matters at length with Abdullah as well, but since he had essentially told Nehru that he did not want to correspond with him nor did he want to meet, he was hesitant to write to him.[84]

Abdullah had swung too far to the extreme for Nehru to continue to turn a blind eye. The position in Kashmir was 'distinctly odd when the Chief Minister [*sic.*], while retaining his position as such, begins functioning as the leader of the opposition,' wrote Nehru to C. Rajagopalachari, a close friend and at that time chief minister of Madras State, on 31 July.[85] The threat that Abdullah would take a desperate step as he got further isolated within his own party seemed real. On the day of Abdullah's dismissal, 9 August, Nehru wrote to Indira Gandhi that the crisis in Kashmir had boiled over and Abdullah's campaign against India, and Nehru himself, had reached a level of bitterness that could no longer be ignored.[86] In any case, with the plebiscite option foundering on the question of demilitarization and looking ever more unlikely, India no longer needed Abdullah to deliver the Valley to India. And, as the Press Information Bureau noted, 'This chain of surmise, speculation and rumour and conclusions based thereon', resulting from Abdullah's activities and speeches followed by press reports, needed to be brought to an end.[87]

A set of instructions appended to a 31 July 'Top Secret' Intelligence Bureau report on the rifts within the upper echelons of the NC sealed Abdullah's fate. Noting that 'the present drift and resulting confusion cannot be allowed to go on', it emphasized the need to clearly state the policy of the J&K government regarding the future of the state. A majority should abide by this policy, but if a minority refused to, then the continuation of the present government was not possible. The head of state needed to step in at this point and ask for the resignation of the government, and if it was not forthcoming, the government should be dismissed. Once the new government was in place, it should issue a statement regarding the policy of the government, clean out corrupt officials, suspend those whose loyalty was suspect, and maintain law and order.[88]

These instructions most likely had Nehru's approval. But it is important to note that they did not include a directive for Abdullah's arrest, a step that was taken at the behest of the NC leadership. A later report of the Intelligence Bureau that described the meetings in Abdullah's house on 3 and 4 August had a note appended to it which illustrates knowledge of the actual date of the event: 'It is reported that the expected developments may take place next Saturday.'[89] 8 August 1953 was a Saturday, and Abdullah was dismissed and arrested in the early hours of Sunday morning, 9 August.

## THE DISMISSAL

It was late summer in Kashmir and the atmosphere in Abdullah's residence charged with tension as he confronted members of his cabinet and other NC leaders on 4 August. He first challenged Sadiq and Dogra, asking them whether they agreed with the CPI's stand on Kashmir. Sadiq, with whom Abdullah had always had an argumentative relationship, responded that he did. He defended the PP agitation, saying that the people of Jammu had been treated poorly since independence and their grievances needed to be addressed. Dogra said that he did not agree with the CPI's stance and was for Kashmir's independence. Abdullah then moved on to asking Bakshi and Sadiq why, in their public speeches, they were challenging the view on the future of Kashmir that had been agreed upon in previous meetings. Bakshi countered that he had never gone back on the agreed upon stance. Sadiq, again, responded that the content of Abdullah's speeches, which he disagreed with, had forced him to speak out publicly.[90]

Abdullah then tried to convince them that they needed to speak with one voice by issuing a joint statement on the future of Kashmir and its relationship to India. Since Bakshi and some of the others at the meeting knew that Abdullah would be gone in a matter of days, Bakshi suggested that this would require meetings of the NC working committee and general council, which were set for the end of August. The elections were similarly postponed. Abdullah then focused on the corruption allegations against Bakshi's brother, which were in the process of being investigated. At this point, Bakshi left the meeting.[91]

In desperation, Abdullah had begun to home in on such charges against members of the cabinet and party in an attempt to weed out those who were working against him, as well as prove himself to be above such malfeasance. At a cabinet meeting on 7 August, Abdullah asked for the resignation of his health minister, Shyam Lal Saraf, based on charges of bribery and negligence of duty. Saraf refused to resign, since at that very moment, the cabinet was in the process of drafting a memorandum expressing lack of confidence in the government. Abdullah's authority was at a low ebb. He wrote a defensive letter to Masoodi on 8 August, explaining his action in dismissing Saraf and also his recent speeches, in which he claimed he had never spoken bitterly against Nehru or Azad. He admitted that he had indeed said that with some exceptions, no one had spoken out against the PP's 'basic stand although their methods and approach have been condemned', but he was willing to 'exchange views on problems of Kashmir with friends coming from India'.[92]

This must have sounded disingenuous at this stage, even to Abdullah himself. And yet from the letters he wrote to Masoodi and the speech he made on the eve of his dismissal in which he clearly stated that Kashmiris were not confined to a choice between India and Pakistan, and had a third alternative—to stay independent and maintain good relations with both[93]—it seems as though he was not aware of his impending fate. Perhaps his faith in his friendship with Nehru remained unshaken. Karan Singh, who invited Abdullah to his residence to discuss the situation on 8 August, was astonished when he claimed that there was no difference of opinion within his cabinet and blamed the Indian press for misrepresenting the situation as a constitutional crisis, also pointing to a possible 'external solution' to the Kashmir issue. Then he brushed aside Karan Singh's suggestion for the cabinet to meet in the evening at his home to resolve their issues, and proceeded to Gulmarg with his family as he had planned. It was at this moment that his dismissal became inevitable.[94]

For Nehru, leaving aside his personal relationship with the man, Abdullah served a very particular purpose. As Puri recalled Nehru telling him when the former had accused him of imposing a corrupt regime headed by Abdullah on the people of J&K, 'Yes, of course, he may be a *goonda*; he may be corrupt, but national interest demands that we should compromise on these things. After all, idealism is not everything. Democracy is not everything. After all, we have gambled in Kashmir, we cannot afford to lose it.'[95] By 1953, Abdullah had outlived his usefulness. Rather than bringing Kashmir closer to India, he seemed intent on separating from it, and Nehru was willing to have him removed for the same reasons that he had supported him in the first place.

Abdullah's relationship with India had been complicated from the start. He viewed sovereignty in terms of personalities and personal relationships, and not institutions of the state. He had, in effect, inherited Kashmir's sovereignty from the Maharaja and believed that he should have the same relationship with India that the Maharaja had with the British Indian Empire. But these were no longer the days of the Raj. Nehru did not hold absolute power; he headed a centralizing postcolonial nation state whose emergent institutions and the individuals that embodied them were in the process of charting India's territorial extent and consolidating their indivisible sovereignty and authority over the resultant geo-body. With the territorial dismemberment of India as a result of Partition looming large, the geographical, followed by political, integration of princely states became especially critical to this endeavour. As David Gilmartin has noted, 'It was partition, far more than independence from Britain, that irrevocably fixed the territorial definition of the nation-state', for both India and Pakistan.[96]

But Kashmir was keeping India from fixing the boundaries of its territory and hence preventing the process of territorial consolidation. Abdullah clashed repeatedly with the States Ministry and the Ministry of Home Affairs as they attempted to integrate J&K into the Indian Union. He was convinced that they had begun a whisper campaign against him as soon as he became head of the administration of Kashmir.[97] Patel had always been sceptical of Abdullah's proclivities towards India and often expressed his worries to Nehru.[98] This mutual distrust just got worse as Abdullah's rhetoric against India became more strident. From the perspective of the ministries, they were upholding the writ of the Indian constitution, according to which India was a union of states, from which no state had the right to secede.

Unfortunately, Abdullah was arrayed against far greater forces than one individual, no matter how well-meaning, could control. As the Indian polity defined itself in the wake of Independence and the Indian National Congress's nationalist consensus of India as a secular state, to which J&K was central, it had to contend with the increasingly insistent voices of Hindu communalism. These voices demanded that the Indian nation and state identify itself in terms of its Hindu majority. In J&K, with its Muslim majority and Muslim leadership personified in Abdullah, as well as its unsettled position within India, the purveyors of these views found an easy target. And by creating the conditions that ultimately led the Indian government to support Abdullah's dismissal, Hindu communal forces were successful in challenging the Congress and its secular, plural vision for India.

The international scenario did not help matters, with various powers playing their own strategic games over the Kashmir issue. The Anglo-Americans supported Pakistan's claim over the state while the

Russians had turned to supporting India more openly by 1952. Abdullah was a factor for the Western bloc because he was seen as harbouring communists and might be one himself. He was also preventing the plebiscite because he wanted autonomy for the Valley. But beyond reassuring themselves that he was not a communist and lending him an ear, the Americans certainly did little else to support Abdullah's dreams of independence.

As the Cold War deepened, Abdullah's contact with Americans became the ostensible reason for his communist comrades to abandon him in favour of India as they followed Russia's stance and took up cudgels against the imperialist-capitalist designs of the new superpower, America. The fact that he might be in league with America in demanding Kashmir's independence also made the Indian government, increasingly wary of American designs, more unlikely to enter into any kind of dialogue with him.

Ultimately, what undid Abdullah was the Valley itself, as well as his inability to garner support beyond it. By coopting or silencing critics, he had undercut the very bases of his own political support. The NC was no longer a movement against autocracy, it was now the bastion of autocracy itself. Abdullah thought of himself as a divinely ordained messiah placed on earth for the deliverance of the Valley's people,[99] so when Kashmiri Muslims grew weary of him, he became desperate. He began to remind them of why they had supported him in the first place—because he had delivered them from the clutches of a repressive Hindu ruler—and why they should continue to support him—because he was prepared to do the same again by freeing them from a Hindu-majority India. Not only was this not enough for Kashmiri Muslims, but it also permanently alienated the other parts of the state, not to mention India itself.

In any case, he had always wanted a more autonomous status for Kashmir than the Indian government was prepared to concede under the constitutional imperative of creating a robust, unified state. And by 1953, this was looking even more unlikely given the level of ire in India against Abdullah's statements, Nehru's own position both within India and on the international stage, and America moving ever closer to Pakistan.

As Nehru had noted in a letter to Pandit as early as 1950, there were 'too many forces at play in Kashmir' that were pulling Abdullah in multiple 'different directions'.[100] And so it happened that in the chilly early hours of 9 August in Gulmarg, where he had retreated for the weekend with his family, Abdullah was served the no-confidence memorandum from his own cabinet and his dismissal orders signed by Karan Singh. According to the orders, Abdullah had failed to maintain unity and harmony within his cabinet, which was thus unable to function. He (Karan Singh) had asked him to resolve these differences in a meeting at his home, but Abdullah had declined to attend, and therefore, he had no choice but to dissolve the council of ministers. Abdullah was also handed an arrest order, which Karan Singh made clear to Nehru went against his own wishes, but to which he had to agree because the new government felt that law and order could not be maintained if Abdullah was free.[101]

Once Bakshi received news that Abdullah had been served his dismissal and arrest orders, he agreed to be sworn in as prime minister. The news was conveyed to a nervously waiting Nehru and his coterie at Teen Murti, where everyone present heaved a sigh of relief. Abdullah, meanwhile, asked to say his morning prayers, and after consoling his family and handing over his official files to his private secretary, R.C. Raina, gave himself up for arrest at 9 a.m. on 9 August.[102]

Abdullah most likely recognized that these actions of his cabinet colleagues, supported by the Indian government, would get him what had proved elusive in the past few years—the instantaneous restoration of his image as the symbol of Kashmiri sovereignty and self-determination. He also perhaps believed that given that fact, he would not stay in prison for long. He noted years later in his autobiography, *Aatish*, 'I must admit I was terribly shocked but there was nothing to do except to be patient.'[103] Little did he realize that he would have to exercise patience for a long time, as the complicated confluence of internal, domestic, regional and international factors would keep him behind bars for much of the next two decades.

# 5

# Reprising the Role of Revolutionary, 1953–1958

BALRAJ PURI, AN ERSTWHILE MEMBER OF THE NATIONAL CONFERENCE (NC) from Jammu, member of the Praja Socialist Party and noted political commentator on Kashmir affairs, penned an article entitled 'Political Mind of Abdullah' in 1957. Published just prior to Abdullah's impending release and reissued in 1958 in the context of the conspiracy charges filed against him, the article made the point that it was curious for Abdullah to be condemned by some as a Pakistani agent while others claimed him as a true Indian patriot. Puri observed that although Abdullah derived his popularity from the anti-India sentiments whipped up in the wake of his dismissal and arrest in 1953, for Abdullah and his supporters, there was a subtle difference between being anti-India and pro-Pakistan. Abdullah symbolized Kashmiri nationalism to the people of Kashmir; indeed, India itself had held Abdullah up as the sole symbol of Kashmiri nationalism not that long ago in the hope of curtailing pro-Pakistan sentiments and Muslim communalism.

But this was possible, Puri continued, only if Kashmir was allowed a measure of autonomy to create a space for the free expression of Kashmiri nationalism. This is precisely what Abdullah was attempting to do by making the case against full accession after the Delhi Agreement to ensure that Kashmiris stayed on the side of accession to India. Puri argued that even now, Abdullah, who carried 'a semi-religious halo around him', could carry the people against pro-Pakistan elements if only India would be willing to concede Kashmir's special identity and grant it more autonomy. Having declared victory for Kashmiri nationalism, Abdullah could then make a more effective case for Kashmir's association with India. Kashmiris were not against India, but the Indian government; if he was given something to work with, Abdullah could bring about popular backing for a stronger relationship between the centre and state.[1]

Puri captured the central dilemma that shaped Abdullah's political life: How was he to balance his stature as a representative of Kashmiri nationalism while remaining a loyal Indian who did not question India's absolute sovereignty over Kashmir? He had always felt himself to be more Kashmiri than Indian in any case, although he was happy to promote Kashmir's association with India as long as the latter recognized the state's special position. In postcolonial India, however, such dual loyalties were simply not acceptable, particularly in the case of a state such as Jammu and Kashmir (J&K), which was on the border and also claimed by Pakistan. From the Indian government's perspective, it was preferable to compromise on democratic principles and maintain a quisling government in the state that accepted its sovereignty without question. But in doing so, and in persecuting and prosecuting Abdullah for his views, it ensured that rather than reining in pro-Pakistan sentiment, Abdullah was transformed into its very symbol. It also had the effect of building up Abdullah's international reputation as a freedom fighter taking on a neocolonial order.

His opponents, in particular Bakshi's regime that replaced his, played no small part in painting him as an anti-India, pro-Pakistan figure who had conspired to bring about Kashmir's independence. This was cemented when Pakistan instantly appropriated him after his dismissal, elevating him to the status of a martyr for the cause of Kashmiri self-determination. In India, on the other hand, suspicion of his intentions ran deep among the political establishment and bureaucracy. This, coupled with the fact that India did not allow any viable opposition to emerge in J&K, meant that Abdullah became the embodiment of Kashmiris' mounting political grievances. His supporters kept his memory alive in Kashmir by circulating stories about his spiritual prowess among people at shrines and other community gatherings. To the younger generation coming of age in the late 1950s and 1960s Kashmir, the figure of an incarcerated Abdullah was to take on powerful symbolism.

The creation and appropriation of this image would eventually, quite as much as his physical confinement, imprison Abdullah and limit his ability to manoeuvre. Without his personal popularity among Kashmiri Muslims—ironically re-created as a result of his arrest and imprisonment—he was politically obsolete, and to maintain their support, Abdullah had to live up to the image of an anti-India firebrand created for him as much by his detractors as his supporters.

## RE-MAKING THE REVOLUTIONARY

Had Abdullah not been dismissed and arrested on 9 August 1953, he was to deliver a speech on the day of Id, 21 August 1953, that would have surely led to his dismissal. This would have been a speech by a man who felt that Kashmir's relationship to India had run its course and could not be sustained without a change in direction. Not only did the text of the speech call the accession to India provisional, but it also stated that Pakistan had come to occupy the position of a party directly concerned with the Kashmir issue, and thus any resolution of the problem had to include Pakistan. It noted that the Security Council was also a party to the dispute, and as a result, a resolution by the state's constituent assembly to ratify the accession to India would mean very little.

A large portion of the speech expressed Abdullah's sense of injury at the Praja Parishad (PP) agitation, which it labelled as the main reason for the current impasse with regard to Kashmir. It had weakened his ability to rally support for India among Kashmiri Muslims and when he attempted to address their concerns, he was branded a turncoat: 'Must I or not carry the support of the majority community with me? If I must then it becomes necessary that I should satisfy them to the same extent that a non-Muslim is satisfied that his future hopes and aspirations are safe in India.' Middle-class Kashmiri Muslims, it warned, were deeply disturbed not only by the communal nature of the PP agitation and its anti-Muslim overtones, but also because the state's relationship with India had allowed Hindus and Sikhs to ameliorate their lot while Muslims stagnated. The Muslim intelligentsia was looking for a definite stake in India but instead all it felt was fear, frustration and near-disillusionment.[2]

The NC, Abdullah declared further, stood by the state's accession to India and the Delhi Agreement, but what was to prevent India from changing this relationship and coercing the state into a more subservient position in the future, he asked. Besides, he wondered whether even the unchanged relationship was good for the state as a whole: 'Would it be possible under this relationship to overcome the difficulties presented by geography and nature which stand in the way of all-round economic prosperity of the State?'[3]

These were the ideas of a man who realized that he was caught between Kashmir and India and could no longer legitimately claim to represent the interests of both. Once he was dismissed and placed in detention, in a sense, the choice was made for him, and he would hone these ideas into a strident campaign against India in an attempt to force it to deliver its promises to the Kashmiri people. No longer encumbered by the fetters of power and as head of a regime with a reputation for repression and corruption, his dismissal had the effect of wiping the slate clean, while catapulting him to the position of a revolutionary willing to sacrifice his own freedom for the sake of Kashmiri self-determination. But, if Kashmir was the cage within which he was imprisoned, India was the much larger prison within which this cage was located.

As Abdullah cooled his heels in an Udhampur guest house in August 1953, followed by a detention camp in Kud, with Delhi's political class expressing 'sober satisfaction' at the 'timely action' taken by the Sadar-i-Riyasat,[4] Bakshi's government set about constructing a narrative around him that would pursue Abdullah for the rest of his life. Kashmiri leftists, such as D.P. Dhar and G.M. Sadiq, who had been completely against Abdullah's stand in the early 1950s, now took control over the party and its propaganda machine. Sadiq Ali and Madhu Limaye, two prominent members of the Praja Socialist Party who visited Kashmir in late September and early October 1953, noted in their report that the Bakshi regime was busy presenting the coup as the result of the intervention of foreign powers in Kashmir, particularly the US, which they claimed had been supporting the independence option espoused by Abdullah. According to the report, this was in accordance with the official stance of the Communist Party of India (CPI). It also noted that while the Americans were clearly interested in Kashmir, and perhaps also in its independence, there was little evidence of a 'regular organised conspiracy' in which they had colluded with Abdullah.[5]

The most concrete result of the regime's propaganda was a book entitled *Conspiracy in Kashmir* by Ghulam Mohammad Mir Rajpori and Manohar Nath Kaul, published in 1954. It argued that Abdullah had been in league with the US and other capitalist powers to gain independence for Kashmir, which had made his removal necessary. The book was based almost entirely on a decontextualized reading of Abdullah's speeches and American newspaper reports.[6] Informing the Government of India about the publication of the book, K.N. Bamzai noted that it was clearly sponsored by the J&K government and was replete with 'conjecture', making numerous charges against Abdullah and foreign diplomats and others who had allegedly been conspiring with him. This was problematic in itself, but the book also, perhaps unwittingly, supported the stand of the Hindu Mahasabha and Jan Sangh on Kashmir. In his note on the file, M.O. Mathai, Nehru's private secretary, agreed that it was 'neither dignified nor politic' to run down Abdullah by making vague charges against him, a point that he would bring to the J&K government's notice.[7]

Nehru too was uncomfortable with rumours that maligned Abdullah. In a speech to parliament on 17 September 1953, he stated that Abdullah was not in the process of fleeing to Pakistan or in league with the US before his removal, but he did want independence, which the people of Kashmir were against. Hence his colleagues decided to detain him, for which Nehru was very sorry. In private as well, Nehru expressed his regret at Abdullah's arrest and detention in numerous letters to Bakshi in the immediate aftermath of the event and the following years. Fearing the longer-term consequences of the arrest in a letter dated 15 August 1953, he noted, 'I do not like things done in the dark and in the middle of the night. I have insisted from the very beginning that constitutional procedure should be followed. Technically this was done. I confess that it left a bad taste in my mouth.'[8]

He also felt that the process of Indo-Pak dialogue, which was ongoing at that moment and held much promise, had been vitiated by this course of events. As an editorial in the Pakistani daily *Dawn* declared, the dismissal of Sheikh Abdullah was a 'challenge to Pakistan' and it would be foolish to expect the scheduled talks between the prime ministers of India and Pakistan to yield much in the wake of these developments: 'Pandit Nehru has shown that, in his view, anyone in Kashmir who questions the finality of Kashmir's so-called accession to Bharat or talks of people of the State determining their own future is a criminal.'[9]

Nehru was thus right that Abdullah's arrest and continued detention as well as the Bakshi regime's attempts at painting him as the vanguard of a movement for Kashmir's independence firmly entrenched his image as a freedom fighter in Kashmir and beyond, and a traitor in India. Even Abdullah's vehement denials throughout that he had conspired with foreign powers, or indeed even espoused outright independence, had the effect of further cementing these ideas in the popular imagination. This made the possibility of a fair compromise with him—and with Pakistan over Kashmir—less likely as the years went by.

Abdullah was in his late forties, and in fairly good health, at the time of his dismissal in 1953 and potentially had many years ahead in his political life. The Government of India had handed him a boon, in a sense, by approving his dismissal and arrest at the time when his popularity and image were at a low ebb in Kashmir. The Bakshi government was helping further by turning him into a symbol of anti-India grievances and by imprisoning any opposition, even those who were not necessarily pro-Abdullah but nevertheless felt that his dismissal was unjust. In the Kud detention camp—hastily constructed in a forest to house Abdullah and other political detainees—Abdullah was able to renew his relationships with these individuals, many of whom had fallen out with him as a result of his politics during his years in power. With them he developed a concrete path forward. The detention camp was, by his own description, comfortable, and a place where he could kick back a little while indulging in his favourite pastimes of gardening, birdwatching and raising poultry after years of relentless battles on multiple fronts as prime minister of J&K.[10] Although creating worries about the struggles faced by his family on the outside, prison had the effect of rejuvenating him and his image, and of returning him to his political roots.

It was in this atmosphere that the next phase of Abdullah's political career began. Mirza Afzal Beg, who had stayed by his side throughout the 1953 crisis and was the legal mind behind Abdullah's regime and its constitutional negotiations with India, was now a fellow inmate in Kud. So was Ghulam Ahmad Ashai, one of the earliest founders of the movement for Kashmiri Muslim rights, who had not supported the conversion of the Muslim Conference to the National Conference and had subsequently been deeply disillusioned by Abdullah's first regime. Between Abdullah, Ashai, Beg and many other leaders, there was a wealth of political experience at Kud that was deployed to chart the movement's new course. Since the NC's image was now tarnished as it was under the control of the opposition, the group decided to launch a rival organization.

This led to the founding—on the second anniversary of Abdullah's dismissal—of the All Jammu and Kashmir Plebiscite Front (PF) to champion the right of Kashmiri self-determination. At its founding, the organization had sixteen members, of which Abdullah was not, and never would become, one. Beg became its public face as the president, while Abdullah acted as the patron. This was likely a move to shield him from the legal implications of belonging to an organization that questioned J&K's accession to India. Years later during his last days, in an interview with P.N. Jalali—a veteran Kashmiri journalist and one-time member of the NC—Abdullah would admit that becoming the patron of the PF was 'the only option I was left with. My friends drove me to the wall and I had to fight back.'[11]

Beg was able to lay the groundwork for the PF when he announced its founding at the time of his brief release due to ill health in 1955. But since he was soon back in prison, the day-to-day running of the organization fell to individuals such as Munshi Ishaq, its treasurer. This was reminiscent of the Quit Kashmir agitation, when Abdullah and other first-tier leaders were either behind bars or outside of Kashmir and leaders such as Ishaq and G.M. Karra stepped in to fill the breach. As we have seen, Ishaq had been an active member of the NC and provided funding for as well as directed communications during Quit Kashmir. But he had soured on Abdullah after 1947 because he felt that the NC had lost sight of its revolutionary promise once it became the party in power. When Abdullah was dismissed and founded the PF, Ishaq, like many others who had felt the same way, returned to the fold. One of their most important functions, as during Quit Kashmir, was to keep the people's enthusiasm for the movement—with Abdullah at its centre—alive at a time when Bakshi's regime was not only using repressive techniques to control them, but also plying them with cheap rice and other economic incentives to set aside their political grievances.

Beg's letters to Ishaq reminded him to not fall for the enemy's cheap tricks and to remain united in the face of malicious rumours and conspiracy theories. At the practical level, Beg directed Ishaq to focus on keeping the prime objective of an unbiased plebiscite alive while revealing the social, political, economic, constitutional and administrative lapses of the Bakshi government. This would give hope to the people and bring to light the hollowness of the administration. He urged Ishaq to read Abdullah's letters and get hold of other letters written by him to his well-wishers, because they discussed topics from the Quran—such as the battle between right and wrong, patience and resistance, and the importance of faith and its practice—that the quom needed to hear at this moment.[12]

Abdullah's letters to his followers were indeed replete with Quranic ayats (verses) and lessons from the history of Islam. What is particularly striking about these letters is that they are lacking in any practical instructions about the movement, since they were meant to be read out loud in gatherings and were a means for Abdullah to stay in communication with Kashmiri Muslims while in prison. In them, he appears as a spiritual figure far above the mundane affairs of politics, fighting injustice and persecution not unlike the Prophet Muhammad himself. In one of them, he asked his friends and supporters not to be discouraged: 'Those who are not disheartened in the face of privations and miseries, but tenaciously cling to the path of Truth and do not feel horrified to strive and to act, are sure to triumph.' Much like Joseph, who had been given the choice between earthly pleasures and the righteous path that would lead to prison, he, too, had chosen the latter.[13]

As congratulatory messages poured into Kud sub-jail on his fiftieth birthday in December 1955, Abdullah responded to Ishaq's note by thanking him and noting that he had spent the first five decades of his life fighting for a goal greater than his individual material interests. In this pursuit, he had suffered separation from family, deprivation, persecution and hunger, but none of this had shaken his resolve. He hoped that Ishaq would pray for him to spend the next fifty years engaged in the same jihad on the path designated for him by Allah. He reminded Ishaq to keep the faith and the movement alive, for which he had been especially chosen at its time of need. In another letter to Ishaq from 1956, Abdullah reiterated the necessity of keeping the faith in the face of insurmountable difficulties because a tyrant's tyranny could not last forever; Allah had destroyed all quoms that went against truth. He ended the letter with the following couplets: 'Swords and strategies are of no use to the oppressed / Faith alone will break the chains / We who conquer the world with our love have faith in our actions / Jihad is a man's sword in life.'[14]

This spiritual turn was meant to present Abdullah as a victim of the politics of the powerful rather than a major political figure himself. The pirs associated with Kashmir's sacred spaces—who had supported Abdullah's rise to the leadership of the movement in the 1930s—played a significant role in maintaining Abdullah's presence among the people of Kashmir while he was physically absent. One such pir, Rahim Punjabi Sadarbali, is remembered in Srinagar as being instrumental in creating an otherworldly aura around Abdullah.[15] Many of his and others' stories presented Abdullah as a spiritual leader of the masses endowed with divine powers, such as the ability to heal the sick and wounded or bestow a child on a childless woman. But most importantly, their stories reignited memories of Abdullah as a fearless rebel against Dogra authoritarianism, thereby creating a seamless link between the Kashmiri nationalist movement of the 1930s and his present struggles against India.

These stories, recounted at shrines and in people's homes, were woven into Kashmir's vibrant oral traditions as Abdullah achieved an almost mythical status in the minds of younger Kashmiris. Muhammad Yusuf Yattoo and his wife, Fayaaz Alam, both born in the early 1950s, spoke of Abdullah with a reverence reserved for spiritual figures rather than politicians, reciting one of the many songs about him that were sung during their youth by women at weddings:

> Resident of Soura, you are the light of religion,
> You are brave and a river of patience.
> When you were imprisoned in the fort,
> You recited the ayats of the Quran in your heart.
> The power of the ayats caused all your agonies to disappear,
> They built a cauldron of oil for you.
> That too you accepted,
> The cauldron transformed into a beacon of light.
> You entered the Khanqah-i-Mualla [shrine],
> And united the Muslims against Dogra rule.

They also remembered the verses that their pir Sadarbali would recite at gatherings:

> Come, O faithful, take a look at the Sheikh,
> Sher-i-Kashmir will reign over the world.
> Say yes or say no, the government rules,
> Send a message to God and Sher-i-Kashmir.[16]

Mohammad Ishaq Khan, a historian of Islam in Kashmir, was eight years old at the time of Abdullah's arrest, and writes movingly of the deep impression Abdullah's dismissal and arrest had on him as a young boy as he watched his father bereft, and later facing arrest himself as an Abdullah supporter. According to Khan, 1953 was a turning point for

Kashmiri Muslims as their resentment towards the 'Indian occupation' increased. Pro-Pakistan elements were easily able to make the case that Abdullah would not have met this fate had he allied with Jinnah and not the wily Brahmin, Nehru, who ended up subjugating Kashmiri Muslims. He also remembered 'how much hatred the youth in all schools and colleges nursed against Bakshi, his goondas, and the "peace brigade"', which terrorized and silenced Abdullah's supporters.[17]

Although Abdullah's immediate family—his wife and five children—had been rendered political pariahs and were living in straitened circumstances in rented accommodation after his dismissal and arrest, they continued to provide the crucial link between him and the outside world, keeping him apprised of the political situation while also keeping his memory alive among the people. Relying on her mother's financial help and the goodwill of some others, such as Mridula Sarabhai, to support her family during these years, Begum Abdullah worked assiduously behind the scenes to disseminate the Sheikh's letters and protests, while also providing moral and material support to the plebiscite movement.[18]

Meanwhile, as the days turned into months followed by years, with no hope of his release, Abdullah grew impatient about his status. The Bakshi regime had wasted no time in ratifying the Delhi Agreement through the constituent assembly in 1954, which had led to the passage of a presidential order that granted Indian citizenship to all residents of the state as well as empowered the state legislature to endow 'permanent residents' with special rights and privileges through Article 35A of the Indian constitution. Then, as a result of the emergence of the PF the next year, the regime began an intense vilification campaign against Abdullah and the organization, accusing it, among other things, of being funded and directed by Pakistan. The PF itself was not particularly well organized with about 600 members in the Valley by 1956, from schoolteachers to small business-owners, who had joined for a variety of political reasons—including a sense of powerlessness in the face of the nepotism and repression of the Bakshi regime—and not necessarily because they believed in its stated objectives.

As a response to Pakistan's closer ties with the US, apparent in its signing of a military pact with the US and entering into the South-East Asia Treaty Organization (SEATO) in May and September 1954 respectively, India sought Russian backing of its own position in Kashmir and welcomed Russian leaders Nikita Khrushchev and Nikolai Bulganin to India. Both leaders gave their imprimatur to Kashmir's integral position within India during their trip to Srinagar in December 1955.[19] Soon thereafter, in early 1956, Nehru's speech in parliament declared that J&K's accession to India in 1947 was legal and had been ratified by the state's constituent assembly in 1954, thus rendering a plebiscite 'beside the point'.[20] By 1956, Abdullah's attempts at swaying political opinion in Kashmir seemed to be yielding few results as J&K's constituent assembly looked poised to adopt the state's constitution, and along with it drive the final nail towards its integration with the Indian Union.

Although Nehru's attention was diverted from Kashmir during this time by multiple domestic issues such as demands for linguistic reorganization of states and foreign policy issues such as the non-aligned movement, he remained uneasy about Abdullah's continued detention. He was keenly aware of the impact the detention had on India's international reputation and position, especially since India had officially moved away from plebiscite as an option in the wake of the military pacts between the US and Pakistan. But his attempts at having Abdullah released were thwarted by a combination of his own home ministry and the J&K government. In a January 1956 exchange with Sadar-i-Riyasat Karan Singh, who was against Abdullah's release because he felt that he would become the rallying point for disruptionist forces, Nehru pointed out that without Abdullah on board, there could be no resolution of the Kashmir dispute. He further added, 'Sheikh Abdullah may behave very foolishly but the effect of his behaviour is likely to be less now and can be dealt with more easily ... It is bad to live in apprehension all the time. It is best to take the ghost out of our minds and deal with it.'[21] Karan Singh persisted in the view that the proper time for Abdullah's release would be after the state constitution had been enacted and the constituent assembly dissolved, since Abdullah was still technically a member of the assembly and could disrupt this process if released.[22]

Recognizing that he would lose his moral legitimacy if he compromised at this stage, Abdullah refused to budge from his stance. He recollected a conversation with Maulana Abul Kalam Azad, who had told him that he had become 'a voice in the wilderness' at the centre with little influence, because his own community—Indian Muslims—refused to follow him.[23] Abdullah had no intention of being reduced to a Muslim figure in Kashmir or India with no authority or following. He would command greater influence from prison, being remembered and celebrated as a martyr for the cause of Kashmir. In June 1956, Abdullah communicated clearly to Nehru's emissary Dr P. Subbarayan, who visited him in jail, that he would not issue any kind of statement or meet Nehru until his position had been vindicated. He reiterated his stand on the plebiscite, which he noted was in accordance with the demands of the movement as well as international resolutions on the issue.[24]

Following this, he wrote to his erstwhile colleague G.M. Sadiq, now president of the J&K constituent assembly, demanding that the assembly desist immediately from meeting in a future session to discuss and adopt a constitution for the state. This was because after the August 1953 coup that led to his removal and arrest, the assembly was no longer representative, did not answer to the people and therefore had no right to adopt a constitution on their behalf. The democratic right to face a motion of no confidence had been denied him, while Bakshi was catapulted to power through a motion of confidence in an assembly from which several members, including himself, were missing. He accused this new regime of widespread repression and atrocities against the opposition, and 'sabotag[ing] the great movement of which I have been the spearhead since 1931'.[25] This exchange of letters between Abdullah and Sadiq from August to October 1956 brings out the extent to which the events of 9 August 1953 became a pivot around which Abdullah organized and legitimized his stand from henceforward.

Not to be outdone, Sadiq mounted a strident defence of those actions in his lengthy response, as well as the assembly's right to ratify the state's constitution, mainly by using Abdullah's vacillating stance in the past as a way to undermine his charges in the present. He pointed out that in

Abdullah's opening speech to the constituent assembly in 1951, he had himself hailed Kashmir's ties to India and the need to speedily write and ratify the state's constitution to delineate the legal nature of these ties with more clarity. But once this task was taken up, according to Sadiq, Abdullah's priorities began to shift and all manner of prevarication and drift took over. This became worse after the signing of the Delhi Agreement, which again, Abdullah hailed in his subsequent speech to the constituent assembly. Until August 1953, Sadiq charged, he and his colleagues had attempted to work out the basic principles with regard to the constitution, but had noticed a tendency of 'drifting away not only from the basic commitments but also from the ideals which we held so dear'.[26]

Sadiq reminded Abdullah that the process of constitution-making and the final ratification of the Delhi Agreement were stymied over two issues—the applicability of the fundamental rights section of the Indian constitution to J&K and the ability of the Supreme Court of India to enforce these rights in the state. As these matters were being thrashed out by a subcommittee, Abdullah peremptorily informed the members that the application of Indian fundamental rights was an unnecessary discussion since he no longer believed in the basis of the state's relationship with India. Sadiq quite clearly alluded to Beg as the culprit who refused to give ground on these matters, keeping everyone embroiled in legal minutiae while egging Abdullah on against India. This began, according to Sadiq, the protracted search for alternatives to the state's association with India, leading to confusion, fanning of communal passions and general disruption. At this point, a parting of the ways with Abdullah became unavoidable. Answering Abdullah's accusation of widespread repression by the Bakshi government by taking a swipe at the record of Abdullah's own regime, Sadiq pointed out that civil liberties had been considerably expanded in the state since 1953. This was in large part because the constituent assembly had taken the step of applying the fundamental rights of the Indian constitution to the state and vesting the authority to enforce them to the State High Court and the Supreme Court of India.[27]

Abdullah was furious at this letter, especially at the way that Sadiq had sidestepped the 'coup', as Abdullah saw it, referring to it instead as a 'ministerial change'. Therefore, in his response, he returned to the unconstitutionality of his removal in August 1953, noting that the only course open to the new government, if it wanted to live up to its so-called democratic credentials, was to seek a fresh vote of confidence from the electorate through elections before ratifying a constitution. He denied that he had been in favour of the state's independence in 1953, but rather that he had wanted the issue to be settled through a plebiscite that even Sadiq himself at the time had considered the fairest option. He continued to accuse the Bakshi regime of suppressing the opposition and attempting to buy people's allegiance through economic measures.[28] Sadiq refused to give ground, accusing Abdullah of harbouring dreams of independence and creating confusion in the state. He noted that even now Abdullah's stand on the issues was unclear as the organizations he was associated with, particularly the PF, advocated plebiscite but refused to take a stand on accession. Such organizations evoked little sentiment in the people, who were happy with the course of the state's politics and economy under Bakshi.[29]

Abdullah responded yet again, in a final letter dated 28 October 1956, sounding more infuriated than ever. He reiterated that the 1953 coup had thwarted democratic procedure and robbed him of the opportunity to place his views before the general council of the NC so that the members could make up their own minds. He then reminded Sadiq of his leadership of the Kashmiri nationalist movement since 1931 and the milestones within it, including the 'death-defying Quit Kashmir struggle'. Abdullah pointed out that when he was serving time in prison and being tried for his initiation of the movement, Sadiq, along with 'your present chief, Bakshi Ghulam Mohammad had deemed discretion as better part of valour and left the state to enjoy the salubrious climate of Lahore'.[30] In the wake of the tribal raids, India came to Kashmir's aid, but promised the people the right to express their wishes about accession. Just because Pakistan had entered into military pacts with another country did not absolve India of its responsibility of seeing this promise through. After all, he noted, quoting Nehru himself, 'Kashmiris are not mere chattel that they can be bartered away on the free will of India or Pakistan or anyone else.' He ended the letter by saying that he was no longer inclined to continue the exchange and asked Sadiq to place this correspondence before the house.[31]

Needless to say, Sadiq did not bring the correspondence to the floor of the state assembly, which ratified the state's constitution, and along with it the state's accession to India, on 17 November 1956. As member of the Indian Constituent Assembly, Abdullah was a signatory to the Indian constitution, but his signature is missing from J&K's constitution for which he had fought so hard. This was a bitter pill to swallow. The movement he had led from its inception had been coopted by his lieutenants; they claimed to be following in his footsteps to implement his agenda that, according to them, he had lost sight of. But perhaps all this was for the best because this was not the constitution he had envisioned. He was now more determined than ever to fight the bigger fight, to ensure that Kashmiris received what they had been promised—a voice in their political future.

## REBEL AMONG THE PEOPLE

In March 1957, it looked like Abdullah had been politically defeated. He was still in prison, lonely and cut off from developments outside, with only sheep and fowl that he raised himself, and occasionally his visiting family members, for company. Meanwhile Bakshi was elected prime minister in J&K's first legislative assembly elections under the new constitution. Abdullah's ghost, however, haunted the regime, as his continued detention without charge or trial tarnished its legitimacy. Neither could it live down the mounting accusations of widespread intimidation and corruption that hounded its functionaries. An internal split in the party itself, with the leftists threatening to go their own way, further complicated the situation. The only solution seemed to be to release Abdullah and create a situation that would make his imprisonment again inevitable, this time on a serious charge.

Abdullah's well-wishers had been outspoken against his imprisonment and campaigning for his release ever since his dismissal and detention. C. Rajagopalachari, who felt that rather than shutting the door on him altogether Abdullah should have been offered the alternative of autonomy, expressed his discontent to Nehru soon after the events.[32] B.P.L. and Freda Bedi, despite having fallen out with Abdullah by the time of his arrest and despite it being against the CPI's official position at the time, came out with a scathing statement against his detention in late August 1953, warning that 'it may cost India dearly, even to the extent of losing Kashmir itself'.[33]

Maulana Masoodi, general secretary of the NC and member of the Indian parliament from J&K, had not agreed with Abdullah's sudden turn towards breaking off relations with India, but he had been shocked and distressed by Abdullah's dismissal and detention. Since he was located in Delhi at the time of the event, he issued a public statement condemning the actions, expressing his 'deep regret that an old comrade [Sheikh Abdullah] should have gone the way he did', while calling on India to exercise restraint and win over the hearts of Kashmiris.[34] He conveyed his disquiet to Nehru in person on the turn of events, intervening on Abdullah's behalf and begging Nehru to undo the actions of 9 August. But Nehru told him that although he was heartbroken at the situation, he could do nothing about it. Masoodi also attempted to meet with Abdullah, but was thwarted by Bakshi. As the leftists took over control of the NC, Masoodi was shunted out of the organization to be replaced by Bakshi's brother, Abdul Rashid, as general secretary, but continued to work quietly to disseminate Abdullah's perspective and secure his eventual release.[35]

Meanwhile, Mridula Sarabhai took up cudgels against the Jan Sangh and the Bakshi regime, which were engaged in a propaganda war against Abdullah, and kept the outside world informed of Abdullah's struggles against the tyrannical government. She founded an organization called the Friends of New Kashmir—of which Masoodi and Balraj Puri were also members—with the specific intent of countering the Jan Sangh's activities in J&K and the Punjab. She publicly accused the Bakshi regime of dismantling the NC, stifling dissent and engaging in widespread

Saaduddin Shaal, Ghulam Ahmad Ashai and Sheikh Abdullah (seated in the back), Srinagar, c. early 1930s. *(Courtesy Anwar Ashai.)*

Sheikh Abdullah (seated on the left), Jawaharlal Nehru, Mian Iftikharuddin (seated on the right) and others, Lahore, January 1938. *(Nehru Memorial Museum and Library Photo Collection, courtesy Jawaharlal Nehru Memorial Fund.)*

Khan Abdul Ghaffar Khan and Jawaharlal Nehru being welcomed by Sheikh Abdullah, Srinagar, 1940. *(Courtesy Hakim Ghulam Geelani.)*

Jawaharlal Nehru being greeted by Sheikh Abdullah at Srinagar Airport for his first official visit to Jammu and Kashmir after the Maharaja signed the document of accession, November 1947. *(Courtesy Photo Division, Government of India.)*

Sheikh Abdullah and Gopalaswami Ayyangar at Palam Airport, New Delhi, on their return from the United Nations conference at Lake Success, New York, February 1948. *(Courtesy Photo Division, Government of India.)*

Jawaharlal Nehru, Maulana Azad and Sheikh Abdullah in a boat procession on the Jhelum during freedom day celebrations, Srinagar, May 1948. *(Courtesy Photo Division, Government of India.)*

Jawaharlal Nehru being received by Sheikh Abdullah at Srinagar Airport, September 1949. *(Courtesy Photo Division, Government of India.)*

Sheikh Abdullah, Chief Minister of Jammu and Kashmir, 1978. *(Courtesy Photo Division, Government of India.)*

Gutted remains of Sheikh Abdullah's mansion in Soura, 2016. *(Photo by author.)*

Sheikh Abdullah's tomb, Hazratbal, Srinagar, 2015. *(Photo by author.)*

Sheikh Abdullah's grave, Hazratbal, Srinagar, 2015. *(Photo by author.)*

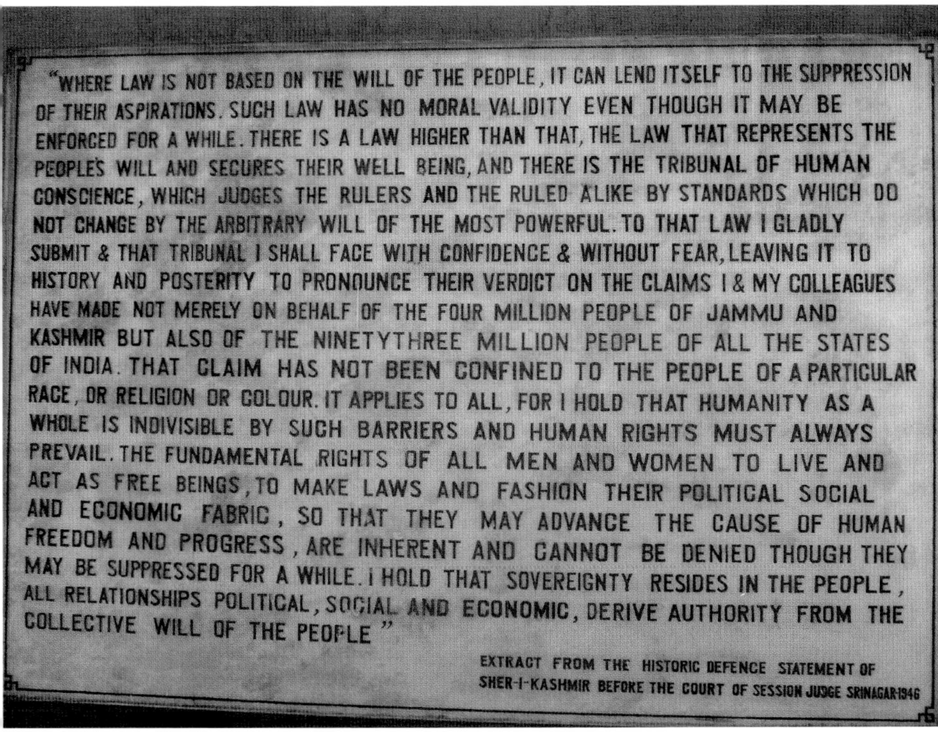


Plaque on the entrance to Sheikh Abdullah's tomb, Hazratbal, Srinagar, 2015.
*(Photo by author.)*

Hazratbal shrine, Srinagar, 2010. *(Photo by author.)*

corruption and nepotism. She wrote letters to the J&K legislative assembly imploring them to take action against the illegitimate government, and to not fall victim to the '*khayalon ki ladai*' (battle of ideas) being waged within and beyond Kashmir by anti-national elements to undermine Indian democracy.

She even wrote to Bakshi himself, explaining why she felt compelled to raise her voice in defence of Abdullah. She pointed out that physical union had to be accompanied by mutual confidence, goodwill and inter-reliance, and this was true of all states in India, not just J&K. Instead, by forcibly integrating J&K, Bakshi's regime was merely aiding the enemy.[36] She attempted to clear misunderstandings, especially among Indians, about Abdullah's mission by, among other things, publishing his Id day speech and several pamphlets that disseminated his views as well as the exchange of letters between Abdullah and Sadiq. She also financially supported Abdullah's family and arranged for his defence once he was brought to trial on charges of conspiracy.[37]

Abdullah himself was eager to be released so that he could reconnect with his base and remind them of why he was literally and symbolically the tallest leader of Kashmiris. A confluence of circumstances in 1957–8 made this possible. In the course of the elections in J&K, the rift between the leftists (led by Sadiq and Dhar) and Bakshi came to the fore, as the latter attempted to consolidate his position within the NC. After the victory of the NC, Bakshi sidelined the leftists, which led them to break from the party and form the Democratic National Conference (DNC) in 1957. The stand of this organization was that it stood for the true, 'democratic' principles of the NC, which under Bakshi had fallen by the wayside. Although they remained in favour of J&K's accession to India, the DNC leaders began to murmur about Abdullah's continued imprisonment by Bakshi as a way to undermine the latter further.[38]

Across the border, Pakistan, using Abdullah's continued detention as a pretext, took the Kashmir issue back to the UN Security Council in early 1957. This was just in time for the Congress in India to make its Kashmir policy into a campaign issue for the second general elections. Although the Congress faced numerous challenges in its first term, the opposition was still too splintered in 1957 to pose a serious threat in these elections. As a result, the Congress secured a comfortable victory, even increasing its vote share from the first general elections by a few percentage points. Having received the country's imprimatur on its performance and policies, Nehru felt more comfortable taking a more decisive stand on Abdullah's detention. Since Abdullah's dismissal in 1953, he visited Srinagar for the first time in December 1957 and in a speech expressed his sorrow at Abdullah's imprisonment. In private, he forced Bakshi's hand to release Abdullah immediately.[39]

If Bakshi was to be forced to release his arch nemesis, he was determined to manage the method of the release as well as the narrative surrounding it. So in January 1958, he sent his inspector general (IG) of police to Kud to move Abdullah in the dead of night to the jail in Srinagar. Abdullah was too shrewd a politician to not recognize what this meant and was equally determined to be in charge of the manner of his own release, especially to ensure that he was given a grand reception as he triumphantly entered Srinagar. He thus refused to budge, demanding that he either be released in Kud itself or be left in prison. The IG was loathe to give in but eventually contacted the government, and finally through Nehru's intervention, Abdullah was released in Kud and moved to a dak bungalow on 8 January. On catching wind of his release, the press began to arrive in Kud to interview Abdullah, who set up the narrative for his own vindication by declaring that he had not betrayed India in 1953: 'Sheikh Abdullah does not sell his conscience for official position or monetary considerations. Nor does he fear military might. He bows to God alone. Prime Ministership for him is only a means to implement convictions and not an end in itself.'[40]

The real challenge was to find transport to Srinagar but the authorities in Kud made no effort to help Abdullah and his companions secure it—in part by denying him access to a working telephone—since they did not want Abdullah to be feted as he arrived in Srinagar.[41] Eventually, the party organized transport and left for Srinagar on 11 January on a journey that was beset, recalled Abdullah, with numerous roadblocks and a ban on public gatherings put in place by the government. When they crossed Banihal into Verinag, the guesthouse was locked so that they had no place to have a meal and break their journey. Abdullah was angry to see Masoodi waiting for him in Verinag because he was convinced that Masoodi had played a role in his dismissal, suspicions that he now expressed to Masoodi. But he nevertheless sent Masoodi back to Srinagar to put up welcome arches in a few prominent spots in the city to encourage people to come out to show their support, thereby thwarting Bakshi's plans of a quiet arrival.[42]

As the group proceeded further into the Valley, people burst forth from villages and towns—Anantnag, Bijbehara, Awantipur, Pampur—to welcome the Sher-i-Kashmir back into their midst. At every stop Abdullah gave stirring speeches, reminding people of his deep connection with them:

> I have been kept away from you for a long, long time. My opponents cried themselves hoarse claiming that my people had forgotten me. But I would not believe them. They said they had bought your conscience in return for free rice. But I would tell them that my people were not saleable. I am seeing now that they were wrong, while I was right. By God's grace, we are together once again ... Those who are intimidating you are themselves cowards. They are afraid for their conscience is uneasy. Do not be afraid of them. You have fought temptation and oppression so bravely that history will always remember you.[43]

Eventually, the crowds became so thick that they halted the progress of the convoy into Srinagar, and by his own admission, Abdullah had to wield a stick against them so that the convoy could enter the city, where a rousing reception awaited them. Ever sensitive to symbolism, Abdullah made his way to the Khanqah i Mualla shrine—the sacred centre of his political influence in the city—where he said his prayers before retiring for the day.[44]

And thus began the three-month tussle between Bakshi and the Indian press on the one side and Abdullah on the other that would end with the latter in prison once again. A *Times of India* article on 9 January declared that the Kashmir government had released Abdullah in 'good faith' and was 'prepared to let bygones be bygones', but only if he 'stands by his original commitment on Kashmir's accession to India ... It is now for Sheikh Abdullah to adjust himself to the new conditions in the State and co-operate in the venture of building up a new Kashmir.' It ended with a warning that Abdullah would be 'ill-advised to abuse his freedom', because no Kashmir government 'can permit anyone to disrupt the peace of the State or endanger its security'.[45] Abdullah had altogether different ideas; he felt that this was his moment to seize the limelight back from Bakshi by demonstrating that he was the only true leader of the Kashmiri people and that no level of economic incentives would turn them away from him.

If that had been the end of it, he would perhaps have been easier to ignore, but Abdullah took it a step further by asserting that it was his duty as their true leader to demand their right to self-determination. Perhaps his aim was to push Bakshi into re-arresting him so that Kashmiris would turn against Bakshi completely and towards the idea of plebiscite. This is because he recognized that while Kashmiris revered him, they also liked Bakshi, who had been much more connected to the working classes and their concerns throughout the anti-Dogra movement; they also appreciated the efficiency and order that Bakshi had brought to the administration, not to mention the cheap rice that was now available to them. And most were unsure about how a plebiscite would impact their lives. Abdullah also hoped that his re-arrest would galvanize the international community to put pressure on India to resolve the Kashmir issue.

Bakshi, for his part, was happy to oblige, and was making every effort to prove that Abdullah continued to pose a threat to Indian sovereignty. This involved providing the Indian Intelligence Bureau with the resources it needed to amass evidence demonstrating Abdullah's, his family's and his supporters' links to Pakistan.[46] According to the memoirs of B.N. Mullik, the director of the Intelligence Bureau (IB) at this time, Pakistan was indeed funnelling money to a number of Kashmiri organizations, including the PF, with the intention of inciting revolt against the Bakshi regime and India. By late 1957, he notes, the IB had enough evidence against the PF as a whole and Begum Abdullah, Beg and other specific individuals in particular of being involved in an anti-India conspiracy with Pakistan.[47]

Abdullah's speeches following his release provided the rest of the ammunition for the propaganda campaign that had been active throughout the years that he had been in prison, then had heated up right before his release, and now gathered steam in its wake. For instance, the Indian press downplayed the welcome Abdullah had received in Kashmir after his release, while highlighting certain aspects of his speeches so as to frame them in such a way that made him sound like an anti-national traitor and partisan of Pakistan.[48] Reporting on one such speech, *The Times of India* noted that Abdullah had loudly proclaimed that the accession of Kashmir to India was not final and irrevocable just because Bakshi called it so; the true power to change this decision rested with the people. The report added that Abdullah had referred to the present government of J&K as '"goondas, opportunists and thieves" and accused the Government of India of "conniving at this state of affairs"'.[49]

Abdullah remained uncompromising in public and in private. On the frigid morning after his arrival, he made his way to Hazratbal shrine, another centre of his political authority and Kashmiri sovereignty. Thousands of people thronged the area around the modest wooden structure of the shrine in freezing temperatures in a scene reminiscent of the days of the movement's height in the 1930s, eager to hear what Abdullah had to say. He began as he used to with Quranic ayats, followed by Iqbal's verses, then reminded people that Kashmir did not belong to Bakshi or the leaders in Delhi, Moscow or Washington, but to them. In speeches at sacred spaces across the city, he drew on stories from Islamic history and the Quran to liken his own persecution and that of his supporters to that of the Prophet and his supporters in Mecca. He told audiences that prison had given him the opportunity to consider some of his earlier failures and how he could do better if given another chance. Almost always, he ended his speeches by noting that Kashmir's accession was not a settled fact and could only be decided by its people: 'As a matter of fact, India has been misguided. It is unfair to say that a decision has been taken unless it is supported by the people ... Self-determination is the people's right. Our slogan will continue and our struggle will go on till this slogan does not take a practical shape.'[50]

Before ending up at the Eidgah ground for his Id speech, he drove through the city in a jeep, personally offering his good wishes to party workers and families of jailed supporters. In the speech, he recalled the sura of the Quran that recounts the battle between Moses and the Pharaoh, which is won by Moses. Waves of excitement ran through his audiences, reminding them of their own sacrifices and reconnecting them to the earlier fervour of the movement. He not only reasserted his—and the Kashmiri people's—claim to the sacred spaces of the city, which had been so critical to his emergence as leader, but also undertook the construction of a new mosque in his birthplace, Soura, thereby expanding his influence further. Abdullah further renewed his contacts with the people by visiting localities where his supporters lived and by holding court at his home in Soura, which once again became abuzz with political activity.[51] He confirmed his status for Kashmiris as a great spiritual leader, above and beyond politics.

At the same time, Abdullah attempted to reach out to Indians by reprising his image as Kashmir's Gandhi, a simple man who was willing to stand and fight for Gandhian values such as non-violence and secularism, which postcolonial India seemed to have forgotten. He issued a statement on Gandhi's tenth death anniversary, appealing to the millions of followers and admirers of Gandhi in the subcontinent to 'make truth and non-violence as the only standards of their conduct in speaking or thinking about the Kashmir question and to help in finally resolving this long-standing dispute in the light of these two principles'.[52] In the same vein, he made overtures to Kashmir's Hindus and Sikhs, reminding them of his commitment to their protection and safety. In her regular reports on the situation in Kashmir, Sarabhai likewise emphasized the image of Abdullah as a Gandhian figure—a deeply spiritual yet secular leader taking on a mighty state through non-violent means.[53]

While presenting himself as a spiritual figure, as he had encouraged his followers to do from prison, Abdullah also wanted to ensure that

Kashmiris as well as India and the world were very clear about his political stance. In the pamphlet *Raishumari Kyun?* (Why Plebiscite?), issued soon after his release, Abdullah carefully questioned the notion that Kashmir's accession to India was final, arguing that its ratification by the J&K constituent assembly did not render it legitimate because the assembly itself was illegitimate at that time. He further asserted that the charges of conspiracy and corruption against him were baseless; he had been labelled a communalist by Indian newspapers since 1931 but had proven them wrong every single time. He was a committed secularist, and the plebiscite demand did not go against the principles of secularism. He was not the one who had reversed his stance; it was the Government of India that had reneged on its promise to the people of Kashmir. He reiterated these ideas in speeches all over the Valley, noting that the state's accession to India was not a settled issue and that he simply could not give up on the idea of self-determination for Kashmiris. He argued that at independence, the states had the option to join India or Pakistan, or remain independent, and the accession by the Maharaja to India was supposed to be temporary. As a Gandhian, he would not give up on truth.[54]

As Abdullah went door to door in Kashmir canvassing support for his views and even flew around the country, including to Bombay and Hyderabad, the din against him in the Indian press increased. He came across as unhinged in press reports, one describing him as 'highly fanatical, oozing revenge against India and deadset on a dangerous path whose consequences to himself, India and Pakistan, he seemed unmindful of… a danger to the peace of the entire region'. It also noted that Abdullah was bitter against the Indian press for its coverage of his activities.[55] Meanwhile, Bakshi's regime continued to spread rumours that Abdullah was attempting to foment revolt and kept up the pressure by curtailing people's freedom of movement and expression while arresting many for their political activities. Abdullah's strident resistance to the repression was reported in the press as calling for his supporters to rise up against the state police to 'crush the traitors'.[56]

Masoodi wrote to Sarabhai in March, appealing to her to spread the word in India, if not among common people then at least the elites, that

Abdullah's intentions were honourable and Bakshi's regime was treating political prisoners, some of them former friends of Pandit Nehru himself, like cattle. Kashmiris, he added, needed to feel that they deserved justice as much as they deserved subsidized rice. The only way forward was through dialogue between Abdullah and Nehru, which was not possible in the current climate of repression.[57]

By April, deeply frustrated and with conspiracy charges mounting against him, Abdullah wrote to Nehru, complaining about the Bakshi regime's actions and appealing to him for his intervention. He expressed his dismay at the mass arrests and the poor treatment of prisoners, many of whom were lawyers, doctors and businessmen, likening it to the treatment of inmates in Nazi war camps. Reminding Nehru that this did not look good for India's claims of being a secular state, he noted, 'I am watching this silently to see how Indian democracy functions in this Muslim-majority state.' He pointed out that Bakshi was a traitor who had stabbed his own mentor in the back and was thus not to be trusted. He hoped fervently that Nehru would not be deceived again by such an individual or else they were all doomed. Recalling their relationship and Nehru's promises to Kashmir, he wrote:

> You have always known that I do not get involved in conspiracies, but I am against the Indian government's policy towards Kashmir, which I have always made public. I think that Kashmiris deserve the right to self-determination, which you too at one time endorsed with much enthusiasm. I am of the belief that our demand is based on justice and the day is not far when world opinion will be with us and Hindustan will have to concede our demands. I have no desire to spread dissension in the state or to dethrone the present government. But I undoubtedly want to create strong opinion among the people of Kashmir and Hindustan to end conflict between India and Pakistan and get Kashmiris the right to express their opinion without any internal or external interference. Despite the events of 1953, I believe that the key to resolving the situation lies in your hands.[58]

Nehru did not respond to the letter; by this time he was under intense pressure from his own home ministry and the Intelligence Bureau to rein in Abdullah by charging him with conspiracy. Even as his concerns about Abdullah's activities and speeches mounted, Nehru remained reluctant to paint Abdullah as a pro-Pakistan conspirator. He felt that the image of India would be damaged if Abdullah was tried for being in league with Pakistan after Nehru himself had gone the distance to present him to the world as staunchly pro-India. But he finally relented and Abdullah was re-arrested at the end of April 1958 and charged with conspiracy.[59] The reasons for his arrest, according to Bakshi, included 'rousing communal passions, preaching the two-nation theory, trying to subvert Kashmir's link with India, organizing an Ansar force, describing the Indian army as an occupation force and above all receiving money from Pakistan for his subversive activities'.[60] As soon as Abdullah was re-arrested, Sadiq, who had earlier made overtures to Abdullah to ally with him against Bakshi and been turned down, issued a statement condemning the action.[61]

Although Abdullah had known, in some ways, that his freedom would be short-lived, it was still a shock for him to be thrown back in prison so quickly. But the charges against him and the subsequent trial allowed him to retain his position in the public consciousness in Kashmir, India and the world at large. As the noted American broadcaster Edward Murrow proclaimed in a CBS news report on 1 May 1958, 'It is ironic that the Lion of Kashmir who fought so long for freedom has been jailed again by a freedom-loving state. The Lion exemplifies the spirit of Thoreau, who said, "I was not born to be forced. Freedom isn't something to be won and then forgotten. It must be renewed like soil after yielding good crops."'[62] At the same time, on the other side of the border, Abdullah's erstwhile colleague and opponent Chaudhuri Ghulam Abbas was also thrown into prison by the Pakistani authorities for founding the Kashmir Liberation Front with its slogan 'Kashmir Chalo', which demanded action on Kashmir. Although the two would meet during Abdullah's visit to Pakistan after his release in 1964, neither was able to move the needle on the Kashmir issue.

## ASSESSING THE REVOLUTIONARY

Any assessment of Abdullah during these years as a prisoner of India interspersed with a bout of freedom has to be placed in the context of Indian postcolonial politics as well as the regional Indo-Pak relationship. This was the moment when India was beset by a variety of crises in centre–state relations as the party in power, the Congress, set about putting in place a centrist federation as envisioned in the constitution. Since the constitution left little room for the accommodation of religious, or even linguistic, demands for provincial reorganization, challenges from the regions abounded, from linguistic demands in south India to claims based on regional and religious nationalisms in the Northeast and J&K. While the state was much better at accommodating linguistic demands, J&K represented a particularly thorny problem because it was not just strategically located, but was also the only Muslim-majority state in India that was in an internationally recognized dispute with Pakistan.

Abdullah became, for India, an embodiment of this crisis. Secular, Muslim and Kashmiri at once, he challenged the Indian state to face up to its majoritarianism despite its claims of secularism, and did so on an international stage. His revolt hit at the very heart of India's identity as a democratic, secular republic and was, therefore, met with the harshest possible response, which in turn weakened these very aspects of the Indian identity. In the end, Abdullah's life illustrates that it was impossible to be both a patriotic Kashmiri Muslim and a loyal Indian at once. In Pakistan, where he had been eulogized after his dismissal and arrest in 1953, his image as a revolutionary leader dedicated to the causes of Kashmiri self-determination and for bringing about Indo-Pak rapprochement was further burnished after his brief release and re-arrest in 1958. An article in the *Pakistan Horizon* noted:

> His efforts during the short spell of his qualified freedom were directed towards a lasting and permanent solution of the Kashmir problem. Had he been interested in a show of force or contest of power in Kashmir he most probably would have executed his plans but since he believed that the Kashmir problem was part and parcel of the

> Indo-Pakistan relations and it could not be isolated, his attempts were directed towards an understanding between the two countries.[63]

The article ended on a sombre note: 'Abdullah's rearrest has deprived Kashmir and the sub-continent of all hopes of settlement.'[64] The Indo-Pakistan relationship was indeed entering a particularly difficult phase, which would gravely impact Abdullah's relationship with India in the next few years.

For Abdullah himself, India and Pakistan were secondary; what mattered to him most was that he was still the tallest leader in Kashmir, his home and centre of his political identity. During this period, as anti-India feelings grew in Kashmir, they coalesced around him since he was India's prisoner, and he became an enduring symbol of an anti-India opposition. As Noor Ahmad Baba has written, 'He became instrumental in socializing the post-partition generation in Kashmir in accepting it as an unresolved dispute.'[65] Whether he wanted to or not, Abdullah represented separation from India—an image that he then had to live up to, in a sense, to remain relevant in Kashmir. He was willing to be a rebel for Kashmir and its people, and spend years in prison for them, but he also wanted to bring them justice, which he could only do if he was free and moderated his rhetoric. This tussle would define his political life and determine his political decisions for the next decade.

# 6

# On Trial, 1958–1965

IN A BBC INTERVIEW RECORDED IN LONDON ON 10 MARCH 1965, SHEIKH Abdullah sounds quietly confident as he corrects the interviewer when asked why there had been a change since 1949–50 in his view, and perhaps also in that of the Kashmiri people, as to the finality of the territory's accession to India. 'The people of Kashmir have never taken that attitude that the accession of Kashmir to India was final because they always considered this accession as provisional,' he notes, adding that there was 'enough proof in the records of the Indian government and parliament that India, too, considered this accession as provisional'. Going further in the answer to the follow-up question about whether he thought India and Pakistan would consider the possibility of a plebiscite to determine the will of the Kashmiri people, he quite clearly states that Pakistan had been pressing for an implementation of those promises to the people of Kashmir, but it was India 'where you find a change'. One can sense a deep, simmering undercurrent of frustration beneath his calm exterior.[1]

And Abdullah was indeed an angry and frustrated man in 1965, with most of his ire directed at India. He had been in detention since 1953 with the Indian government's imprimatur, with a brief period of freedom in 1958 that ended in disaster. He and his followers had held high hopes for this most recent release in early 1964, but that too was not turning out much differently. To Abdullah, it was clear that India had changed since he was first interned in 1953, but it seemed for the worse, especially after Jawaharlal Nehru's death in May 1964. As he travelled through European and Arab capitals during his hajj travels in spring 1965, news of the heavy-handedness with which the Jammu and Kashmir (J&K) government was repressing his supporters who were offering peaceful protest against the merger of the National Conference (NC) into the Congress, followed him. As a result, despite being aware that the damning words he was uttering about India would foreclose all possibility, if any remained, of his coming to a rapprochement with its political leadership, he continued to make such speeches and comments, raising awareness and gaining support for the Kashmiri movement for self-determination, a movement of which he claimed leadership.

But the truth was that although Abdullah enjoyed immense personal popularity in Kashmir—and among the Indian political elites that had pinned all their hopes of the resolution of the Kashmir issue on him—his political influence itself was on the wane. He had been in detention for a decade and much had changed on the political scene in Kashmir as well as India and Pakistan in the interim, which he had not quite come to grips with. In fact, the agitation in late 1963 over the disappearance of the holy relic from Hazratbal shrine that had been the catalyst for his own release also brought out the challenges and challengers to his authority in Kashmir. The Plebiscite Front (PF), the organization through which he had been carrying out the movement since its founding in 1955, was itself divided along moderate and extremist lines.

He might have been able to re-assert his influence in the Valley had he made any sort of headway in the direction of the promises generated by his release—to bring about some sort of a resolution to the Kashmir issue between India and Pakistan, admittedly a tall order. But by early 1965, the situation looked worse than before. The economic policies of the Bakshi government had created a Kashmiri Muslim middle class while at the same time widening the wealth gap between those who were its beneficiaries and those who could not access its patronage. All social groups were chafing at the bit as their political, and for many also economic, aspirations continued to be denied. Indian secularism and socialism—ideas that Abdullah himself had strongly espoused in the past—had lost their promise and were being replaced, especially among the youth, by the powerful alternatives offered by Islamist groups.

Much like earlier in his political life, Abdullah was caught in the throes of larger forces over which he had little control. The India–Pakistan balance of power had shifted with India's military defeat at the hands of China in 1962 and the attenuation of Nehru's power in its wake. But Abdullah seemed incapable of recognizing this, and by insisting on Indo-Pak rapprochement on Kashmir as the only way forward, lost the initiative when his 1964 visit to Pakistan failed to produce any tangible results. Meanwhile, Pakistan, while upholding him as a martyr for Kashmir's cause, continued to pursue its plans of bringing India to its knees at its moment of weakness. And in India, the need to appear strong was more imperative than ever after Nehru's passing, leaving little tolerance for Abdullah's shenanigans around the world. It was no surprise, then, that Abdullah was greeted by an arrest party when his plane landed at Palam Airport on 8 May 1965 and was whisked away to Ootacamund, followed by a bungalow in Kodaikanal in Tamil Nadu, where he would spend the next three years in detention.

By this time, Abdullah was used to being removed from the political scene when he became an inconvenience for India. In the twelve years since his first arrest in independent India, he had rebuilt his image as a formidable revolutionary who refused to bend his knee to the postcolonial state no matter the cost. This meant that if he were to settle his differences with India (as he finally formally did in 1975), he risked alienating his base permanently, and if he continued to act as the anti-India rebel, he would not be able to come to terms with the country whose support he needed to deliver justice to Kashmir and its people.

This struggle to remain politically salient defined Abdullah's public life in this period and continued to determine his politics even after he had finally accepted India's overlordship. In the process of reconciling with his new status as a defendant on trial for criminal conspiracy against the Indian state, Abdullah embraced the image of a crusader not just for Kashmiri self-determination, but also Indo-Pak amity. Although he spoke like a regional and sometimes even global statesman, his political aspirations began and ended with the Kashmir Valley, from whose people and sacred spaces he drew legitimacy while simultaneously defending their sovereignty.

## BATTLING CONSPIRACY

A case was lodged in Jammu in May 1958 against Mirza Afzal Beg and twenty-five others on charges of conspiracy against the state for espousing the cause of independent Kashmir. Abdullah was not one of the accused because Nehru was reluctant to give his permission, but he was eventually pressured into giving his consent. Therefore, a supplementary charge sheet was filed against Abdullah in October 1958. The accused were now transferred to a building complex in Jammu that had a special prison to house them as well as a courtroom where the judicial proceedings were carried out.

Abdullah's reminiscences about these years in the Jammu jail as the case dragged on until 1964 are tinged almost with nostalgia. Here the environment was much more collegial and purposeful than at Kud, where Abdullah had felt somewhat solitary and in limbo. As he narrated years later, 'We had carved a home of our own in the special jail.'[2] The prisoners took it upon themselves to organize their daily affairs as well as manage the court case in the manner of an administration, with committees dedicated to defence, health, public relations, kitchen matters, gardening and so on. Abdullah was able to indulge his passion for gardening again in the land around the prison, describing the activity as 'subduing' the arid land of Jammu to yield variegated flowers, vegetables and even the Chinar tree. It was almost as if through the act of cultivation he was claiming sovereignty over Jammu by transforming it into the Valley. There was regular exercise in the form of badminton games, sometimes with jail staff, who also sat down to the meals that Abdullah himself often prepared, especially on festivals such as Id. Most importantly, the case against them was such a 'farce' that, as Abdullah remembers, 'We considered ourselves fortunate in having a forum where we were exposing relentlessly the duplicity of the Indian leadership.'[3]

In general, Abdullah's release in 1958, followed by his re-arrest and the filing of the case against him had the effect of solidifying support for him among his erstwhile critics from J&K—Balraj Puri and P.N. Bazaz among them—as being the only hope for a resolution of the Kashmir problem. Puri, who was roughed up when he showed up to support Abdullah on the opening day of the trial, kept up a correspondence with him in prison, subtly nudging him to not allow his politics to be shaped wholly by Kashmiri public opinion. In response to a memo written by Abdullah on the 'greater neutralisation of Kashmir', which Puri felt would be unacceptable to India, while receiving Pakistani support, he noted: 'I would not like you to be content with remaining a mere symbol of the changing moods of the people—which you admirably do with your present attitude—but would wish you to aspire to have a hand in shaping the destiny of your people.'[4]

In August and October 1960 respectively, the statements of Beg and Abdullah to the court sought to demolish the government's case altogether. First, both noted that the charges—of attempting to bring down the J&K government through Pakistan's help with the ultimate aim of the state's merger with Pakistan—were preposterous. Second, the charge of conspiring with Pakistan was baseless and cheaply used and hurled against all opponents of the party in power for political ends. At one time, they had been labelled Congress stooges when their stand aligned with the Congress, and today they had become the stooges of Pakistan because their position was the same as Pakistan's official stand. Third, it did not matter what India or Pakistan believed about Kashmir's future because it was up to the Kashmiri people to decide. Fourth, India had promised not to take political advantage of the Kashmiris' plight in 1947. Was it the fault of the Kashmiris that India's position had changed and thus also Kashmiris' attitude? Rather than persecuting them for it, it made more sense to delve into the root causes and address them.[5]

Finally, the statement by the accused pointed out that plebiscite was the only solution to the problem of Kashmir. Far from fomenting revolt, the main organization promoting this view, the PF, was responsible for keeping 'fissiparous and communal tendencies' at bay by ensuring that people's attention was focused on self-determination. If not for the PF, vested interests would have been successful in promoting far more communal ideas after Abdullah's dismissal and arrest. It was a travesty to suggest that the slogans for the movement were inspired by Pakistan, since its inspiration came from India's and Kashmir's long freedom struggle.[6]

What these statements were arguing, in strikingly Gandhian terms, was that the movement for self-determination—and Abdullah himself—was not pro-Pakistan, but rather committed to working within the Indian framework by making sure that India lived up to its own promise(s). The struggle was not against India itself, which professed the same ideals as the movement, but the Nehru government, which was not following them.

As the case dragged on and became more farcical, with the prosecution presenting Abdullah's letters to his supporters from prison as evidence of a conspiracy, India's image around the world took a severe knock, while Abdullah's grew larger. Domestically, the Congress was being challenged by a far more consolidated opposition by the turn of the 1960s, with the Communist Party of India (CPI) on the left and the Swatantra Party on the right making gains in the 1962 general elections. This was followed by the devastating Chinese attack on India in late 1962, which weakened Nehru's power even further as opposition party candidates took several open seats in the 1963 bye-elections. As the opposition became increasingly critical of the government's Kashmir policy, public opinion began to turn against the case.

Following a three-week visit to the Valley in June 1962, P.N. Bazaz wrote to Nehru, explaining to him that even those who had been critics of Abdullah's regime, such as himself, felt that he was Kashmir's only salvation. While Kashmiris were economically better off under the Bakshi regime—Bakshi had been re-elected to power in the February 1962 assembly elections—they were deeply disgruntled with its denial of their civil liberties. Years in prison had 'burnished Abdullah's image' and people felt that if an honourable settlement was arrived at with him, tensions would ease in Kashmir. Abdullah might not abandon the idea of self-determination, but he could be convinced to carry it out in such a way that would be amenable to all parties. Abdullah was the only leader who could bring on board even the most fanatical pro-Pakistan elements.[7] Nehru's terse replies to Bazaz made no mention of Abdullah, instead blaming Pakistan for creating a climate that made it necessary for Bakshi's government to suspend civil liberties.[8] Undeterred, in another letter in the wake of the Sino-Indian War, Bazaz suggested to Nehru that Pakistan's anti-India propaganda could be neutralized if India reached a settlement with Abdullah that the Kashmiri leadership then announced publicly.[9]

India's relationship with the US, which was getting warmer since the election of John F. Kennedy as president in 1961, became closer with the promise of American arms aid to India in the wake of the Sino-Indian War that led the Chinese to wrest control of the Aksai Chin region of Ladakh from India. Along with this came American pressure to negotiate with Pakistan to resolve the Kashmir problem for good, as a result of which India and Pakistan went through six rounds of bilateral talks that began in late 1962 and ended in mid-1963.[10] American diplomats and spies on the ground in Pakistan and India held the view shared by many others in the subcontinent who wanted an equitable resolution of the Kashmir issue: that Abdullah was its only 'rational hope'. US Embassy Reports from Delhi and Karachi in 1963 described him as the 'dominant' and 'strongest single political force' on both sides of Kashmir, one noting that even the president of the Pakistani part of Kashmir, K.H. Khurshid, was prepared to admit this.[11]

The talks provided an opportunity for renewed public debate on a variety of potential solutions to the issue as well as calls for Abdullah's release, including from within the Valley itself. The American and British Embassies received several open letters and petitions from the Valley's inhabitants with suggestions for points of discussion that could be included in the ongoing talks. A group of 125 residents of Kashmir from a cross section of society sent a proposal to the US Embassy in Delhi to convert the Valley into a neutral zone as an interim phase until the details of the form of self-determination its people would exercise could be determined. People in the neutral zone would have free access to both India and Pakistan, and enjoy the fundamental rights of both. The Embassy notes pointed out that there was a good chance that this was along the lines of what Abdullah had in mind, too. Another letter from the 'religious divines' of Kashmir, the managers and administrators of its shrines—Abdullah's base—demanded his release so that he could participate in the talks with the leaders of India and Pakistan to arrive at a just solution.[12]

Writing in the 29 May 1963 issue of *The Hindu*, B. Shiva Rao, noted journalist and former member of the Constituent Assembly of India, urged the Indian government to continue talks with Pakistan even though they seemed to have yielded little. It was incumbent on India to take the higher moral ground and release leaders such as Abdullah without whom a solution was not possible. In fact, he noted, it would be akin to the British colonial state drawing up India's constitution when the entire Congress leadership was in prison. He went further to suggest that India should offer to give up the part of Kashmir it controlled so that it could be unified with the other parts of Kashmir (controlled by Pakistan) and become independent, with its security to be guaranteed by India, Pakistan, Afghanistan, Britain, America and the USSR. The real threat to India, he posited, came not from Pakistan, but rather China, and India needed to resolve its differences with Pakistan over Kashmir if it were to have any initiative in its dealings with China.[13]

Feeling the pressure on all fronts, Nehru attempted to have the case against Abdullah withdrawn in April 1962 and September 1963, the latter after the bilateral talks ended in failure, but was dissuaded both times by Bakshi, Karan Singh and B.N. Mullik, the director of the Intelligence Bureau.[14] By 1964, however, it was no longer feasible or justifiable to continue with an inconclusive case that seemed to serve no obvious purpose and into which the government was pouring crores of rupees.

## THE LION ROAMS AGAIN

Events within Kashmir itself provided the impetus for the dismissal of the case and Abdullah's release. In December 1963, the Valley was a tinderbox. The unpopular Bakshi had resigned earlier that year under

Nehru's Kamaraj Plan—meant to strengthen the image of the Congress after its poor showing in the elections and India's defeat at the hands of China—but evidence of the nepotism and corruption of his regime was everywhere. It did not look like anything would change under his hand-picked successor, Shamsuddin.[15] The latest series of talks between India and Pakistan to resolve their differences over Kashmir had yielded little. The best hope for change, Abdullah, was still battling for his own freedom. It was in this environment that on 27 December, news spread that the hair of the Prophet Muhammad, which was housed in Hazratbal shrine, had disappeared. The Valley instantly went up in flames.

Braving the bitter cold, Kashmiris poured out into the streets in protest, demanding the restoration of the holy relic and the prosecution of those responsible for its disappearance. Spontaneous kitchens sprung up in neighbourhoods to feed the demonstrators as people donated food, oil and firewood, while traders sold commodities at cheap rates. This vociferous reaction provided a legitimate space for the rise and consolidation of a political opposition to the Indian-backed regime.[16] Although its immediate aim was to restore the holy relic to its rightful place, the Action Committee for the Recovery of the Moi-e-Muqqadas—organized by Masoodi and other stalwarts of the original nationalist movement—became representative of Kashmiri grievances as a whole. It also allowed for the rise of Moulvi Muhammad Farooq (the erstwhile Mirwaiz Yusuf Shah's nephew)—who had been appointed Mirwaiz of Kashmir by Bakshi in 1962 and was now installed as the president of the Action Committee[17]—as a potential contender for the leadership of the Kashmiri Muslim community.

The Government of India was in a panic as protests continued unabated within Kashmir and their spillover effects became visible in sectarian violence in northeastern India and East Pakistan. The foreign press descended on Delhi to report on the unrest and Pakistan used the opportunity to point out the serious flaws in India's administration of Kashmir, taking the issue back to the Security Council and stepping up military pressure along the Ceasefire Line. India's position in Kashmir seemed gravely threatened for the first time since Abdullah's dismissal a decade earlier. American diplomats were concerned that the episode would lead to war between the two countries and felt that Abdullah's release was critical to restoring peace.[18] Nehru made urgent appeals for calm over All India Radio, to little effect. As the upheaval continued, he sent Mullik to Srinagar to deal with the situation, and the relic was restored to its proper place through the efforts of the intelligence community. The Indian government made the announcement of the reappearance of the relic in Hazratbal on 4 January, but did not divulge who was responsible for its disappearance, or indeed its reappearance.[19]

Balraj Puri wrote later that the affair could not have been 'handled more badly' by the Indian government, with the home minister labelling the episode as a Pakistani-orchestrated conspiracy.[20] Other speculations included that it was Bakshi's work, to demonstrate to India how quickly the situation in Kashmir would fall apart if he was not in control; or that G.M. Sadiq and D.P. Dhar had orchestrated the entire affair to embarrass Bakshi's puppet, Shamsuddin, so that Sadiq could take over as prime minister; or that Abdullah's supporters were behind it to bring about his release.[21]

Abdullah himself, watching the events unfold from the Jammu jail, seized the moment and wrote to President Radhakrishnan in January 1964, hammering home the point that this was the final straw in India's morally bankrupt policies towards Kashmir: 'Whereas the 1953 intrigue was aimed at decimating the people politically, the present event was brought about to deprive them of their spiritual anchorage in their misfortune. What has happened will only complete the process of their political, spiritual and moral disintegration.'[22] He was right, because the Indian government had come to the realization that its Kashmir policy had created a disastrous situation and had to change. Moderate elements within the government, led by Lal Bahadur Shastri, whom Nehru had appointed his heir apparent after his stroke, brought about an end to the Bakshi era by replacing Shamsuddin with Sadiq as prime minister of J&K in February 1964. This began an era of 'liberalization' under Sadiq, who recognized the value of allying himself with Abdullah at this critical juncture when public opinion was so against his government. He thus supported the suspension of the conspiracy case, leading to Abdullah's release on 8 April 1964.

This moment was perhaps one of the most crucial of Abdullah's political life. And like many such moments, Abdullah's own actions—based either on a lack of awareness or a misreading of the larger context as well as powerful forces beyond his control—ensured that it ended in disappointment for himself and his followers. The hopes vested in him at this moment were too high. Everyone from the Americans to many Indians and Pakistanis as well as Kashmiris felt that he would somehow be able to bring India and Pakistan to the table to negotiate a just settlement to the Kashmir issue. At the same time they expected him to fill the political vacuum in Kashmir left by Bakshi and restore democracy to J&K. Some even hoped that he would take over the leadership of the Indian Muslim community, which had been adrift since Maulana Azad's death in 1958.[23] This was a tall order indeed for any one individual, particularly when the political climate in India, Pakistan and Kashmir was at a delicate juncture, leaving little room for a negotiated settlement among them, however much certain sections of their populations might have desired it.

In India, Nehru's influence was at its lowest ebb, and his chosen successor, Shastri, had to defend his policies on multiple fronts, including within the Congress itself. While some members of parliament (MPs), particularly Muslim ones, were hopeful about the role Abdullah could play in Kashmir and India, most MPs remained suspicious of his goals. The CPI and Hindu right-wing parties such as the Jan Sangh were ratcheting up rhetoric against Abdullah's release. Following Nehru's lead, Shastri was taking a gamble that Abdullah would recognize the changing situation in India and contain the tenor of his rhetoric while calming down the atmosphere in Kashmir.[24] For this reason, he and other moderate supporters of Abdullah felt that it was crucial for Abdullah to visit Delhi right after his release and only then make his way to Kashmir. This would have the effect of reassuring Indians regarding his intentions before he had the opportunity to make intemperate statements, which he was more likely to do in the Valley.[25]

Fresh from prison, Abdullah was revelling in his freedom. He met with Bakshi and Sadiq in Jammu, both of whom appeared contrite and conciliatory, and for a moment he felt vindicated. But reality set in soon enough. Nehru's 'soft and affectionate' letter inviting Abdullah to Delhi as his guest so they could have an informal chat was waiting for Abdullah as soon as he emerged from the Jammu jail.[26] Abdullah was faced with a difficult choice at this point—he could either first go to Delhi as Nehru's guest and work out a deal with the Indian leadership or he could go straight to the Valley to reconnect with the people and then make his way to Delhi.

Abdullah chose the latter path, in part because he could not envision himself as anything other than a leader of Kashmiri Muslims, which required him to gauge their mood to ensure that he continued to be a leader whom they were prepared to follow. He could sense that a new, younger leadership with more Islamist views—not surprisingly from the family of his old opponents, the Mirwaiz—had emerged in the wake of the holy relic episode and seriously threatened his own influence over the Valley's Muslims and the future direction of its politics. The danger of being painted as an Indian mouthpiece was too great for him to take the risk. The outpouring of affection he received as people gathered in droves to greet him on his way to Kashmir from Jammu by road, and the celebrations in Kashmir as news of his release spread, confirmed that he had made the right choice. Unsurprisingly, soon after his return to the Valley, Abdullah began collecting funds to rebuild Hazratbal shrine.

Chester Bowles, the American ambassador to India, wrote to the US secretary of state that Abdullah's decision to make his way to Kashmir was a 'profound blow to hopes of moderate elements within the Government of India', who had been prepared to give him a hearty welcome in Delhi, have him speak in favour of communal harmony and then even negotiate a favourable status for Kashmir within India, such as that of Sikkim, or along the lines of the status of Puerto Rico within the US. This was especially the case because soon after his release, even the usually highly critical Indian press was well-disposed towards him and prepared to give him the benefit of the doubt.[27] As the *Hindustan Times* commented on 21 April 1964:

> What after all is the substance of Sheikh Abdullah's statements? This, that the future of Kashmir has to be decided by the people of Kashmir and that it has to be done in a manner that the dispute about it between India and Pakistan is amicably ended. With a little imagination it is possible to see that this clear and principled stand of the Kashmiri leader opened for India a wonderful opportunity that could be exploited to the advantage of all concerned.[28]

Bowles pointed out that had Abdullah chosen to visit Delhi soon after his release, his tactical position would have been so strong that he could have 'written his own ticket, including some form of autonomy; once the process had passed a certain stage, GOI would have been powerless to prevent it'.[29]

By not doing so, Abdullah allowed his critics—from the left and the right—to gather their forces and provided them with ample ammunition to start a vicious campaign against him as well as Shastri for pushing for his release. Although 'thrown off balance' by Abdullah's decision, the moderates continued to hold out hope that he could be persuaded to visit Delhi before the Id celebrations on 23 April, so that he could return to Srinagar in a more temperate mood for his speech that day.[30] Nehru was reportedly unhappy about the gathering furore and had criticized Shastri in private, although his comments in public asked for restraint in passing judgements at this early stage.[31]

Abdullah attempted to reassure Nehru and his other supporters in India that he would be in a better position to accept a deal with the Indian government after he had established himself as the foremost leader in the Valley. He knew that this time around, he had more leverage in his dealings with the Indian government than he had ever before and was determined to use it to his advantage. Thus, in his initial comments, he spoke in generalities and just enough to secure his political base in the Valley while testing the waters of Indian intentions without giving India cause to re-arrest him. He repeated that his basic stand on the issue had not changed, which was that the Kashmir issue was not settled and that the only answer was to bring about a settlement through negotiations with all parties concerned, including Kashmiris. As the US Central Intelligence Agency (CIA) report issued soon after his release noted, the challenge for the Indian government was to go beyond merely tolerating his statements and 'show enough flexibility in their policies toward and in Kashmir to meet Abdullah's as yet unspecified minimum requirements and to persuade the Sheikh that he has a good reason to stay out of the comfortable confinement he has just left'.[32] It was a tricky moment for both sides.

When Abdullah met Nehru, after eleven years, in a series of meetings in late April and early May, the tide of Indian public opinion was already turning against him. Beg and Masoodi, the latter acting as facilitator, joined them for tea but left soon after to give Abdullah and Nehru a chance to speak alone. Abdullah's reminiscences of these meetings and Nehru's notes on them are strikingly different. For Abdullah, Nehru was a much-diminished man, eager to make amends, and allowed Abdullah to lay out his proposals for the future of Kashmir. He also wholeheartedly agreed with Abdullah's prescriptions on Indo-Pak relations.[33]

Nehru's notes on the meetings, on the other hand, present an exchange in which Abdullah appears to be more interested in laying out his grievances about the treatment meted out to him in the past than in discussing concrete proposals to address the present and future of Kashmir. The only point he repeatedly made, according to Nehru, was that Kashmir's internal problems would be resolved if India and Pakistan came to a resolution of the dispute between them, but had little to offer in terms of how to go about this. To Nehru, Abdullah seemed unaware of the numerous times the two countries had engaged in dialogue in the past eleven years since Abdullah was dismissed, the most recent having ended in failure in 1963.[34]

M.C. Chagla, the minister of education, sat in on the 1 May meeting and told Abdullah that his departure from secular principles would cause a lot of issues in India. Abdullah's response was that he continued to hold firm on those principles, but he was against the declaration that J&K's accession to India was irrevocable. When Nehru asked him why that was the case, he noted that the agreement in 1947 was for accession on three subjects only and the accession had not been ratified by the will of the people. From Nehru's perspective, this stance was untenable; he attempted to explain to Abdullah why plebiscite had not been possible in the past and had become increasingly impossible with Pakistan joining alliances with the US, and more recently as a result of the Chinese invasion of India. Nehru's repeated attempts to pin Abdullah down on a specific idea on how to move forward with Kashmir yielded generalities, such as that it 'would depend on many factors and especially the attitude India took up', and the need to speak to all colleagues, including those outside the Congress, before any decision could be taken.[35]

The talks were inconclusive at best. But Abdullah continued to meet with people from across the political spectrum in Delhi while travelling across the country giving speeches regarding his position. In Delhi, he met with the Indo-Pak reconciliation group, whose members included J.J. Singh, J.P. Narayan and B. Shiva Rao. In Madras, he met with C. Rajagopalachari, and in Sevagram with Vinoba Bhave. These leaders were concerned about the mounting criticism of Abdullah's stance in the press, especially his statements regarding accession not being final since it had not been approved by the Kashmiri people. Shiva Rao was troubled in particular by the former defence minister Krishna Menon's 'debilitating propaganda' against Abdullah, which was being supported by communist journals.[36] They themselves were also coming under criticism in the press for encouraging this 'lotus-eater's dream', by suggesting impracticable solutions such as a confederation among India, Pakistan and Kashmir.[37]

Shastri wrote to Rajagopalachari, asking him to advise Abdullah not to make provocative speeches because it was hardening the stance of many within the cabinet and party. Rajagopalachari agreed that Nehru was in no position to withstand the chauvinism that had begun to grip Delhi at this time, and suggested to Abdullah to keep the matter of accession out of his speeches as well as to consider running for a fresh set of elections in the state as a means of resolving the matter. Abdullah declined, saying that he had no intention of running for office in a corrupt and rotten system, but he did express fear that his freedom would be short-lived if public opinion continued on this path.[38]

However, there were still a few individuals within the Indian government who were determined to make the most of the opportunity provided by Abdullah's release to hammer out a solution that would be acceptable to all parties. Among them was Y.D. Gundevia, the foreign secretary, who had felt for some time that a resolution of the Kashmir issue needed a new line of thinking and that nothing would change, as he wrote to G. Parthasarathy, India's high commissioner to Pakistan, 'till Kashmir is taken away from the hands of the Home Ministry'.[39] On 8 May, Gundevia met with Abdullah, along with Parthasarathy and Badruddin Tyabji, Aligarh Muslim University's vice chancellor, at the prime minister's house. To Gundevia, much like he had appeared to Nehru, Abdullah seemed out of touch, especially when it came to the Indo-Pak relationship. According to Gundevia, he kept repeating the line that India and Pakistan should improve relations as though they had never attempted to negotiate prior to that moment. Indeed, during the 1963 talks, India had offered to make the Ceasefire Line the international border, but Pakistan had rejected it as the offer from a defeated nation.[40]

But at the same time, Abdullah was able to get across the dilemma that faced him at this moment, which explains, in part, why he was being so cagey regarding specifics. The image of him painted by the Bakshi regime as a pro-Pakistani, anti-Indian agitator for plebiscite had sunk deep into the minds of Kashmiris, especially the younger generation that had not known him or his politics prior to his incarceration in 1953. When he was released, all anti-Indian elements had flocked to him, but it would take him time to change the image of India in their minds and to win them over to an ideology that appealed to their self-respect without, at the same time, betraying his own Gandhian ideals. It did not help that Bakshi, now out of power, had done a volte-face and was carrying on a campaign against Abdullah labelling him India's lackey who would ultimately accept a deal with India that maintained the status quo with few changes. So Abdullah was implying that his anti-India rhetoric was for political purposes only, to keep the anti-India elements on his side, rather than losing them to the increasingly radical opposition that had recently strengthened in Kashmir. For this very reason, they needed to come up with a formula for settlement that would be acceptable to Pakistan, or at least one that it could not turn down in the face of world opinion.[41]

Abdullah felt that there were a couple of possibilities for such a settlement, including a joint Indo-Pak condominium over Kashmir and a confederation among India, Pakistan and Kashmir. It is important to note that while the group regarded the first possibility as impracticable due to the divergent foreign policy goals of India and Pakistan, especially with regard to China, the second was seriously considered. They told Abdullah that it was worth pursuing and not just as a trap for the resurrection of an Akhand Bharat (united India), as long as the larger settlement between India and Pakistan was tied to the protection of the welfare of minorities in both countries. Gundevia later wrote to V.K.T. Chari, a distinguished lawyer who was advocate general for Madras State—and who also happened to be Parthasarathy's brother-in-law—to send him a note on the legal implications of a confederation, in which India and Pakistan would remain sovereign states, while Kashmir would be brought into the confederation.[42] Abdullah made no mention of self-determination or plebiscite during these talks.

## MISSION TO PAKISTAN

The stage was set for Abdullah's visit to Pakistan to meet with President Ayub Khan and Kashmiri leaders from Pakistani Kashmir. But this was an inopportune moment from the perspective of both India and Pakistan to build bridges between them. Shiva Rao met with Abdullah to get a sense of where he stood at this moment and sent notes on the meeting to the American Embassy, which seemed to have vested a considerable amount of hope in Abdullah being able to bring about a resolution of the dispute. Abdullah was resentful of the rising tide of criticism against him and told Rao that not only had the treatment meted out to him in the past been unfair, but also that India had applied double standards in its dealings with Kashmir and Junagadh. He quoted from statements made by Indian leaders about the provisional nature of accession and its resolution through a reference to the will of the people. Rao explained to him that the political conditions in India simply did not allow a rethinking of the terms of the accession and Nehru was no longer politically or physically strong enough to carry public opinion with him. Given this, he advised Abdullah to not go for a quick and easy solution, but instead to ascertain Ayub's views while in Pakistan.[43]

Abdullah seemed to think, perhaps overly optimistically, that he could persuade Ayub Khan to relinquish Pakistan's control over the Pakistani part of Kashmir so that conditions could be created for a plebiscite in the entire territory of J&K as per UN resolutions. He told Shiva Rao that he preferred plebiscite to a general election as a means of ascertaining the views of the people in every possible version of a solution.[44] Again, Abdullah did not seem to appreciate how far both countries were from being in a position to accept these conditions. In Pakistan, although Abdullah was celebrated as a hero, as evident from the welcome he received on his visit, senior state officials viewed him as Nehru's envoy and were in no mood to be cooperative with India. They felt that India was in a weakened position at this time due to its defeat at the hands of China as well as Nehru's physical state, which augured a transition of power in the near future. In particular, Zulfikar Ali Bhutto, Pakistan's foreign minister, believed that rather than coming to terms with India, this was the time to strike it, before the country became too strong in a few years as a result of US military aid.[45]

In some ways, then, despite the expectations vested in Abdullah's visit to Pakistan, at least in some quarters, it was doomed from the start and even before Nehru's death brought about its untimely end. Abdullah himself sincerely believed that he had been put through the test of the past eleven years just so that he could serve to bridge the divide between the two countries. When asked by a journalist on 12 May whether he was going to Pakistan as an Indian citizen, he said, 'I am going as Sheikh Muhammad Abdullah; I am going as a human being.'[46] This was his attempt at transcending the narrow confines of nationalism to appeal to Indians, Pakistanis and Kashmiris across national divides. It came to light later that in his passport application, he had identified himself as 'Kashmiri Muslim' rather than 'Indian'.[47] Of course, all of this confirmed the hawks' suspicions of him.

As he met with Nehru again at Teen Murti House on 20 May for a final round of talks before his departure for Pakistan, he felt that his 'greatest friend' and also his 'captor' was with him and his mission in spirit. This would be their last meeting. Before his departure, Abdullah issued a statement reiterating his belief in secularism and the need to repair the relationship between the two countries for the sake of their minorities, which faced the brunt of the violence when this relationship deteriorated. An 'amicable solution' to the problem of Kashmir had to be found, 'a solution that gives neither party a sense of defeat, a solution that does not weaken the secular foundations of India either. It should also ensure the freedom and dignity of the people of our state.'[48] Thus, accompanied by his son Farooq, nephew Sheikh Rashid, Masoodi, Beg, Om Saraf (Mulk Raj Saraf's son, a one-time member of the NC from Jammu, and at that time a Reuters journalist) and several others as well as a bevy of Indian journalists, Abdullah set off on what was intended to be a two-week visit to Rawalpindi, Pakistani Kashmir, and, he hoped also, East Pakistan.

As Abdullah's plane landed on 24 May at the airport in Rawalpindi—that city with deep links to Kashmir that had been rent asunder by Partition—his heart leaped at the thought of being there again and reconnecting with old friends that he had not seen in years. His old rival Mirwaiz Yusuf Shah came up to the ramp and held him in a tight embrace while Ghulam Abbas waited at the tarmac to do the same. Many other Kashmiris crowded the airport for a chance to meet with him—some had worked with him in the heady days of the Kashmir movement, and others, who had been too young to do so, knew him as a legend.[49] Zulfikar Ali Bhutto represented the Pakistani government in welcoming him. Abdullah let the adulation of the people lining the streets to greet his vehicle as it made its way to the city wash over him. He was impressed with Ayub Khan's physical presence and commitment to Pakistan after their first meeting, in which they exchanged pleasantries and Abdullah presented him with that quintessentially Kashmiri musical instrument in walnut wood, the santoor. His assessment of Ayub Khan at the end of the visit was that 'Pakistan had ultimately got its saviour after its share of trials and tribulations'.[50]

In the evening, Abdullah addressed a large public gathering in Rawalpindi that was hosted by Ghulam Abbas. Abbas's welcome speech was emotional, but also portentous, because it captured the mood among the Pakistani elite regarding India. Tellingly, Abbas introduced China as a party to the dispute over Kashmir, overplaying the friendship between China and Pakistan, while downplaying the Indo-Pak relationship.[51] According to Shabir Masoodi, Maulana Masoodi's son, his father was surprised at how little the Pakistani governing class, especially Bhutto and his coterie, seemed interested in a negotiated settlement with India. Bhutto allegedly intimated to Abdullah that China and Pakistan would join hands in attacking India, leaving it with no choice but to compromise on Kashmir. Even Ayub Khan, it was said, might not have been privy to some of the machinations of the Pakistani establishment with regard to India.[52] Notwithstanding the truth behind these claims, the fact remained that Abdullah was swimming against the tide.

His own speech, in which he lauded Indian secularism and emphasized Indo-Pak amity as critical to the resolution of the Kashmir issue, was not appreciated by the Pakistani press. The newspaper *Dawn,* which had issued Abdullah a hearty welcome on his arrival, noted acerbically:

> People here feel that the shabby and inhuman treatment to which Muslims are subjected in India should be an eye-opener for the Sheikh who now appears from his statements to have taken up the role of an apostle of peace and friendship between Pakistan and India rather than that of a leader of Kashmir whose prime objective should be to seek their freedom from Indian bondage.[53]

This shift in tone reflected Pakistani public opinion at large, which had expected Abdullah to act as an advocate of the political rights of the Muslims of Kashmir and was disappointed to see him acting as an emissary of India instead. Nonetheless, there was hope that Abdullah would not give up on the demand for plebiscite, which the Pakistanis believed would render a pro-Pakistan verdict given India's record in J&K. This illustrates the fine line that Abdullah was treading on his mission to Pakistan—staying true to his status as the defender of Kashmir's right to self-determination without compromising his role as peacemaker between the two countries.

Abdullah, along with Beg, met with Ayub Khan again on 26 May for a four-hour-long meeting, of which there are conflicting reports. According to Ayub Khan's book *Friends, Not Masters,* published in 1967, Abdullah had been sent to Pakistan by Nehru with the sole purpose of proposing the idea of confederation as a means of settling the dispute and pushed for this during their meeting. Miffed at this representation, Abdullah wrote Ayub Khan a letter reminding him that all he had emphasized was the need for the two parties to meet to discuss all perspectives and had not presented any final proposal at their meeting.[54]

The more likely scenario is that the men discussed a variety of options, including confederation, which Ayub Khan rejected out of hand. According to the veteran journalist Inder Malhotra, who was part of the press corps accompanying Abdullah, Ayub told Abdullah that such an arrangement was not viable because, among other things, it would lead to demands by other regions, such as Bengal and Rajasthan, or even the Sikhs, to join the confederation as autonomous units.[55] Nevertheless, Abdullah was able to persuade him to visit Delhi to meet with Nehru in the middle of June, and presented this in itself as a major accomplishment.[56]

The next day, Abdullah's party set off for Muzaffarabad amidst much excitement. Abdullah was keen to survey the conditions in this part of Kashmir with his own eyes and meet with people there to assess their feelings. But the festivities in Muzaffarabad were not to be, as on the way there, they got the news that Nehru had passed away. Abdullah was devastated; not only had he lost a close friend with whom he had a turbulent relationship over the decades, but he could also see the Indo-Pak rapprochement that he had taken such care to foster withering on the vine. His own position and perhaps freedom, too, he knew, was now in jeopardy. After a desultory meal at the home of President Khurshid in Muzaffarabad and a public meeting that focused on mourning the loss of Nehru, the party turned back for Rawalpindi and arrived there amidst an atmosphere of uncertainty. Ayub Khan appeared uneasy about the impending transition in India and its repercussions for Pakistan and seemed to have put aside all thought of talks with India. Bhutto accompanied Abdullah's party back to Delhi to pay respects at Nehru's funeral.[57]

According to Om Saraf, Abdullah felt forlorn at this time, abandoned by fate. His greatest advocate was no more and the project on which he had staked his freedom, as well as that of the people of Kashmir, was now in jeopardy. He was not officially invited to Nehru's funeral, and nobody paid attention to this tall man, stooped over, crying uncontrollably as his friend's body, and Kashmir's future, went up in flames.[58]

## THE AFTERMATH

A collection of essays published in the June 1964 issue of *Seminar* attempted to come to terms with the meaning of Abdullah's release for India, Kashmir and Indo-Pak relations. As a whole, the issue made a case for providing Abdullah with the space to help mend the relationship between Kashmir and India—hitherto a story of missed opportunities—and perhaps also serve as a conduit between India and Pakistan. Kashmir was not the cause of the crisis in Indo-Pak relations, but rather it was Indo-Pak relations that had led to the crisis in Kashmir. For many of the contributors to the journal, this was an opportunity to take stock of the performance of the postcolonial Indian state, which they argued had abjectly failed in many arenas, especially in terms of centre–state relations, evident most starkly in the case of J&K.[59]

Surindar Suri noted that the grievances being expressed in Kashmir were not unique and that people in a number of states felt the same about India's political leadership. The difference was that for Kashmiris there was an alternative, which made their expression of discontent seem like a much larger threat: 'Kashmir today is a mirror of India's future. Disillusionment among Kashmiris is of the same kind as that among a great many people in India, but in Kashmir it has a means of expressing itself which renders it dramatic and ominous.' He pointed out that when Abdullah stated that accession was not complete, it did not necessarily mean that Kashmir had no ties to India or that it should leave India, but rather that the Indian state had performed terribly poorly with regard to Kashmir.[60]

By the time these essays were published, an era had ended and Abdullah faced a much more hardened climate in India. Within the Congress, Shastri faced a battle to succeed Nehru as prime minister, which he eventually won, pledging to carry on his predecessor's policies. But his adversary for the position, Gulzari Lal Nanda, consolidated an opposition to the pro-Kashmir policies—including Abdullah's release and Indo-Pak dialogue—that had been advocated by Nehru and Shastri before the former's death. Abdullah returned to Kashmir, his final emotional link with India broken, only to find himself locked in an ideological struggle for leadership with Mirwaiz Farooq.

Abdullah was convinced that Farooq had been elevated to the position of Mirwaiz by Bakshi, and later to the position of chairman of the Holy Relic Action Committee by Masoodi, to undermine his position as sole leader of Kashmiri Muslims.[61] After his release, Abdullah had suggested to Farooq that the Action Committee should be disbanded since it could prove to undermine the PF. But instead, Farooq had immediately formed a new political party, the Awami Action Committee (AAC), to agitate for self-determination at any cost, with the hope that a plebiscite would bring a pro-Pakistan verdict.[62] The schisms of the 1930s, between the Shers and Bakras, reappeared with renewed vigour in an altered political landscape. Now that his bid to bring about reconciliation between India and Pakistan had failed, Abdullah was caught in a bind yet again. Was he to go back to an insistence on plebiscite, which he had not done for the past few weeks, instead keeping the focus on Indo-Pak dialogue? If he did not, he risked losing ground to the Mirwaiz, who could easily, as a leader more in touch with the concerns of the younger, more anti-India generation, take the initiative away from him.

In stark contrast to the steadfast stand represented by the Mirwaiz, Abdullah vacillated and appeared unsure of what to do next, as was his wont in such situations. He most likely felt that he had no choice but to begin courting communal elements, since secularism had become a dirty word associated with Indian designs on Kashmir. But this alienated the more progressive sections that had hoped that Abdullah would mend bridges with India, not to mention that it provided ammunition for his detractors in India. Reflecting on Abdullah in the context of the struggle between him and the Mirwaiz, Bazaz noted that Abdullah's ambition for absolute popularity and power was a misfortune for Kashmir; it had rendered him into an unsteady leader, always changing his stand on public affairs. At times he was a steadfast, progressive revolutionary in the face of severe opposition and at other times he caved to reactionary forces: 'He wants at once to be a communalist as well as a secularist, little realising that the two are incompatible roles, impossible to unite.'[63] In reality, Farooq was not nearly as popular as Abdullah at that time and was unlikely to replace him as the foremost Kashmiri leader in the near future. But Abdullah's insecurity about losing his primacy was so great that he took steps that ended up costing him the support of other key groups that he needed to achieve his agenda.

In the meantime, mainstream politics in J&K was moving in the direction of the state's greater integration with India. Bakshi had begun a campaign against the Sadiq government soon after Nehru's death by attempting to win over legislators to his side and bringing a motion of no confidence against the government in the state legislature. But the government turned the tables on Bakshi by arresting him on corruption charges. This move prompted Sadiq to regain control of the NC with the help of Mir Qasim by purging it of pro-Bakshi elements, and eventually, in his mind, re-vision it by merging it with the Congress. Recognizing its deleterious repercussions, Nehru had warned against establishing a branch of the Congress in Kashmir in late 1963 so as not to undermine the NC.[64] By late 1964, Sadiq had not just undermined the NC, but had also decimated the very identity of the party, which was now renamed the Pradesh Congress Committee. The Kashmiri journalist Shamim Ahmed Shamim noted that the move was akin to attempts at reviving a rotting corpse. The stench of the organization's misdeeds could not be hidden under the cloak of the Congress, he wrote.[65]

This was an especially low point for Abdullah; he appeared to have reached a blind alley. He had returned empty-handed from Pakistan, India was tightening its grip over Kashmir, and now the political party that he had founded and that stood for Kashmir's freedom struggle had lost its identity to the Congress. To rub salt in these wounds, the opposition, led by Mirwaiz Farooq, was alleging that since its very inception the NC had been a branch of the Congress, which had always directed the nationalist movement in Kashmir. This was a powerful assertion, one that ran the risk of tainting Abdullah's entire political career. A drastic step had to be taken to send a message to his detractors. Observing the situation at the time, P.N. Jalali wrote that Abdullah was utterly frustrated, and 'a man like Sheikh Abdullah in frustration can be a danger both to people and the government'.[66]

Abdullah issued a call for a boycott (*tark-i-mawalat*) of the new organization as well as a social boycott of its members. It appears that he took this call almost unilaterally, and it is worth noting that he does not mention it in his autobiography. In his speeches, he condemned the organization and those who chose to continue to be its members, as well as India for allowing this to happen. In a particularly strident speech at Hazratbal on 9 January 1965 (that he later recanted), he called the merger a move against Islam, which necessitated its boycott.[67] In another speech at Hazratbal on 15 January, he pointed out that Nehru's successors were not interested in completing what he had begun, but instead had decided to alienate the people of Kashmir further by imposing the Congress on them. Just as the Prophet's companions had socially boycotted their enemies, it was incumbent upon freedom-loving Kashmiris to do the same.[68]

The response within Kashmir and the rest of India was swift. PF workers on the ground bore the brunt of the government's wrath against the boycott, even as families and friends were divided over the move. The Mirwaiz-led AAC refused to join in the call for boycott and the atmosphere in Kashmir appeared more vitiated and riven than ever before. In India, meanwhile, Abdullah was condemned as a communalist who had finally revealed his true colours, with him and his supporters being labelled 'political mullahs' for using religion to further their political ends.[69] *The Times of India* quoted the Kashmiri MP Syed Nazir Hussain

Samnani as saying that Abdullah's 'fatwa to Muslims that they would fail to be Muslims if they joined the Congress had pained every patriot', and demonstrated that Abdullah had 'abandoned the national outlook'.[70] Shastri, who was struggling to maintain control within the Congress and over his own cabinet in the context of a food crisis in India, had little other than goodwill to impart to Abdullah at this moment, especially as the latter's speeches became increasingly vociferous against India. Events appeared to be hurtling towards a reprise of April 1958.

At this crucial moment, a demoralized Abdullah decided to withdraw from the domestic scene and take his campaign on the road. Leaving the PF in Masoodi's hands, much to the chagrin of Mirwaiz Farooq—who had hoped that he would have been handed the reins of the movement—Abdullah, accompanied by his wife and trusted friend Beg, left Srinagar to undertake the hajj in the first week of February.[71] He also intended to visit a few Arab and European capitals along the way. His speech on 10 February 1965 before his departure from India was portentous of things to come:

> Kashmir simply wants its right—that does not mean that we hate you. In fact, even today if India is threatened, a Kashmiri will lay down his life for India's freedom. He knows that without India, Kashmir cannot survive. All we are asking from you is to keep your promises. If you cannot go forward, at least do not go backwards. Burying the National Conference and hoisting flags of the Congress will make no difference nor will pouring money into the state or saying that Kashmir is an integral part of India (Atoot Ang), unless Kashmiris agree. This path can only lead to India's destruction. This is not a matter of religious affiliation, it is a matter of self-determination.[72]

If even respected senior leaders of the Congress, such as Morarji Desai, he said, accused Muslims of disloyalty to India, then what could one expect from the Jan Sangh? Although he assured Indian audiences that this would not be a political trip during which he would badmouth India, to Kashmiris he promised that he would place their wishes in front of world leaders. He asked them to be patient and stay non-violent in his absence.[73]

Abdullah knew that such words, especially uttered abroad, would lead to his imprisonment once he returned to India. But perhaps that is exactly what he wanted. He had reached a dead end with India, and if he was able to get the world on board for Kashmiris, then some pressure might be brought to bear on Indian leaders. It would also be good for his image in Kashmir in the long run, especially with the younger, more radical generation. As he wound his way through Egypt, Saudi Arabia and Algeria, he was gratified at being treated as a state guest and entertained by high officials. Carried away by this attention, he did not stop to consider the consequences of meeting with the Chinese premier, Chou En-Lai, at a state dinner in Algeria.

He always maintained that this was a casual meeting during which the two men focused on Sino-Indian relations and not the Kashmir issue,[74] but he misjudged the depth of anti-Chinese feelings in India in the wake of the 1962 war, thus providing his Indian detractors with a perfect reason to vilify him further. Opposition MPs, such as the Jan Sangh's Atal Bihari Vajpayee, raised a furore in the two houses of parliament demanding clarification on the issuance of a passport to Abdullah prior to his travels despite the fact that he had identified himself as a Kashmiri Muslim rather than an Indian.[75] Even his supporters, such as Balraj Puri, felt that meeting the Chinese premier had been an error of judgement on Abdullah's part. In a letter to the editor of the *Hindustan Times*, Puri noted that Abdullah had always lacked sincere friends who would give him sound advice and critique his actions, 'for his misfortune is that he is never criticized. He is either abused or eulogized.'[76]

The situation reached a tipping point in Britain, where Abdullah went next, giving interviews to outlets such as the BBC, in which he pointed out that India and Pakistan needed each other and Kashmir could serve as a bridge between them, while exhorting India to live up to the promises it had made to the Kashmiri people. Writing in the *Observer*, Guy Wint noted that the tall and usually vigorous Abdullah looked 'somewhat fragile after his long incarceration', but was determined to ensure that Kashmir's wishes were no longer subservient to those of India and Pakistan in any discussion of the solution.[77] As Abdullah continued his international campaign, pressure from India mounted, and he was asked to return to India or have his passport impounded and his Indian citizenship revoked.

Abdullah returned, even though Pakistan made a show of offering him a Pakistani passport if he chose not to do so. In this he had no choice, because for Abdullah the Valley was home and the heart of his political influence, and it lay in India. If he was to have any kind of political career at all, he had to go back to India, regardless of the consequences. This time he was banished from J&K altogether, to live in detention in the southern state of Tamil Nadu.

## ADRIFT

Abdullah had reached a crossroads in 1965. India–Pakistan relations were at an all-time low and his peacemaking attempts had yielded little. He was fully aware that while he was lauded as the arch nemesis of the Indian state and a champion of Kashmiri rights in Pakistan—a slew of biographies published in the early 1960s described him as a hero and martyr—he could never truly shed the image of being an Indian proxy among the Pakistani elites. For the Pakistani state, he was not much more than a convenient bludgeon with which to beat India and advance its own foreign policy agenda vis-à-vis its enemy; as Bhutto declared on Abdullah's detention: 'We have to act now with cold determination to meet this challenge and put an end, once and for all, to the neo-colonialist Indian usurpation and tyranny.'[78]

Other than individuals such as Vinoba Bhave, who lodged a protest against Abdullah's arrest,[79] he seemed to have few friends in India, where he was persona non grata for having maligned India and cavorted with the Chinese and Pakistanis while abroad. Most importantly, his revolutionary credentials seemed to be wearing thin in the Valley itself, where a radical younger generation demanded an immediate resolution of its political and economic grievances. These were mounting as the Sadiq government took symbolic and literal steps to hollow out Article 370 and forcefully integrate the state with India. Not only did the NC, the embodiment of Kashmiri nationalism, no longer exist, having been merged into the Congress, the embodiment of Indian nationalism, but also the post of prime minister of the state was now replaced with that of chief minister. J&K was now like any other Indian state. Protests by Abdullah's supporters and those of the Mirwaiz at these measures had been brutally repressed.

Abdullah seemed impotent in the face of larger forces. The Nehruvian era was over in India, and Pakistan was in a belligerent mood. Kashmir was in disarray, its very nationhood in peril. He was in detention once again and this time as a far older man. Time was running out for him, and for Kashmir, and he would soon have to find a way to reconcile his revolutionary credentials with a more conciliatory stand with India.

# 7

# Coming to Terms, 1965–1974

A CARTOON IN AN ENGLISH DAILY CAPTURED SHEIKH ABDULLAH'S image both inside and outside Kashmir in the wake of his decision to sign an accord with the Indian prime minister, Indira Gandhi. Gone was the fierce Sher-i-Kashmir of yore, replaced by a toothless lion whose dentures had been ripped out, with Indira Gandhi looming over the lion with a whip; the caption read: 'He will roar but cannot bite.'[1] By the end of 1974, Abdullah was no longer a revolutionary, having made the pragmatic decision to come to terms with the Indian centre and accept the position of chief minister of the state of J&K within the Indian Union.[2] It had been one of the most difficult and momentous decisions of his political life and rankled him to his very core, but one that he felt he had no choice but to make.

Even by subcontinental standards, the decade that began in 1965 was a politically tumultuous one. Within this period, India and Pakistan saw dramatic transitions of power with ruling parties facing multiple internal and external challenges. The countries fought two wars against each other and struggled with food shortages as well as contestations of the central authority that left Pakistan dismembered and India in the throes of a constitutional crisis that ended with the imposition of Emergency rule. Jammu and Kashmir (J&K) was directly or indirectly implicated in several of these events, and their consequences were so momentous that Abdullah could hardly choose to remain above them as he considered his relationship to India and Pakistan. Inevitably, they determined his course of action, while also shaping the Indian centre's response to him. Torn as he remained between India and Kashmir, his course of action had to also account for the changes within Kashmir itself, where an increasingly restive, uncompromising professional class was clamouring for justice for the Kashmiri nation. After all, Abdullah himself had created the concept of the Kashmiri nation and, for many, had come to embody it in the past two decades by crusading against India for its rights.

Much as he would have liked to reconcile the role of a towering leader of Kashmiri Muslims leading the Kashmiri nation to success with that of a devoted Muslim champion of Indian secular nationalism, he himself, as much as his detractors in India and Kashmir, had played a large part in making this impossible. It was also clear that despite engaging in two wars, India and Pakistan were no closer to a just or equitable resolution of the Kashmir issue. By the early 1970s, Abdullah had reached the end of the road. Meanwhile, most of his compatriots who had battled on the same middle ground between Kashmir and India, had, by and large, made their choices, or voluntarily or involuntarily bowed out of public life.

The two concerns on either side of the central fault line of his political career—an enduring commitment to his Kashmiri homeland and working with and within the Indian nation state—came to a head towards the end of Abdullah's life, as evident within the pages of his autobiography, *Aatish-i-Chinar*. He found himself in a race against time, with his physical health declining and his political relevance being called into question by a younger, more belligerent generation of Kashmiris. And, even as the geopolitical dynamic of the subcontinent shifted in favour of India, Abdullah made the decision to work within the system. The call of power was perhaps too great, but he also genuinely hoped that he could reform the state's broken institutions from within, making them healthier for future generations. This, however, was not enough to placate Kashmiri Muslims, to whom he now appeared as the worst kind of traitor—one who had built up their aspirations only to sell them down the road to the enemy.

## 'STRANGE PRISONER'

In his 1965 essay in *Foreign Affairs*, Abdullah drew the world's attention to the possible solutions to the Kashmir problem, which he implied had the support of 'distinguished leaders of Indian public opinion such as Mr. Rajagopalachari, Mr. Jayaprakash Narayan [JP] and Mr. Shiva Rao':

> This might take the shape of independence for Kashmir, with its defence guaranteed by the United Nations; or of its being made a trusteeship of the United Nations for a period of ten years, at the end of which the question of its accession to India or Pakistan or its remaining independent could be decided by a plebiscite held under United Nations auspices; or of a confederation of India and Pakistan with Kashmir one of its constituent units.[3]

When this article appeared, the time for such solutions was long past, even though Abdullah was still propagating them on his tour of the Middle East and Europe. Indeed, many of the personages he mentions in the essay felt that the views expressed in the article were inadvisable and feared that Abdullah's utterances and other actions abroad would lead to his detention upon his return.[4] Their fears were not unfounded, as police boarded Abdullah's plane as soon as it landed in Delhi early on 8 May, serving him and Afzal Beg with orders under the Defence of India Rules to proceed to Ootacamund and remain within its municipal limits. Two hours later, both men were on a plane to Bangalore.[5]

The press communique issued by the Government of India regarding the men's detention stated that during his travels Abdullah had been 'hobnobbing with India's enemies', China and Pakistan in particular, and seeking their assistance as well as that of countries friendly to India 'for the highly prejudicial act of seeking the independence of Kashmir', thereby 'misusing the freedom permitted to him by the law and the Constitution'. It alleged that 'in the course of his political career, Sheikh Abdullah, "has not shown any genius for loyalty to any leader, his colleagues, or even to any ideology"'.[6] His loyalties once again openly in question, Abdullah was removed from the scene, leaving his followers in Kashmir to fend for themselves.

Visiting Kashmir in late May in the wake of Abdullah's detention, Balraj Puri found its politics in disarray and his followers demoralized and disillusioned. They had already been suffering under government repression when Abdullah left on his travels after issuing a call for the boycott of the newly established state Congress party, and this had only intensified as a result of his activities abroad, especially his meeting with the Chinese premier, Chou En-Lai. Although they recognized Abdullah as the supreme leader, nobody within the ranks of the Plebiscite Front (PF) or the Awami Action Committee (AAC ) defended the boycott or his meeting with the Chinese leader.

As Maulana Masoodi and G.M. Karra attempted to maintain calm in the city at the news of his detention, to them as well as to Puri, Abdullah seemed out of touch with the practicalities of politics on the ground. Their only hope was that JP and others might intervene with the Indian authorities to have his detention cut short.[7] Opposition organizations, including Karra's Political Conference (PC) and the Mirwaiz's AAC, joined hands with the PF to organize a civil disobedience movement to protest Abdullah's detention.[8] G.M. Shah, Abdullah's son-in-law, declared in an article that 'Sheikh Abdullah is Kashmir and Kashmir is Sheikh Abdullah', and, therefore, was the only person capable of resolving the Kashmir situation, for which he needed to be allowed to return to Kashmir.[9]

Pakistan's infiltration into the state in early August 1965 in the hope of fomenting rebellion among the Kashmiri Muslim population, however, put paid to these dreams of an early release and further complicated the position of the opposition. Although the Kashmiri population did not rise up against India to aid the invaders, it nonetheless came under intense suspicion as full-scale hostilities between India and Pakistan intensified. Masoodi and Karra called off the satyagraha and other public meetings scheduled to agitate for Abdullah's release, but the authorities were not impressed by this show of faith and the harassment of political workers continued, even as public hostility against the police and army increased exponentially.[10] The Tashkent Declaration, which formally ended the war in early 1966, did little to ease tensions between the two countries over Kashmir or indeed the situation on the ground in the Valley. Shastri's death in Tashkent soon after the declaration was signed added yet another hurdle to securing Abdullah's release.

Writing in 1969, the American political scientist D.E. Lockwood noted that Kashmiri politics had been radicalized in the wake of the war, with students demanding action and the Mirwaiz encouraging more extremist postures. Moderates within the opposition camp, such as Masoodi and Karra, were being marginalized in the process. This was evident in their reception at a rally at Hazratbal where they were booed off the stage for being Indian proxies. In response, they were forced to take a more definitive stance towards student arrests and police brutality, which, in turn, led to their own arrests. The ruling Pradesh Congress was itself deeply disillusioned at the failure of the policy of liberalization.[11]

As the situation in Kashmir was reaching a nadir, Abdullah was living in isolation in hill stations in the south of India, untouched by the depth of feelings aroused in India and Kashmir following his actions, arrest and then the Indo-Pak war. He was first taken to Ootacamund, but moved to a bungalow in Kodaikanal soon thereafter because he became a tourist attraction in Ooty, with people gathering around him at the mosque on Fridays. At the Kohinoor Bungalow in Kodaikanal, where his wife and youngest daughter, Suraya, lived with him, Abdullah had the chance to be a family man again, spending time cooking elaborate Kashmiri dishes with his wife and taking walks with his wife and daughter within the municipal limits of the town, to which his movements were restricted. Here, too, he was somewhat of a curiosity, held in awe by the local population as they watched this tall rebel from the faraway, exotic place in the north—Kashmir—striding through their town, or saw him at his desk by the window, reading and writing, with a bowl of red Kashmiri apples at his elbow.[12]

In the relative calm of Kodaikanal, he was able to renew his relationship to his wife—who had chosen to live with him even though she was free to live anywhere in the country other than J&K—coming to rely on her increasingly for political advice. This was also the first time that his daughter was able to spend time with him, getting to know him more intimately as a father and getting acquainted with his political views. She recalled that he was loath to waste time, keeping himself busy learning Tamil from a tutor, and even engaged a tutor for her to learn shorthand and typing.[13] Despite leading a regulated life, he got weaker as his blood sugar levels increased, and as they could not be brought under control by the doctors who had been assigned to him, his sense of persecution increased. According to Suraya, he felt that he was being slowly poisoned by the Government of India. This feeling was compounded by the coldly aloof attitude of the representatives of the Indian government who were sent to look him up every other week.[14] The interviewer who spoke at length to him after his release in 1968 remarked that Abdullah was the 'most expensive prisoner of Hindustan'; he was also a 'strange prisoner', who lived in relative comfort and freedom with his family, but was yet not free.[15]

Attempts to orchestrate his release from this 'strange' prison, however, were underway soon after hostilities between India and Pakistan came to an end in September 1965 through the intervention of the USA and USSR. In a meeting with an associate of JP and Vinoba Bhave in October, Abdullah remained defiant, refusing to condemn Pakistan's actions outright, noting that the infiltrators had raised the slogan of Kashmiri self-determination, a point that India refused even to acknowledge, let alone act upon. He stated that he was willing to consider the fullest regional autonomy for Kashmir, since it appeared that de-accession and a referendum would be impossible to carry out.[16]

By the spring and summer of 1966, Abdullah had toned down his rhetoric, sending word to J.J. Singh and JP through his son-in-law, G.M. Shah—who had spent two weeks with him in Kodaikanal—that he was willing to come to an honourable agreement with India, which, if not reached under duress, could be presented to Pakistan jointly by him and Indian representatives. He was still insistent on self-determination, but its meaning had changed quite significantly to any agreement between him and India that was ratified by the Kashmiri people.[17] Undoubtedly, Begum

Abdullah and his son-in-law played a role in impressing on him that time was running out and persuaded him to be more conciliatory towards India, so that he would be allowed back into Kashmir and perhaps even allowed to participate in the upcoming general elections.

Kashmir, meanwhile, continued to simmer under a seemingly calm exterior. J.J. Singh—a once-vociferous proponent of the rights of Indians in the US through the India League of America, now a member of the Indo-Pak reconciliation group—who visited Srinagar in June, wrote to his close friend JP that Kashmir was 'disquietingly quiet', but people bore tremendous resentment against India while pro-Pakistan feelings ran high. It was a 'garland of razors around India's neck', waiting to erupt into bloodshed if no steps were taken to mitigate these feelings. Singh met several prominent individuals, many of whom had pinned their hopes on Abdullah's release, but worried that he would not be able to carry the young, extremist, pro-Pakistan elements with him. These elements had been using him as their own symbol for propaganda purposes and would cease to support him as soon as they realized that he was working on a deal with India.

Mir Qasim, for instance, felt that it would be best if after his release Abdullah talked to leaders in Delhi and then visited Pakistan prior to returning to Kashmir. This would give his deal with India legitimacy in the eyes of Kashmiris and make it easier for them to accept it. Kashmiri Pandits also recognized that Kashmiri Muslim public opinion had turned so anti-India that even Abdullah would not be able to change it and 'deliver the goods'. Chief Minister G.M. Sadiq, not surprisingly, was categorically against Abdullah's release, noting that everyone involved with the PF, including Abdullah, had received funding from Pakistan, a view that was widely held within the government.[18]

Having received several of these communications from Singh, JP wrote directly to Indira Gandhi—by this time chosen by the Congress to lead the party and hence the Indian prime minister—on the matter of Abdullah's release. In this lengthy 23 June 1966 letter, he impressed on her the absolute necessity of resolving the Kashmir situation, which 'has distorted India's image in the world as nothing else has done', and implored her to release Abdullah, the only man capable of helping achieve this goal within the limits of accession. Abdullah, while 'indiscreet', was not a traitor and deserved an opportunity to clear his name of the wild charges that had been made against him. In any case, he argued, keeping Abdullah in prison would not make him change his mind, if that was the objective of the imprisonment. And if he was released because he had changed his mind, then he would have no political utility for India, since he would cease to hold any sway over Kashmiris. Recognizing the core of Abdullah's predicament, he wrote:

> I am sure that on his release Sheikh Saheb would again reiterate the right of the Kashmiris to decide their future; he would again declare that the accession was not final ... We should have the maturity enough to understand that and not to denounce him as a Pakistani agent. He can never hope to persuade the Kashmiris to accept an autonomous position within India if he did not make it clear that it was they and not anybody else who was to take that decision. Instead of that, if he came out and declared that the issue had been settled already when he was in prison ... his voice would carry no more weight than that of Bakshi Saheb did or Sadiq Saheb does.[19]

He then noted that the best way for Abdullah to achieve the goal of allowing the people to decide would be to fight the elections of 1967 on the basis of his agreement with India. But none of this was possible without his unconditional release.[20]

Indira Gandhi, unfortunately, much as she might have liked to take JP's advice, was in no position to do so at that time. She was facing an extraordinary array of challenges when she first took office, including a Mizo rebellion in the Northeast, unrest brought on by food shortages due to the failure of monsoons and a dip in foreign exchange reserves that demanded devaluation. Her own position within the party was not well-established enough to take such an unpopular step, especially when opposition parties were mounting a serious challenge to the Congress in many states. Several friends and advisors strongly cautioned Mrs Gandhi against releasing Abdullah and allowing him to participate in the

1967 elections. Karan Singh, the governor of J&K, argued that when the world found out about Abdullah's willingness to negotiate with India, he would be assassinated by Pakistan upon his release, with the blame being pinned on India. This would enflame the Valley and bring down the prime minister, who was simply not entrenched enough to take the risk. Abdullah's release could be considered once she had established herself and the party in the 1967 elections.[21]

The prime minister did, however, grant JP permission to visit Abdullah in person in Kodaikanal in August 1966. Abdullah, who realized the significance of this visit, assured JP that he was willing to work within the limits of accession as long as there was a guarantee of full autonomy for Kashmir. The meeting, however, caused a furore, with the vernacular media in particular labelling JP 'a meddlesome fool who should better be behind prison bars'. Sadiq led the charge, claiming that the visit would send the wrong signal and give the impression that the government was in talks with Abdullah. On hearing from JP's associate regarding Abdullah's stance, Sadiq remained unconvinced, claiming that Abdullah's words always held a double meaning. JP, who was furious at Sadiq's reaction to his visit, dismissed these claims as 'too ridiculous for words'.[22] In general, the visit did not lead to any significant change, much to the disappointment of the PF, which had placed some hope in its leading to Abdullah's release.

The situation began to shift in the aftermath of the February 1967 general elections, which delivered a victory to the Congress at the national level, albeit with a more slender margin than ever before. Politics in J&K too began to heat up as the Congress performed better there than in other states in the legislative assembly elections, in part because it was the ruling party and because the PF decided to boycott the elections. Some members of the PF, such as Shabir Masoodi, Maulana Masoodi's son, decided to contest the elections regardless and were expelled from the organization as a result. The National Conference (NC) had been revived by Bakshi to challenge the ruling Congress based on taking the state back to the 1947 position—he had even made overtures to Abdullah to forget the past and join hands with the party—but did not perform as well as Bakshi had hoped. The low voter turnout in the Valley—a mere 37 per cent in Srinagar and 51 per cent in Baramulla—further helped the Congress, and also signalled the people's alienation from the political process.[23]

In May 1967, R.K. Patil, JP's associate, met with Afzal Beg, who had been allowed to leave Kodaikanal for medical treatment in Delhi. Beg railed against the Indian government's policies in Kashmir, noting that they had produced vehemently anti-Indian feelings among the people that would be difficult to assuage with any deal. He and Abdullah had been willing to contest the elections, but they had not been released, forcing the PF to boycott the elections. He was prepared to use his influence to persuade Abdullah to come to a settlement with the government, but Indian leaders had to recognize that if Abdullah compromised too much, he would have little influence left with the people and thus no utility for the government. In general, Beg seemed amenable to a settlement within the framework of the Indian constitution.[24]

The seething discontent evident to any observer of Kashmir finally erupted into communal violence in September and October 1967, partly in reaction to a young Pandit girl marrying her Muslim boss. Her parents and Hindu organizations alleged that she had been abducted and forced to convert to Islam to marry the Muslim man. As Hindus clashed with Muslims and the police, Srinagar was placed under curfew, and it appeared that Sadiq's government was losing control of the situation. It was clear that something needed to be done to placate public opinion; the only man who seemed capable of doing so was Abdullah. By late 1967, a large group of MPs, including some from the Congress, had signed a petition advocating for his release.[25]

By this time, Abdullah had been moved from Kodaikanal to a comfortable bungalow on Kotla Lane, Delhi, since the capital provided better access to medical facilities that he required due to his various ailments. Abdullah settled into his new life, maintaining a flourishing garden in which he grew flowers of all kinds as well as Kashmiri leafy vegetables that he liked to cook, while also attending diplomatic parties to which he was invited.[26] Beg occupied the bungalow next door. Beg's son, Mehboob Beg, who visited his father often during this time, noted how close the two men were as they considered Kashmir's options vis-à-vis India. On their long walks, Abdullah expressed deep anxieties about his continued absence from Kashmir and the impact it was having on his standing as a leader. He noted that many Kashmiris who spent winters in Delhi had ceased to visit him. To the younger Beg, Abdullah appeared fatigued by the long struggle and wanted a resolution.[27]

But before Abdullah could be released, the Indian government had to ascertain his views and decide for itself whether he was willing to negotiate with India, as his many supporters had been claiming. This task was deputed to T.N. Kaul, the foreign secretary and a member of Indira Gandhi's inner circle of advisors. The choice of Kaul as the interlocutor made sense—not much younger than Abdullah himself, Kaul was born and educated in the Valley, spoke Kashmiri, had known Abdullah for thirty-six years and was a career diplomat committed to India's interests. He clarified that he was meeting with Abdullah in a personal capacity to exchange views with him as an old friend and not as a representative of the Indian government, and therefore the content of their conversations should not be disclosed to the press.[28] Abdullah agreed, but presented his views as he would have to an Indian official and hoped that they would bear some fruit. These talks, in many ways, laid the foundation for the negotiations between Afzal Beg and G. Parthasarathy that culminated in the 1975 Accord between Abdullah and the Indian government.

Abdullah and Kaul met three times during the course of October and early November 1967 in Kotla Lane. The first meeting was initiated by Kaul and included Abdullah's wife and daughters as well as a few other Indian officials. Kaul tried to sound Abdullah out on what he thought of the contemporary world situation, at which Abdullah expressed concern about the rising power of China. China had allied with Pakistan as a counter to India, while for Pakistan this alliance provided security against India. When Kaul protested that India had no designs on Pakistani territory, Abdullah pointed out that many in Pakistan felt that influential sections within India had not reconciled themselves to the fact of Partition. Eventually, Abdullah began talking about the circumstances of the state's accession to India and subsequent events, providing his perspective on the dismissal of his regime and its aftermath. While cordial, Abdullah was strident in impressing certain points on Kaul, which he clearly wished to be transmitted to the Indian government.[29]

The next meeting was the result of Abdullah's invitation to Kaul, which Kaul accepted after consulting with the home secretary and home minister. This time, they had the opportunity to discuss matters in private for two hours. Abdullah told Kaul that he was not bitter but sorrowful at the Indian government's policies that had allowed the situation in Kashmir to drift almost to the point of no return. He was no miracle worker and could not instantly wipe out anti-India feelings among the population that were the result of India's removal of his regime and decades of political repression. He worried that even if it was possible to go back to the pre-1953 position, the people of Jammu and Ladakh would oppose such a move, and that Article 370 had been eroded to the extent that it meant little to the people of Kashmir. He would be willing to work with the Indian government if it did not treat him as it had done in the past and gave him full trust and confidence. But while he had confidence in the prime minister, he was not sure whether all political parties would be on board, and he needed that assurance before making any kind of deal.[30]

In his comments on the meeting, Kaul noted that Abdullah appeared to be reconciled to 'the idea of [an] autonomous Kashmir within the Indian Union, but with proper guarantees against whittling down the autonomy'. He also warned, 'It will not be easy to deal with him if he resumes leadership of Kashmir again. He will make demands which will not be easy to satisfy ... But it is possible that once he sees the reality of the situation he may become more pragmatic and reasonable.'[31] Kaul felt that it was worthwhile to consider releasing him after further talks which made clear that India would not accept any solution that involved giving away the Valley.

The third and final meeting between Abdullah and Kaul on 30 October was the least cordial, as Abdullah insisted on the point that Pakistan was a party to the dispute and in a stronger position than it had been earlier. Kaul responded that to the contrary, Pakistan was in a much weaker position than before 1965. But Abdullah viewed Pakistan from the perspective of Kashmiris, and from that point of view, the country was a very real player in the issue and becoming more so as Kashmiris grew increasingly disillusioned with India. Abdullah told Kaul that by supporting a series of corrupt and repressive governments in Kashmir, India had created a Frankensteinian monster that would destroy the fabric of Indian secularism.[32]

The conversation grew more heated when Kaul asked Abdullah which Kashmiri organizations to bring into the talks and Abdullah mentioned the PF. When Kaul responded that this was not possible because of what the PF stood for, Abdullah accused the Indian government of acting like the British colonial state in its attitude to the Congress. The PF was not only a representative organization of Kashmiris, but also committed to containing communal elements and maintaining peace, and yet it had been and continued to be persecuted. He wondered how India could agree to negotiate with the Nagas, who had declared war on India, but not the PF, whose only demand was that India live up to its own commitments.[33]

When asked by Kaul at the end of this meeting if they could meet again, Abdullah replied that he had said all there was to say and it was now time for the Indian government to make the next move. Kaul's assessment of Abdullah from these meetings was that 'he was bitter at times but for a man who had been imprisoned for a total of twenty years, he was large-hearted'. He was also insistent that the 'wrongs done since his arrest in 1953 must first be undone' before any further steps could be taken.[34]

Abdullah's notes on the meetings reflect his satisfaction at how vociferously he had presented his views, which remained unchanged since his dismissal and arrest in 1953.[35] He was likely hopeful that given the climate in parliament, which was turning against the Defence of India Rules under which he had been detained, his release might be imminent. When, in January 1968, the prime minister lifted the state of emergency that led to the institution of the Defence of India Rules, Abdullah was unconditionally released from house arrest and was free to travel anywhere in the country.

## THE PERILS OF FREEDOM

'I will not give in to allurements or to any other consideration at the cost of the basic mission of getting for the people of Kashmir a place of honour, dignity and status of freedom,' Abdullah assured a group of Kashmiri students who called on him soon after his release in 1968.[36] This was his most challenging constituency, if it could be called that, since for most Kashmiri youth, Abdullah was not much more than a symbol; their support for him did not run deep. They were more drawn to smaller, militant organizations, such as Al Fatah and the Students and Youth League, that had emerged in the Valley in the mid-1960s. In this meeting, it was almost as though Abdullah was attempting to prove his credentials as a legitimate leader of Kashmiri Muslims: describing his concern for the plight of working-class Kashmiris from an early age, his role in Kashmir's freedom struggle, and his realization that the exploitation of the poor cut across religious and other divides and so the struggle had to include non-Muslims. This latter point, in particular, was significant, because the extremist, pro-Pakistan, mostly young and urban student and professional class that had hijacked Abdullah's image, as P.N. Jalali noted, 'does not sustain itself on the old traditional images of anti-feudal struggle, but looks up to Pakistan as centre of inspiration'.[37]

Abdullah faced a complex political landscape upon his release. While his own views had not changed much since his last release in 1964, politics in India and Pakistan as well as in Kashmir were now very different. Even in 1964, he had to maintain a delicate balance between his role as the foremost leader of Kashmiri Muslims and a leader that India would be willing to negotiate with on an honest basis. The room to be able to strike such a balance had narrowed considerably since then; in particular, his incessant refrain of India and Pakistan coming to terms on Kashmir, which he repeated on his release in 1968, was likely to fall on deaf ears, both in India and across the border in Pakistan. In Kashmir meanwhile, he still had a loyal following in rural areas, but his support base in urban areas—especially among the economically and socially marginalized middle and lower classes, who were increasingly drawn to the Jamaat-i-Islami's idea of an Islamic polity as an alternative to the secular state espoused by Abdullah[38]—was rapidly shrinking.

Abdullah did not return to Kashmir immediately after his release, as he had done in 1964. Instead, he chose to remain in Delhi to lay out his views, meeting President Zakir Husain and visiting the ambassadors of Saudi Arabia, the United Arab Emirates, Turkey and Iraq, hoping that the Government of India would initiate a formal dialogue with him. But he was careful not to give Kashmiris the impression that he was abandoning their demands by making speeches and giving interviews in which he came across as holding steadfast to the principle of self-determination.

He gave his first speech on the day of his release on 2 January, which was Id. After offering Id prayers at the Eidgah, he declared unequivocally that he had not changed his mind after fourteen years of imprisonment. He had made certain promises to the people of Kashmir that he would fulfil at the cost of his own life. He was not prepared to make any deals with the leaders of India or Pakistan that would compromise on those promises. He exhorted the Muslims of India to remain united, not be fearful, consider Hindustan their mulk and not be embarrassed at the formation of Pakistan, because everyone had a hand in its creation. It would be Muslims who would suffer the most in both countries in the event of a conflict between them.[39] In an interview with *The Times of India*, he seemed overly insistent on Indo-Pak reconciliation, noting in response to a question regarding the possibility of an Indira Gandhi–Ayub Khan summit, 'We have to bring them closer. We have to force them to become friends.' Afzal Beg, who was present, chimed in, 'We will order them to love each other.'[40]

Abdullah's statement at a press conference at his bungalow a couple of days later—in which he stood flanked by Beg on one side and J.J. Singh on the other, and which was attended by 250 journalists—declared that his life would continue to be dedicated to amity between India and Pakistan, sovereignty for Kashmiris, and religious tolerance and protection of minorities in India and Kashmir. In response to questions, he made it clear that he felt that a peaceful resolution to the Kashmir issue had become even more imperative after the 1965 war. He also said that even if this made Indians hate him, he believed that Pakistan had a right to exist, be strong and play a role in world affairs. There was dead silence after this statement.[41] Such comments might have endeared him in Kashmir, but in India, they were considered anathema.

As Abdullah continued his round of speeches, interviews and meetings with, among others, Union Home Minister Y.B. Chavan and the prime minister herself, concerns about his position emerged within the Congress, and the Jan Sangh began an outright campaign against him. Abdullah's statements that the Kashmir issue remained unresolved caused particular consternation in the context of his refusal in an interview to declare that he was an Indian citizen. K. Hanumanthaiya, deputy leader of the Congress, stated:

> We feel greatly perturbed that Sheikh Abdullah is again trying to bring the Kashmir issue to the level of an international conflict. All the goodwill that he expresses has actually no foundation in the light of his refusal to admit that he is an Indian citizen. This refusal in particular has made every Indian apprehensive about his intentions.[42]

In general, there was consensus among Congress members that Abdullah should not be allowed to visit Pakistan or another foreign country.[43] Adding to the negative press, the president of the Jan Sangh, Deendayal Upadhyaya, told reporters that the 'Kashmir question could not be solved through his [Sheikh Abdullah's] mediation', because 'he had no authority to speak on behalf of the people of Kashmir',[44] and Indira Gandhi was about to 'repeat the mistakes of her father in giving undue importance to Sheikh Abdullah'.[45]

Undeterred, Abdullah gave a wide-ranging, biographical interview to Aiwan Publications at his home on Kotla Lane, Delhi, for several days in January. The interviewer noted in his introduction to the published interview that when he first laid eyes on Abdullah, he looked like an individual who had spent his entire life fighting the vagaries of life and had taken the world's sorrows on himself. His voice was thunderous, but also filled with innocence. He answered all questions without hesitation, and it was as though fourteen years of imprisonment had left no mark on him. There was pain and sorrow in his eyes, but also truth. His courage and determination remained unshaken. The interviewer also noted that Afzal Beg was often around during their conversations and was so close to Abdullah that 'it was difficult to tell where one person ended and the other began'.[46] For Abdullah (and Beg), this interview was an opportunity to remind Kashmiris of—and tell the rest of India and Pakistan about—the story of his life and accomplishments, thus renewing his image as the most significant leader of Kashmir, and indeed, in some ways, one of the most significant of the subcontinent as a whole.

The interview, which was published in Rawalpindi as a book titled *Sheikh Abdullah: Dost ya Dushman?* (Sheikh Abdullah: Friend or Enemy?), rehearses the events in Abdullah's early life and career first laid out in Bazaz's *Kashmir ka Gandhi* in 1935 and brings the story forward to 1968. Abdullah's answers focused on presenting himself as a warrior and martyr for the cause of justice and freedom. Much like the Prophet Muhammad, whose life lessons he followed, Abdullah had not strayed from the truth despite the persecution he had suffered. The interview presents even the rare glimpse into his personal life and his relationships with his children in terms of his dedication to the quom. His daughter Suraya notes that ever since she could remember, she saw her father struggle for Kashmir and realized early on that he loved the Kashmiri people more than his own children.[47]

The interviewer pointed out to Abdullah that he seemed solely focused on Kashmir and its problems and asked whether he would be willing to extend his leadership to help Indian Muslims. Should they, he continued, form their own political party to protect their interests? Abdullah's response was that Kashmir was his 'special field' and once he had discharged his duty towards Kashmir, he might consider the issues of Indian Muslims, whose problems he was interested in but had not given too much specific thought to. As a result, he did not feel capable of giving them advice, including about forming their own political party. He did think, however, that Indian Muslims needed to 'unite to form a common platform for themselves' rather than being splintered into many groups with different and sometimes competing agendas.[48]

Throughout the interview, Abdullah did not spell out any concrete terms for resolving the dispute over Kashmir. Instead, he reiterated time and again that he was no traitor to India, which he considered his mulk, but India had broken its promises to Kashmiris. Kashmir did not, he said, belong to India or Pakistan because it was not a piece of property that could be divided. It belonged to the people, whose hopes and dreams were tied up with the place. He was a soldier for peace between India and Pakistan, and precisely because he was a friend of India, he could not be an enemy of Pakistan. He categorically stated that he had no intention of becoming chief minister of J&K; all he wanted was the resolution of the Kashmir issue that was amenable to India, Pakistan and Kashmir. The interviewer, duly impressed, ended by noting that Abdullah reminded him of 'a mountain amidst barren lands and frightening caves ... his heart beating with that of the people'. He appealed to the public to learn from Abdullah's life 'so that Gandhi does not have to die again, Bahadur Shah Zafar does not have to be exiled again, Rani of Jhansi does not have to be sacrificed again, and Tipu Sultan does not have to lose his life again'.[49]

Such florid descriptions might have appealed to Pakistani public opinion at the time but did little to convince those in India—who had already labelled Abdullah a traitor—about his patriotic bona fides. But the biggest test was whether publications such as this made any difference to his political stature in Kashmir. Despite what he had been saying in interviews and speeches, the PF was not the only representative organization of Kashmiris. As Jalali noted, there were many political groupings in Kashmir; the pro-Abdullah camp was a heterogeneous collection of these groupings representing different Muslim religious and economic interests that had rallied around him as a leader because he was seen as commanding universal respect and devotion of the people in the Valley. Beyond that, they had little in common and often worked at cross purposes, trying to encroach on each other's turf. The major point of contention among them was whether to declare openly for accession to Pakistan. Abdullah wanted to keep the possibility of a third option open, which is why he maintained a scrupulous balance between India and Pakistan in his public pronouncements.[50]

Political organizations such as the PF, AAC and PC were anticipating Abdullah's return to Kashmir 'with anxiety and scepticism'.[51] Many among the leadership described him as a Zulaikha-like figure, 'vain, temperamental, and ambitious', but with a secular outlook and the only individual capable of leading the people. At the same time, the moderates among them were concerned that if some sort of a resolution was not reached soon, Abdullah would be unable to control the angry and frustrated youth at universities and colleges.[52] Beg attempted to lay the groundwork for his return by making overtures to the Mirwaiz to accept Abdullah's leadership through Bakshi's mediation. Bakshi, as head of the revived NC, had made common cause with Abdullah by this time. Although the Mirwaiz accepted Abdullah as the 'leader of us all', it was clear that his followers were not particularly enamoured of Abdullah. In addition, in Jammu, Balraj Puri and Karan Singh had organized the Autonomy Forum, which was pushing for the autonomy of linguistic units within the state.[53]

Thus, when Abdullah returned to Kashmir in March amidst less than the usual fanfare, he attempted to seize the initiative by making fiery speeches that alleged that India was in forcible occupation of Kashmir and that 'freedom was never given, but taken'.[54] This caused a firestorm in Delhi, where Home Minister Chavan attempted to placate the fury of the MPs in the Lok Sabha regarding these statements, urging 'restraint and caution'. He suggested that Abdullah had to be given time after his release to grapple with the political realities on the ground in Kashmir and India before any conclusions could be drawn about his stand, which, Chavan admitted, had been 'contradictory'.[55] Trying to make sense of Abdullah's ever-changing stance, K.S. Khosla, writing for *The Times of India*, opined that this was his attempt at forging some kind of unity within his camp, which consisted of disparate elements pursuing their own political and economic interests. Within the camp itself, Abdullah seemed to be moving away from the moderating influence of Maulana Masoodi and towards the more extremist posture of Mirza Afzal Beg. Abdullah was building up Beg in his speeches, even as Radio Pakistan was also presenting Beg as a leader of almost equal importance as the Sheikh.[56]

Abdullah was clearly in a bind; his vacillations between being a secularist in India and an Islamist in Kashmir had left all sides unsatisfied. He had to find a way to allow the varied parties in J&K, which had been stifled for two decades, to air their views, and do so in a forum that would be acceptable in India. The best way would be to organize a State People's Convention; as he wrote to JP when requesting him to inaugurate the event, the central problem of Kashmir was its people, who had been the principal victims of the irresolution of the conflict and were as a result becoming increasingly restive and eager to settle the issue. For this reason, he had decided to organize a convention of 'liberal-minded and intellectual citizens' to offer their opinions on the matter.[57] He also invited his erstwhile colleague P.N. Bazaz to co-convene the event.[58] The convention, which took place in October 1968, gave Abdullah the opportunity to preside over the entire gamut of political views within the state of J&K. Even as participants presented their lengthy papers laying out their views on the subject, Abdullah's own speech was carefully neutral, keeping both India and Pakistan in play as parties to the dispute.[59]

The general consensus about the convention was that it was dominated by the pro-India viewpoint, while the extremist secessionists were sidelined.[60] JP's inaugural speech—in which he unequivocally stated that plebiscite was out of the question and Pakistan had no role to play in the dispute that had to be settled between Kashmir and India within the confines of the Indian constitution—set the tone for the rest of the occasion. The reaction at the convention was swift and left Abdullah in an uncomfortable position. He wrote later to JP that he was dismayed that JP could have expressed such opinions at the event. He denied that he had ever supported autonomy within the Indian Union, instead pointing out that Pakistan had to be a party to the dispute since Kashmiris had become so pro-Pakistan. Pakistan's endorsement of the settlement between India and Kashmir was essential for it to be viable.[61]

The convention ended with Abdullah's appointment of a steering committee, composed of Beg, Puri and Bazaz, charged with putting together a report of the viewpoints expressed at the event. In keeping with Puri's views on the subject, the report, presented in February

1969, contained the broad outlines of an internal constitutional set-up for the Indian state of J&K to create a federal character with maximum devolution of power at the Panchayati level. This was meant to ensure that all constituent units were equally represented and no one region felt dominated by the other. The report did not concern itself with Pakistan or its endorsement.[62]

Writing to Abdullah after the conclusion of the convention, B. Shiva Rao suggested that it would be a mistake for the PF to boycott the upcoming bye-elections and Panchayati elections since they provided an opportunity to make the legislature representative and clean up the Kashmir administration. Electoral participation would also put Abdullah in a stronger position to negotiate with the centre when the time came.[63] By early 1969, Abdullah and Beg were considering this as a real possibility, in the hope that it would illustrate their seriousness to India. Abdullah, and in particular Beg, had no illusions about India, but they could see that time was running out and the likelihood of Pakistan being a real player in the negotiations was slim. Such actions did not bode well for Abdullah's support base.

While to Indian leaders Abdullah continued to insist that Pakistan was a party to the dispute, as he had written to JP, his public actions in Kashmir seemed to be veering in the opposite direction. The PF was split on the issue of elections, with many members feeling that participating in elections meant accepting that Kashmir was an inalienable part of India and leaving the Kashmiris on the other side of the border in Pakistan altogether out of the equation.[64] Some of Abdullah's most vehement critics in contemporary Kashmir are the descendants of these PF workers who parted ways with Abdullah at that moment. Munshi Ishaq—who had been with the Kashmir movement since its early days in the 1930s, had grown disillusioned with Abdullah's first regime, but who had rejoined the movement after his arrest and the formation of the PF—expressed his fierce disagreement with this change of policy. He walked out of the PF's meeting in which a resolution was passed to pave the way for participation in the upcoming 1969 elections in J&K as well as the next general elections.

Subsequently, he held a press conference to point out that participating in the elections went against the very constitution of the PF, which stood for a neutral plebiscite in the entire state, and so he urged its followers to join the PC and AAC instead. According to Ishaq, when he called attention to the unconstitutionality of the resolution to Beg, the latter brought out the constitution, and noted that in it, self-determination applied only to the part of Kashmir occupied by India and there was no mention of the other party, Pakistan. Ishaq then went to Abdullah, who ignored his entreaties altogether and asked him to begin preparing voter lists. When he persisted, they began a media campaign against him and expelled him from the organization.[65] Ishaq passed away soon thereafter, recognizing during his last days that years of detention had not changed Abdullah's personality or his response to challenges to his authority.[66]

Even as he alienated his closest colleagues, Abdullah attempted to explain the change in policy to his support base, while ensuring that India understood the risk he was taking and the risks involved in leaving the situation unresolved. The mood in the general council meeting of the PF on 24 May 1969 was tense, and murmurings of dissent arose as Abdullah presented a rather feeble defence stating that he had never been against elections, but instead had wanted them to be free and fair before participating in them. Friends had convinced him that participation itself would lead to freer and fairer elections. He added that a group of angry youth had come to meet with him and had blamed him for the current impasse while threatening to take up the gun in pursuit of the cause. Youth the world over were restive, and if Kashmiri youth began to focus on the situation and take violent steps to resolve it, it would have grave consequences. This, he knew, would resonate in India, where youth unrest was endemic and had turned into a Maoist insurgency in West Bengal.[67]

To compensate for what would appear to Kashmiris as his political backtracking, Abdullah focused his efforts on maintaining the direct support of the people, going door to door to raise funds to rebuild Hazratbal shrine and appealing to them in public gatherings to donate money towards this sacred endeavour. When he was in Srinagar, he would offer prayers at Hazratbal on Fridays and personally collect donations from the thousands of pilgrims and worshippers who gathered there on the holy day. In sharing their meagre earnings, they, in turn, sought the blessings not just of Allah, but also of their beloved saint-leader.[68] The Kashmiri poet Mirza Kamaluddin Shaida penned the following verses in Urdu in praise of Abdullah for his vision for Hazratbal, popularly known as the Dargah Sharif:

> By your tresses, resembling 'The Night'!
> Kashmir has the backing of the Holy Hair.
> I too have been honoured with praising you,
> The star of Shaida's fortune has brightened.
> The one who was honoured with the construction of the dargah,
> God has made the fortune of that lucky man.
> That self-aware man, the son of Kashmir,
> He loves Kashmir and Kashmir loves him.
> Sunk in your love, day in and day out,
> His fate is adorned by serving you.
> An embodiment of the nation's devotion and services,
> Is what the artist has carved out of stone.[69]

But such paeans could not mask the subtle changes that were detectable in Abdullah's stance even when he was outside Kashmir, in Delhi and in other parts of India. At a press conference at the Press Club of India on 15 October, he stated that he was neither anti-India nor anti-Pakistan and believed in Kashmiris' right to self-determination, but that plebiscite was not the only option to ascertain the people's will. 'We are not wedded to one particular solution,' he repeatedly noted during the conference.[70] While he was away in India, both his pro-India and anti-India opponents in Kashmir began to consolidate their positions against him. For the Mirwaiz, this was an opportunity to remind the people that he continued to be committed to a plebiscite while Abdullah cavorted with Indian leaders in Delhi.[71] The pro-India faction within the Pradesh

Congress, jittery at the possibility of the PF fielding candidates in elections and facing their own obsolescence as a result, emphasized certain aspects of Abdullah's speeches in India, particularly his commitment to secularism, with the hope that this would turn the Kashmiri public against him.[72]

Returning to Kashmir from a ten-week tour of India in early 1970, Abdullah defended his stance, noting in public speeches that his mind remained unchanged and the people should not believe the lies being spread by the likes of Sadiq and the Mirwaiz, who were traitors to the mulk. J.N. Sathu, who began his career as a journalist for the *Hamdard* and was now working for the London *Telegraph* from Srinagar, wrote to Bazaz that his own conversations with Muslims revealed growing anti-Sheikh feelings amongst them. Many said that he was undependable, was unable to deliver the goods and should retire; others even felt that he might have made a deal with India already because he had lost the courage and the will to stick to his principles.[73]

Abdullah was well-aware of his waning popularity and knew that the secessionists had to be placated in some way, allowed to express their views so that they felt included. The next State People's Convention, slated for June 1970 at Mujahid Manzil, the centre of the movement since the late 1930s, provided the opportunity to do just this. In fact, Balraj Puri had a falling out with Abdullah over the inclusion in the steering committee of the convention of two pro-Pakistan members rather than the two Muslim members from Jammu whom Puri had recommended. According to Puri, who resigned from the committee over this issue, Abdullah did not want to include the two members from Jammu because these were well-known men in their own regions, one being from Poonch, and he did not want to give them a forum to express their views and gain more prominence. On the other hand, Abdullah wanted to continue to use Pakistan as a bargaining chip, and thus invited the pro-Pakistan leaders into the committee.[74]

The convention received sixty-two proposals in both Urdu and English from within J&K, across the Ceasefire Line and Kashmiris living in the UK. While allowing the secessionists to blow off steam—

particularly the Jamaat, which insisted that the term 'secular-democratic state' be expunged from any potential solution to the Kashmir problem—Abdullah steered a middle course in his own inaugural speech to the convention. He reiterated his commitment to secularism, 'that all people have equal rights irrespective of their faith and religious persuasions, and that everybody should respect the other's feelings'. Despite attempts by the Hindu right-wing at poisoning the atmosphere in Kashmir, the majority community had always respected and protected the rights and lives of minorities in the state, he stated. Recognizing the recent rise of communal violence against Indian Muslims as alarming and casting doubt on Indian secularism, he nevertheless noted that without secularism 'the entire basis on which the political structure of India is built will be completely knocked out'. One had to believe that not all Hindus in India felt the same way towards Muslims as did Hindu right-wing communal organizations and were instead ashamed at the violence, but afraid to speak out. It was thus their responsibility to help Hindus in India to stand up against the atrocities, so as not to leave the field open to individuals such as Madhok, Vajpayee and Golwalkar.[75]

Abdullah also emphasized the importance of Indo-Pakistan amity as critical to the solution, and focused specifically on two proposals at two ends of the spectrum: one that advocated accession to Pakistan and the other a solution within the Indian constitutional set-up. To the proposal that advocated accession to Pakistan, he responded that unequivocal stances such as this could only result in stalemate because it would encourage the state's Hindus to demand accession to India. To the other proposal, by the Jammu journalist Ved Bhasin, that advocated integration with India, he argued at length that India had failed to live up to its promises to the Kashmiri people and their freedom struggle would not be suppressed. But he left unclear how exactly Kashmiri self-determination would be achieved.[76]

It was the Draft Manifesto of the convention that spelled out more concretely what Abdullah and his close circle of advisors at this time—some of whom were members of the steering committee of the convention, including Beg, Bazaz, Ragho Nath Vaishnavi, G.M. Shah,

Ghulam Hassan Khan and Mubarak Shah Naqshbandi—were considering as the ideal solution to the problem of Kashmir. The manifesto reiterated that the situation on both sides of the border needed to be remedied, but the Kashmir issue was so complicated that it would have to be settled in phases. During the transition period before the resolution, people on both sides of the Ceasefire Line should be allowed complete freedom to build democratic institutions by participating in free and fair elections to form representative governments, and enjoy autonomy to run the internal administration of their respective territories. Besides defining the limits of autonomy, the government on this side of the line would pave the way for the implementation of the five-tier constitutional set-up as accepted by the convention. During this period, India would have authority over defence, foreign affairs, and currency and communications. Similar changes would also have to be made on the other side of the line.[77]

During the transition period, the Srinagar–Muzaffarabad road should be thrown open for traffic and trade, with all nationals of J&K being allowed to return to their ancestral homes if they chose to do so. Then in the fullness of time, when good relations had been established between India and Pakistan and the governments on the two sides of the Ceasefire Line had worked together, the legislative assemblies on both sides would meet separately. And through an expression of free will they would take the final decision to end the Ceasefire Line and unite the two parts, thus restoring the state to the August 1947 position. This resurrected state could choose to assume complete sovereignty or enter into treaty relations with India or Pakistan, entrusting defence, foreign policy and communications to one or both. 'This process will obviate the necessity of holding a plebiscite or a referendum,' noted the manifesto. The transition period was to be no more than ten years.[78]

Two points are noteworthy about this manifesto. First, it explicitly endorsed participation in elections and the formation of a democratically elected government in J&K. Second, while it did away with plebiscite as a practicable option, it did envision an independent J&K as the final solution to the problem of Kashmir. In this, it reflected the mindset of the plurality of the convention, which had received the most number of proposals in favour of independence. Needless to say, the latter point was completely unacceptable to India (and as much to Pakistan, despite its official claims to the contrary). Indira Gandhi paid a hasty visit to Kashmir in July, categorically stating in her speech from the Polo Ground in Srinagar that the issue of Kashmir had been settled twenty-three years ago and the people with vested interests who were attempting to reopen it should realize that this was not possible.[79] The issue of a truly representative government in J&K, however, remained. And as it turned out, India was unwilling to concede even this recommendation of the convention manifesto.

## 'HE WILL ROAR BUT CANNOT BITE'

In an interview with the *Rahnuma-E-Deccan* on 11 May 1971, Abdullah clearly came out in support of the Pakistani state against the movement in East Pakistan. By this time, the Pakistani government headed by General Yahya Khan had annulled the results of the 1970 elections—in which the Awami League, the main political party in East Pakistan, had won a majority in the National Assembly—and launched a systematic military attack on East Pakistan to subdue its movement for self-determination. Abdullah noted that even though his heart bled for the East Pakistani people's right to self-determination and he understood their grievances, Yahya Khan had no choice but to follow the course he did to preserve the integrity of Pakistan. He himself had been against Pakistan's creation, but now that it existed, he could not support its dissolution. As far as India was concerned, over the past decades it had not played the role of conciliator between India and Pakistan well enough; besides, it was following the same course in Kashmir as West Pakistan was in East Pakistan and, therefore, had no moral authority to question Pakistan's actions.[80]

By the time he gave this interview, Abdullah was yet again an exile, living in the bungalow on Kotla Lane that he had left two years earlier. The PF had been banned, thus preventing its members from participating in elections. It is no surprise, then, that Abdullah sounded critical of India in the interview. However, his defence of Pakistan can be chalked up to far more than mere bitterness towards India or even hypocrisy, as he was accused of by the Indian press. After his dismissal in 1953, Abdullah had taken the decision to embrace Pakistan as a party to the dispute, in part because Pakistan gave moral and financial support to the Kashmir movement at a time when it had few powerful backers. Equally importantly, it allowed him to stay relevant both in India and in Kashmir. Support for him in Kashmir did not translate into support for India; indeed, through the decades, he had become the centre of the anti-India, pro-Pakistan opposition. And India needed this external threat, he knew well, to negotiate with him on an equal level. But by the end of the year, with India entering the war to support the East Pakistani insurgency led by the Mukti Bahini, and the subsequent defeat of West Pakistani forces and the creation of the sovereign state of Bangladesh, Pakistan could no longer play this role. Abdullah had to rethink the basis of his—and Kashmir's—relationship to India.

Karan Singh, first as governor of J&K and then as an MP from the Udhampur district in Jammu, regularly updated Indira Gandhi on the situation in the state. Now civil aviation and tourism minister in her government, he wrote to her on 23 November 1970, making a strong case against allowing the PF to participate in the upcoming general elections:

> While it has always been our policy to adopt a liberal attitude to political problems in the State, and even permit Sheikh Abdullah and his colleagues to hold a series of conventions in the hope that this may lead to a basic rethinking by them, it is quite a different matter when it comes to actually allowing a party like the Plebiscite Front the opportunity to capture political power.[81]

He noted that the basic ideology of the party remained secessionist—whether that meant accession to Pakistan or independence was immaterial—and it received regular funding from Pakistan. In light of these facts, it would be unwise to legitimize the organization by allowing it into the electoral arena. Once it received permission to contest elections, it would, he argued, step up its organizational and propaganda campaign, with its leaders questioning the finality of the state's accession to India. This would, in turn, communalize the atmosphere in the state and demoralize the Pradesh Congress, which was in disarray in any case. The communalization of the atmosphere would guarantee that the PF would win a considerable number of seats, as would the Jan Sangh in Jammu, leading to a deadlock in the assembly and embarrassment for the Congress in the state and nationally. Singh urged the prime minister to take swift action to address the situation that was developing in the state.[82]

Mrs Gandhi, for her part, was just recovering from a split in the Congress while also battling right-wing forces within her wing of the party, which were against Abdullah and dead set against the resolutions passed at the Kashmir conventions. Meanwhile, the Indian press had stepped up its campaign against Abdullah, presenting the PF as wanting to participate in the elections to wreck the constitution from within. Reports of 'increasing secessionist activities and anti-national propaganda in the interior parts of the Kashmir Valley' began to circulate with more frequency.[83] With the midterm parliamentary polls coming up in March 1971, Mrs Gandhi could not take any chances of, among other things, a decimation of the already weak Congress in J&K.[84] In January 1971, she gave her imprimatur to Abdullah's externment for actions that 'have for some time past been and continue to be prejudicial to the security of the state' and the banning of the PF.[85] He was not allowed to return to Srinagar even to attend the *rukhsati* (sending off) ceremony of his daughter Suraya after her wedding.

Abdullah was livid at the order; he wrote to JP that the 'Kashmir Government, in collusion with the Centre, is sparing no effort to re-enact the sordid drama of 9th Aug, 1953', by attempting, among other things, to link the PF to the 30 January hijacking of the Indian Airlines flight from Srinagar to Jammu. But all their efforts would come to naught.[86] He also issued a strident press statement defending the PF and pointing out that the order banning it was a mere ploy to 'conveniently' remove its 'politically conscious members' from the field of the upcoming elections. Regardless, he had not given up hope of fighting the ruling candidates in the elections.[87]

An equally frustrated Masoodi wrote to Sarabhai that he was increasingly exhausted by events such as those of August 1953 and January 1971 because they obscured the real issue—a lasting solution to the Kashmir problem. Nonetheless, he pointed out the steps that the PF was taking to ensure that the Congress did not win in the upcoming elections. These included running independent candidates close to the PF in key constituencies such as Srinagar.[88] For instance, Abdullah persuaded the journalist Shamim Ahmed Shamim, who had filed papers to run from Anantnag, to run from Srinagar instead to oppose Bakshi. (The Congress had joined hands with Bakshi in the hopes that they could capture Srinagar through him.) Begum Abdullah herself flew to Srinagar from Delhi to campaign for Shamim, officially announcing the PF's support of his candidacy.[89] Interestingly, Shamim ran as an independent candidate on a pro-accession platform, vowing to improve relations between the centre and state by demanding a redress of people's grievances, and won. Nevertheless, the Congress did well in other constituencies, but the exclusion of the PF benefitted parties such as the Jamaat-i-Islami and the Jan Sangh the most, both of which recorded impressive poll results.[90] The Jamaat, for instance, entered into a strategic understanding with the Congress and emerged victorious in five constituencies.[91]

At the national level, the people handed the Congress wing led by Indira Gandhi—which had campaigned on the populist platform of poverty reduction—a landslide victory. JP wrote to her after the elections in March, requesting her to lift the externment order against Abdullah, which would allow him to return to Kashmir. The J&K assembly elections were scheduled for 1972 and this would allow him to participate in them.[92] But by this time, the confrontation between West and East Pakistan was gathering steam, and India was soon involved in the conflict. In December 1971, Pakistan lost its Eastern wing as Bangladesh came into existence with India's help. Not only was Pakistan obviously weakened, Bhutto, the new Pakistani prime minister, did not want Kashmir on the table in the post-war negotiations with India that culminated in the Shimla Agreement. Indira Gandhi, meanwhile, was now stronger than ever, her name synonymous for many with India itself. At this point, the government did not see any point in lifting the ban against the PF or the externment order against Abdullah. Mrs Gandhi could afford to wait for Abdullah to come to her, allowing her to become the leader who had not only cut Pakistan to size, but also brought J&K finally into India's fold while at the same time making the Congress dominant in the state.

It was obvious to Abdullah and his coterie that their room for manoeuvre had shrunk considerably in light of recent events. There was a furious exchange of meetings and letters among Abdullah, Beg, Masoodi, Karra, Bazaz, Puri and Shah in order to figure out how to respond to these external events as well as the internal situation, with Mir Qasim taking over as chief minister after Sadiq's passing in 1971 and the impending assembly elections in J&K.[93] Moderates such as Masoodi were in favour of participating in the elections by fielding independent candidates, while others such as Beg were now for boycotting them to bolster their secessionist credentials. The question of participation was settled when the Kashmir authorities imprisoned Karra and Masoodi and banned Begum Abdullah from entering the state.

As to the larger question of Kashmir's position in the subcontinent, in private, even Beg had come around to accepting accession to India. He and Abdullah had realized, several years prior to the war and its unfavourable outcome, what was evident to most observers and stated clearly by T.N. Kaul to Jalali: that Abdullah was an ageing man while Indira Gandhi was much younger, and if he chose to die as a martyr for the cause, then all the government could do was build him an impressive mausoleum in Srinagar.[94] Mir Qasim, moreover, appeared much more willing to work with Abdullah and encouraged him to enter into negotiations with the centre. Abdullah's own family members, in particular Begum Abdullah, who had been forced to live apart for long stretches of time and at times suffer financial hardships, played no small part in convincing him to bury the hatchet so that he—and they—could live peaceably and comfortably at the end of his life and into the future.[95]

By the spring of 1972, Abdullah had begun to make overtures to the prime minister through the intercession of several individuals, including Karra and Puri. Karra met with the prime minister in May, informing her that Abdullah was a 'changed man', but he could not speak definitively on the subject of accession in public for fear of undermining his authority in Kashmir.[96] Puri reported to Mrs Gandhi on his conversations with Abdullah and Beg, noting that while Abdullah had accepted accession, he did not want to give in on the question of the state's autonomy within India. He also wanted to ensure that the reasons for the erosion of trust between the centre and the state, which were tied to the erosion of its autonomy, were addressed. He no longer appeared to be rigid on the matter of a plebiscite, stating that any broad means of ascertaining the will of the people would be acceptable. Beg also endorsed similar ideas, claiming that any agreement with Abdullah was tantamount to a plebiscite. Abdullah wanted talks to begin at lower levels, with Beg as his representative, and he would get involved once they had progressed further.[97]

Puri's assessment was that Abdullah needed the minimum reassurance that Kashmir's status within India was not a closed question, but before being given that assurance he should be asked to accept the irrevocability of accession and some sort of consensus between the leaders of the three regions of the state on its future. He noted further that many secessionist leaders were also rethinking their stand in light of the changes in the broader political context, but were waiting for Abdullah to provide the lead. The Mirwaiz was more anti-Abdullah than pro-Pakistan, and could be persuaded to support Indian interests if the state was to revert to a pre-1953 status, which would ensure more freedom for Kashmiris, especially Abdullah's opponents. Many younger leaders had joined the Mirwaiz's group because of personal or generational differences with Abdullah and not all were necessarily against India. Both Karra and Shah were angling to increase their own political influence in the set-up that might result from the negotiations with India by isolating Beg and neutralizing Abdullah.[98]

Later in May, Abdullah was invited to the prime minister's residence and the two officially decided to 'forget the past' and begin negotiations to start a new chapter. In practice, this meant that not India but Abdullah had to forget the past, forgive the Indian leadership and come to terms with the centre, all of which he agreed to do. By early June, Beg, Begum Abdullah and Abdullah himself were back in Srinagar. His speech at Hazoori Bagh, in which he deputed Beg to represent him at the talks with the prime minister's representative, G. Parthasarathy, signalled the volte-face on the horizon:

> I met Indira Gandhi ... and we will take steps to find an honourable way of removing our misunderstandings. Some people talk of Pakistan being a party to the issue. I don't know of anybody here who has got a letter of attorney from Pakistan. If Pakistan has the might, it should prove its credentials. I appeal to you not to turn to Pakistan or to China for the solution to your problems. We have to solve them ourselves. This land belongs to us, and only we can decide its future.[99]

So thoroughly had his position undergone a change that these words must have been jarring even to his close supporters, who were somewhat aware of Abdullah's change of heart. No doubt it was the burden of securing his family's future in the context of intimations of his own mortality—after all, he was close to seventy and not in particularly good health—as well as the dismemberment of Pakistan that rendered it a spent force no longer in any position to provide moral and material support to Kashmir, which informed this change of heart.

Kashmiris were further alienated when the negotiations themselves were carried out in complete secrecy, and made no attempt to consider the resolutions and manifestoes of the past two conventions, or to bring on board any other Kashmiri leaders—such as the Mirwaiz—let alone the populace. Many leaders, including Masoodi, themselves refused to participate in the negotiations because they felt that the talks were an elaborate charade, since it was impossible to return to the pre-1953 position.[100] The seeds of the Kashmir insurgency were sown at this very moment.

Abdullah himself was quite aware of this and busied himself with the task of shoring up his legitimacy through two acts: the construction of an elaborate medical institute in his birthplace, Soura, and the rebuilding of Hazratbal shrine. But as the Beg–Parthasarathy talks continued behind the scenes, these acts would not quell the speculation among Kashmiris that he had given up on his principles and decided to join the mainstream. Writing to the prime minister on his visit to Srinagar in June 1974, Karan Singh noted that Abdullah had received him warmly, and while there was excitement at the political changes in the offing, many were feeling 'nervous and frustrated' at what was to come.[101]

As the rumours swirled and his legitimacy continued to slip away, Abdullah hastily organized another State People's Convention in August 1974 to quell the growing allegations that he had capitulated to India and to make a gesture towards including other leaders as well. In his inaugural speech at the headquarters of the NC, Mujahid Manzil, Abdullah told the gathering that he did not know how to convince the Muslim majority of the state that their future, dreams and civilization were safe in India, and that 1953 would not happen again. He had moved on from bitterness against India, but how could he expect Kashmiris to do the same? He appealed for help in finding answers to these questions.[102]

But it was already too little, too late. As Mirwaiz Farooq warned India in an interview in September 1974, 'One person and one party is not the entire valley. The Sheikh is not the sole representative of the people here ... India would do well to gain the confidence of the youth and not to rely on the "old guard" and its leadership.'[103] At the same time, Abdullah's opponents on the other end of the political spectrum from Jammu, such as the Jan Sangh, were equally critical of the talks, demanding that they be called off immediately because any agreement resulting from them would curtail the state's integration with India.[104] The defanged lion was in a precarious political position in late 1974.

## THE BETRAYAL

For many Kashmiris such as Z.G. Muhammad, who was born in 1948, Abdullah was the lodestar of their political education and represented his generation's aspirations of self-determination and freedom. These were shattered when Abdullah agreed to come to terms with the centre. The towering man Muhammad had idolized since childhood—and whose incendiary speeches after his release from prison in 1958 Muhammad had run from home to hear—had submitted to his own sworn enemy. It was the worst kind of betrayal, according to Muhammad, who now spends his time exposing the flaws in the nationalist movement led by Abdullah.[105]

Anwar Ashai (b. 1941), Ghulam Ahmad Ashai's son, had similarly harsh words for Abdullah and the accord, which he called a fraud. Abdullah was a man of no convictions, he believed; his father before him had believed the same and had told his son during his last hours in 1964 that Abdullah was untrustworthy and would sell Kashmir and Kashmiris in the future.[106] Indeed, many of the individuals vehemently against the accord were part of the state bureaucracy, where they had for many years straddled the line between working for India while nursing pro-Pakistani sentiments.[107]

As ever re-inventing himself according to the circumstances, Abdullah hoped that by bringing about change from within the system, he would be able to persuade Kashmiri Muslims that he still had their interests at heart in his new avatar as chief minister of J&K. He had no intention of being compliant with the centre and every intention of asserting the state's autonomy, but this turned out to be a much harder task than even he could have imagined. Just as he had been crushed between India and Pakistan with neither side truly accepting him, now he was caught between the centre and Kashmir as he attempted to straddle the line. By the end of his life, Abdullah was in an uneasy truce with the centre, but at the cost of burning all bridges with his own people.

# 8

# The Final Stand, 1975–1982

SHEIKH ABDULLAH'S POSTHUMOUSLY PUBLISHED AUTOBIOGRAPHY, *Aatish-i-Chinar: Ek Aap Biti*, is dedicated to the 'July 13 martyr, who before his last breath, told the narrator, "We have done our duty; from henceforward it is your responsibility. Tell the quom not to forget its duty."' This is followed by a couplet by Faiz Ahmed Faiz—'*Qatal gahon se chun kar hamare alam / Aur niklenge ushaak ke qafile*' (Collecting the flags from the hands of the martyrs in the battlefield / And with them will march out the caravan of patriots).[1] Narrated by Abdullah in the waning years of his life (1979 to 1982) to M.Y. Taing, his amanuensis, *Aatish* is not just a life narrative, but a political intervention, an attempt to forge a particular image of Abdullah that would make his life synonymous with the life of the Kashmiri nation itself. Abdullah told Taing that the autobiography was to be his last act of service for, and the fulfilment of his final obligation towards, Kashmir and its people, thus reminding them of his role in shaping Kashmir's past, present and future.[2]

This last act of service belied the bitter disappointments and deep regrets of a man who prided himself as a revolutionary and sacrificed many years of his own freedom for Kashmiris' right to self-determination, but in the end compromised it permanently in the process of coming to terms with India. It was thus even more imperative for the life narrative to ensure that his political legacy as a whole—now passed on to his son and residing in the National Conference (NC)—was not judged merely by what many saw as his capitulation at the tail end of his life. He did not want to be remembered as a defanged lion, or indeed as R.K. Laxman's caricature portrayed him—lazily lounging under an apple tree with several half-eaten apples strewn around him.[3]

Ultimately, his decision never sat well with him (or with the centre) and he spent the entire period of his chief minister-ship compensating for it by taking on the centre and the ruling party, the Congress, on a number of fronts. But this was no longer enough to satisfy his Kashmiri political constituency, which was by now fractured and far more radicalized than in years past, its anger fuelled further by the growing corruption and nepotism of his administration. He died a sad, broken man, crushed under the weight of his unfulfilled promises to the Kashmiri people and harbouring serious doubts about his own successor's ability to shepherd the political movement he had founded and launched.

## THE TRANSITION

In his speech to the people on Radio Kashmir on 26 February 1975, the newly installed chief minister of Jammu and Kashmir (J&K) did not mention the accord that he had signed two days prior and that had led him to this point. Instead, he thanked the people for reposing their trust in him again after twenty-one years of trials and tribulations; the power that they had vested in him was a means to an end, which would allow him to achieve the cherished ideals that he had worked for all his life. He could not, he said, stand by and watch his beloved Kashmir go to ruin, steeped as it was in corruption, separation of families across borders, inflation and the unemployment of the educated. The desire to fix these problems had driven him to come back to power to rebuild a New Kashmir. He would also continue to work towards the goal of friendly relations between India and Pakistan, for which he had offered the Indian prime minister his services.[4]

Abdullah fervently hoped that Kashmiris would forget the past and focus on the future so that he was not remembered as a toothless lion. But that was hardly possible; after all, following years of fighting for plebiscite, Abdullah had dismissed it as 'irrelevant' in his speech after signing the accord. He had also re-affirmed his 'shared ideals and common objectives' with India that had made him a signatory to the Indian constitution and led him to consent to the state's accession to the Indian Union, again dismissing the period of his incarceration and falling out with the central government as 'very brief'.[5] Newspapers across the globe, including *The New York Times, The Jerusalem Post, The Guardian* and even the *Hartford Courant* carried the news that India had 're-instated' the Kashmiri leader, who had given up his earlier demands, noting also that the Pakistani prime minister Zulfikar Ali Bhutto had registered Pakistan's protest to the agreement by calling for a general strike by Pakistanis and Kashmiris around the world.[6] As *The Guardian* put it bluntly—giving voice to the way Abdullah's actions were being interpreted within and outside Kashmir—while the loss of the 'Pakistan option' after the Bangladesh war was a significant factor in the Sheikh's decision, 'At 69 the Sheikh no doubt saw this agreement as his last chance of regaining power.'[7]

Abdullah himself would soon realize what Kashmiris already knew—that the accord was merely a working arrangement between him and the centre, the terms of which could be changed by the latter to suit its own interests. He spent the rest of his life attempting to erase the indelible mark the accord had left on his reputation. He had allowed India to dictate the terms, but now he intended to regain his reputation as a warrior for Kashmiris and return Kashmir's honour. Instead, he alienated even his most ardent supporters and grew increasingly estranged from his close friends and colleagues, even as he presided over one of the most corrupt and nepotistic administrations in the history of the state.[8]

The Indira–Sheikh Accord, made public on 24 February 1975, was a far cry from the self-determination, or indeed even autonomy within the Union of India, that Abdullah had promised the people of Kashmir. It merely confirmed the status quo, designating J&K as one of India's constituent units that would 'continue to be governed under Article 370' of the Indian constitution. Since Article 370 had been systematically denuded of its efficacy over the years, leading to the state's effective integration into India, this meant little. The state legislative assembly was given residuary powers to make laws, with the Indian parliament retaining the right to make laws against threats to the integrity of the Indian Union. The state assembly could review the laws that had been applied to J&K after 1953 and decide which ones needed amendments. But no such review took place, and no laws were amended.[9]

Prior to the signing of the accord, the then chief minister, Mir Qasim, graciously agreed to step down as leader of the Pradesh Congress, proposing Abdullah's name instead. The party then unanimously elected Abdullah, hence paving the way for his assumption of the office of chief minister. Abdullah recognized how arbitrary this move would appear to Kashmiris, and in an effort to endow the process with at least a semblance of democratic legitimacy, he had argued that elections to the assembly be held instead. But Indira Gandhi overruled him, assuring him that the Pradesh Congress would allow him to carry out his policies and programmes without obstruction.[10] In reality, many members of the party were not enamoured of Abdullah—who never officially even joined the Congress—and, as he would soon discover, expected him to fall in line with their priorities once he had assumed power. Once again, India—and not just its central leadership but quite as much the opposition—had put its faith in one individual to bring Kashmir and Kashmiris over into its fold.

Once he became chief minister, Abdullah was faced with an array of issues, including an administration that had no concrete agenda or political ideology. As a *Times of India* editorial pointed out, one of the 'ticklish problems' left unresolved by the accord was 'the relationship between the Congress, which has voluntarily handed over power to him, and the Sheikh's followers'.[11] Abdullah himself was neither a member of the Congress nor the Plebiscite Front (PF), the latter being defunct after the accord in any case. Balraj Puri wrote to him in May 1975, noting that the people who were loyal to him were confused as his administration drifted without an organization or direction, and as the two parties continued to exist without any plans of merging.[12] From Abdullah's perspective, as the daily quibbles with the Congress over cabinet positions and other issues became the norm, the question of joining the Congress or merging the PF with it did not arise.

The best way to legitimize his own administration, while also pushing back at the Congress, he felt, was to revive the NC, the party of Kashmiri nationalism. This would also give him the most room to manoeuvre and shape the policies of his administration as well as ensure the preservation of his own legacy by allowing him to choose his successor. He wrote to Beg in May 1975 that it was time to fill the political vacuum created by the dissolution of the PF by reviving 'our bonds with the old values of that name—National Conference—and move forward with renewed determination to achieve our aims and fulfil the dreams which stand documented in "Naya Kashmir" and to which we have dedicated the thirty long years of our movement'.[13] The intervening period, during which Abdullah had taken up cudgels against the NC through the PF, was to be relegated, quite literally, to history's dustbin, as records from this period disappeared from all official historical repositories.[14]

P.N. Bazaz, who was severely disappointed with Abdullah for the way in which he had come to terms with India, pointed out that the dissolution of the PF and the revival of the NC would spell the death knell of the accord. During the 1970 State People's Convention, he noted, Abdullah and Beg tried their utmost to squash the pro-Indian perspective and then suddenly did a political somersault by making a deal with India that even their own supporters could not justify or support. Rather than allow the convention's steering committee to do its job by bringing people around to an acceptable solution, Abdullah, being 'an ambitious man who lacking both patience and tolerance, yearned for some spectacular achievements in the shortest possible time. Cooperative endeavour is not to his liking.'[15] And now, in yet another pendulum swing, Abdullah was reviving the NC when he should have joined the Congress instead and reorganized it from within. This latest move was sure to create an atmosphere of enduring confrontation between the two organizations, he wrote to Abdullah, and was incompatible with the terms of the accord. The revival of the NC would have made sense had the accord achieved complete autonomy for the state within the Indian Union, but given that it accepted J&K as an integral part of India instead, there was no room for the NC as the sole representative political body of the state.[16]

Bazaz was prescient, because the revival of the NC in July 1975 permanently turned the Congress against Abdullah and set the two organizations on a warpath. This is not surprising, given that they had fundamentally opposing views on the interpretation of the post-1953 period in the state, with the Congress refusing to accept the NC's claim that it was a 'dark patch of 23 years'. After all, the Congress was for the complete, albeit gradual, integration of J&K into India, while the NC under Abdullah had always advocated maximum autonomy for the state. The NC's revival also meant that the Congress had the potential to become defunct in J&K, since the NC now represented the secular, democratic forces that the Congress had stood for in the state.[17]

Added to this was the fact that after his offer to the Congress to merge with the NC was rejected, Abdullah began to lure members of the Pradesh Congress into the NC with the hope of achieving the same end in time. Starting with Mir Qasim, he wrote personally to many of them, inviting them to join the resurrected NC:

> I sincerely and affectionately invite you, your other friends, to forget individual differences, personal preferences, past bitterness and imaginary apprehensions, to join the National Conference ... I am confident that the resurrection of the National Conference will restore the great historical continuity which, due to some unpleasant situation, had been snapped for some time, and which produced an ominous vacuum in our political history.[18]

In the run-up to the municipal elections in 1976, several members of the Congress defected to the NC. Besides turning the Congress against Abdullah, these moves did little in the way of rendering the accord any more palatable to Kashmiris.

Meanwhile, organizations such as the Awami Action Committee (AAC) and Jamaat-i-Islami continued to maintain that Abdullah's government was unrepresentative and that the Kashmir issue remained unresolved despite the formalization of the accord.[19] Statements such as the one by Beg in the wake of the revival of the NC, referring to their eighteen years in the PF as '*aawaragardi*' (loafing) did not help matters.[20]

To bring them and their constituents to his side and to marginalize the Congress, Abdullah began courting both organizations as well as the Jan Sangh to enter into poll alliances with the NC with the aim of fielding candidates against the Congress in the municipal elections. This created a space for right-wing extremist parties on the state's political landscape that would have far-reaching consequences.

At that moment, it allowed Abdullah to present himself as standing up to the central government by attacking its puppet—the Pradesh Congress—in the state. In his fiery Id speech in September 1976, he accused the centre of not living up to its promises, pointing out that he could hold himself responsible for commitments made until 1953 and not beyond. He declared that the corrupt Congress should have been dissolved after the revival of the NC and he would never bow his head to the central government. He then defended the appointment of his sons and daughter-in-law to important positions within the administration.[21] He was also defensive about his administration's decision to end the subsidy on rice in 1975, which was going to save the government several crores that could be better directed towards development projects.[22] This subsidy had been put in place after his dismissal in 1953 to provide cheap rice to the people to win them over, and putting an end to it was his way of thumbing his nose at the centre. Asserting his own and the state's independence in yet another way, in January 1977 Abdullah visited the tomb of Yusuf Shah Chak—the last ruler of the Chak dynasty who had been exiled when Kashmir became a part of the Mughal Empire—in Bihar. He hailed Yusuf Shah as the 'last king of independent Kashmir' and erected a commemorative stone in his honour.[23]

Abdullah's bluster against the centre was limited, however, to the politics of the state and did not extend to national politics, since he mostly maintained a studied silence on the Emergency that had been declared by Indira Gandhi in June 1975. He did not want to unnecessarily antagonize the prime minister, even though it was clear to him that the accord had already ceased to be of much importance to her.

For the Pradesh Congress, his actions and words were tantamount to a declaration of war. Some within the party, such as Qasim, were willing to work with Abdullah to iron out differences, but others, such as Mufti Mohammad Sayeed, the president of the party, were completely against him. Matters came to a head after the post-Emergency general elections of March 1977, which led to the victory of the Janata Party over the Congress.[24] According to Abdullah, Indira Gandhi approached him for an NC–Congress alliance prior to the elections, to which he agreed, fielding his wife from the Srinagar constituency. Begum Abdullah won the seat by a thin margin, reflecting the public's sinking opinion of the Abdullahs and the NC. The Pradesh Congress seized this opening to cut Abdullah down to size by withdrawing support from his government, hoping to form its own. Instead, Abdullah called their bluff by blocking the attempts by Mufti Sayeed to form a government and persuaded the governor, L.K. Jha, to dissolve his own government and call fresh elections to the assembly.[25]

In many ways, this is what Abdullah had been waiting for, since it gave him the opportunity to shrug off the Congress's influence and even the constraints of the accord itself. The elections would allow him to reclaim power as the legitimately elected representative of the people of Kashmir rather than an Indian plant. He knew that he had little time left, given his health, to ensure his legacy was not forever tainted by the accord. The election and the administration that came out of it was his final hope to erase this taint.

## THE CAMPAIGN TRAIL

In an article entitled 'Sheikh Sahab Kya Kare?' (What Should Sheikh Sahab Do?), written in the aftermath of the 1977 assembly elections that handed the NC a resounding victory, Shamim Ahmed Shamim noted that even Abdullah's critics had to acknowledge his greatness as not just a political leader, but a symbol and an institution. But he also issued a warning about certain worrying trends that the election results and the campaign that preceded it had revealed, particularly for Abdullah's leadership. Most importantly, he noted that Abdullah had won as a leader of the Muslims of the state, not a state leader, because the NC had won only those areas of Jammu, for instance, where Muslims were in a majority. And even though Abdullah's leadership in the Valley was not in doubt, he had chosen to focus exclusively on issues that appealed to Kashmiri Muslims during the election campaign. Thus, he had emerged not as a leader of all three regions of the state, but rather as leader of the Muslims of the three regions, a less than satisfactory outcome for a man who claimed to be secular and represent the entire state.[26]

Besides inevitably having to deal with the problems emerging from this regional/religious imbalance, Abdullah faced the challenge, Shamim pointed out, of redirecting the energies of the youth that he had fed on slogans of freedom, self-determination and plebiscite during the campaign. It was they who helped him sail to victory, and their desire for freedom would not remain unsatiated. Shamim then advised Abdullah to take the opportunity that the mandate had handed to him to make a real difference in the politics of the state by passing the baton of chief minister to Beg or Shah and assuming the role of elder statesman. He could then more effectively guide the youth to work for the betterment of the state, resolve the divisions that plagued the polity, such as the Sher–Bakra divide, and strengthen non-communal and democratic forces in the state.[27] 'Sheikh Sahab talks,' wrote Shamim, 'of following Gandhian principles, but until now he has acted contrary to them. His way is to seek revenge against his political rivals and blacklist them, and he lures people from other organizations with the temptation of power. These actions are not Gandhian and do not behoove him.'[28]

Shamim was one of several prominent leaders—including Masoodi, Karra and Bazaz—who had once been Abdullah's supporters and colleagues but had chosen to join hands against him in the 1977 elections, so disillusioned were they with Abdullah's leadership and the terms of the accord. This coalition of individuals came from a dizzying variety of political backgrounds and even included the Mirwaiz—who set aside his anti-election stand to campaign for the candidates—united merely by the desire to defeat Abdullah and the NC and expunge both from Kashmiri politics.[29] Bazaz noted that the 1977 elections were fought by parties on issues concerning the electorate, and for once there was a serious challenge to the 'monopolistic leadership of Sheikh Abdullah and his party, National Conference, from secular minded sections most of whom in the valley consisted of Muslims, who had rallied under the banner of [the] Janata Party'.[30]

Masoodi was named head of the ad hoc committee of the J&K Janata Party and several members of the NC and Congress defected to join it. An assessment of the elections in *The Times of India* observed, 'In fact, party loyalty and public postures are very ephemeral in the state. The style has been set by the Sheikh himself. He has the reputation of saying one thing today and another tomorrow.'[31] This was not a Janata wave, as in other parts of the country, but an anti-Abdullah wave. Abdullah had, thus, united Kashmiris with opposing political views as never before.

But he was not one to give up so easily. He realized that the situation was worrisome for himself and his party, and his first move was to reach out to the Janata Party at the centre to form an alliance with them in the state. The national leadership of the Janata Party, most likely at the suggestion of local Kashmiri leaders, instead suggested that a merger of the NC with the party would work better. Abdullah was livid; in an irate letter to the president of the Janata Party, Chandra Shekhar, he demanded to know why, 'if the Janata Party can make alliances with the Akali Dal, the DMK, the CPI (M), and many other regional and national parties', it was insisting on 'winding up the NC and seek[ing] its merger with your party'. He also lambasted the party for holding an ambiguous position on Article 370, pointing out that he had accepted the invitation of Indira Gandhi to turn the deteriorating situation in Kashmir around and assume the office of chief minister 'only on the basis of the position as it existed on 8 August 1953'. Beyond that, it was up to the J&K assembly to decide which laws that applied to the state would continue to be honoured.[32]

Chandra Shekhar did not respond to the letter, and Abdullah reverted to his time-honoured strategy of restoring his sinking popularity by invoking the far more vehement anti-India feelings among the Kashmiri populace. The NC ran a masterful campaign on a pro-Article 370, anti-India and pro-Pakistan platform, with Abdullah making intense speeches that threatened secession from India if Kashmir was not accorded a place of honour within the country. It painted the Janata members as anti-

Muslim, pro-India Jan Sanghis, thereby reviving the decades-old schisms between Sher–Bakra, Hindu–Muslim and Shia–Sunni, since the Bakras, Hindus and Shia supported the Janata coalition. Beg reportedly carried a lump of rock salt (called Pakistani salt in Kashmir) wrapped in a green handkerchief at election rallies, taking it out of his pocket and displaying it to the audience with a flourish as his speech reached a climax.[33]

A vote for the NC candidates was thus presented as a plebiscite—a vote against Hindu India and Indian parties such as the Janata Party and the Congress—to prevent the future mass murder of Muslims. The NC organized bands of young men, drunk on extremist rhetoric, to carry out the campaign and terrorize the opposition and their followers. News reports of clashes between Abdullah's and the Mirwaiz's supporters became rife throughout June. According to one report, 'Small children, young women and elderly people take part in the campaign, attend election meetings and indulge in violence.'[34] As Bazaz pointed out, by June 1977, when the elections were held, anger against Abdullah for signing the accord had subsided to an extent to be replaced by anger against India.[35]

And then Abdullah launched his masterstroke, some would say, that all but guaranteed the NC a victory in the elections—he fell seriously ill. If the Janata candidates spoke out against him, it appeared that they were attacking a dying man. He himself gave taped speeches from his sickbed, leading people to collapse into fits of weeping when they heard his words. As shrines across the Valley echoed with prayers for his recovery, which turned into poll rallies, Prime Minister Morarji Desai felt compelled to express his sympathy. The NC utilized his illness to devastating effect, basically presenting the election as a choice between a dying martyr and pro-India candidates. The NC was Abdullah and Abdullah was the NC, and as a result, when people voted for the NC, they did so for Abdullah, not the candidates themselves. This explains, in part, why the Janata Party, despite fielding stalwarts such as Karra and Masoodi, registered such a poor showing at the polls when compared to the NC, which fielded unknown, unlettered grocers and shopkeepers from many constituencies.[36] It was during this time that Begum Abdullah once again became a visible political presence, standing in for her husband at campaign rallies across the Valley.[37]

Abdullah had saved face—for the moment. His party had won in a landslide and he could claim a popular mandate for his new administration. On the occasion of his seventy-second birthday in December 1977, *Nawa-i-Subuh*, the organ of the NC, published a special 'Sher-i-Kashmir' issue in which Abdullah was presented as history, an era and the quom itself, with his birthday being celebrated as a 'national festival'.[38] But these plaudits obscured the much larger challenges raised by the elections, as Shamim had warned, that grew more insistent as the months passed. There was no question of Abdullah taking a backseat and passing on the baton, which might have allowed him to salvage some part of his reputation in the long run. Instead, he continued as chief minister, becoming embroiled in almost daily battles with the centre, which was more wary of him now that he had come to power on an anti-India platform and the consequent consolidation of the Muslim vote.

## THE END OF THE ROAD

'They have gulped us; do not allow them to digest you,' Abdullah told Ghulam Ahmad, his principal secretary in the last year of his life.[39] Ever since he took office in 1975, Abdullah had been haunted by the idea that he no longer commanded the respect and adulation of the people of Kashmir. He was furious at himself for having compromised with India and was determined to prove to the Kashmiris—and himself—that he still had the capacity to battle with the centre for their rights. But until he came to power on his own merit in 1977, he mostly restrained himself, other than criticizing the Emergency regime for Jayaprakash Narayan's (JP's) arrest in 1975 and the shootings of residents of the Turkman Gate area of Delhi for protesting the demolition of their homes in 1976. After 1977 and until his death in 1982, Abdullah once again became a fiery critic of the centre, specifically in terms of its relationship to J&K, even as he battled within the state itself on multiple fronts. He was fighting a losing battle, not just because Kashmiris remained unconvinced of his sincerity, but also because the late 1970s and 1980s ushered in an era of centralization in India that severely constrained states' autonomy.

In some ways, Abdullah's final administration bore significant similarities to his first administration; in both cases, he came to power through the centre's blessing and subsequently ran afoul of it as he asserted the state's autonomy within an India that he imagined as a federal union. To an extent, his own plummeting popularity within Kashmir drove him in both instances to take this stand. And while he was able to reclaim his revolutionary image as his first regime ended with his dismissal and arrest, even his death that ended his final regime could not dampen the years of accumulated fury felt by Kashmiris against the centre, of which he now became the target. No longer the symbol of Kashmir's freedom, he instead became the embodiment of its enduring humiliation at the hands of India.

Youth in Kashmir were now more riled up than ever before and further isolated from the mainstream of Indian life. They were unlikely to be placated by platitudes such as the one made by Abdullah in the 'Sher-i-Kashmir' issue, calling them the 'real architects of the future' and noting that, 'we have removed the obstacles in front of them and now they have to create the world of their own dreams'.[40] Alongside this, regional tensions were once again on the rise in Jammu as large sections of the population began to feel alienated from Abdullah's administration. Abdullah could sense his legacy hanging in the balance, with much depending on whom he picked as his successor. And that caused unending heartache, because it involved family and close friends. These were knotty problems for even the most robust individual to take on, and when he came back to power in July 1977, Abdullah was a much-diminished man—both physically and mentally due to his illness and the pace of the election campaign. These challenges only hastened his end.

As Ahmad, his principal secretary, wrote later about these years spent working with him, Abdullah had become an insecure man. Haunted as he was by the past and eager as he was to secure his family's future in the politics of the state, he saw conspiracies and threats against him everywhere.[41] He was convinced that the officers within the state bureaucracy held him in disdain for signing the accord with India, which, to an extent, was true. He was not even convinced of the loyalty of his own cabinet members and went so far as to make them swear an oath of loyalty to him. And one of the ways they had to prove this loyalty was by voting against Afzal Beg, his long-time friend and colleague, who had never once wavered in his support of Abdullah for nearly five decades no matter the cost to his own personal life and career. This was a cherished association for Abdullah as well; he had once reportedly said that he and Beg were so close that they should be buried together in one grave.[42]

But now, at the very end of his life, Abdullah was convinced, possibly by his son-in-law G.M. Shah and others who wanted to ensure that Beg did not inherit his mantle, that Beg was working with the centre to dislodge him. According to some, the centre wanted to sow seeds of discord between the two so that they would not insist on the implementation of those sections of the accord that returned Kashmir's autonomy.[43] As a result of a combination of these reasons, Beg, who was serving as the deputy chief minister, was forced to resign from the cabinet and expelled from the NC in September 1978. With Beg gone from his inner circle, Abdullah was left surrounded by sycophants and family members, most of whom had solely their own interests at heart. In photographs accompanying an interview with *The Hindu* in the same month as Beg's dismissal, Abdullah appears visibly aged and grim, the battle scars of his multiple past and present battles inscribed into the lines running across his face.[44]

Beg's statement to the state legislative assembly about his dismissal made public his private feelings about Abdullah and the anguish Beg felt at this betrayal, further damaging Abdullah's image. Beg noted that he had remained loyal to the movement and the organization for forty-seven years, but he had also felt that it was equally important to remain loyal to the movement's symbols. Abdullah was the most significant symbol of the principles and values of the movement, and he had never flinched from standing by him despite his arrogance and his contradictory nature. 'Friends,' he said, 'accused me of being an individual-worshipper, of intellectual backwardness, but I bore it because I felt that my opponents would realize the purity of my friendship.' But his loyalty had been rewarded with dismissal, without being given a chance to defend himself.[45]

Beg was not the only friend and colleague who publicly aired his views on Abdullah at the time. Finally tiring of Abdullah's repeated accusations that he was part of the conspiracy to remove him from office in 1953, Masoodi gave a tell-all interview to Shamim, the English translation of which was published in the 12 July 1978 issue of *The Illustrated Weekly of India* that had Abdullah on its cover. According to Masoodi, Abdullah suffered from 'numerous fixations and obsessions' that had become a part of his personality, which was further given to not caring about others' opinions and wanting his own ideas to be accepted as the gospel truth. Despite not being in agreement with his views on the state's relationship with India, Masoodi had tried his utmost to work towards Abdullah's release in the years after 1953.[46]

The interview was accompanied by an article on Abdullah that charged him with suffering from megalomania, a conspiracy complex and a 'dictator's sense of insecurity', evident most recently in his dismissal of Beg.[47] Shamim kept up a steady anti-Abdullah drumbeat in his weekly journal *Aina*, pointing out Abdullah's penchant for using people and casting them off when it no longer suited his or his progeny's interests. According to Shamim, when Abdullah talked about working for the honour and dignity of the people of Kashmir, he meant his own family.[48]

By 1978, Abdullah had also fallen out with Balraj Puri, who had supported him throughout his incarceration and played a prominent role in easing the way to the accord. Subsequently, he had stood behind Abdullah's decision to revive the NC and become its provincial vice-president from Jammu. He had even contested the 1977 elections from the Jammu constituency on an NC ticket, but had lost to a Jan Sangh candidate. According to Puri, soon after the elections, as the internal power politics among the NC's top leadership—particularly Beg, Shah, Farooq Abdullah and D.D. Thakur (finance and planning minister in Abdullah's cabinet)—heated up, Puri came to be seen as a liability because he was Abdullah's close advisor. They put pressure on Abdullah to dismiss

Puri from the NC on various grounds, including that he would convert the Jammu NC into a unit of the Janata Party because of his relationship with JP.[49] Puri would say later that despite having a rocky relationship with Abdullah when he was in power, he always believed that he 'was a symbol of Kashmiri personality and he represented the entirety of the Kashmiri people, politics, culture, and everything'.[50]

As Abdullah grew more isolated and the same issues that he had grappled with in his previous administration came back to trouble him, he felt cornered and his responses turned increasingly dictatorial. He repressed the protests that erupted in Jammu in December 1978 over the imbalances of resource distribution among the three regions of the state and the corruption, nepotism and favouritism of his administration by passing and then utilizing the draconian Jammu and Kashmir Public Safety Act. This Act has since continued to be used to suppress all forms of protest in Kashmir. Karan Singh made a statement in parliament and wrote to JP, condemning Abdullah for his authoritarian ways, which he felt disqualified him from office. He noted that Abdullah had repudiated the 1968 Gajendragadkar Commission Report, which had offered suggestions for balancing regional tensions in the state. And when the people responded by organizing an all-parties committee to examine the grievances of the people of Jammu and Ladakh, he let loose a 'reign of terror' against everyone involved, including the student protestors and Karan Singh himself.[51]

JP wrote to Abdullah expressing his concern over the situation as matters became more pressing through 1979.[52] Gathering steam were demands for regional autonomy on the one hand and the separation of Jammu from the Valley with its complete integration into India on the other, which was led by none other than Balraj Madhok himself.[53] Soon after its founding in 1980, the Bharatiya Janata Party (BJP) began to issue calls for an abrogation of Article 370, with Ladakh joining in the agitation for complete integration with India.

These demands infuriated Abdullah, but he appointed a commission, headed by S.M. Sikri, to examine and suggest solutions on issues related to regional imbalances. However, this issue was much larger than one commission could resolve; it was rooted in the Kashmiri nationalist movement itself with Abdullah as its leader, whose influence beyond the Valley had always been in question. This was apparent in his first term in office; indeed, his refusal to address this issue was germane to his dismissal in 1953. The regional–communal lines along which the NC had been returned to office in 1977 bore testament to the issue's continuing potency. And, just as it had during his first regime, the issue would cause an enduring rift between the centre and the state during Abdullah's final years in office.

The only solace for Abdullah during these years was the completion and opening of the grand new structure of Hazratbal shrine on the banks of the Dal Lake in 1979. Abdullah's claim to represent Kashmiri sovereignty had long been tied to this sacred space, and now he had successfully had it rebuilt in marble along the lines of the Prophet's mosque in Medina. Even his detractors had to admit then (as do they now) that he had done a great service to Kashmir by seeing through this project. He also applied himself to the development of the Auqaf Trust or Muslim Endowment Board, originally established in 1940, bringing more prominent shrines dotting the Kashmir Valley, such as the Kashmiri mystic Nund Rishi's shrine in Chrar, within its ambit.[54] This allowed the NC to manage and control the properties attached to these shrines and the people who lived and worked in the surrounding regions.

But the goodwill generated by Hazratbal's reopening did not last long. With the victory of the Congress and the return of Indira Gandhi to the office of prime minister in January 1980, the stage was set for the confrontation between the centre and state. Mrs Gandhi was now a battle-hardened politician, determined to impose the centre's writ on the states; with Assam and Punjab heating up, she was not likely to take regional intransigence lightly. For her, this matter went beyond personal loyalty, and so she was willing to take on Abdullah and even play the communal card to maintain Congress control of the state despite the fact that he had supported her candidacy during the 1980 elections. Since it had carte blanche from the centre, the Pradesh Congress stepped up its attacks on Abdullah's regime for its corruption and nepotism. This was not a difficult case to make, since Abdullah had installed his sons and other family members in important positions within the administration.

In many ways, the clash between Indira Gandhi and Sheikh Abdullah was not surprising, since they were quite similar in what would turn out to be the final years of their lives. Mrs Gandhi felt that she embodied the Indian nation and Abdullah saw himself quite as much as the embodiment of the Kashmiri nation. Much like Abdullah, Indira Gandhi too was deeply mistrustful of those around her and surrounded herself with sycophants and family members. Both were equally concerned with naming and establishing their successors within their respective political parties: Mrs Gandhi wanted to ensure that her son Sanjay, and after his death, Rajiv, took over the Congress mantle while Abdullah was torn between his eldest son, Farooq, and son-in-law, G.M. Shah, as potential successors. And through all the wars that they were fighting on multiple fronts, both felt increasingly embattled and isolated.

Abdullah felt beleaguered, not just by the Pradesh Congress's attacks, but also by the increasingly vocal Islamist challenge from parties such as the Jamaat, organizations that he had himself encouraged with the objective of sidelining the Congress. Worryingly for him, along with the wealthy orchard owners who formed the Jamaat's support base in rural areas, the Kashmiri peasantry, disillusioned with the failure of Abdullah's rural poverty alleviation schemes, had also begun to turn towards the organization.[55] The Jamaat itself had grown into a much more powerful organization through the 1970s, opening madrasas, mosques and schools throughout the Valley with the patronage of states such as Saudi Arabia that were keen to spread their influence through petrodollars.[56]

The organization's youth wing, Jamaat-i-Tulba, and another youth organization, the People's League, became thorns in Abdullah's side, whipping up the youth that had been ripened for revolt in part by his own actions and rhetoric. A leader of the People's League, Farooq Rehmani, accused Abdullah of using Kashmir's sacred spaces to catapult himself to power and then separating the concept of self-determination from religion, speaking instead the language of secularism, socialism and nationalism. In the context of the economic and political crises as well as the more strident rhetoric of the Hindu right in India, Kashmiri youth were drawn to these ideas of an Islamist society and polity, resulting in street battles between angry youth and the police. As violence escalated and the Indian Army became involved, even many ordinary Kashmiris began to lean towards the anti-accord forces.[57] Abdullah's response was to lash out at the centre, accusing it of curtailing the states' ability to function independently. In an interview on 31 July 1980 with Aroon Purie, *India Today*'s editor, he asserted the right of the states, in particular J&K, to have more powers within a federal structure:

> Article 370 defines the powers of the states and the centre. There we have a certain independence, we can function independently. In 1947, the country was in a chaotic condition. To preserve the integrity of the country, the army had disintegrated, the civil services had disintegrated, and there was a need for a strong centre that would arrest this. So more powers were given to the centre. After 30 years, the situation is not the same. We now have an organised army, civil service—we can manage. So we can afford to release some powers which the centre does not need, and hand them back to the states. After all, the states are the training ground for the centre. Unless they experience there, they cannot function successfully at the centre. You have to trust and train people in the states, and you cannot do that by controlling everything. Even if you want to sneeze, you have to get the permission of the centre—may I sneeze Sir?[58]

But the attacks against Abdullah continued relentlessly, with the Pradesh Congress creating a 'Red Book' that detailed his and his family's assets, badly tarnishing his reputation. The coup de grâce, according to his principal secretary, Ahmad, was the Income Tax Department raids in April 1981 on the prominent business families of the Valley that had connections to his regime. Abdullah wrote to Indira Gandhi, demanding to know how she expected Kashmir to be emotionally integrated into India in such an atmosphere.[59] But the prime minister was in no mood to conciliate him; she was no Nehru, as was evident from the fact that she visited Jammu in the same month to strengthen the Congress's appeal with the non-Muslim constituency by expressing sympathy with the Hindus for their struggles in a Muslim-majority state.[60] In this way as well Abdullah and Indira Gandhi were alike, neither having any compunctions about playing the communal card when it suited their interests.

This was apparent in Abdullah's refusal to consider the grant of state subject status to Hindu refugees (or their children) who had moved to the state from West Punjab to escape the violence during Partition. According to him, 'If once the gates are opened to outsiders they will buy the whole state and local people will have nothing left.'[61] Karan Singh was irate at this characterization, and was even more so when the NC, with Abdullah's full support, introduced the J&K Resettlement Bill, which granted any Kashmiri state subject who had migrated to Pakistan between 1947 and 1954 the right to return to and resettle in the state.[62] This caused a furore both in the state—further alienating from Abdullah's regime the Hindus and Sikhs in Jammu who had settled on evacuee property—and in the rest of India, where the bill was seen as an opportunity for Pakistani spies and saboteurs to enter India's territory and gain Indian citizenship.[63]

Abdullah felt debilitated—physically and emotionally—from his punishing schedule as chief minister, and the cycle of attacks and counter-attacks that he seemed to have become embroiled in. He felt like he was destined to relive his past time and again, and became convinced that, much like her father, Indira Gandhi was about to dismiss him from office. In a frank note to the prime minister, B.K. Nehru—whom Mrs Gandhi had appointed governor of J&K in February 1981—categorically stated that despite his speeches to the contrary, Abdullah remained the strongest pro-secular force in the Valley. But he was feeling extremely threatened at that moment, convinced that the centre was making plans to remove him, which explained his sometimes 'wild utterances'. B.K. Nehru stated that as long as Abdullah was alive, India had no option but to accept his rule in Kashmir, where no candidate could come to power without his support. The charges against his government of being corrupt were true, but his government was less corrupt than many other state governments across the country that had the centre's support.[64]

The Pradesh Congress's attitude towards Abdullah and his policies was leading to a confrontation between the centre and the state that was 'not advisable', Nehru warned. The prime minister's own actions and words, such as meeting with Pradesh Congress leaders but not Abdullah on her visits to the state, and statements that she could get rid of any government within half an hour if she so chose coupled with the income tax raids in J&K, had hurt Abdullah deeply, adding to his sense of insecurity. The only way to deal with Abdullah, according to Nehru, was for the prime minister to have a frank conversation with him 'without hurting his ego or vanity, both of which he has in abundant measure'. She had to reassure him while getting reassurances in return: These would include not attacking the prime minister; pushing back against secessionist and communal organizations such as Jamaat-i-Islami, the RSS and the BJP; not arousing communal passions; and increasing the number of outsiders in his administration. In return, the prime minister would have to stop attacking him in public and ensure that the regional Congress organization toed the line on this as well.[65]

The prime minister took the governor's advice and visited Kashmir in August 1981 with the express purpose of having this conversation with Abdullah, and it even placated him—for a short while. She reassured him that the Congress would function as a disciplined opposition in the state. She also agreed on a matter that was exercising Abdullah quite as much, if not more: that she would support his son, Farooq, as his successor as long as he supported Rajiv as her successor at the centre. Rajiv Gandhi even went so far as to make a statement that the Pradesh Congress had to learn to stand on its own two feet in the state rather than trying to take on the NC in the streets.[66] The very next day after the meeting, on 21 August 1981, Abdullah made the announcement appointing Farooq the president of the NC at a large gathering in Iqbal Park, Srinagar. In his speech, he presented Farooq as the representative of the younger generation of Kashmir, comparing himself to Motilal Nehru passing the baton on to his son Jawaharlal:

> After 50 years, the time has come when I pass the torch that was given to me by the martyrs of 1931 on to the next generation. I have led the

> boat out of the storm and now want to pass the oars on to the youth. I hope that you will take this boat to its destination. Motilal Nehru passed the presidency of the Congress in 1930 to Jawaharlal, who incidentally happened to be his son. And then the world witnessed the result of the wise Brahman's farsightedness. Today, fate has brought me to the same delicate point. I am handing over the leadership and presidency to Dr. Farooq Abdullah. This crown is full of thorns and I hope that he will succeed in living up to the expectations of his quom.[67]

Tellingly, in his acknowledgment of those who had supported the movement throughout its existence, Abdullah mentioned the martyrs of the 1931 movement, Mahatma Gandhi, Nehru, Azad, Khan Abdul Ghaffar Khan, JP and Mridula Sarabhai, but not a single Kashmiri leader. This speaks to how isolated he was at this time and how much of a family business the NC had become.

In private, Abdullah was plagued by his choice of successor and regretted it, because he did not think Farooq capable of steering the quomi ship.[68] He did not have a particularly close personal relationship with his son, who grew up during the thick of the movement when Abdullah was generally away from home. By the time Farooq was sixteen, his father had been dismissed and imprisoned, remaining under arrest on and off for the next two decades. A medical doctor trained in Jaipur, Farooq had eventually settled in Britain with his British wife and their children, and returned to Srinagar along with them in 1976 to try his hand at politics, most likely at his mother's insistence. But he was unschooled in the ways of politics and reportedly led a hedonistic lifestyle that embarrassed Abdullah and the family.[69] Farooq's children, who visited their grandparents every evening with their parents, remember Abdullah as a stern, distant figure, not particularly interested in anything other than politics. He inspired fear not only in the grandchildren but also in his own adult children.[70] Interestingly, Abdullah's five children barely find mention in his autobiography, since they had been of little importance to his political life. And yet, now one of them was to be his successor.

After his announcement, Abdullah not only regretted his choice, but also ended up alienating his own daughter Khalida in the process, since her husband, G.M. Shah, had long wanted to succeed him as president of the NC. This caused a deep rift in the family, with family members being forced to take sides, while Abdullah felt that neither Farooq nor Shah were worthy successors. Instead, as he told Ahmad, he wanted the working committee of the NC to come together to pick a president who could lead the organization through the stormy times that lay ahead.[71] But Begum Abdullah, who had suffered the most due to her husband's political choices and stood by him nonetheless, was now determined that her son should take on her husband's mantle before his death so that the family's political power remained entrenched.[72] The centre's calculation in supporting Farooq's candidacy was most likely influenced by the views of Mir Qasim; he felt that since Farooq had his father's blessing, he would be more acceptable to the people, and if he failed spectacularly, then he could be replaced by Shah, who had been cultivating the central leadership for some years.[73]

By mid-1982, Abdullah was a shadow of his former self. But he continued to attack the centre; in a speech at Hazratbal at the end of May, he 'drew a grim picture of a north Indian Hindu cabal poised to strip his state of its Muslim character'. Pondering on how his tirades would be countered by Mrs Gandhi, who was facing a host of other issues in the country, *India Today* noted:

> Home Ministry sources discern a disturbing similarity between communal arguments being propagated in both Kashmir and Punjab. Ultimately, the Sheikh has to be handled with kid gloves; everybody who knows him intimately agrees that he is a towering egotist. The tragedy is that he is similar in this and other traits to Mrs Gandhi. These similarities have widened the gulf between them in the last five years. But Kashmir does not deserve pettiness; it needs wisdom and statesmanship.[74]

A heart attack in June brought Abdullah's public bluster to an end. Visiting him two weeks after the episode, Bilquees Taseer, the widow of his one-time friend M.D. Taseer, saw a man whose usually sonorous voice 'rose barely above a whisper', although he remained mentally alert.[75] Abdullah told Balraj Puri, who also visited him during his last days, 'At this stage of my life, I have become lonely,' and beseeched him to forgive him for his past mistakes, especially for dismissing Puri from the NC.[76] Khalida ministered to her father day and night, and his heart ached to watch her because he felt that he had let her down. He had recently asked Shah to step down from the cabinet to pave the way for Farooq after his death. But he had little time or strength left to undo what had already been done. Indira Gandhi, who had flown into Srinagar with Rajiv, Sonia and the grandchildren, met with him a week after his heart attack to affirm Farooq as his successor and to get his pledge that the J&K legislative assembly would vote for her choice for president, Zail Singh.[77]

Abdullah was so weak that even his last will and testament was drafted by those around him, more with the interests of the party in mind than him, and his signature stamp was affixed on it after it had been approved by Farooq and Begum Abdullah.[78] As always when her husband was indisposed or absent, Begum Abdullah stepped into the breach—tirelessly meeting well-wishers, diplomatically mediating between her husband and political figures such as Indira Gandhi, organizing his care, keeping the household running,[79] and advising Farooq on administrative and other affairs to ensure that Sheikh Abdullah's legacy remained intact for him and future generations of Abdullahs. The will and testament read, in part, as follows:

> There will be many phases of disloyalty and dissension when you will miss my presence, but remember that the only way to preserve my memory is to strengthen and join the National Conference. This is the organisation that has provided us with shade, and I have irrigated with my own blood. National Conference's existence is a sign of quomi identification and if you want to maintain your existence and identity, then you have to consistently support it. I am leaving this legacy behind for you and if you want to express your love for me, support the National Conference.[80]

## THE EMBERS OF THE CHINAR

Abdullah's autobiography, *Aatish*, which translates variously into 'fire', 'flame', 'anger', 'passion', derives its title from one of Iqbal's verses that he wrote with Kashmir in mind: '*Jis khak ke zameer mein ho aatish-e-chinar / Mumkin nahi ki sard ho woh khak-e-arjmand*' (The heart of the soil that embodies within itself the fire of the chinar / It is not possible that such bountiful soil will ever turn cold). This is one of three epigraphs to the autobiography, the other two being verses by Kalhana in *Rajatarangini*, 'Kashmir can be conquered by the power of spirit, not by the sword', and by the Kashmiri mystic Nund Rishi, 'I broke my sword and made it into a sickle'.

By the time Abdullah began narrating his life story to Taing in 1979, he was acutely aware that he was no longer the tallest leader of the Kashmiris, as he had been for decades past. The Kashmiri cartoonist Bashir Ahmad Bashir captured the feelings of the people in a series of cartoons in the *Srinagar Times* that poked fun at post-accord Abdullah, but one stood out in particular. In it, Abdullah is striding towards the chair of the chief minister while a grave in the background marked 'Liberation Front' cries out, 'Meri kahani bhoolne wale, tera jahan aabaad rahe' (Oh you, who forget my story, may your world prosper).[81] Thus, for Abdullah, *Aatish* was his final opportunity to exercise some control over the way that his story would be told to posterity and the place that he would occupy in Kashmir's history.

He had already given up on his successor's ability to do justice to his memory, which meant that it was even more crucial that the narrative stand in for his life and legacy. The epigraphs as much as the text itself were meant to remind readers that much like Kashmir, his spirit remained unvanquished until the very end as it continued to smoulder with the fiery embers of resistance against external interference, and the political and economic exploitation of the poor and underprivileged. Equally importantly, that his vision of nationalism and secularism was not incompatible with religious faith: 'It was my firm conviction that a true Muslim could be simultaneously a nationalist. Similarly, a true Hindu could at the same time be a patriot … Mahatma Gandhi, who repeatedly called himself a committed Hindu, was not suspect as a patriot.'[82]

*Aatish* does not provide a satisfactory answer, if one at all, to why the thundering revolutionary of 1931 would stoop to accept the post of chief minister in 1975. And that may be because Abdullah did not dare ask himself that question. Thus, the narrative is in no way self-reflexive, but rather an apologia for Abdullah's actions that descends into a bitter screed against those who betrayed him through his political career—among them Maulana Azad and Rafi Ahmed Kidwai, both of whom he blamed for urging Nehru to dismiss him in 1953. He went so far as to say that Azad and Kidwai had great 'potential' as leaders, 'but neither had a popular base within his community … I guess they did not like the regard and loyalty people showered on me. I believe they were jealous.'[83] For Kashmiri Pandits, he had choice words, addressing them directly in a chapter entitled 'Those Sprightly Sons of Brahmans!':

> Kashmir is a bouquet incomplete without its tulip—Pandits—with their beaming faces and cultured demeanour. But it is necessary that they outgrow their feudal tendency. They should come out of their obsession with government services and stop acting as moles for central leaders … and share the joys and sorrows of their brethren.[84]

These comments reflect his state of mind at the end of his life, furious at those whom he felt had prevented him from fulfilling his promise to the Kashmiri people and embittered with himself for having allowed them to do so. As reviewers of the book noted—some with genuine regret—it read like the last, almost strangled, roar of a caged and muted lion, the once magnificent and defiant Sher-i-Kashmir. To others, his attempts at setting the record straight came across as the musings of an arrogant, opinionated, egotistical and self-righteous man.[85]

Abdullah died a forlorn man on 8 September 1982. His friends and comrades from the generation that dared take on the colonial state, the Dogra state and then the far more powerful Indian state had either died or were permanently alienated from him. Nehru, who had, according to him, made him a 'scapegoat' to appease the Hindu right,[86] but for whom he continued to hold a soft spot, had long since passed away. Abbas died in 1967, leaving behind an unfulfilled dream of a united and free Kashmir, a dream that Abdullah had once shared with him; and Bakshi and Sadiq, by whom Abdullah felt particularly betrayed, passed away in the early 1970s. Beg, his closest companion, never quite recovered from Abdullah's dismissal of him from his cabinet, and died a few months before him; and Bazaz, one of his earliest supporters, who became a fierce detractor, and then a supporter again before becoming disillusioned with him yet again, died a couple of years after him. Finally, Masoodi, towards whom Abdullah nurtured an abiding mistrust, but who continued to fight for him until he joined the Janata coalition against Abdullah in 1977, had withdrawn from politics after these elections. (He would fall to an assassin's bullet in 1999, in large part due to his past association with Abdullah and the NC.)

Abdullah yearned deeply to mend fences with the ones who were still alive during his last days, but the choices he had made between friendship and power could not be undone. Politics had so consumed his life that he had never quite been able to form truly close relationships with anyone, including his own family members. In any case, the events of 1953 had left an indelible mark, making it almost impossible for him to trust anyone. What cut most deeply was that his people, the Kashmiris, for whom he had sacrificed his youth, middle-age, lasting friendships and family life, were deeply disappointed in him. Even his supporters who remembered him fondly many decades later noted that he permanently tarnished his image by coming to terms with India in the way that he did. In a final injury and profound irony, his coffin was draped in the Indian tricolour, even as the people of Kashmir wept and wailed around the body of their once-great leader. The postcolonial nation state had claimed him at last.

# Epilogue
# The Legacy

IT WAS WINTER, USUALLY A QUIET TIME IN THE VALLEY, WHEN PEOPLE huddle around their warm hearths sheltering from the bitter cold outside. But the winter of 1984–5—not unlike the winter of 1963–4, when the Moi-e-Muqqadas agitation erupted—was different. Regal and Palladium, the two famous cinema halls in the heart of downtown Srinagar, abandoned their usual fare of Bollywood films to screen instead the 1981 Hollywood film *Lion of the Desert.* The screenings of this anti-colonial film depicting the resistance organized by the Bedouin leader Omar Mukhtar against the Italian army during the interwar period were met with a rapturous, boisterous reception in Kashmir.[1] For young Kashmiri men, here was a true rebel, a martyr to the cause of Libya's freedom, who had refused to submit to Italian authorities no matter the material inducements offered him and no matter the cost.

And what a contrast he was to the Kashmiris' supposed hero Sheikh Abdullah, who had succumbed to the Indian state and sold out their dreams of dignity and freedom. Could Abdullah not have withstood the lure of power, even if it meant giving up everything, even his life, for the cause? They came out of the movie theaters in droves, shouting pro-aazadi, anti-Abdullah slogans, and tearing down posters and banners of Abdullah in the downtown localities as well as outside the main offices of the National Conference (NC), which they also pelted with stones. Abdullah's legacy was finally being openly repudiated.[2]

The publication of his autobiography, *Aatish-i-Chinar*, a year later in 1986, did little to convince these young men that Abdullah was the icon of freedom that he purported to be or that his organization, the NC, had the intention of fighting for the Kashmiri right to self-determination. Some of these young men would go on to form or join the Muslim United Front (MUF), which ran against the NC in the 1987 elections. But since their victory in these elections was thwarted and they were imprisoned rather than being accepted into the halls of power, they became the leaders of an insurgency against the Indian state instead. In 1990, they burned down Abdullah's multi-storey home in Soura—once the bustling heart of political activity to free Kashmir from autocratic rule—leaving it in gutted ruins.[3] Kashmir had found new saviours to deliver her from the chains of servitude.

As Kashmiris abandoned their former idol and the insurgency gathered force, the Indian state clung ever more firmly to Abdullah's memory as an exemplary Muslim. *Aatish* was awarded the Sahitya Akademi Award for Urdu literature in 1988—the only autobiography to ever win in this category—albeit over protestations in parliament due to what were perceived as its distasteful remarks about Jawaharlal Nehru.[4] And in 1990, the Lok Sabha's Eminent Parliamentarians Monograph Series dedicated its annual volume to Abdullah. Eliding his strained relationship with India through the decades, the seven articles in the volume emphasized his contribution to the Indian freedom movement, his unqualified opposition to the two-nation theory that gave birth to Pakistan, and his staunch defence of the Indian ideal of secularism. They eulogized Abdullah as the indelible link between Kashmir and India at a time when this connection was being openly called into question by the insurgency. As the introductory profile on his life noted:

> His powerful personality provided the much needed balance between divergent regional and communal aspirations within his State on [the] one hand and in harmonising the aspirations of Kashmiri sub-

> nationalism with those of Indian nationalism on the other without damaging his own much acclaimed image of an ardent lover of Kashmir and its distinct identity.[5]

This description homed in on the central unresolved tension of Abdullah's political life, because it was precisely his inability to balance the competing aspirations of regions within Jammu and Kashmir (J&K), or indeed to reconcile Kashmiri with Indian nationalism, that had led to the contemporary impasse between Kashmir and India. But, at the same time, his attempts to resolve this tension connected him to India in ways that ultimately made him a pariah in Kashmir.

As Balraj Puri wrote in February 1984, in Kashmir, Kashmiri regionalist/nationalist, Islamic fundamentalist, Muslim communalist, pro-Pakistan, anti-centre and anti-Congress sentiments combined and overlapped. Abdullah, by the sheer force of his personality and stature, had been successful for the most part in keeping the pro-Pakistan and Islamic extremist elements at bay by bolstering Kashmiri nationalist sentiments that were imbued with anti-centre and anti-Congress rhetoric. His successor, Farooq Abdullah—not nearly as charismatic or politically savvy as his father—was unable to do the same, leading to the consolidation of extremist forces. Moreover, he became a victim of the bitter enmity between the NC and Congress that Abdullah's stint as chief minister of J&K had entrenched in the state's politics.

Indeed, the only reason that Kashmiris voted for the NC in the 1983 legislative assembly elections was to prevent the Congress from taking power in the state. The Congress, now in the opposition, set about attacking the new chief minister (Farooq) at every juncture, utilizing the rift within the NC between Farooq and his brother-in-law G.M. Shah—also a legacy of Abdullah's final days—to join hands with the latter to topple the Farooq government. However ineffectual Farooq was as chief minister, Puri warned, it would be inadvisable for the centre to pressure the governor of J&K, B.K. Nehru, to dismiss his government.[6]

B.K. Nehru himself refused to do so because he recognized that the Congress's machinations, besides being unconstitutional, would only serve to harden Kashmiri attitudes further towards both the Congress and the centre. In his letters to Indira Gandhi, he expressed his concern with Farooq's ability to lead a government, but at the same time, pointed out that he would not be party to the dismissal of an elected chief minister simply because a number of members of the legislative assembly had expressed their discontent with him. He reminded her of what a Kashmiri Muslim bureaucrat had said a year ago of the Abdullah family: the father is senile, the son-in-law is a rogue and the son is a fool. And while the father was now out of the picture, the son and son-in-law still remained and remained unchanged.[7] He was suggesting that it might be easier for the centre to deal with the fool rather than the rogue.

It was clear that Mrs Gandhi felt differently; her response to Mir Qasim's letter of June 1983—in which he condemned the Pradesh Congress's behaviour in the state, such as its attacks on Abdullah and the Indira–Sheikh Accord, and the more recent assaults on Farooq—was dismissive. She noted that the accord was never meant to annihilate the Congress in J&K, and given the rise of divisive and extremist forces, it was imperative that the party continue to function as a significant force in the state.[8] Not surprisingly, she replaced Nehru with Jagmohan Malhotra as the state's governor, since he was far more amenable to do the centre's bidding.

Farooq Abdullah ratcheted up the rhetoric, attacking his opponents for trying to destroy what his father had painstakingly built, and warning that Sheikh Muhammad Abdullah was 'not just the name of a person, but the name of an emotion and a belief that would survive the physical death of the man. He courses through the veins of his people like warm blood'.[9] It was to no avail. In a reprise of August 1953, Jagmohan dismissed Farooq's government in June 1984, hammering it home to Kashmiris that democracy held little meaning in Kashmir. This sentiment was further confirmed when Farooq came back to power a mere two years later through an accord with the centre to form a government in alliance with the ruling Congress party. To Kashmiris, it was clear that the son was not only no different from the father, but was also most likely far worse, since at least the father had fought the centre for decades before reaching a compromise. The subsequent formation of the MUF and the rigging of the following year's assembly elections made the insurgency all but inevitable.

The insurgency rallied around slogans of azaadi, bringing together the two strains within Kashmiri politics, both anti-India, which Sheikh Abdullah knew overlapped but had managed to play against each other throughout his career: the irredentists, those who wanted the state's accession to Pakistan, and the separatists, those who wanted the state to become autonomous. The central driving force of the upsurge, which received broad-based mass support within the Valley, was freedom from India. Anything linked to India—in particular Abdullah and his successors, his ideology of secular nationalism, and his organization the NC—had to be expunged from Kashmir, by force of arms if necessary, in favour of a specifically Islamic identity.

*Kashmiriyat,* Kashmir's tradition of communal harmony and syncretic religious culture that was fashioned under Abdullah's first government, became a dirty word held responsible for bringing Kashmir to this pass by forcing upon it a sub-nationalistic identity acceptable to India. This also has to be placed in the larger context of the demise of the secular consensus and the ascendance of Hindu majoritarianism in the Indian political and electoral contexts as a whole, traceable to the same moment as the start of the insurgency. But at a basic level, the insurgency was a struggle to preserve the state's special (Muslim) identity in the face of concerted attempts by the state and central governments to denude it.

In this sense, the Kashmir insurgency is very much a part of Sheikh Abdullah's legacy, since it was Abdullah who built his entire career around Kashmir's special status within India, promoting himself as its protector. But he cannot be held solely responsible for failing to accomplish this task; in critical instances he was left with little choice by much more powerful entities and events far beyond his control. The manner of the subcontinent's decolonization made it likely that the princely state of J&K, its people and he as their leader would be crushed between India and Pakistan. Resist as he might, Abdullah had to work within the parameters of the two postcolonial states, which were themselves driven by larger strategic concerns shaped by the tumultuous postwar global scenario. And depending on these needs, he was either built up as a hero or torn down as a traitor. He knew that he would never completely satisfy India or Pakistan, because he was not secular enough for one and not Muslim enough for the other; but to his lasting regret, he failed to convince his own people, Kashmiri Muslims, that he was sincere in his efforts to get the best deal for Kashmir given the circumstances.

It did not help that his most visible legacy, the NC, did not inspire much confidence. Once electoral politics was re-instated in the state, like other mainstream regional parties in J&K, the NC found a space for itself between complying with the centre and stoking nationalist and religious sympathies of the Kashmiri Muslim populace. Although in 2009 the people were willing to bring the NC and along with it Abdullah's dynasty back to power as his grandson Omar Abdullah took over as chief minister, the latter's mismanagement of several incidents of excesses by Indian security forces soon soured them again towards the party. The next assembly elections in 2014, with the Hindu right-wing Bharatiya Janata Party (BJP) government already at the centre, clearly divided the state's electorate along regional and religious lines, with the BJP winning a majority in Jammu and the People's Democratic Party (PDP) in the Kashmir Valley. This resulted in a BJP–PDP coalition government that predictably collapsed in 2018 amidst a renewed wave of protests by the generation of Kashmiri youth raised during the insurgency and nurtured on the hatred of Indian troops.[10] The state was once again under the centre's direct rule, with the BJP government finally in a position to cut the state and its people down to size.

What Sheikh Abdullah had fought for his entire political career—a struggle that the insurgency carried forward for three decades, albeit with a less secular tinge—was dismantled on 5 August 2019 by the central government. On that day, the newly re-elected BJP government fulfilled its long-held campaign promise: it announced that Article 370 of the Indian constitution had been abrogated, and to add insult to injury for Kashmiris, J&K had lost its statehood. It had been divided into the two union territories of J&K and Ladakh. Article 35A, which prevented outsiders from buying property and settling in the state, was also nullified. In one fell swoop, Kashmiri fears of legally and symbolically losing the Muslim-majority character of the state had been realized.

For the Hindu right, Abdullah had always been suspect—his secularism never quite convinced them, in part because secularism as an ideology was itself suspect in their eyes. As a result, in this scenario, with the dispute laid to rest and Kashmiris brought to heel, the preservation of Abdullah's memory served no purpose whatsoever for the BJP. In 2020, without much fanfare, the central government removed his birth anniversary from the list of official holidays in the union territory of J&K. In 2022, his image was removed from J&K police medals and replaced by the emblem of the Government of India. Despite Twitter posts by the leaders of the NC in response, such as ones using the hashtag 'ShereKashmirliveson',[11] Abdullah had simply been erased, much like the state that he had devoted his entire adult life to and the constitutional article that had ensured its special status.

Sheikh Abdullah's was a fundamentally twentieth-century life, shaped by the global and regional forces of that turbulent century. He was born and raised at the peripheries of the British Empire in India, his political personality forged in the inequities of the princely state system and burnished in the flames of early twentieth-century anti-colonial nationalisms. Like many Muslims around the colonial world at this time, his political world view was shaped by Islamic universalism alongside a fervent attachment to a regional identity that produced what can be termed a vernacular, particularistic nationalism, with a dash of socialist ideals thrown in. He saw a kindred spirit in Jawaharlal Nehru and his organization the Indian National Congress, which espoused a pluralism and socialism that he found absent from Muhammad Ali Jinnah's two-nation theory that seemed comfortably feudal even as it pitted Hindus and Muslims against each other. But it was more than that: He did not want Kashmir's identity and autonomy, and by extension his own leadership, to be subsumed in the entity that succeeded the British in the subcontinent.

And a federal India made up of semi-autonomous units, rather than Pakistan, offered the best possibility of realizing his aspirations for Kashmir and himself.

Decolonization, accompanied by the partition of British India into India and Pakistan, put paid to these dreams. Deeply disappointed and fearful of what the years ahead held for Kashmir, he weighed the pros and cons of joining both states, but as its future hung in the balance, he was left with no choice than to accept the state's accession to India. This turned out to be a Faustian deal that would haunt him for the rest of his political career. From 1947 onwards, Abdullah became a participant in as well as a victim of the postcolonial state's agenda of integrating and centralizing its diverse territories. Postcolonial India's anxieties about nation, territory and sovereignty expressed themselves most acutely at its frontiers, in this particular case in J&K—a Muslim-majority state integral to its secular identity and security and also claimed by Pakistan—where the fiction of the centre's exercise of unitary sovereignty under a composite Indian nationalism was most apparent. Abdullah, as votary of a fierce regional nationalism, became both the face of these anxieties as well as the sole means of their alleviation.

This dual role captures the fraught nature of centre–state relations as well as the complexities of state politics in postcolonial India. In particular, it illustrates the Indian centre's troubled relationship with and response to identarian and other demands from its restive peripheries, which it has sought to control through a mixture of personalities, governance strategies and economic incentives designed to mollify their populations. This has had the effect not only of creating 'insurgent subjects',[12] but also of recreating the centre–region relationship within the states themselves, with a dominant regional centre imposing its will on its sub-regions.

In many ways, Abdullah is a perfect embodiment of the abject failure of these policies. For it is the continuous cycle of building him up as the symbol of the state's identity and its people's sole representative regardless of his actions towards them, then tearing him down when he failed to toe the line, only to build him up yet again, and finally reinstating him as what the Indian centre thought was its puppet that is directly responsible for the gridlock in Kashmir today. Abdullah himself played no small part in this, leveraging Pakistan against India while calling up the bogey of 'Islam in danger' and the idea of Kashmir's special status to rally his base at critical moments, before finally seemingly compromising with the Indian state. The battle lines that both shaped and were shaped by his political life—between centres and regions, between religion and secularism, between the exploited and the exploiters, and between India and Pakistan—continue to haunt the subcontinent today.

# Acknowledgements

THIS BOOK HAS BEEN LONG IN THE MAKING—A CULMINATION OF nearly three decades of research and writing on the history of the Indian subcontinent—and as a result, the debts I have accumulated along the way are manifold. Foremost, I want to express my eternal gratitude to the people of Jammu and Kashmir, who have encouraged and supported my work in every way and recognized the value of academic writing despite the daily struggles of their own lives. They have given me physical and intellectual sustenance by sharing their songs, stories, histories, ideas, manuscripts and much else besides. Special thanks to Shabir Masoodi, Anwar Ashai, Ghulam Hassan Munshi, Mehboob Beg, Ashraf Beg, Sheikh Showkat Hussain, K.N. Pandita, Qurat-ul-Ain, Javid Ahmad Dar, Mirwaiz Umar Farooq, Z.G. Muhammad, Rajinder Singh Rana, Khalida Shah, Farooq Abdullah, Sheikh Zaffar, Muhammad Yusuf Yattoo, Fayaaz Alam, Noor Ahmad Baba, Ravinder Kaur, Gull Mohammad Wani, Siddiq Wahid, Hakim Ghulam Geelani, M.H. Zaffar, Gulshan Majeed, Peerzada Muhammad Ashraf, Muhammad Yusuf Taing, Om Saraf, Ellora Puri, Karan Singh and Bhushan Bazaz.

The research for the book, which began in earnest in 2014 and continued into 2022, was made possible through two sabbaticals from William & Mary (W&M) and the generous support of a W&M Plumeri Award as well as a Senior Fellowship from the American Institute of Indian Studies. My professional home, the Harrison Ruffin Tyler

Department of History at W&M, funded several research trips through the Harrison Ruffin Tyler Faculty Research Award Endowment, James Pinckney Harrison Chair of History research funds, and Keith Dauer and Sandy Senior-Dauer Research Award Endowment. Research funds from W&M's Class of 1962 Professorship allowed me to complete the last bits of follow-up research for the book. A word of thanks to the staff at the institutions, libraries and archives that I have frequented over the past decade for this project, in particular W&M's history department; the University's Swem Library and its interlibrary loan department; the Nehru Memorial Museum and Library (NMML) and the National Archives of India in Delhi; and the United States National Archives and Records Administration in Maryland. Much gratitude to Rakesh Kapur for his generosity in organizing safe and comfortable places to stay during my numerous research trips to Delhi.

The bulk of this book was written during the simultaneously quiet and noisy isolation imposed by the pandemic, with my young sons milling about in my study, wondering why Mama spent so much time 'writing a book' and why they were not allowed to touch her papers. They have thus lived with this book in more intimate ways than usual and in a sense grown up with it. My husband has been my sounding board since the very inception of the idea of this biography, while my parents and sister cheered me on from afar as travel to see them became impossible.

Ramachandra Guha, the doyen of biographical writing, approached me with the idea of publishing the manuscript in the Indian Lives series and transformed it for the better with his sharp editorial suggestions, while Udayan Mitra at HarperCollins Publishers India and Jaya Chatterjee at Yale University Press ensured the smooth sailing of the book through the publication process. I am particularly grateful for the detailed and insightful comments of the anonymous reviewers at Yale, which pushed me to dive deeper into certain facets of Abdullah's life, and to the copy editing team at HarperCollins, which did a masterful job of editing the book in a timely fashion. Thanks to Saanika Patnaik for her diligent research assistance in sourcing some of the images included in the book. Andrew Whitehead, fellow Kashmir scholar and biographer of Freda

Bedi, was generous with his words of encouragement and in sharing sources, wherever he came across them. Mahesh Rangarajan, as director of the NMML and beyond, was ready with a word of advice whenever needed and offered countless suggestions and ideas.

Finally, the publication of this book is a testament to the support of three exemplary individuals who are no longer with us. Sunil Kumar, scholar, colleague, friend, made Delhi feel like home, and would have been delighted to see my daily research trips through the sweltering heat materialize into this book. Shujaat Bukhari, intrepid journalist from the Valley who always strove to publish the truth, put me in touch with vital contacts, shared his keen insights and kept reminding me of the importance of the project I had undertaken. And my uncle Dr R.K. Zutshi, dedicated physician and avid reader, with whom I had many spirited discussions about politics, life and our family history, and who perhaps more than anyone else believed in my scholarship and wanted to see this book in print. I hope that the book lives up to their faith in the indispensability of impartial scholarship.

**Chitralekha Zutshi**
**Williamsburg, VA**
**August 2023**

# Notes

## Introduction: The Lion of Kashmir

1. See Ghulam Ahmad, *My Years with Sheikh Abdullah: Kashmir, 1971–1987* (Srinagar: Gulshan Books, 2008), pp. 77–8; D.D. Thakur, *My Life: Years at the Bar, Bench and in Kashmir Politics* (Gurgaon: LexisNexis, 2017), pp. 308–09; Mohammad Farooq Rehmani, *Sheikh Abdullah ke Nakush* (Srinagar: Aflaq Publications, 1988), pp. 24–7.
2. Sheikh Muhammad Abdullah, *Aatish-i-Chinar: Ek Aap Biti* (Srinagar: Ali Muhammad and Sons, 1986).
3. Muhammad Maroof Shah, 'Revisiting the Life and the Work', *Greater Kashmir Magazine*, 4 December 2014, http://m.greaterkashmir.com/news/gk-magazine/revisiting-the-life-and-the-work/181699.html, accessed 15 March 2021.
4. P.N. Bazaz, *Kashmir ka Gandhi, yane Batasveer-i-Sawan-i-Hayat Sheikh Muhammad Abdullah* (Srinagar: Kashmir Publishing Company, 1935), p. 155. All translations from Urdu and Kashmiri are mine, unless otherwise noted.
5. R.K. Kak, 'Pandit Kashyap Bandhu: Some Reminiscences', *Vitasta Annual Number* XXXIII (1999–2000): 97.
6. Daniel R. Meister, 'The Biographical Turn and the Case for Historical Biography', *History Compass* 16, 1 (2018): 5.
7. Nyla Ali Khan, ed., *Sheikh Mohammad Abdullah's Reflections on Kashmir* (New York: Palgrave Macmillan, 2018).

8. Sheikh Muhammad Abdullah, *The Blazing Chinar: Autobiography*, translated by Mohammad Amin (Srinagar: Gulshan Books, 2013), p. 22.
9. Sheikh Muhammad Abdullah, *Flames of the Chinar: An Autobiography*, translated and abridged by Khushwant Singh (New Delhi: Viking, 1993).
10. Sardar Ibrahim Khan, *The Kashmir Saga* (Lahore: Ripon Press, 1965); Muhammad Yusuf Saraf, *Kashmiris Fight—For Freedom*, Vol. I, *1819–1946* (Lahore: Ferozsons Ltd, 1977); Vol. II, *1947–1978* (Lahore: Ferozsons Ltd, 1979).
11. Chaudhuri Ghulam Abbas, *Kashmakash* (Lahore: Lahore Urdu Akademi, 1950).
12. See, for instance, Kalim Akhtar, *Sher-i-Kashmir Sheikh Mohammad Abdullah: Tarikh-i-Hurriyat-i-Kashmir ke Aaine Mein* (Lahore: Isteqlal Press, 1963); Sayed Mahmud Azad, *Sher-i-Kashmir Sheikh Mohammad Abdullah: Maazi aur Haal ke Aaine Mein* (Rawalpindi: Zamindar Book Depot, 1964).
13. Examples of recent Urdu biographies include, Aashiq Hussain Bhatt, *Sheikh Muhammad Abdullah: Shaksiyat aur Karname* (Srinagar: Watan Publications, 2009); S. Ghulam Mohammad, *Hayat-i-Sher-i-Kashmir Sheikh Muhammad Abdullah* (Srinagar: Shaheen Book Stall and Publishers, 1988).
14. Ajit Bhattacharjea, *Sheikh Mohammad Abdullah: Tragic Hero of Kashmir* (Delhi: Roli Books, 2008).
15. Altaf Hussain Para, *The Making of Modern Kashmir: Sheikh Abdullah and the Politics of the State* (London & New York: Routledge, 2019).

## 1. First among Equals, 1905–1934

1. Muhammad Yusuf Saraf, *Kashmiris Fight—For Freedom*, Vol. I, *1819–1946* (Lahore: Ferozsons Ltd, 1977), p. 505.
2. P.N. Bazaz, *Kashmir ka Gandhi, yane Batasveer-i-Sawan-i-Hayat Sheikh Muhammad Abdullah* (Srinagar: Kashmir Publishing Company, 1935), pp. 1–2.
3. The Kashmir Province was majority Muslim (about 94 per cent); the Jammu Province, though home to 90 per cent of the state's Hindus, had a sizeable minority of Muslims (about 40 per cent); and Ladakh, though primarily Buddhist, was also home to a minority Shia Muslim population.
4. Sheikh Muhammad Abdullah, *The Blazing Chinar: Autobiography*, translated by Mohammad Amin (Srinagar: Gulshan Books, 2013), pp. 38–9.
5. Abdullah, trans. Amin, *Blazing Chinar*, pp. 40–1.

6. Abdullah, trans. Amin, *Blazing Chinar*, pp. 33–4; C. Bilquees Taseer, *The Kashmir of Sheikh Muhammad Abdullah* (Lahore: Ferozsons Ltd, 1986), pp. 272, 280.
7. Nagin Bazaz, *Ahead of His Times: Prem Nath Bazaz, His Life & Work* (New Delhi: Sterling Publishers, 1983), pp. 19–25.
8. Chaudhuri Ghulam Abbas, *Kashmakash* (Lahore: Lahore Urdu Akademi, 1950), p. 20.
9. Abbas, *Kashmakash*, pp. 34–38; Taseer, *Kashmir of Sheikh Muhammad Abdullah*, p. 180.
10. Interview with Anwar Ashai (Ghulam Ahmad Ashai's son), 24 June 2016, Srinagar, Kashmir.
11. Interview with Shabir Masoodi (Muhammad Sayyed Masoodi's son), 26 May 2015, Srinagar, Kashmir; Taseer, *Kashmir of Sheikh Muhammad Abdullah*, p. 169.
12. Saraf, *Kashmiris Fight*, Vol. I, p. 364.
13. Rajiv Kumar, 'Pandit Kashyap Bandhu: The Karam-Yogi Par Excellence', *Vitasta Annual Number* XXXIII (1999–2000): pp. 9–10.
14. Interview with Ghulam Hassan Munshi (Munshi Ishaq's son), 21 May 2015, Srinagar, Kashmir; Taseer, *Kashmir of Sheikh Muhammad Abdullah*, pp. 240–1.
15. Taseer, *Kashmir of Sheikh Muhammad Abdullah*, pp. 135–40; Hafsa Kanjwal, 'Building a New Kashmir: Bakshi Ghulam Muhammad and the Politics of State-Formation in a Disputed Territory (1953–63)' (University of Michigan: PhD Dissertation, 2017), pp. 25–6.
16. For a longer discussion, see Chitralekha Zutshi, *Languages of Belonging: Islam, Regional Identity, and the Making of Kashmir* (New York: Oxford University Press, 2004), pp. 101–17.
17. Zutshi, *Languages of Belonging*, pp. 197–204.
18. B.P.L Bedi, *Oral Transcript*, No. 270, pp. 27–9 (New Delhi: Nehru Memorial Museum and Library).
19. Bedi, *Oral Transcript*, pp. 24–5; Taseer, *Kashmir of Sheikh Muhammad Abdullah*, pp. 229–30; Abdullah, trans. Amin, *Blazing Chinar*, p. 47.
20. Bazaz, *Kashmir ka Gandhi*, p. 5; Abdullah, trans. Amin, *Blazing Chinar*, p. 44.
21. Bazaz, *Kashmir ka Gandhi*, p. 7; Abdullah, trans. Amin, *Blazing Chinar*, pp. 45-6.
22. Abdullah, trans. Amin, *Blazing Chinar*, p. 47; Taseer, *Kashmir of Sheikh Muhammad Abdullah*, p. 312.

23. Taseer, *Kashmir of Sheikh Muhammad Abdullah*, pp. 286–7.
24. Interview with Sheikh Showkat Hussain, 30 October 2014, Srinagar, Kashmir.
25. Bazaz, *Kashmir ka Gandhi*, pp. 12–13; Abdullah, trans. Amin, *Blazing Chinar*, p. 48.
26. Abdullah, trans. Amin, *Blazing Chinar*, pp. 49–50.
27. The Majlis-e-Ahrar, or Ahrar for short, was a political organization of Khilafatist Muslims founded in Lahore in 1929; its membership was drawn from a cross section of educated lower to middle classes and men of commerce and religion who espoused an anti-imperialist, pro-Indian nationalist ideology. It became active in J&K's politics in the early 1930s. In this, the party came into conflict with the Ahmadi movement, which began as a small-town, middle-class religious resurgence in 1889, whose founder, Mirza Ghulam Ahmad, claimed to be the *mahdi* (messiah). Ahmadis had begun to speak on behalf of Kashmiri Muslims long before the Ahrars entered the scene. For details on the origins and ideologies of the two sects, see Ayesha Jalal, *Self and Sovereignty: Individual and Community in South Asian Islam since 1850* (New York: Routledge, 2000), chapter 6.
28. Interview with Anwar Ashai, 24 June 2016; Interview with Shabir Masoodi, 26 May 2015.
29. Taseer, *Kashmir of Sheikh Muhammad Abdullah*, pp. 240–1; Bazaz, *Kashmir ka Gandhi*, p. 19; Interview with Ghulam Hassan Munshi, 21 May 2015.
30. Interview with Anwar Ashai, 24 June 2016.
31. Saraf, *Kashmiris Fight*, Vol. I, pp. 356–7.
32. Bazaz, *Kashmir ka Gandhi*, pp. 22–3.
33. Abdullah, trans. Amin, *Blazing Chinar*, pp. 64–5.
34. N.N. Raina, *Oral Transcript*, No. 580, Vol. I, p. 67 (New Delhi: Nehru Memorial Museum and Library).
35. Bazaz, *Kashmir ka Gandhi*, p. 31.
36. Saraf, *Kashmiris Fight*, Vol. I, pp. 359–60.
37. Saraf, *Kashmiris Fight*, Vol. I, p. 361.
38. For a more detailed discussion of these events, see Zutshi, *Languages of Belonging*, pp. 211–6.
39. Bazaz, *Kashmir ka Gandhi*, pp. 38–9.
40. Saraf, *Kashmiris Fight*, Vol. I, p. 368.
41. Abdullah, trans. Amin, *Blazing Chinar*, p. 75.

42. Bazaz, *Kashmir ka Gandhi*, pp. 45–6.
43. Bazaz, *Kashmir ka Gandhi*, pp. 49–53.
44. Saraf, *Kashmiris Fight*, Vol. I, p. 391.
45. Saraf, *Kashmiris Fight*, Vol. I, p. 392.
46. Interview with K.N. Pandita, 19 November 2014, Jammu City, Jammu.
47. Bazaz, *Kashmir ka Gandhi*, pp. 152–4.
48. Abdullah, trans. Amin, *Blazing Chinar*, p. 107.
49. Abdullah, trans. Amin, *Blazing Chinar*, p. 93.
50. Taseer, *Kashmir of Sheikh Muhammad Abdullah*, p. 240.
51. 'Telegram from the Resident in Kashmir', 11 November 1931, Crown Representative Papers of India, Foreign and Political Department R/1/29/823, p. 7, India Office Records (London: British Library).
52. Saraf, *Kashmiris Fight*, Vol. I, pp. 454–65.
53. Abbas, *Kashmakash*, p. 108.
54. Sheikh Muhammad Abdullah, 'Some instances of Muslims receiving Discriminative Treatment', 13 January 1932, Political Department 23/22/PL/1932, Government of Jammu & Kashmir (Jammu: Jammu State Archives).
55. Abdullah, 'Some instances'.
56. Abbas, *Kashmakash*, pp. 126–7.
57. B.J. Glancy, *Report of the Commission Appointed under the Order of His Highness, the Maharaja Bahadur dated 12th November 1931 to Enquire into Grievances and Complaints* (Jammu: Ranbir Government Press, 1933), pp. vi–vii.
58. 'Representation of Sanatan Dharma Youngmen's Association to Prime Minister', 2 May 1932, Crown Representative Papers of India, Foreign and Political Department R/1/29/886, p. 21, India Office Records (London: British Library).
59. R.K. Kak, 'Pandit Kashyap Bandhu: Some Reminiscences', *Vitasta Annual Number* XXXIII (1999–2000): 97.
60. Saraf, *Kashmiris Fight*, Vol. I, pp. 392–3.
61. Babu Fakirullah Khan Sahab, *Safinaye Nooh, almaroof Sach Aawaaz* (Amritsar: Ahmadiyya Press, 1932).
62. *Mousiki Kashmiri ka Nava Hissa* (Lahore: Inqilab Steam Press, 1932), pp. 4–5.
63. *Mousiki Kashmiri ka Dassva Hissa* (Lahore: Inqilab Steam Press, 1933), p. 2.

64. Chief Secretariat, Political Dept. 139/PS–51/1932, Government of Jammu & Kashmir (Jammu: Jammu State Archives).
65. Abdullah, trans. Amin, *Blazing Chinar*, p. 69.
66. Raina, *Oral Transcript*, Vol. I, p. 59; Vol. II, p. 382.
67. For a longer discussion of the historical underpinnings of this schism, see Chitralekha Zutshi, 'Contesting Urban Space: Shrine Culture and the Discourse on Kashmiri Muslim Identities and Protest in the Late Nineteenth and Early Twentieth Centuries', in *Kashmir: History, Politics, Representation*, edited by Chitralekha Zutshi (New Delhi: Cambridge University Press, 2018), pp. 51–69.
68. Interview with Shabir Masoodi, 26 May 2015; Saraf, *Kashmiris Fight*, Vol. I, p. 482.
69. 'Welcome Change in Affairs in Kashmir: S.M. Abdullah's View', *The Civil & Military Gazette*, Lahore, 9 July 1932, Political Department 83/1931 (Jammu: Jammu State Archives).
70. 'Presidential Address by Sheikh Mohammad Abdullah at First Session of All Jammu and Kashmir Muslim Conference', 15–17 October 1932, Srinagar, in *The Political Struggle of Kashmiri Muslims, 1931–1939: Selected Documents*, edited by Mirza Shafiq Hussain (Srinagar: Gulshan Publishers, 1991), pp. 219–29.
71. Raina, *Oral Transcript*, Vol. II, pp. 446–7.
72. Saraf, *Kashmiris Fight*, Vol. I, p. 491; Interview with Mirwaiz Umar Farooq, 21 May 2015, Srinagar, Kashmir.
73. Raina, *Oral Transcript*, Vol. I, p. 58.
74. Abbas, *Kashmakash*, p. 150.
75. Mir Qasim, *My Life and Times* (New Delhi: Allied Publishers, 1992), pp. 9–10.
76. Raina, *Oral Transcript*, Vol. I, pp. 197–200.
77. Taseer, *Kashmir of Sheikh Muhammad Abdullah*, p. 245; Saraf, *Kashmiris Fight*, Vol. I, pp. 494–5; Abdullah, trans. Amin, *Blazing Chinar*, pp. 145–7.
78. Abdullah, trans. Amin, *Blazing Chinar*, p. 147.
79. 'Presidential Address by Mirwaiz Mohammad Yusuf at First Session of Jammu and Kashmir Azad Party Conference', 3 December 1933, Srinagar, in *The Political Struggle*, ed. Hussain, p. 265.
80. General Department 132/P–18/1932, Government of Jammu & Kashmir (Jammu: Jammu State Archives).
81. Abdullah, trans. Amin, *Blazing Chinar*, pp. 313–4.

82. R.G. Wreford, *Census of India, 1941,* Vol. XXII, *Jammu and Kashmir* (Jammu: Ranbir Government Press, 1943), p. 5.
83. Saraf, *Kashmiris Fight,* Vol. I, pp. 497–9.
84. Abbas, *Kashmakash,* pp. 153–4.
85. Abbas, *Kashmakash,* pp. 155–6.
86. Abdullah, trans. Amin, *Blazing Chinar,* p. 197.
87. Kashyap Bandhu, 'A Kashmiri Leader', *Vitasta Annual Number* XXXIII (1999–2000): p. 60.

## 2. Defining the Leader and the Movement, 1935–1946

1. P.N. Bazaz, *Kashmir ka Gandhi, yane Batasveer-i-Sawan-i-Hayat Sheikh Muhammad Abdullah* (Srinagar: Kashmir Publishing Company, 1935).
2. Mulk Raj Saraf, *Fifty Years as a Journalist* (Jammu: Raj Mahal Publishers, 1967), pp. 157–8.
3. Bazaz to Gandhi, 8 May 1934; Gandhi to Bazaz, 15 May 1934, *Hamdard,* 29 August 1936: 1–3.
4. Nagin Bazaz, *Ahead of His Times: Prem Nath Bazaz, His Life & Work* (New Delhi: Sterling Publishers, 1983), pp. 50–1.
5. Bazaz, *Kashmir ka Gandhi,* pp. sheen, swad, to.
6. Bazaz, *Kashmir ka Gandhi,* p. 18.
7. Bazaz, *Kashmir ka Gandhi,* p. 113.
8. Bazaz, *Kashmir ka Gandhi,* pp. 130–1.
9. Bazaz, *Kashmir ka Gandhi,* p. 141.
10. Bazaz, *Kashmir ka Gandhi,* p. 161.
11. Nehru to Bazaz, 8 July 1936, *Hamdard,* 29 August 1936: 4–5.
12. Jawaharlal Nehru, 'Advice to the Youth of Kashmir', *Hamdard,* 27 June 1936.
13. Ghulam Muhammad Basati and Ghulam Rasool, 'Kya Deen-i-Islam Mazhabi Dhakosla Hai?', 1937 (New Delhi: Bhushan Bazaz Private Collection).
14. Sheikh Muhammad Abdullah, 'Statement to the Press', 1937 (New Delhi: Bhushan Bazaz Private Collection).
15. Sheikh Muhammad Abdullah, *The Blazing Chinar: Autobiography,* translated by Mohammad Amin (Srinagar: Gulshan Books, 2013), pp. 166–7; N.N. Raina, *Oral Transcript,* Vol. I, No. 580, pp. 73–4 (New Delhi: Nehru Memorial Museum and Library).

16. Abdullah, trans. Amin, *Blazing Chinar*, pp. 167–8.
17. Raina, *Oral Transcript*, Vol. I, pp. 73–4.
18. Chaudhuri Ghulam Abbas, *Kashmakash* (Lahore: Lahore Urdu Akademi, 1950), pp. 189–90.
19. Abbas, *Kashmakash*, pp. 196–7. Hindus made up about 6 per cent of the population of the Valley, while in Jammu they constituted nearly 50 per cent of the population.
20. Abdullah, trans. Amin, *Blazing Chinar*, p. 191.
21. Muhammad Yusuf Saraf, *Kashmiris Fight—For Freedom*, Vol. I, *1819–1946* (Lahore: Ferozsons Ltd, 1977), pp. 528–9.
22. Sheikh Muhammad Abdullah, 'Statement to the Press', 16 June 1938 (New Delhi: Bhushan Bazaz Private Collection).
23. Meem, 'Kashmir Mein Zimmedar Nizam-e-Hukumat ki Zarurat', *Hamdard*, 31 July 1938: 55.
24. *Hamdard*, 31 July 1938: 6.
25. *Hamdard*, 3 April 1938: 9.
26. C. Bilquees Taseer, *The Kashmir of Sheikh Muhammad Abdullah* (Lahore: Ferozsons Ltd, 1986), pp. 23–6, 258; Andrew Whitehead, 'The People's Militia: Communists and Kashmiri Nationalism in the 1940s', in *Partition: The Long Shadow*, edited by Urvashi Butalia (New Delhi: Zubaan, 2015), pp. 134–7.
27. 'Notice', Secretary, Kashmir Mazdoor Sabha, 14 September 1937 (New Delhi: Bhushan Bazaz Private Collection).
28. P.N. Jalali, *Oral Transcript*, No. 834 (New Delhi: Nehru Memorial Museum and Library); Balraj Puri, *Oral Transcript*, 2 Vols, No. 818 (New Delhi: Nehru Memorial Museum and Library).
29. Raina, *Oral Transcript*, Vol. I, pp. 64–5, 174–6, 382–3.
30. 'Memorandum of Silk Workers to Legislative Assembly', 1937 (New Delhi: Bhushan Bazaz Private Collection); *Hamdard*, 10 July 1938: 11.
31. Abdullah, trans. Amin, *Blazing Chinar*, p. 171.
32. Abdullah, trans. Amin, *Blazing Chinar*, pp. 174–5.
33. 'Central Intelligence Officer's Note', 12 December 1939, Political Department, Political Branch 2 (24)-P (Sec)/39, 1939, Government of India (New Delhi: National Archives of India).
34. Raina, *Oral Transcript*, Vol. I, pp. 205–6.
35. Abbas, *Kashmakash*, pp. 203–5, 212–7.
36. Jawaharlal Nehru, *Selected Works of Jawaharlal Nehru*, Vol. Eleven (New Delhi: Orient Longman, 1978), pp. 267–9.

37. Political Department E 206/1940, Government of Jammu & Kashmir (Jammu: Jammu State Archives).
38. Abbas, *Kashmakash*, p. 218.
39. 'Central Intelligence Officer's Note', 12 December 1939.
40. Begum Abdullah to P.N. Bazaz, 12 March and 4 May 1940 (New Delhi: Bhushan Bazaz Private Collection).
41. Interview with Farooq Abdullah, 22 May 2015, Srinagar, Kashmir.
42. Begum Abdullah to P.N. Bazaz, 12 March 1940; Sheikh Muhammad Abdullah to Munshi Muhammad Ishaq, 9 August 1941 (Srinagar: Ghulam Hassan Munshi Private Collection).
43. *Trust Deed* (Srinagar: All Jammu Kashmir Muslim Auqaf Trust, 1973), pp. 1–3.
44. Interview with Sheikh Zaffar, 21 June 2016, Srinagar, Kashmir.
45. Jalali, *Oral Transcript*, p. 61; Raina, *Oral Transcript*, Vol. II, p. 449.
46. Abdullah, trans. Amin, *Blazing Chinar*, pp. 201–3.
47. Bazaz, *Ahead of His Times*, pp. 72–6.
48. Kashyap Bandhu, 'Why I Left National Conference', *Vitasta Annual Number* XXXIII (1999–2000): pp. 45–6.
49. Abdullah, trans. Amin, *Blazing Chinar*, pp. 179–80, 185.
50. Bandhu, 'Why I Left', pp. 46–7.
51. Raina, *Oral Transcript*, Vol. II, p. 597.
52. Jalali, *Oral Transcript*, pp. 67–8.
53. Saraf, *Kashmiris Fight*, Vol. I, pp. 658–9.
54. B.P.L Bedi, *Oral Transcript*, No. 270, pp. 202–3 (New Delhi: Nehru Memorial Museum and Library); Abdullah, trans. Amin, *Blazing Chinar*, p. 213.
55. Abbas, *Kashmakash*, pp. 227–8.
56. Abbas, *Kashmakash*, pp. 249–50.
57. Bedi, *Oral Transcript*, pp. 159–60.
58. Jalali, *Oral Transcript*, p. 53.
59. M.A. Jinnah to Sheikh Abdullah, 29 April 1944, in *Quaid-I-Azam Mohammad Ali Jinnah Papers*, edited by M.A. Zaidi, Second Series, Vol. X (Islamabad: Quaid-i-Azam Papers Project, 2004), pp. 327–8.
60. Abbas, *Kashmakash*, pp. 256–60; Altaf Hussain Para, *The Making of Modern Kashmir: Sheikh Abdullah and the Politics of the State* (London & New York: Routledge, 2019), p. 106.
61. Abdullah, trans. Amin, *Blazing Chinar*, p. 226.

62. *The Civil & Military Gazette*, 22 June 1944: 7.
63. Abbas, *Kashmakash*, pp. 260, 265.
64. *Hamdard*, 30 July 1944.
65. *The Civil & Military Gazette*, 25 April 1945: 4.
66. Sheikh Muhammad Abdullah, 'Kashmir: Towards the Future', in *Naya Kashmir* (Srinagar: All Jammu and Kashmir National Conference, 1944), pp. 3–15.
67. Andrew Whitehead, *The Lives of Freda: The Political, Spiritual and Personal Journeys of Freda Bedi* (New Delhi: Speaking Tiger, 2019), p. 163.
68. *Naya Kashmir*, pp. 17–77.
69. Abdullah, trans. Amin, *Blazing Chinar*, p. 217.
70. Whitehead, *Lives of Freda*, pp. 161–2.
71. Whitehead, *Lives of Freda*, pp. 158–60.
72. Quoted in Mohammad Farooq Rehmani, *Sheikh Abdullah ke Nakush* (Srinagar: Aflaq Publications, 1988), p. 62.
73. *The Civil & Military Gazette*, 7 August 1945: 9.
74. Sheikh Muhammad Abdullah, 'Khutba-i-Sadarat', All Jammu and Kashmir National Conference Annual Session, Sopore, 3, 4, 5 August 1945, pp. 3, 6–7.
75. Abdullah, 'Khutba', pp. 14, 18, 21–2.
76. Abdullah, 'Khutba', p. 7.
77. Jawaharlal Nehru, *Selected Works of Jawaharlal Nehru*, Vol. Fourteen (New Delhi: Orient Longman, 1981), pp. 388–91.
78. Nehru, *Selected Works*, Vol. Fourteen, p. 393.
79. *The Civil & Military Gazette*, 7 August 1945: 9.
80. *The Civil & Military Gazette*, 11 August 1945: 4.
81. Sonia Gandhi, ed., *Two Alone, Two Together: Letters between Indira Gandhi and Jawaharlal Nehru, 1940–1964* (London: Hodder & Stoughton, 1992), p. 499.
82. Raina, *Oral Transcript*, Vol. I, p. 224.
83. Saraf, *Kashmiris Fight*, Vol. I, p. 657.
84. Raina, *Oral Transcript*, Vol. I, p. 236.

### 3. From Revolutionary to Prime Minister, 1946–1951

1. A.G. Noorani, *Article 370: A Constitutional History of Jammu and Kashmir* (New Delhi: Oxford University Press, 2011), p. 96.

2. Srinath Raghavan, *War and Peace in Modern India* (New York: Palgrave Macmillan, 2010), p. 28.
3. Sheikh Muhammad Abdullah, *Quit Kashmir: Memorandum to the British Cabinet Mission* (Srinagar, 1946), p. 2.
4. Jawaharlal Nehru, *Selected Works of Jawaharlal Nehru*, Vol. Fifteen (New Delhi: Orient Longman, 1982), pp. 368–9.
5. Nehru, *Selected Works*, Vol. Fifteen, pp. 391–2.
6. Nehru, *Selected Works*, Vol. Fifteen, pp. 403–10.
7. Quoted in Andrew Whitehead, 'The People's Militia: Communists and Kashmiri Nationalism in the 1940s', in *Partition: The Long Shadow*, edited by Urvashi Butalia (New Delhi: Zubaan, 2015), p. 128.
8. Nyla Ali Khan, *The Life of a Kashmiri Woman: Dialectic of Resistance and Accommodation* (New York: Palgrave Macmillan, 2014), pp. 38–9.
9. Interview with Khalida Shah, 28 May 2015, Srinagar, Kashmir.
10. N.N. Raina, *Oral Transcript*, Vol. I, No. 580, pp. 267–8 (New Delhi: Nehru Memorial Museum and Library).
11. Raina, *Oral Transcript*, Vol. I, p. 293.
12. Letters exchanged among Sheikh Muhammad Abdullah, Bakshi Ghulam Muhammad, G.M. Sadiq, G.M. Karra and Munshi Muhammad Ishaq, August 1946–August 1947 (Srinagar: Ghulam Hassan Munshi Private Collection).
13. Sheikh Muhammad Abdullah to Freda Bedi, 2 October 1946 (courtesy Andrew Whitehead).
14. Sheikh Muhammad Abdullah, 'Speech on 3 January 1946', in *Irshadat-e-Baba-e-Quom*, edited by Abdul Majid Kishtwari, Trilok Singh and Maharaj Krishan (Srinagar: Ghulam Muhammad and Sons, undated), p. 3.
15. Bakshi Ghulam Muhammad to Munshi Ishaq, 3 June 1947 (letters among Abdullah, Bakshi, Sadiq and others).
16. Raina, *Oral Transcript*, Vol. II, p. 352.
17. Sheikh Muhammad Abdullah, *The Blazing Chinar: Autobiography*, translated by Mohammad Amin (Srinagar: Gulshan Books, 2013), pp. 268–9.
18. Jawaharlal Nehru, *Selected Works of Jawaharlal Nehru*, Second Series, Vol. Three (New Delhi: Oxford University Press, 1985), p. 217.
19. Jawaharlal Nehru, *Selected Works of Jawaharlal Nehru*, Second Series, Vol. Four (New Delhi: Oxford University Press, 1986), pp. 263–4.
20. Raina, *Oral Transcript*, Vol. II, p. 352.
21. Sheikh Muhammad Abdullah, 'Speech on 29 September 1947', in *Irshadat-e-Baba-e-Quom*, p. 5.

22. C. Bilquees Taseer, *The Kashmir of Sheikh Muhammad Abdullah* (Lahore: Ferozsons Ltd, 1986), pp. 52–4.
23. Abdullah, trans. Amin, *Blazing Chinar*, p. 268.
24. RG56, Box 6071, File 3, Central Decimal Files, 1945–1949, p. 6 (Maryland: National Archives and Records Administration).
25. RG56, Box 6071, File 2, Central Decimal Files, 1945–1949, p. 2 (Maryland: National Archives and Records Administration).
26. Muhammad Yusuf Saraf, *Kashmiris Fight—For Freedom*, Vol. II, *1947–1978* (Lahore: Ferozsons Ltd, 1979), pp. 709–13.
27. Comrade Habibullah, 'Sheikh Muhammad Abdullah ke Khayalat ka Post-Mortem', *Hamdard*, 16 October 1947: 2.
28. A Friend, 'Sheikh Abdullah: The Kashmir Leader', *The Hindustan Review* 82 (January 1948): 62–4.
29. V.K. Chinnammalu Amma, 'Sheikh Muhammad Abdullah', *Swatantra* (22 May 1948): 24.
30. Interview with Anwar Ashai, 24 June 2016, Srinagar, Kashmir.
31. Interview with Shabir Masoodi, 26 May 2015, Srinagar, Kashmir.
32. Dwarkanath Kachru to Jawaharlal Nehru, 4 October 1947 (Jammu: Balraj Puri Private Collection).
33. Christopher Snedden, *The Untold Story of the People of Azad Kashmir* (New York: Columbia University Press, 2012), pp. 39–45; Sardar Muhammad Ibrahim Khan, *The Kashmir Saga* (Lahore: Ripon Press, 1965), pp. 69–80.
34. See Andrew Whitehead, *A Mission in Kashmir* (New Delhi: Penguin, 2007), for a detailed discussion of the events in Baramulla.
35. Chitralekha Zutshi, *Kashmir: Oxford India Short Introductions* (New Delhi: Oxford University Press, 2019), pp. 109–10.
36. For the Maharaja's letter acceding to India, Mountbatten's response accepting the accession and the Instrument of Accession, see Durga Das, ed., *Sardar Patel's Correspondence, 1945–50,* Vol. I, *New Light on Kashmir* (Ahmedabad: Navajivan Publishing House, 1971), pp. 339–43.
37. Raghavan, *War and Peace*, pp. 58–9. The plebiscite, which was held in Junagadh in February 1948, much after the Indian Army had annexed the princely state in November 1947, resulted in an overwhelming vote for India.
38. For more details on Gilgit's revolt and its aftermath, see Martin Sökefeld, '"Not Part of Kashmir, but of the Kashmir Dispute": The Political Predicaments of Gilgit-Baltistan', in *Kashmir: History, Politics,*

*Representation*, edited by Chitralekha Zutshi (New Delhi: Cambridge University Press, 2018), pp. 132–49.

39. B.P.L. Bedi, *Oral Transcript*, No. 270, p. 239 (New Delhi: Nehru Memorial Museum and Library).
40. See Ilyas Chattha, 'Escape from Violence: The 1947 Partition of India and the Migration of Kashmiri Muslim Refugees', in *Refugees and the End of Empire: Imperial Collapse and Forced Migration in the Twentieth Century*, edited by Panikos Panayi and Pippa Virdee (New York: Palgrave Macmillan, 2011), pp. 196–218. In a particularly gruesome case of Muslim mass murder, Jammu Muslims were asked by Dogra officials to gather at the state grounds under the false promise that they would be given safe passage to Pakistan. Instead, the convoy was redirected and the Muslims were executed. See Shahla Hussain, *Kashmir in the Aftermath of Partition* (New Delhi: Cambridge University Press, 2021), p. 91.
41. Raina, *Oral Transcript*, Vol. II, p. 392.
42. Khan, *The Life of a Kashmiri Woman*, pp. 124–5.
43. Sheikh Muhammad Abdullah, 'Speech in November 1947', in *Irshadat-e-Baba-e-Quom*, p. 7.
44. Bedi, *Oral Transcript*, p. 239.
45. Andrew Whitehead, ed., 'Krishna Misri: 1947, a Year of Change', https://www.andrewwhitehead.net/krishna-misri–1947-a-year-of-change.html, accessed 25 May 2021; Rafiq Kathwari, *Diary of Khwaja Ghulam Mohammed Kathwari*, 'Nine Days in October 1947 That Mapped the Future of Kashmir', https://3quarksdaily.com/3quarksdaily/2015/11/pages-from-my-fathers-diary.html, accessed 25 May 2021.
46. *The Hindustan Times*, 28 December 1947, p. 1.
47. B.P.L. Bedi and Freda Bedi, *Sheikh Abdullah: His Life and Ideals* (Srinagar, 1949), pp. 14–5.
48. Bedi and Bedi, *Sheikh Abdullah*, p. 16.
49. Bedi and Bedi, *Sheikh Abdullah*, p. 13; Chinnammalu Amma, 'Sheikh Muhammad Abdullah', pp. 24–5.
50. For two ends of the spectrum in thinking about democracy, see Gyan Prakash, *Emergency Chronicles: Indira Gandhi and Democracy's Turning Point* (Princeton, N.J.: Princeton University Press, 2019), pp. 11–2.
51. Sheikh Muhammad Abdullah, 'Speech in November 1947', in *Irshadat-e-Baba-e-Quom*, p. 7.
52. Andrew Whitehead, '"I Shall Paint My Nails with the Blood of Those that Covet Me": Kashmir Women's Militia and Independence-Era Nationalism', *History Workshop Journal* (2022): 8.

53. Interview with Qurat-ul-Ain, 1 November 2014, Srinagar, Kashmir; Interview with Mirwaiz Umar Farooq, 21 May 2015, Srinagar, Kashmir.
54. Jai Lal Tamiri to Editor, *Janata*, 25 November 1948, J.P. Narayan Papers, IIIrd instalment, File no. 87, pp. 21–3, p. 22 (New Delhi: Nehru Memorial Museum and Library).
55. Raina, *Oral Transcript*, Vol. II, pp. 466–7; Andrew Whitehead, *The Lives of Freda: The Political, Spiritual and Personal Journeys of Freda Bedi* (New Delhi: Speaking Tiger, 2019), pp. 187–9.
56. D.D. Thakur, *My Life: Years at the Bar, Bench and in Kashmir Politics* (Gurgaon: LexisNexis, 2017), p. 100.
57. Raina, *Oral Transcript*, Vol. II, p. 404.
58. Josef Korbel, *Danger in Kashmir* (Princeton, N.J.: Princeton University Press, 1966), p. 208. The UNCIP, whose five-member team was established on 20 January 1948 with the objective of determining the Ceasefire Line and submitting truce proposals to India and Pakistan, visited both sides of the erstwhile princely state on a fact-finding mission in the summer of 1948.
59. Munshi Muhammad Ishaq, *Chodvi Sadi Hijri ke Iptidayee aur Wusta Daur ke Chand Ikhtebasaat* (Self-Published, 1950), pp. 71–5.
60. Tamiri to Editor, *Janata*, 25 November 1948, pp. 21–3, p. 22.
61. Karan Singh, *Heir Apparent: An Autobiography* (Delhi: Oxford University Press, 1982), pp. 77, 81–3.
62. According to Karan Singh, these allegations were baseless, but as Ilyas Chattha persuasively argues, the killings of Jammu's Muslims were part of a programme of ethnic cleansing that involved the Dogra army and had the official sanction of the Dogra state. See Chattha, 'Escape from Violence'.
63. Hari Singh to Sardar Patel, 6 June 1948, in *Sardar Patel's Correspondence*, Vol. I, pp. 212–5.
64. J.P. Narayan Papers, Ist and IInd instalments, File no. 56, pp. 14–18 (New Delhi: Nehru Memorial Museum and Library).
65. *Sardar Patel's Correspondence*, Vol. I, pp. 230–2.
66. Jawaharlal Nehru to Vijayalakshmi Pandit, 17 May 1949, Vijayalakshmi Pandit Papers, Correspondence, Nehru, Jawaharlal, N.7 (V), Ist instalment, p. 62 (New Delhi: Nehru Memorial Museum and Library).
67. Jawaharlal Nehru to Sardar Patel, 4 October 1948, in *Sardar Patel's Correspondence*, Vol. I, p. 233.

68. Indira Gandhi to Jawaharlal Nehru, May 20 1948, in *Two Alone, Two Together: Letters between Indira Gandhi and Jawaharlal Nehru, 1940–1964,* edited by Sonia Gandhi (London: Hodder & Stoughton, 1992), p. 555.
69. Sheikh Abdullah to Sardar Patel, 7 October 1948, in *Sardar Patel's Correspondence,* Vol. I, pp. 233–41.
70. Sardar Patel to Sheikh Abdullah, c. 11 October 1948, in *Sardar Patel's Correspondence,* Vol. I, p. 245.
71. Singh, *Heir Apparent,* p. 81.
72. Sardar Patel to Jawaharlal Nehru, 2 June 1949, in *Sardar Patel's Correspondence,* Vol. I, p. 280.
73. Singh, *Heir Apparent,* pp. 103–4.
74. Taseer, *Kashmir of Sheikh Muhammad Abdullah,* p. 26.
75. Raghavan, *War and Peace,* p. 63.
76. Raina, *Oral Transcript,* Vol. II, p. 498.
77. Korbel, *Danger in Kashmir,* p. 109.
78. Raina, *Oral Transcript,* Vol. I, p. 298.
79. Bedi, *Oral Transcript,* p. 247.
80. N. Gopalaswami Ayyangar to Sardar Patel, 15 October 1949, in *Sardar Patel's Correspondence,* Vol. I, p. 302.
81. Sardar Patel to Gopalaswami Ayyangar, 16 October 1949, in *Sardar Patel's Correspondence,* Vol. I, p. 305.
82. Korbel, *Danger in Kashmir,* pp. 147–8.
83. Interview with *The Scotsman,* 14 April 1949, in *Sardar Patel's Correspondence,* Vol. I, pp. 266–8.
84. RG59, Box 6113, File 2, Central Decimal Files, 1945–1949, p. 3 (Maryland: National Archives and Records Administration).
85. Oral History Interview with J. Wesley Adams, Harry S. Truman Library and Museum, https://www.trumanlibrary.gov/library/oral-histories/adamsjw, accessed 25 May 2021, p. 98.
86. RG59, Box 6113, File 2, Central Decimal Files, 1945–1949, p. 4 (Maryland: National Archives and Records Administration).
87. RG59, Box 6113, File 2, Central Decimal Files, 1945–1949, pp. 1–3.
88. RG59, Box 6113, File 2, Central Decimal Files, 1945–1949, p. 4.
89. RG59, Box 6113, File 2, Central Decimal Files, 1945–1949, p. 2.
90. RG59, Box 6113, File 2, Central Decimal Files, 1945–1949, p. 10.
91. A.G. Noorani, 'The Dixon Plan', *Frontline,* 25 October 2002, https://frontline.thehindu.com/the-nation/article30246359.ece, accessed 23 May 2020.

92. Singh, *Heir Apparent*, pp. 120–1.
93. Josef Korbel, 'The National Conference Administration of Kashmir, 1949–54', *Middle East Journal* 8, 3 (Summer 1954): pp. 284–5.
94. Raina, *Oral Transcript*, Vol. II, p. 594.
95. Sadiq Ali and Madhu Limaye, 'Report on Kashmir', October 1953, J.P. Narayan Papers, Ist and IInd instalments, File no. 237, pp. 21–4 (New Delhi: Nehru Memorial Museum and Library); Korbel, 'National Conference Administration', pp. 285–6.
96. Ministry of States, Kashmir Branch, Government of India 1-K, 1950 (New Delhi: National Archives of India).
97. Ministry of States, Kashmir Branch, Government of India 19 (9)-K/52, 1952, p. 4 (New Delhi: National Archives of India).
98. Sardar Patel to Gopalaswami Ayyangar, 10 October 1950, in *Sardar Patel's Correspondence*, Vol. I, p. 320.
99. See Raghavan, *War and Peace*, chapter 3.
100. Sheikh Muhammad Abdullah, 'Speech in March 1951', in *Irshadat-e-Baba-e-Quom*, p. 16.
101. Ministry of States, Kashmir Branch, Government of India 8(12)-K/51, 1951 (New Delhi: National Archives of India).
102. Korbel, 'National Conference Administration', p. 287; Ministry of States, Kashmir Branch, Government of India 8(25)-K/51, 1951 (New Delhi: National Archives of India); see also, Ashutosh Varshney, 'India, Pakistan, and Kashmir: Antinomies of Nationalism', *Asian Survey* 31, 11 (November 1991): 1009.
103. Interview with Rajinder Singh Rana, 21 March 2015, Jammu City, Jammu.
104. Noorani, *Article 370*, p. 98.
105. Noorani, *Article 370*, pp. 102–3.
106. Singh, *Heir Apparent*, p. 131.
107. Noorani, *Article 370*, pp. 105–7.
108. Mridula Sarabhai, ed., *Sheikh-Sadiq Correspondence [August to October 1956]* (Self-Published, undated), p. 7.
109. See http://autarmota.blogspot.com/2012/09/come-near.html, accessed 15 March 2022.
110. Nehru, *Selected Works*, Second Series, Vol. Four, p. 321.
111. Nehru, *Selected Works*, Second Series, Vol. Four, p. 322.

## 4. The Turning Point, 1952–1953

1. Jawaharlal Nehru to Maulana Abul Kalam Azad, 1 March 1953, J.N. (S.G.) Papers, File no. 167 (II), p. 22 (New Delhi: Nehru Memorial Museum and Library).
2. Morarji Desai to Jawaharlal Nehru, 5 August 1953, J.N. (S.G.) Papers, File no. 192 (II), p. 344 (New Delhi: Nehru Memorial Museum and Library).
3. Memorandum to Sheikh Abdullah, J.N. (S.G.) Papers, File no. 194 (I), pp. 34–7 (New Delhi: Nehru Memorial Museum and Library).
4. Karan Singh to Sheikh Abdullah, 8 August 1953, J.N. (S.G.) Papers, File no. 194 (I), pp. 32–3.
5. G.M. Sadiq to Mehmooda Ali Shah, 15 June 1953, J.N. (S.G.) Papers, File no. 186, p. 109 (New Delhi: Nehru Memorial Museum and Library).
6. Interview with Karan Singh, 19 September 2014, New Delhi.
7. N.N. Raina, *Oral Transcript*, Vol. I, No. 580, pp. 335–6, 338–41 (New Delhi: Nehru Memorial Museum and Library).
8. Jawaharlal Nehru to Sardar Patel, 27 September 1947, in *Sardar Patel's Correspondence, 1945–50*, Vol. I, *New Light on Kashmir*, edited by Durga Das (Ahmedabad: Navajivan Publishing House, 1971), pp. 45–7.
9. A.G. Noorani, *Article 370: A Constitutional History of Jammu and Kashmir* (New Delhi: Oxford University Press, 2011), p. 124.
10. Noorani, *Article 370*, pp. 125–7.
11. Noorani, *Article 370*, pp. 127–8.
12. For further details, see Noorani, *Article 370*, pp. 133–8.
13. Noorani, *Article 370*, p. 8.
14. Noorani, *Article 370*, p. 164.
15. Noorani, *Article 370*, pp. 198–205.
16. Karan Singh, *Heir Apparent: An Autobiography* (New Delhi: Oxford University Press, 1982), p. 145. The J&K constituent assembly elected Karan Singh Sadar-i-Riyasat on 15 November 1952 for a period of five years.
17. Ministry of States, Kashmir Branch, Government of India 8(9)-JK/52, 1952, p. 29 (New Delhi, National Archives of India).
18. Balraj Madhok, *Kashmir Problem: A Story of Bungling* (New Delhi: Bharti Sahitya Sadan, 1952).
19. Ministry of States, Kashmir Branch, Government of India 8(6)-K/51 Vol. I, 1951 (New Delhi: National Archives of India).

20. Balraj Puri, *Oral Transcript*, Vol. I, No. 818, pp. 39, 103, 124–5 (New Delhi: Nehru Memorial Museum and Library).
21. Singh, *Heir Apparent*, p. 150.
22. Balraj Puri, Untitled Note, c. 1952, J.P. Narayan Papers, Ist and IInd instalments, File no. 237, pp. 5–7 (New Delhi: Nehru Memorial Museum and Library); Intelligence Bureau, 'A Note on the Praja Parishad Agitation', J.N. (S.G.) Papers, File no. 159 (I), pp. 357–62 (New Delhi: Nehru Memorial Museum and Library).
23. Ministry of States, Kashmir Branch, Government of India 8(25)-K/51, 1951 (New Delhi: National Archives of India).
24. Mulk Raj Saraf, *Fifty Years as a Journalist* (Jammu: Raj Mahal Publishers, 1967), p. 131.
25. Jawaharlal Nehru to Sheikh Abdullah, 27 November 1952, J.N. (S.G.) Papers, File no. 54 (I), p. 98 (New Delhi: Nehru Memorial Museum and Library). Nehru first visited Leh in July 1949.
26. Sheikh Abdullah to Jawaharlal Nehru, 23 December 1952, in *Jammu and Kashmir, 1949–64: Select Correspondence between Jawaharlal Nehru and Karan Singh*, edited by Jawaid Alam (New Delhi: Penguin/Viking, 2006), p. 83fn2.
27. Jawaharlal Nehru to Sheikh Abdullah, 16 December 1952, J.N. (S.G.) Papers, File no. 157 (I), pp. 57–8 (New Delhi: Nehru Memorial Museum and Library).
28. Sadiq Ali and Madhu Limaye, 'Report on Kashmir', October 1953, J.P. Narayan Papers, Ist and IInd instalments, File no. 237, pp. 6–8 (New Delhi: Nehru Memorial Museum and Library).
29. See, for instance, Rajbans Krishen, *Kashmir and the Conspiracy against Peace* (Bombay: People's Publishing House, 1951).
30. G.M. Sadiq to Mehmooda Ali Shah, 16 June 1953, J.N. (S.G.) Papers, File no. 186, p. 109 (New Delhi: Nehru Memorial Museum and Library).
31. Meenu Gaur, 'Kashmir on Screen: Region, Religion and Secularism in Hindi Cinema' (School of Oriental and African Studies, London: PhD Dissertation, 2010), p. 128.
32. J.N. (S.G.) Papers, File no. 192 (II), p. 344 (New Delhi: Nehru Memorial Museum and Library).
33. Sheikh Muhammad Abdullah, *Izhar-i-Haq: Kashmir Saazish Case* (Delhi: Kohinoor Printing Press, 1961), pp. 37–8.
34. See Munshi Muhammad Ishaq, *Chodvi Sadi Hijri ke Iptidayee aur Wusta Daur ke Chand Ikhtebasaat* (Self-Published, 1950).

35. *The Times of India*, 8 February 1953, p. 9.
36. Jawaharlal Nehru to Sheikh Abdullah, 23 February 1953, J.N. (S.G.) Papers, File no. 166 (I), p. 163 (New Delhi: Nehru Memorial Museum and Library).
37. Jawaharlal Nehru to Syama Prasad Mookerjee, 5 February 1953, J.N. (S.G.) Papers, File No. 164 (I), pp. 142–4 (New Delhi: Nehru Memorial Museum and Library).
38. Syama Prasad Mookerjee to Sheikh Abdullah, 13 February 1953, in Mir Qasim, *My Life and Times* (New Delhi: Allied Publishers, 1992), p. 208.
39. Sheikh Abdullah to Syama Prasad Mookerjee, 18 February 1953, in Qasim, *My Life and Times*, p. 209.
40. Sheikh Abdullah to Jawaharlal Nehru, 27 February 1953, J.N. (S.G.) Papers, File no. 167 (II), p. 19 (New Delhi: Nehru Memorial Museum and Library).
41. Jawaharlal Nehru to Sheikh Abdullah, 1 March 1953, J.N. (S.G.) Papers, File no. 167 (II), p. 21.
42. Jawaharlal Nehru to Maulana Azad, 1 March 1953, J.N. (S.G.) Papers, File no. 167 (II), p. 22.
43. B.N. Mullik, *My Years with Nehru: Kashmir* (New Delhi: Allied Publishers, 1971), pp. 18–20.
44. Singh, *Heir Apparent*, pp. 127–8.
45. RG56, Box 6113, File 2, Central Decimal Files, 1945–1949, p. 5 (Maryland: National Archives and Records Administration).
46. B.P.L Bedi, *Oral Transcript*, No. 270, p. 246 (New Delhi: Nehru Memorial Museum and Library).
47. RG59, Box 6113, File 2, Central Decimal Files, 1945–1949, p. 1 (Maryland: National Archives and Records Administration).
48. Jawaharlal Nehru to Sardar Patel, 12 May 1948, in *Sardar Patel's Correspondence*, Vol. I, pp. 186–7.
49. Jawaharlal Nehru to Vijayalakshmi Pandit, 18 July 1950, Vijayalakshmi Pandit Papers, Correspondence, Nehru, Jawaharlal, N.7 (V), Ist instalment, p. 140 (New Delhi: Nehru Memorial Museum and Library).
50. Raina, *Oral Transcript*, Vol. II, p. 505.
51. Singh, *Heir Apparent*, p. 153.
52. Bakshi Ghulam Muhammad to Jawaharlal Nehru, 19 January 1953, J.N. (S.G.) Papers, File no. 161 (I), pp. 63–4 (New Delhi: Nehru Memorial Museum and Library).
53. Bedi, *Oral Transcript*, pp. 251–2.

54. Sarvepalli Gopal, *Jawaharlal Nehru: A Biography*, Vol. II, *1947–1956* (Cambridge, MA: Harvard University Press, 1979), pp. 127–8.
55. Alam, ed., *Jammu and Kashmir, 1949–64*, pp. 114–7.
56. Srinath Raghavan, *War and Peace in Modern India* (New York: Palgrave Macmillan, 2010), p. 224.
57. *The Times of India*, 25 June 1953, p. 7.
58. Mridula Sarabhai, 'Note on the Immersion of Dr. Mookerjee's Ashes', 16 July 1953, Mridula Sarabhai Papers, Reel no. 59 (New Delhi: Nehru Memorial Museum and Library).
59. Jawaharlal Nehru to J.P. Narayan, 8 July 1953, J.P. Narayan Papers, Ist and IInd instalments, File no. 240, pp. 10–12 (New Delhi: Nehru Memorial Museum and Library).
60. Singh, *Heir Apparent*, p. 154.
61. Ali and Limaye, 'Report on Kashmir', p. 3.
62. Speech on 23 July 1953, J.N. (S.G.) Papers, File no. 190, p. 202 (New Delhi: Nehru Memorial Museum and Library).
63. Ali and Limaye, 'Report on Kashmir', p. 3.
64. J.N. (S.G.) Papers, File no. 188 (II), pp. 220–4 (New Delhi: Nehru Memorial Museum and Library).
65. Ali and Limaye, 'Report on Kashmir', pp. 7–8.
66. *The Times of India*, 10 August 1953, p. 6.
67. Ali and Limaye, 'Report on Kashmir', p. 4.
68. Sheikh Abdullah to Jawaharlal Nehru, 4 July 1953, J.N. (S.G.) Papers, File no. 188 (II), pp. 27–30 (New Delhi: Nehru Memorial Museum and Library).
69. Abdullah to Nehru, 4 July 1953, pp. 28–9.
70. Abdullah to Nehru, 4 July 1953, p. 27.
71. Jawaharlal Nehru to Sheikh Abdullah, 8 July 1953, J.N. (S.G.) Papers, File no. 188 (II), pp. 33–4 (New Delhi: Nehru Memorial Museum and Library).
72. Maulana Azad to Sheikh Abdullah, 9 July 1953, J.N. (S.G.) Papers, File no. 188 (II), p. 37 (New Delhi: Nehru Memorial Museum and Library).
73. Sheikh Abdullah to Jawaharlal Nehru, 15 July 1953, J.N. (S.G.) Papers, File no. 189 (II), pp. 349–50 (New Delhi: Nehru Memorial Museum and Library).
74. *The Times of India*, 16 July 1953, p. 6.
75. Bakshi Ghulam Muhammad to Jawaharlal Nehru, 17 July 1953, J.N. (S.G.) Papers, File no. 189 (II), pp. 356–7.

76. Bakshi to Nehru, 17 July 1953, pp. 354–6, p. 356.
77. Mridula Sarabhai to Jawaharlal Nehru, 18 July 1953, J.N. (S.G.) Papers, File no. 189 (I), pp. 184–5 (New Delhi: Nehru Memorial Museum and Library).
78. Jawaharlal Nehru to Mridula Sarabhai, 3 August 1953, J.N. (S.G.) Papers, File no. 192 (II), p. 184 (New Delhi: Nehru Memorial Museum and Library).
79. Mullik, *My Years with Nehru*, p. 41.
80. Ajit Bhattacharjea, *Sheikh Mohammad Abdullah: Tragic Hero of Kashmir* (Delhi: Roli Books, 2008), p. 187–8.
81. Desai to Nehru, 5 August 1953, J.N. (S.G.) Papers, File no. 192 (II), p. 344 (New Delhi: Nehru Memorial Museum and Library).
82. J.N. (S.G.) Papers, File no. 187 (II), p. 336 (New Delhi: Nehru Memorial Museum and Library).
83. Jawaharlal Nehru to Bakshi Ghulam Muhammad, 24 July 1953, J.N. (S.G.) Papers, File no. 190, p. 201 (New Delhi: Nehru Memorial Museum and Library).
84. Jawaharlal Nehru to Bakshi Ghulam Muhammad, 30 July 1953, J.N. (S.G.) Papers, File no. 191 (II), pp. 170–2 (New Delhi: Nehru Memorial Museum and Library).
85. Jawaharlal Nehru to C. Rajagopalachari, 31 July 1953, C. Rajagopalachari Papers, Vth instalment, File no. 123, p. 186 (New Delhi: Nehru Memorial Museum and Library).
86. Jawaharlal Nehru to Indira Gandhi, 9 August 1953, in *Two Alone, Two Together: Letters between Indira Gandhi and Jawaharlal Nehru, 1940–1964*, edited by Sonia Gandhi (London: Hodder & Stoughton, 1992), p. 596.
87. 20 July 1953, J.N. (S.G.) Papers, File no. 189 (II), p. 346 (New Delhi: Nehru Memorial Museum and Library).
88. J.N. (S.G.) Papers, File no. 191 (II), pp. 222–3 (New Delhi: Nehru Memorial Museum and Library).
89. J.N. (S.G.) Papers, File no. 192 (II), p. 193 (New Delhi: Nehru Memorial Museum and Library).
90. Sheikh Abdullah to Maulana Masoodi, 8 August 1953, in *Sheikh-Sadiq Correspondence [August to October 1956]*, edited by Mridula Sarabhai (Self-Published, undated), pp. 48–9.
91. Abdullah to Masoodi, 8 August 1953, pp. 49–50.
92. Abdullah to Masoodi, 8 August 1953, p. 50.
93. Ali and Limaye, 'Report on Kashmir', p. 4.

94. Singh, *Heir Apparent*, p. 160–1.
95. Puri, *Oral Transcript*, Vol. I, p. 161.
96. David Gilmartin, 'Pakistan, Partition, and South Asian History: In Search of a Narrative', *The Journal of Asian Studies* 57, 4 (November 1998): 1089.
97. Sheikh Muhammad Abdullah, *The Blazing Chinar: Autobiography*, translated by Mohammad Amin (Srinagar: Gulshan Books, 2013), p. 322.
98. Sardar Patel to Jawaharlal Nehru, 3 July 1950, in *Sardar Patel's Correspondence*, Vol. I, p. 317.
99. Puri, *Oral Transcript*, Vol. I, p. 124.
100. Jawaharlal Nehru to Vijayalakshmi Pandit, 10 August 1950, Vijayalakshmi Pandit Papers, Correspondence, Nehru, Jawaharlal, N.7 (V), Ist instalment, p. 147 (New Delhi: Nehru Memorial Museum and Library).
101. Karan Singh to Jawaharlal Nehru, 9 August 1953, in *Jammu and Kashmir, 1949–64*, ed. Alam, p. 121.
102. Abdullah, trans. Amin, *Blazing Chinar*, pp. 400–1.
103. Abdullah, trans. Amin, *Blazing Chinar*, pp. 400–1.

## 5. Reprising the Role of Revolutionary, 1953–1958

1. Balraj Puri, 'Political Mind of Abdullah', *Kashmir Affairs* 2, 7 (September–October 1960): 20–3.
2. Sheikh Muhammad Abdullah, 'Id Speech', in *Sheikh–Sadiq Correspondence [August to October 1956]*, edited by Mridula Sarabhai (Self-Published, undated), pp. 45–6.
3. Abdullah, 'Id Speech', p. 47.
4. *The Times of India*, 10 August 1953, p. 1.
5. Sadiq Ali and Madhu Limaye, 'Report on Kashmir', October 1953, J.P. Narayan Papers, Ist and IInd instalments, File no. 237, p. 2 (New Delhi: Nehru Memorial Museum and Library).
6. Ghulam Mohammad Mir Rajpori and Manohar Nath Kaul, *Conspiracy in Kashmir* (Srinagar: Social & Political Study Group, 1954).
7. Ministry of States, Kashmir Branch, Government of India 7.18 (2)-K/54, 1954, pp. 1–3 (New Delhi: National Archives of India).
8. Jawaharlal Nehru to Bakshi Ghulam Muhammad, 15 August 1953, J.N. (S.G.) Papers, File no. 194 (II), p. 239 (New Delhi: Nehru Memorial Museum and Library).
9. Quoted in *The Times of India*, 11 August 1953, p. 9.

10. Sheikh Muhammad Abdullah, *The Blazing Chinar: Autobiography*, translated by Mohammad Amin (Srinagar: Gulshan Books, 2013), pp. 429–33.
11. P.N. Jalali Papers, File no. 40, p. 38 (New Delhi: Nehru Memorial Museum and Library).
12. Mirza Afzal Beg to Munshi Muhammad Ishaq, 8 September 1956 (Srinagar: Ghulam Hassan Munshi Private Collection).
13. Sheikh Muhammad Abdullah to Mohammad Abdullah Ganai, 8 February 1957, in *Letters of Sh. Muhammad Abdullah, Produced by the Prosecution in the Kashmir Conspiracy Case* (Srinagar: Kashmir People's Printing Press, 1959), pp. 49–51.
14. Sheikh Abdullah to Munshi Muhammad Ishaq, 9 December 1955 (Srinagar: Ghulam Hassan Munshi Private Collection).
15. Interview with Javid Ahmad Dar, 27 May 2015, Srinagar, Kashmir.
16. Interview with Muhammad Yusuf Yattoo and Fayaaz Alam, 17 June 2016, Srinagar, Kashmir.
17. Mohammad Ishaq Khan, 'Evolution of My Identity Vis-à-Vis Islam and Kashmir', in *The Parchment of Kashmir: History, Society, and Polity*, edited by Nyla Ali Khan (New York: Palgrave Macmillan, 2012), pp. 14–18.
18. Nyla Ali Khan, *The Life of a Kashmiri Woman: Dialectic of Resistance and Accommodation* (New York: Palgrave Macmillan, 2014), pp. 49–54.
19. B.N. Mullik, *My Years with Nehru: Kashmir* (New Delhi: Allied Publishers, 1971), pp. 49–51; Jawaid Alam, ed., *Jammu and Kashmir, 1949–64: Select Correspondence between Jawaharlal Nehru and Karan Singh* (New Delhi: Penguin/Viking, 2006), p. 182fn1.
20. Sumantra Bose, *Kashmir: Roots of Conflict, Paths to Peace* (Cambridge, MA: Harvard University Press, 2003), pp. 71–2.
21. Jawaharlal Nehru to Karan Singh, 11 January 1956, in *Jammu and Kashmir, 1949–64*, ed. Alam, pp. 187–8.
22. Karan Singh to Jawaharlal Nehru, 11 January 1956, in *Jammu and Kashmir, 1949–64*, ed. Alam, pp. 185–6.
23. Abdullah, trans. Amin, *Blazing Chinar*, p. 410.
24. A.G. Noorani, ed., *The Kashmir Dispute, 1947–2012*, Vol. I (New Delhi: Tulika Books, 2013), p. 188.
25. Sheikh Abdullah to G.M. Sadiq, 16 August 1956, in *Sheikh–Sadiq Correspondence*, ed. Sarabhai, pp. 1–3.
26. Sadiq to Sheikh Abdullah, 11 September 1956, in *Sheikh–Sadiq Correspondence*, ed. Sarabhai, p. 9.

27. Sadiq to Sheikh Abdullah, 11 September 1956, in *Sheikh–Sadiq Correspondence,* ed. Sarabhai, pp. 10–14.
28. Sheikh Abdullah to Sadiq, 26 September 1956, in *Sheikh–Sadiq Correspondence,* ed. Sarabhai, pp. 15–24.
29. Sadiq to Sheikh Abdullah, 22 October 1956, in *Sheikh–Sadiq Correspondence,* ed. Sarabhai, pp. 25–32.
30. Sheikh Abdullah to Sadiq, 28 October 1956, in *Sheikh–Sadiq Correspondence,* ed. Sarabhai, p. 39.
31. Sheikh Abdullah to Sadiq, 28 October 1956, in *Sheikh–Sadiq Correspondence,* ed. Sarabhai, pp. 39–40.
32. Mullik, *My Years with Nehru,* p. 47.
33. RG59, Box 4164, File 1, Central Decimal Files, 1950–1954, pp. 1–2 (Maryland: National Archives and Records Administration).
34. Maulana Muhammad Sayeed Masoodi, 'Public Statement', 13 August 1953, J.N. (S.G.) Papers, File no. 194 (I), pp. 178–80 (New Delhi: Nehru Memorial Museum and Library); *The Times of India,* 11 August 1953, p. 1.
35. 'Maulana Masoodi Speaks', 12 November 1978, *The Illustrated Weekly of India,* pp. 31–5.
36. Mridula Sarabhai to Jammu & Kashmir Legislative Assembly, 31 March 1956; Mridula Sarabhai to Bakshi Ghulam Muhammad, 6 December 1955 (Jammu: Balraj Puri Private Collection).
37. C. Bilquees Taseer, *The Kashmir of Sheikh Muhammad Abdullah* (Lahore: Ferozsons Ltd, 1986), p. 247.
38. P.N. Bazaz, 'The Role of Communists in Kashmir Politics' (unpublished MS, undated) (New Delhi: Bhushan Bazaz Private Collection).
39. Abdullah, trans. Amin, *Blazing Chinar,* p. 447.
40. Abdullah, trans. Amin, *Blazing Chinar,* pp. 448–9.
41. Mridula Sarabhai, 'Press Statement', 11 January 1958, J.P. Narayan Papers, Ist and IInd instalments, File no. 238, p. 75 (New Delhi: Nehru Memorial Museum and Library).
42. Abdullah, trans. Amin, *Blazing Chinar,* pp. 450–1; 'Maulana Masoodi Speaks', 12 November 1978, *Illustrated Weekly,* pp. 31–5.
43. Abdullah, trans. Amin, *Blazing Chinar,* pp. 451–2.
44. Abdullah, trans. Amin, *Blazing Chinar,* p. 453.
45. *The Times of India,* 9 January 1958, p. 6.
46. Mullik, *My Years with Nehru,* p. 71.
47. Mullik, *My Years with Nehru,* pp. 64–70.

48. Mridula Sarabhai, 'Please Cooperate: A Fervent Appeal to the Press', 15 January 1958, J.P. Narayan Papers, Ist and IInd instalments, File no. 238, pp. 115–8 (New Delhi: Nehru Memorial Museum and Library); Abdullah, trans. Amin, *Blazing Chinar*, p. 453.
49. *The Times of India*, 14 January 1958, p. 9.
50. 'Sheikh Mohammed Abdullah's Speeches—I and II', J.P. Narayan Papers, Ist and IInd instalments, File no. 238, pp. 37–47, p. 45 (New Delhi: Nehru Memorial Museum and Library).
51. Abdullah, trans. Amin, *Blazing Chinar*, pp. 461–2.
52. 'Sheikh Mohammed Abdullah's Speeches—III', J.P. Narayan Papers, Ist and IInd instalments, File no. 238, p. 47 (New Delhi: Nehru Memorial Museum and Library).
53. Mridula Sarabhai, 'Jammu and Kashmir State Newsletter No. 34', J.P. Narayan Papers, Ist and IInd instalments, File no. 238, pp. 119–21 (New Delhi: Nehru Memorial Museum and Library).
54. *Raishumari Kyun? Hazrat Sher-i-Kashmir Sheikh Muhammad Abdullah ka Bayan jo 18 February 1958 ko Srinagar aur Dilli se Jari hua* (Srinagar: K.P. Steam Press, 1958), pp. 5–11.
55. *The Times of India*, 26 February 1958, p. 5
56. *The Times of India*, 3 March 1958, p. 3.
57. Maulana Masoodi to Mridula Sarabhai, 4 March 1958 (Srinagar: Shabir Masoodi Private Collection).
58. Sheikh Abdullah to Jawaharlal Nehru, 11 April 1958 (Srinagar: Shabir Masoodi Private Collection).
59. Mullik, *My Years with Nehru*, pp. 89–91.
60. Hafizur Rehman Khan, 'Abdullah's Release and Re-arrest', *Pakistan Horizon* 11, 2 (June 1958): 108.
61. Abdullah, trans. Amin, *Blazing Chinar*, p. 456.
62. Quoted in N.A. Khan, *The Life of a Kashmiri Woman*, p. 64.
63. H.R. Khan, 'Abdullah's Release and Re-Arrest', p. 109.
64. H.R. Khan, 'Abdullah's Release and Re-Arrest', p. 109.
65. Noor Ahmad Baba, 'Democracy and Governance in Kashmir', in *The Parchment of Kashmir*, ed. N.A. Khan, p. 108.

## 6. On Trial, 1958–1965

1. 1965-03-10_SOUND_ARCHIVE#ABDULLAH, SHEIKH_MOHAMMAD_TEN_O'CLOCK, BBC.

2. Sheikh Muhammad Abdullah, *The Blazing Chinar: Autobiography*, translated by Mohammad Amin (Srinagar: Gulshan Books, 2013), p. 471.
3. Abdullah, trans. Amin, *Blazing Chinar*, pp. 468, 471–3.
4. Balraj Puri to Sheikh Muhammad Abdullah, 5 June 1963 (Jammu: Balraj Puri Private Collection).
5. 'Statement of Mirza Mohammed Afzal Beg [Filed in writing on October 4, 1960]', *Kashmir Affairs* 2, 7 (September–October 1960): 34–42; 'Kashmir Conspiracy Case: The Statement of Sheikh Mohammed Abdullah', *Kashmir Affairs* 2, 7 (September–October 1960): 30–4. See also, *The Kashmir Conspiracy Case*, Report No. 7, *Written Statement Filed by Mirza Mohammad Afzal Beg* (Jammu: Amar Art Press, 1960); *The Kashmir Conspiracy Case*, Report IX (I), *Sheikh Mohammed Abdullah's Brief Reply to Prosecution* (Delhi: Roop Bharti Printers, 1960).
6. 'Statement of Mirza Mohammed Afzal Beg', p. 41.
7. P.N. Bazaz to Jawaharlal Nehru, 29 June and 18 July 1962 (New Delhi: Bhushan Bazaz Private Collection).
8. Jawaharlal Nehru to P.N. Bazaz, 26 July and 7 August 1962 (New Delhi: Bhushan Bazaz Private Collection).
9. P.N. Bazaz to Jawaharlal Nehru, 19 November 1962 (New Delhi: Bhushan Bazaz Private Collection).
10. As Navnita Behera notes, 'The two sides seriously discussed the basis for drawing an international boundary through Kashmir', but the talks foundered because while India was willing to accept the status quo, giving up or partitioning the Valley was unacceptable to Pakistan. For greater detail, see Navnita Chadha Behera, *Demystifying Kashmir* (Washington D.C.: Brookings Institution Press, 2006), pp. 218–9.
11. RG59, Box 3932, File 14, Central Decimal Files, 1963 (Maryland: National Archives and Records Administration).
12. RG59, Box 3932, File 7, 1963 (Maryland: National Archives and Records Administration).
13. RG59, Box 3934, File 3, 1963 (Maryland: National Archives and Records Administration).
14. B.N. Mullik, *My Years with Nehru: Kashmir* (New Delhi: Allied Publishers, 1971), pp. 104–6.
15. Mullik, *My Years with Nehru*, pp. 109–13.
16. Khalid Bashir Ahmad, '27 December 1963: Revisiting the Sacrilege', *Greater Kashmir*, 27 December 2017, https://www.greaterkashmir.com/todays-paper/27-december-1963-revisiting-the-sacrilege, accessed 27 September 2020.

17. Mullik, *My Years with Nehru*, pp. 127–8.
18. RG59, Box 3932, File 1, 1963 (Maryland: National Archives and Records Administration).
19. Mullik, *My Years with Nehru*, chapter 11.
20. Balraj Puri, 'Let Kashmir Not Be Let Down' (unpublished MS, c. early 1964), J.P. Narayan Papers, IIIrd instalment, File no. 93, pp. 224–5 (New Delhi: Nehru Memorial Museum and Library).
21. Abdullah, trans. Amin, *Blazing Chinar*, p. 482.
22. Abdullah, trans. Amin, *Blazing Chinar*, p. 485.
23. RG59, Box 2292, File 3, Central Decimal Files, 1964–1966 (Maryland: National Archives and Records Administration).
24. Central Intelligence Agency Special Report, Office of Current Intelligence, 'Sheikh Abdullah and the Kashmir Issue' (24 April 1964): 4.
25. RG59, Box 2292, File 3, 1964–1966 (Maryland: National Archives and Records Administration).
26. Abdullah, trans. Amin, *Blazing Chinar*, p. 487.
27. RG59, Box 2292, File 3, 1964–1966 (Maryland: National Archives and Records Administration).
28. Quoted in C. Bilquees Taseer, *The Kashmir of Sheikh Muhammad Abdullah* (Lahore: Ferozsons Ltd, 1986), p. 329.
29. RG59, Box 2292, File 3, 1964–1966.
30. RG59, Box 2292, File 3, 1964–1966.
31. CIA Special Report, 'Sheikh Abdullah and the Kashmir Issue' (24 April 1964): 5.
32. CIA Special Report, 'Sheikh Abdullah and the Kashmir Issue' (24 April 1964): 6.
33. Abdullah, trans. Amin, *Blazing Chinar*, pp. 498–500.
34. J. Nehru Notes, 29 April, 30 April, 1 May 1964, J.N. (S.G.) Papers, File no. 753 (III), pp. 367–73 (New Delhi: Nehru Memorial Museum and Library).
35. J. Nehru Notes, 1 May 1964, p. 371.
36. RG 59, Box 2293, File 2, 1964–1966 (Maryland: National Archives and Records Administration).
37. *The Times of India*, 2 May 1964, p. 1.
38. Sheikh Muhammad Abdullah to M.R. Masani, 16 April 1964; Lal Bahadur Shastri to C. Rajagopalachari, 4 May 1964; C. Rajagopalachari to M.R. Masani, 5 May 1964; C. Rajagopalachari to B. Shiva Rao, 12 May 1964, C. Rajagopalachari Papers, IVth instalment, File no. 92, pp. 27–47 (New Delhi: Nehru Memorial Museum and Library).

39. Y.D. Gundevia to G. Parthasarathy, 5 February 1964, Y.D. Gundevia Papers, File No. 4, p. 6 (New Delhi: Nehru Memorial Museum and Library).
40. 'Kashmir—Talk with Sheikh Abdullah', 8 May 1964, Y.D. Gundevia Papers, File no. 4, pp. 20–3 (New Delhi: Nehru Memorial Museum and Library).
41. 'Kashmir—Talk with Sheikh Abdullah', pp. 20–3.
42. Y.D. Gundevia to G. Parthasarathy, 13 May 1964, Y.D. Gundevia Papers, File no. 4, pp. 46–7 (New Delhi: Nehru Memorial Museum and Library).
43. RG59, Box 2293, File no. 2, 1964–1966 (Maryland: National Archives and Records Administration).
44. RG59, Box 2293, File no. 2, 1964–1966.
45. Ayesha Jalal, *The Struggle for Pakistan: A Muslim Homeland and Global Politics* (Cambridge, MA: Belknap Press, 2017), p. 118.
46. P.N. Bazaz, *Sheikh Abdullah, Kashmir Democracy and Indo-Pak Relations* (New Delhi: Pamposh Publications, 1964), p. 8.
47. *The Times of India*, 29 March 1965, p. 9.
48. Abdullah, trans. Amin, *Blazing Chinar*, pp. 501–2.
49. Taseer, *Kashmir of Sheikh Muhammad Abdullah*, p. 331.
50. Abdullah, trans. Amin, *Blazing Chinar*, pp. 503–4, 507–8.
51. Muhammad Yusuf Saraf, *Kashmiris Fight—For Freedom*, Vol. II, *1947–1978* (Lahore: Ferozsons Ltd, 1979), p. 1245.
52. Interview with Shabir Masoodi, 26 May 2015, Srinagar, Kashmir.
53. Quoted in *The Times of India*, 27 May 1964, p. 1.
54. Sheikh Muhammad Abdullah to Ayub Khan, 15 September 1967 (Srinagar: Ghulam Hassan Munshi Private Collection).
55. Inder Malhotra, 'Rear View: Difficulty of Coming Together', *Indian Express*, 16 June 2016, https://indianexpress.com/article/opinion/columns/inder-malhotra-column-difficulty-of-coming-together-2855256/, accessed 28 September 2020.
56. Abdullah, trans. Amin, *Blazing Chinar*, pp. 504–5.
57. Abdullah, trans. Amin, *Blazing Chinar*, p. 507.
58. Interview with Om Saraf, 25 November 2014, Jammu City, Jammu.
59. *Seminar* 58 (June 1964): pp. 1–40.
60. Surindar Suri, 'Basic Weaknesses', *Seminar* 58 (June 1964): 16–9, 19.
61. Muhammad Ishaq Khan, 'The Significance of the Dargah of Hazratbal in the Socio-Religious and Political Life of Kashmiri Muslims', in *Muslim*

Shrines in India, edited by Christian W. Troll (Delhi: Oxford University Press, 1992), pp. 185–6fn52.

62. Abdullah, trans. Amin, *Blazing Chinar*, p. 496.
63. P.N. Bazaz, *The Dialogue between Mirwaiz Farooq and Sheikh Abdullah* (New Delhi: Pamposh Publications, 1964), p. 11.
64. Jawaharlal Nehru to D. Sanjivayya, 22 December 1963, J.N. (S.G.) Papers, File no. 753 (III), p. 522 (New Delhi: Nehru Memorial Museum and Library).
65. Shamim Ahmed Shamim, 'National Conference ka Kaccha Chittha' (June 1964) in *Ainanuma* No. 9, edited by Qurrat-ul-Ain (Srinagar: Self-Published, 2011), pp. 161–6.
66. P.N. Jalali Papers, File no. 7, p. 164 (New Delhi: Nehru Memorial Museum and Library).
67. P.N. Jalali Papers, File no. 7, p. 164.
68. *Falsafa-i-Tark-i-Mawalat* (Srinagar: Mazdoor Press, 1965), p. 6.
69. P.N. Jalali, 'Secession: A Futile Cry', *The Kashmir News*, 22 July 1965, P.N. Jalali Papers, File no. 7, p. 70 (New Delhi: Nehru Memorial Museum and Library).
70. *The Times of India*, 18 January 1965, p. 7.
71. P.N. Jalali Papers, File no. 7, p. 140 (New Delhi: Nehru Memorial Museum and Library).
72. *Mahaz Weekly*, 2, 3 (20 March 1965): 11.
73. *Mahaz Weekly*, 2, 3 (20 March 1965): 12.
74. Abdullah, trans. Amin, *Blazing Chinar*, pp. 514–5.
75. *The Times of India*, 30 March 1965, p. 9.
76. Balraj Puri, Letter to the Editor, *Hindustan Times*, 16 April 1965 (Jammu: Balraj Puri Private Collection).
77. In *The Times of India*, 14 March 1965, p. 13.
78. Quoted in *The Times of India*, 10 May 1965, p. 5.
79. *The Times of India*, 10 May 1965, p. 5.

## 7. Coming to Terms, 1965–1974

1. Ghulam Ahmad, *My Years with Sheikh Abdullah: Kashmir 1971–87* (Srinagar: Gulshan Books, 2008), p. 44.
2. The offices of prime minister and Sadar-i-Riyasat of J&K were replaced with that of chief minister and governor in March 1965, with G.M. Sadiq

becoming the first chief minister and Karan Singh the first governor of the state.

3. Sheikh Mohammad Abdullah, 'Kashmir, India and Pakistan', *Foreign Affairs* 43 (1964–5): 534.
4. Rakesh Ankit, 'Sheikh Muhammad Abdullah of Kashmir, 1965–1975: From Externment to Enthronement', *Studies in Indian Politics* 6, 1 (2018): 90–1.
5. *The Times of India*, 9 May 1965, p. 1.
6. *The Times of India*, 9 May 1965, p. 1.
7. Balraj Puri, 'A Report on the Situation in Kashmir', 26 May 1964, J.P. Narayan Papers, IIIrd instalment, File no. 89, p. 102 (New Delhi: Nehru Memorial Museum and Library).
8. Plebiscite Front, 'Statement of Civil Resisters', 9 June 1965, J.P. Narayan Papers, IIIrd instalment, File no. 89, pp. 122–3.
9. G.M. Shah, 'Sheikh Muhammad Abdullah's Future Role', J.P. Narayan Papers, IIIrd instalment, File no. 89, p. 140.
10. Mridula Sarabhai, 'Letter on Kashmir', 26 August 1965, J.P. Narayan Papers, IIIrd instalment, File no. 89, pp. 173–6.
11. D.E. Lockwood, 'Sheikh Abdullah and the Politics of Kashmir', *Asian Survey* 9, 5 (May 1969): 388–9.
12. Sugata Srinivasaraju, 'Kanyakumari to Kashmir: How a Few South Indians Had Vital Links to Kashmir's History', *The Economic Times*, 18 August 2019, https://economictimes.indiatimes.com/news/politics-and-nation/kanyakumari-to-kashmir-how-a-few-south-indians-had-vital-links-to-kashmirs-modern-history/articleshow/70718004.cms?from=mdr, accessed 8 October 2020; Nyla Ali Khan, 'Conversation with Suraya Abdullah', *Kashmir Lit*, Winter 2010, http://www.kashmirlit.org/conversation-with-suraya-abdullah/, accessed 8 October 2020.
13. C. Bilquees Taseer, *The Kashmir of Sheikh Muhammad Abdullah* (Lahore: Ferozsons Ltd, 1986), pp. 252–3.
14. Khan, 'Conversation with Suraya Abdullah'.
15. *Sheikh Abdullah—Dost ya Dushman? Tarikhi Interview* (Rawalpindi: Faisul Islam Press, 1968), p. 10.
16. 'K. Radhakrishna's Report of His Visit to Sheikh Abdullah in Internment, 1965', in *The Kashmir Dispute, 1947–2012*, Vol. I, edited by A.G. Noorani (New Delhi: Tulika Books, 2013), pp. 216–7.
17. J.J. Singh to J.P. Narayan, 30 April 1966, J.P. Narayan Papers, IIIrd instalment, File no. 87, pp. 288–92 (New Delhi: Nehru Memorial Museum and Library).

18. J.J. Singh to J.P. Narayan, 10 June 1966, J.P. Narayan Papers, IIIrd instalment, File no. 87, pp. 228–31 (New Delhi: Nehru Memorial Museum and Library).
19. J.P. Narayan to Indira Gandhi, 23 June 1966, in *The Kashmir Dispute*, Vol. I, ed. Noorani, p. 222.
20. Narayan to Gandhi, 23 June 1966, pp. 218–23.
21. J.J. Singh to J.P. Narayan, 10 June 1966, J.P. Narayan Papers, IIIrd instalment, File no. 87, p. 228 (New Delhi: Nehru Memorial Museum and Library).
22. R.K. Patil to J.P. Narayan, 6 September 1966, J.P. Narayan Papers, IIIrd instalment, File no. 88, pp. 36–40; J.P. Narayan to R.K. Patil, 12 September 1966, J.P. Narayan Papers, IIIrd instalment, File no. 88, pp. 41–2 (New Delhi: Nehru Memorial Museum and Library).
23. 'The 1967 Elections in the State of Jammu & Kashmir', J.P. Narayan Papers, IIIrd instalment, File no. 91, pp. 97–110 (New Delhi: Nehru Memorial Museum and Library).
24. J.P. Narayan Papers, IIIrd instalment, File no. 87, pp. 112–6.
25. Lockwood, 'Sheikh Abdullah and the Politics of Kashmir', p. 384.
26. Taseer, *Kashmir of Sheikh Muhammad Abdullah*, p. 238.
27. Interview with Mehboob Beg, 17 March 2015, Jammu City, Jammu.
28. T.N. Kaul Papers, Ist, IInd, IIIrd instalments, File no. 12, p. 83 (New Delhi: Nehru Memorial Museum and Library).
29. T.N. Kaul Papers, File no. 12, pp. 83–6.
30. T.N. Kaul Papers, File no. 12, pp. 4–6.
31. T.N. Kaul Papers, File no. 12, pp. 6–7.
32. T.N. Kaul Papers, File no. 12, pp. 72–3.
33. T.N. Kaul Papers, File no. 12, pp. 4–5.
34. T.N. Kaul Papers, Ist, IInd, IIIrd instalments, Articles/Speeches by him, File no. 15, p. 80 (New Delhi: Nehru Memorial Museum and Library).
35. T.N. Kaul Papers, Ist, IInd, IIIrd instalments, File no. 12, pp. 97–100, 6–8.
36. 'Resume of Sheikh Saheb's Talks with Kashmiri Students on January 21, 1968', J.P. Narayan Papers, IIIrd instalment, File no. 87, pp. 9–11 (New Delhi: Nehru Memorial Museum and Library).
37. P.N. Jalali Papers, File no. 9, p. 744 (New Delhi: Nehru Memorial Museum and Library).
38. For more on the Jamaat's ideology and appeal, see Shahla Hussain, *Kashmir in the Aftermath of Partition* (New Delhi: Cambridge University Press, 2021), pp. 156–7.

39. *Sheikh Abdullah—Dost ya Dushman?*, pp. 11–3.
40. *The Times of India*, 3 January 1968, p. 1.
41. *Sheikh Abdullah—Dost ya Dushman?*, pp. 16–7.
42. *The Times of India*, 7 January 1968, p. 1.
43. *The Times of India*, 7 January 1968, p. 1.
44. *The Times of India*, 7 January 1968, p. 6.
45. *The Times of India*, 7 January 1968, p. 9.
46. *Sheikh Abdullah—Dost ya Dushman?*, pp. 7–9.
47. *Sheikh Abdullah—Dost ya Dushman?*, p. 197.
48. Nyla Ali Khan, ed., *Sheikh Mohammad Abdullah's Reflections on Kashmir* (New York: Palgrave Macmillan, 2018), pp. 143–4.
49. *Sheikh Abdullah—Dost ya Dushman?*, p. 210.
50. P.N. Jalali Papers, File no. 9, pp. 599–600 (New Delhi: Nehru Memorial Museum and Library).
51. P.N. Jalali Papers, File no. 9, p. 656.
52. S.G. Dube, 'The Situation in Kashmir: Some Impressions', J.P. Narayan Papers, IIIrd instalment, File no. 91, p. 20 (New Delhi: Nehru Memorial Museum and Library).
53. P.N. Jalali Papers, File no. 9, pp. 657, 665.
54. *The Times of India*, 25 March 1968, p. 8.
55. *The Times of India*, 27 March 1968, p. 12.
56. *The Times of India*, 25 March 1968, p. 8.
57. Sheikh Abdullah to J.P. Narayan, 31 July 1968, J.P. Narayan Papers, IIIrd instalment, File no. 93, pp. 269–70 (New Delhi: Nehru Memorial Museum and Library).
58. Sheikh Abdullah to P.N. Bazaz, 28 May 1968 (New Delhi: Bhushan Bazaz Private Collection).
59. 'Sheikh Abdullah ki Takrir', 17 October 1968, J.P. Narayan Papers, IIIrd instalment, File no. 92, pp. 72–7 (New Delhi: Nehru Memorial Museum and Library).
60. Abdul Aziz, *The Convention: An Analysis* (New Delhi: Nav Kashir Publications, undated), pp. 1–7.
61. Sheikh Muhammad Abdullah to J.P. Narayan, 6 March 1969, J.P. Narayan Papers, IIIrd instalment, File no. 93, pp. 175–7.
62. *Sheikh Mohammad Abdullah's Views Explained: Second Plenary Session, J&K State People's Convention* (Srinagar: New Kashmir Press, 1970), pp. 7–8.

63. B. Shiva Rao to Sheikh Muhammad Abdullah, 28 October 1968, J.P. Narayan Papers, IIIrd instalment, File. no. 93, pp. 188–91 (New Delhi: Nehru Memorial Museum and Library).
64. Munshi Muhammad Ishaq, *Nida-i-Haq* (Srinagar: Falah-i-Am Press, 2003), p. 6.
65. Ishaq, *Nida-i-Haq*, pp. 10–7.
66. Interview with Ghulam Hassan Munshi, 21 May 2015, Srinagar, Kashmir.
67. Mridula Sarabhai, 'Report of Visit to Kashmir', 18 June 1969, J.P. Narayan Papers, IIIrd instalment, File no. 93, pp. 147–8 (New Delhi: Nehru Memorial Museum and Library).
68. Muhammad Ishaq Khan, 'The Significance of the Dargah of Hazratbal in the Socio-Religious and Political Life of Kashmiri Muslims', in *Muslim Shrines in India*, edited by Christian W. Troll (Delhi: Oxford University Press, 1992), pp. 186–7.
69. Mirza Kamaluddin Shaida, Unpublished Poem, c. 1974 (Srinagar: Peerzada Muhammad Ashraf Private Collection).
70. 'Press Conference of Sheikh Mohammed Abdullah', 15 October 1969, J.P. Narayan Papers, IIIrd instalment, File no. 93, pp. 130–6.
71. Maulana Muhammad Farooq, *Muddadall Tafsira* (Srinagar: Awami Action Committee, 1970), pp. 7–11.
72. J.N. Sathu to P.N. Bazaz, 7 March 1970 (New Delhi: Bhushan Bazaz Private Collection).
73. J.N. Sathu to P.N. Bazaz, 7 March 1970.
74. Balraj Puri, *Oral Transcript*, Vol. I, No. 818, pp. 199–200 (New Delhi: Nehru Memorial Museum and Library).
75. Khan, ed., *Sheikh Mohammad Abdullah's Reflections on Kashmir*, p. 104, pp. 103–5. Balraj Madhok, Atal Bihari Vajpayee and M.S. Golwalkar were Hindu right-wing ideologues and members of the RSS (Rashtriya Swayamsevak Sangh).
76. *Sheikh Mohammad Abdullah's Views Explained*, pp. 16–33.
77. 'A Draft Manifesto for Adoption by the J&K State People's Convention, October 1970', pp. 8–9 (New Delhi: Bhushan Bazaz Private Collection).
78. 'A Draft Manifesto', pp. 10–1.
79. Jawaid Alam, ed., *Kashmir & Beyond, 1966–84: Select Correspondence between Indira Gandhi and Karan Singh* (New Delhi: Penguin Random House, 2020), p. 174fn3.

80. *Rahnuma-E-Deccan*, 11 May 1971, J.P. Narayan Papers, IIIrd instalment, File no. 89, pp. 280–3 (New Delhi: Nehru Memorial Museum and Library).
81. Alam, ed., *Kashmir & Beyond*, p. 175.
82. Alam, ed., *Kashmir & Beyond*, pp. 174–7.
83. *The Times of India*, 4 January 1971, p. 1.
84. P.N. Jalali, 'Report on Kashmir', 4 January 1970, P.N. Jalali Papers, File no. 9, pp. 362–3 (New Delhi: Nehru Memorial Museum and Library).
85. Order Dated 7 January 1971, Chief Secretariat, Jammu and Kashmir Government, J.P. Narayan Papers, IIIrd instalment, File no. 93, p. 100 (New Delhi: Nehru Memorial Museum and Library).
86. Sheikh Muhammad Abdullah to J.P. Narayan, 9 February 1971, J.P. Narayan Papers, IIIrd instalment, File no. 93, pp. 81–3.
87. 'Press Statement', 2 February 1971, J.P. Narayan Papers, Sheikh Muhammad Abdullah's Letters, Statements, and Speeches, 1968–71, pp. 18–21 (New Delhi: Nehru Memorial Museum and Library).
88. Maulana Masoodi to Mridula Sarabhai, 2 February 1971, J.P. Narayan Papers, IIIrd instalment, File no. 95, pp. 35–6 (New Delhi: Nehru Memorial Museum and Library).
89. Nyla Ali Khan, *The Life of a Kashmiri Woman: Dialectic of Resistance and Accommodation* (New York: Palgrave Macmillan, 2014), p. 79.
90. P.N. Jalali, 'Report on Kashmir: Election Prospects', P.N. Jalali Papers, File no. 10, pp. 11–8 (New Delhi: Nehru Memorial Museum and Library).
91. Hussain, *Kashmir in the Aftermath of Partition*, p. 297.
92. J.P. Narayan to Indira Gandhi, 26 March 1971, J.P. Narayan Papers, IIIrd instalment, File no. 93, p. 79.
93. P.N. Bazaz to Maulana Masoodi; P.N. Bazaz to G.M. Karra, 3 January 1972 (New Delhi: Bhushan Bazaz Private Collection).
94. P.N. Jalali, 'Report on Kashmir', 26 April 1972, P.N. Jalali Papers, File no. 11, pp. 277–8 (New Delhi: Nehru Memorial Museum and Library).
95. Ahmad, *My Years with Sheikh Abdullah*, pp. 41–2.
96. P.N. Jalali, 'Report on Kashmir', 11 May 1972, P.N. Jalali Papers, File no. 9, p. 71 (New Delhi: Nehru Memorial Museum and Library).
97. Balraj Puri to Indira Gandhi, undated (New Delhi: Balraj Puri Private Collection).
98. Balraj Puri to Indira Gandhi, undated.
99. Sheikh Muhammad Abdullah, *The Blazing Chinar: Autobiography*, translated by Mohammad Amin (Srinagar: Gulshan Books, 2013), pp. 536–7.
100. Interview with Shabir Masoodi, 26 May 2015, Srinagar, Kashmir.

101. Karan Singh to Indira Gandhi, 7 June 1974, in *Kashmir & Beyond*, ed. Alam, pp. 256–7.
102. Sheikh Muhammad Abdullah's Speech, 11–12 August 1974 (Jammu: Balraj Puri Private Collection).
103. Interview with the *Motherland* (New Delhi), 13 September 1974, quoted in G.R. Najar, *Kashmir Accord (1975): A Political Analysis* (Srinagar: Gulshan Publishers, 1988), p. 44.
104. *Hindustan Times*, New Delhi, 11 September 1974, quoted in Najar, *Kashmir Accord*, p. 46.
105. Interview with Z.G. Muhammad, 31 October 2014, Srinagar, Kashmir.
106. Interview with Anwar Ashai, 24 June 2016, Srinagar, Kashmir.
107. See Hafsa Kanjwal, 'Building a New Kashmir: Bakshi Ghulam Muhammad and the Politics of State-Formation in a Disputed Territory (1953–63)' (University of Michigan: PhD Dissertation, 2017), chapter 5.

### 8. The Final Stand, 1975–1982

1. Sheikh Muhammad Abdullah, *Aatish-i-Chinar: Ek Aap Biti* (Srinagar: Ali Muhammad and Sons, 1986).
2. Interview with Muhammad Yusuf Taing, 17 March 2015, Jammu City, Jammu.
3. Kumar Ketkar, *Faces: Through the Eyes of R.K. Laxman* (Mumbai: Bennett, Coleman & Co. Ltd, 2000), p. 67.
4. Chief Minister's Message to the People, Radio Kashmir, 26 February 1975 (Jammu: Balraj Puri Private Collection).
5. *The Times of India*, 25 February 1975, p. 7.
6. *The New York Times*, 25 February 1975, p. 2; *The Jerusalem Post*, 25 February 1975, p. 5; *The Hartford Courant*, 25 February 1975, p. 6.
7. *The Guardian*, 25 February 1975, p. 2.
8. Ghulam Ahmad, *My Years with Sheikh Abdullah: Kashmir 1971–87* (Srinagar: Gulshan Books, 2008), p. 67.
9. Altaf Hussain Para, *The Making of Modern Kashmir: Sheikh Abdullah and the Politics of the State* (London & New York: Routledge, 2019), p. 249.
10. G.R. Najar, *Kashmir Accord (1975): A Political Analysis* (Srinagar: Gulshan Publishers, 1988), pp. 58–9.
11. *The Times of India*, 26 February 1965, p. 6.
12. Balraj Puri to Sheikh Abdullah, 21 May 1975 (Jammu: Balraj Puri Private Collection).

13. Sheikh Abdullah to Mirza Afzal Beg, 23 May 1975, in *The Kashmir Dispute, 1947–2012*, Vol. I, edited by A.G. Noorani (New Delhi: Tulika Books, 2013), p. 267.
14. Para, *The Making of Modern Kashmir*, p. 6.
15. P.N. Bazaz, 'The Secret Negotiations on Kashmir', typescript (New Delhi: Bhushan Bazaz Private Collection).
16. P.N. Bazaz to Sheikh Muhammad Abdullah, 25 October 1975 (New Delhi: Bhushan Bazaz Private Collection).
17. Najar, *Kashmir Accord*, pp. 68–9.
18. Sheikh Muhammad Abdullah to Syed Mir Qasim, 23 May 1975, in *Kashmir Dispute*, Vol. I, ed. Noorani, p. 269.
19. P.N. Jalali, 'Report on Kashmir', 10 March 1975, P.N. Jalali Papers, File no. 11, p. 240 (New Delhi: Nehru Memorial Museum and Library).
20. Rashid Taseer, 'Beg Sahab ki Siyasi Zindagi', *Shiraza* 24 (September–October 1985): 56.
21. P.N. Jalali, 'Report on Kashmir', 10 October 1976, P.N. Jalali Papers, File no. 11, pp. 331–2 (New Delhi: Nehru Memorial Museum and Library).
22. P.N. Jalali, 'Report on Kashmir', 10 October 1976.
23. Toru Tak, 'The Term *Kashmiriyat*: Kashmiri Nationalism of the 1970s', *Economic & Political Weekly* 48, 16 (20 April 2013): 30.
24. P.N. Jalali, 'Report on Kashmir', 10 October 1976.
25. Sheikh Muhammad Abdullah, *The Blazing Chinar: Autobiography*, translated by Mohammad Amin (Srinagar: Gulshan Books, 2013), pp. 552–3.
26. Shamim Ahmed Shamim, 'Sheikh Sahab Kya Kare?' (7 August 1977) in *Ainanuma*, No. 8, edited by Qurrat-ul-Ain (Srinagar: Self-Published, 2009), pp. 236–7.
27. Shamim, 'Sheikh Sahab Kya Kare?', pp. 238–40.
28. Shamim, 'Sheikh Sahab Kya Kare?', p. 241.
29. Ghulam Hassan Shah, *State Politics in India (Sheikh Mohammad Abdullah Voted to Power)* (Delhi: Independent Publishing Company, 1989), pp. 41–5.
30. P.N. Bazaz, 'Kashmir Elections and Their Aftermath', c. 1978, typescript, p. 1 (New Delhi: Bhushan Bazaz Private Collection).
31. *The Times of India*, 22 June 1977, p. 14.
32. Sheikh Muhammad Abdullah to Chandra Shekhar, 26 May 1977, in *Kashmir Dispute*, Vol. I, ed. Noorani, p. 275.
33. Shah, *State Politics in India*, pp. 71–3.
34. *The Times of India*, 22 June 1977, p. 12; *The Times of India*, 12 June 1977, p. 1.

35. Bazaz, 'Kashmir Elections and Their Aftermath', p. 2.
36. Shah, *State Politics in India*, pp. 90–3, 116–7.
37. Nyla Ali Khan, *The Life of a Kashmiri Woman: Dialectic of Resistance and Accommodation* (New York: Palgrave Macmillan, 2014), p. 86.
38. *Nawa-i-Subuh*, Special Issue (1977): 30.
39. Ahmad, *My Years with Sheikh Abdullah*, p. 74.
40. *Nawa-i-Subuh*, Special Issue (1977): 4.
41. Ahmad, *My Years with Sheikh Abdullah*, pp. 66–7.
42. Interview with Mehboob Beg, 17 March 2015, Jammu City, Jammu.
43. Interview with Ashraf Beg, 14 June 2016, Anantnag, Kashmir.
44. *The Hindu Images*, September 1978, https://thehinduimages.com/details-page.php?id=153172564&highlights=Sheikh%20Abdullah, accessed 25 May 2022.
45. M.A. Beg, 'Kabina se Mere Ikhraj ke Vajuhat: Bayan', February 1979, pp. 5–6 (Jammu: Balraj Puri Private Collection).
46. 'Maulana Masoodi Speaks', *The Illustrated Weekly of India*, 12 November 1978, pp. 31–5.
47. *The Illustrated Weekly of India*, 12 November 1978, p. 31.
48. Ahmad, *My Years with Sheikh Abdullah*, pp. 52–4.
49. Balraj Puri, *Oral Transcript*, Vol. I, No. 818, pp. 233, 236–7 (New Delhi: Nehru Memorial Museum and Library).
50. Balraj Puri, *Oral Transcript*, Vol. II, p. 243.
51. Karan Singh to J.P. Narayan, 12 February 1979, J.P. Narayan Papers, IIIrd instalment, File no. 96, pp. 23–6 (New Delhi: Nehru Memorial Museum and Library).
52. J.P. Narayan to Sheikh Abdullah, 19 February 1979, J.P. Narayan Papers, IIIrd instalment, File no. 96, p. 16.
53. Shahla Hussain, *Kashmir in the Aftermath of Partition* (New Delhi: Cambridge University Press, 2021), pp. 226–7.
54. Abdullah, trans. Amin, *Blazing Chinar*, p. 525.
55. Hussain, *Kashmir in the Aftermath of Partition*, p. 165.
56. Hussain, *Kashmir in the Aftermath of Partition*, pp. 299–300.
57. Hussain, *Kashmir in the Aftermath of Partition*, pp. 302–3.
58. *India Today*, 31 July 1980, https://www.indiatoday.in/magazine/interview/story/19800731–sheikh-abdullah-mufti-mohammed-syed-zail-singh-syed-mir-qasim-ghulam-nabi-azad-indira-gandhi-farooq-abdullah-congress-harijan-821320-2014-01–20, accessed 19 March 2021.
59. Ahmad, *My Years with Sheikh Abdullah*, pp. 75–7.

60. Para, *The Making of Modern Kashmir*, p. 271.
61. Jawaid Alam, ed., *Kashmir & Beyond, 1966–84: Select Correspondence between Indira Gandhi and Karan Singh* (New Delhi: Penguin Random House, 2020), p. 313fn1.
62. M.K. Tikoo, *Resettlement Bill: A Solemn Pledge Redeemed* (Srinagar: Government Press, 1982).
63. Alam, ed., *Kashmir & Beyond*, p. 313fn1.
64. B.K. Nehru Papers, Speeches/Writings by him, File no. 59, pp. 1–3 (New Delhi: Nehru Memorial Museum and Library).
65. B.K. Nehru Papers, Speeches and Writings by him, File. no. 59, pp. 5–10.
66. B.K. Nehru Papers, Press Clippings, File. no. 16, pp. 75–7 (New Delhi: Nehru Memorial Museum and Library).
67. Abdullah, *Aatish-i-Chinar*, pp. 941–2.
68. D.D. Thakur, *My Life: Years at the Bar, Bench and in Kashmir Politics* (Gurgaon: LexisNexis, 2017), p. 289.
69. Ahmad, *My Years with Sheikh Abdullah*, pp. 67–8, 81–2.
70. Interview with Safia Abdullah, 22 May 2015, Srinagar, Kashmir.
71. Ahmad, *My Years with Sheikh Abdullah*, p. 68.
72. Ahmad, *My Years with Sheikh Abdullah*, p. 67.
73. Ahmad, *My Years with Sheikh Abdullah*, p. 70.
74. Chaitanya Kalbag, 'Sheikh Abdullah's Hindu Communalists Speech in Hazratbal Sets Nerves Jangling', *India Today*, 30 June 1982, https://www.indiatoday.in/magazine/indiascope/story/19820630-sheikh-abdullahs-hindu-communalists-speech-in-hazratbal-sets-nerves-jangling-771905-2013-10-09, accessed 26 May 2022.
75. C. Bilquees Taseer, *The Kashmir of Sheikh Muhammad Abdullah* (Lahore: Ferozsons Ltd, 1986), p. 85.
76. Puri, *Oral Transcript*, Vol. I, p. 238.
77. Taseer, *Kashmir of Sheikh Muhammad Abdullah*, pp. 86–7.
78. Ahmad, *My Years with Sheikh Abdullah*, pp. 157–8.
79. Taseer, *Kashmir of Sheikh Muhammad Abdullah*, p. 89.
80. Sheikh Muhammad Abdullah, 'The Testament' (Jammu: M.Y. Taing Private Collection).
81. Safeena Wani, 'Bashir Ahmad Bashir: The Wizard of Lines and Curves from Kashmir', *DNA*, 23 May 2014, https://www.dnaindia.com/analysis/standpoint-bashir-ahmad-bashir-the-wizard-of-lines-and-curves-from-kashmir-1988661, accessed 25 March 2021.

82. Abdullah, trans. Amin, *Blazing Chinar*, p. 179–80.
83. Abdullah, trans. Amin, *Blazing Chinar*, p. 428.
84. Abdullah, trans. Amin, *Blazing Chinar*, p. 576.
85. Mohammad Ishaq Khan, 'Evolution of My Identity Vis-à-Vis Islam and Kashmir', in *The Parchment of Kashmir: History, Society, and Polity*, edited by Nyla Ali Khan (New York, Palgrave Macmillan, 2012), p. 27; Muhammad Maroof Shah, 'Revisiting the Life and Work', *Greater Kashmir Magazine*, 4 December 2014, http://m.greaterkashmir.com/news/gk-magazine/revisiting-the-life-and-the-work/181699.html, accessed 15 March 2021; M.L. Kotru, 'The Last Roar', *India Today*, 15 May 1986, http://indiatoday.intoday.in/story/book-review-aatish-e-chinar-by-sheikh-mohammed-abdullah/1/348450.html, accessed 15 March 2021; Saeed Naqvi, 'Timely Memoir: Sheikh's Book in Translation', *India Today*, 15 October 1993, http://indiatoday.intoday.in/story/book-review-flames-of-the-chinar-an-autobiography-of-sheikh-abdullah/1/303078.html, accessed 15 March 2021.
86. Abdullah, trans. Amin, *Blazing Chinar*, p. 388.

## Epilogue: The Legacy

1. Naseer A. Ganai, 'Dismantling Sheikh Abdullah's Legacy One Historical Step at a Time', *Outlook*, 2 January 2020, https://www.outlookindia.com/blog/story/india-news-dismantling-sheikh-abdullahs-legacy-one-historical-step-at-a-time/4148, accessed 20 June 2021.
2. Ganai, 'Dismantling Sheikh Abdullah's Legacy'.
3. Today not even the gutted ruins remain, as the house was demolished in 2018 by the individuals who bought the land and the remnants of the structure that was built on it. 'Sheikh Abdullah's Old Home Is Being Torn Down Brick-by-Brick', *Greater Kashmir*, 13 July 2018, https://www.greaterkashmir.com/srinagar/sheikh-abdullahs-old-home-is-being-torn-down-brick-by-brick, accessed 5 July 2022.
4. Amulya Gopalakrishnan, 'Why the Akademi's Chosen Ones Turned on It', *Times News Network*, 15 October 2015, http://timesofindia.indiatimes.com/india/Why-the-Akademis-chosen-ones-turned-on-it/articleshow/49436581.cms, accessed 21 June 2021.
5. 'Sheikh Mohammad Abdullah: A Profile', in *Sheikh Mohammad Abdullah* (New Delhi: Lok Sabha Secretariat, 1990), p. 11.
6. 'A Note by Balraj Puri', B.K. Nehru Papers, File no. 80, pp. 24–7 (New Delhi: Nehru Memorial Museum and Library).

7. B.K. Nehru to Indira Gandhi, 16 August 1983, B.K. Nehru Papers, File no. 80, pp. 67–71, p. 71 (New Delhi: Nehru Memorial Museum and Library).
8. Mir Qasim to Indira Gandhi, 18 June 1983; Indira Gandhi to Mir Qasim, 2 July 1983, B.K. Nehru Papers, File no. 78, pp. 12–33 (New Delhi: Nehru Memorial Museum and Library).
9. *Dr. Farooq Abdullah's Speech at One-Day Convention of J&K National Conference*, 26 May 1984 (Srinagar: Government Press, 1984), pp. 5–6.
10. For the relationship between electoral and non-electoral politics during the insurgency, see Reeta Chowdhari Tremblay, 'Contested Governance, Competing Nationalisms and Disenchanted Publics: Kashmir beyond Intractability?', in *Kashmir: History, Politics, Representation*, edited by Chitralekha Zutshi (New Delhi: Cambridge University Press, 2018), pp. 220–44.
11. Peerzada Ashiq, 'Sheikh Abdullah's Image Removed from Police Medals in J&K', *The Hindu*, 24 May 2022, https://www.thehindu.com/news/national/other-states/sheikh-abdullahs-image-removed-from-police-medals-in-jk/article65456578.ece, accessed 26 May 2022.
12. Samir Kumar Das, *Governing India's Northeast: Essays on Insurgency, Development and the Culture of Peace* (New Delhi: Springer, 2013), pp. 17–8.

# Bibliography

## PRIMARY SOURCES

### *Archival*

Central Decimal Files, 1964–1966, 1963, 1950–1954, 1945–1949. Government of the United States. Maryland: National Archives and Records Administration.

Crown Representative Papers of India. India Office Records. London: British Library.

General Department Records, Political Department Records. Government of Jammu & Kashmir. Jammu: Jammu State Archives.

Ministry of States, Kashmir Branch. Government of India. New Delhi: National Archives of India.

Political Department Records. Government of India. New Delhi: National Archives of India.

### *Interviews*

Abdullah, Farooq. 22 May 2015. Srinagar, Kashmir.

Abdullah, Safia. 22 May 2015. Srinagar, Kashmir.

Ashai, Anwar. 24 June 2016. Srinagar, Kashmir.

Beg, Ashraf. 14 June 2016. Anantnag, Kashmir.

Beg, Mehboob. 17 March 2015. Jammu City, Jammu.

Dar, Javid Ahmed. 27 May 2015. Srinagar, Kashmir.

Farooq, Mirwaiz Umar. 21 May 2015. Srinagar, Kashmir.

Hussain, Sheikh Showkat. 30 October 2014. Srinagar, Kashmir.

Masoodi, Shabir. 26 May 2015. Srinagar, Kashmir.

Muhammad, Z.G. 31 October 2014. Srinagar, Kashmir.

Munshi, Ghulam Hassan. 21 May 2015. Srinagar, Kashmir.

Pandita, K.N. 19 November 2014. Jammu City, Jammu.

Qurat-ul-Ain. 1 November 2014. Srinagar, Kashmir.

Rana, Rajinder Singh. 21 March 2015. Jammu City, Jammu.

Saraf, Om. 25 November 2014. Jammu City, Jammu.

Shah, Khalida. 28 May 2015. Srinagar, Kashmir.

Singh, Karan. 19 September 2014. New Delhi.

Taing, Muhammad Yusuf. 17 March 2015. Jammu City, Jammu.

Yattoo, Muhammad Yusuf and Fayaaz Alam. 17 June 2016. Srinagar, Kashmir.

Zaffar, Sheikh. 21 June 2016. Srinagar, Kashmir.

## *Newspapers/Periodicals*

*BBC News*, London.

*Civil & Military Gazette, The*, Lahore.

*Dawn*, Karachi.

*DNA*, Mumbai.

*Economic Times, The*, Bengaluru.

*Greater Kashmir*, Srinagar.

*Greater Kashmir Magazine*, Srinagar.

*Guardian, The*, London.

*Hamdard*, Srinagar.

*Hartford Courant, The*, Hartford, CN.

*Hindu, The*, Chennai.

*Hindustan Review, The*, Allahabad.

*Hindustan Times, The*, New Delhi, Mumbai.

*Illustrated Weekly of India, The*, New Delhi.

*Indian Express*, New Delhi.

*India Today*, New Delhi.

*Jerusalem Post, The*, Jerusalem.

*Kashmir Affairs*, New Delhi.

*Mahaz Weekly*, Srinagar, Kashmir.

*Nawa-i-Subuh*, Srinagar, Kashmir.

*New York Times, The*, New York.

*Outlook*, New Delhi.

*Swatantra*, Chennai.

*Times of India, The*, New Delhi, Mumbai.

*Tribune, The*, Lahore.

## Oral Transcripts

Adams, J. Wesley. Independence, Missouri: Harry S. Truman Library and Museum. Available at https://www.trumanlibrary.gov/library/oral-histories/adamsjw.

Bedi, B.P.L. No. 270. New Delhi: Nehru Memorial Museum and Library.

Jalali, P.N. No. 834. New Delhi: Nehru Memorial Museum and Library.

Puri, Balraj. 2 Vols. No. 818. New Delhi: Nehru Memorial Museum and Library.

Raina, N.N. 2 Vols. No. 580. New Delhi: Nehru Memorial Museum and Library.

## *Published Materials/Pamphlets*

Abbas, Chaudhuri Ghulam. *Kashmakash*. Lahore: Lahore Urdu Akademi, 1950.

Abdullah, Sheikh Muhammad. *Quit Kashmir: Memorandum to the British Cabinet Mission*. Srinagar, 1946.

——. *Izhar-i-Haq: Kashmir Saazish Case*. Delhi: Kohinoor Printing Press, 1961.

——. 'Kashmir, India and Pakistan'. *Foreign Affairs* 43 (1964–5): 528–35.

——. *Aatish-i-Chinar: Ek Aap Biti*. Srinagar: Ali Muhammad and Sons, 1986.

——. *Flames of the Chinar: An Autobiography*, translated and abridged by Khushwant Singh. New Delhi: Viking, 1993.

——. *The Blazing Chinar: Autobiography*, translated by Mohammad Amin. Srinagar: Gulshan Books, 2013.

Alam, Jawaid, ed. *Jammu and Kashmir, 1949–64: Select Correspondence between Jawaharlal Nehru and Karan Singh*. New Delhi: Penguin/Viking, 2006.

——, ed. *Kashmir & Beyond, 1966–84: Select Correspondence between Indira Gandhi and Karan Singh*. New Delhi: Penguin Random House, 2020.

Aziz, Abdul. *The Convention: An Analysis*. New Delhi: Nav Kashir Publications, undated.

Bazaz, P.N. *Kashmir ka Gandhi, yane Batasveer-i-Sawan-i-Hayat Sheikh Muhammad Abdullah*. Srinagar: Kashmir Publishing Company, 1935.

——. *The Dialogue between Mirwaiz Farooq and Sheikh Abdullah*. New Delhi: Pamposh Publications, 1964.

——. *Sheikh Abdullah, Kashmir Democracy and Indo-Pak Relations*. New Delhi: Pamposh Publications, 1964.

Bedi, B.P.L. and Freda Bedi. *Sheikh Abdullah: His Life and Ideals*. Srinagar, 1949.

Central Intelligence Agency Special Report, Office of Current Intelligence. 'Sheikh Abdullah and the Kashmir Issue' (24 April 1964): 1–6.

Das, Durga, ed. *Sardar Patel's Correspondence, 1945–50*, Vol. I, *New Light on Kashmir*. Ahmedabad: Navajivan Publishing House, 1971.

*Dr. Farooq Abdullah's Speech at One-Day Convention of J&K National Conference, 26 May 1984*. Srinagar: Government Press, 1984.

*Falsafa-i-Tark-i-Mawalat*. Srinagar: Mazdoor Press, 1965.

Farooq, Maulana Muhammad. *Muddadall Tafsira*. Srinagar: Awami Action Committee, 1970.

Gandhi, Sonia, ed. *Two Alone, Two Together: Letters between Indira Gandhi and Jawaharlal Nehru, 1940–1964*. London: Hodder & Stoughton, 1992.

Glancy, B.J. *Report of the Commission Appointed under the Order of His Highness, the Maharaja Bahadur dated 12th November 1931 to Enquire into Grievances and Complaints*. Jammu: Ranbir Government Press, 1933.

Hussain, Mirza Shafiq, ed. *The Political Struggle of Kashmiri Muslims, 1931–1939: Selected Documents*. Srinagar: Gulshan Publishers, 1991.

Ishaq, Munshi Muhammad. *Chodvi Sadi Hijri ke Iptidayee aur Wusta Daur ke Chand Ikhtebasaat*. Self-published, 1950.

——. *Nida-i-Haq*. Srinagar: Falah-i-am Press, 2003.

*Kashmir Conspiracy Case, The*, Report No. 7, *Written Statement Filed by Mirza Mohammad Afzal Beg*. Jammu: Amar Art Press, 1960.

*Kashmir Conspiracy Case, The*, Report IX (I), *Sheikh Mohammed Abdullah's Brief Reply to Prosecution*. Delhi: Roop Bharati Printers, 1960.

Kathwari, Rafiq. *Diary of Khwaja Ghulam Mohammed Kathwari*. 'Nine Days in October 1947 that mapped the future of Kashmir'. Available at https://3quarksdaily.com/3quarksdaily/2015/11/pages-from-my-fathers-diary.html.

Ketkar, Kumar. *Faces: Through the Eyes of R.K. Laxman*. Mumbai: Bennett, Coleman & Co. Ltd, 2000.

Khan, Babu Fakirullah, Sahab. *Safinaye Nooh, almaroof Sach Aawaaz*. Amritsar: Ahmadiyya Press, 1932.

Kishtwari, Abdul Majid, Trilok Singh and Maharaj Krishan, eds. *Irshadat-e-Baba-e-Quom*. Srinagar: Ghulam Muhammad and Sons, undated.

Krishen, Rajbans. *Kashmir and the Conspiracy against Peace*. Bombay: People's Publishing House, 1951.

*Letters of Sh. Muhammad Abdullah, Produced by the Prosecution in the Kashmir Conspiracy Case*. Srinagar: Kashmir People's Printing Press, 1959.

Madhok, Balraj. *Kashmir Problem: A Story of Bungling*. New Delhi: Bharti Sahitya Sadan, 1952.

*Mousiki Kashmiri ka Nava Hissa*. Lahore: Inqilab Steam Press, 1932.

*Mousiki Kashmiri ka Dassva Hissa*. Lahore: Inqilab Steam Press, 1933.

*Naya Kashmir*. Srinagar: All Jammu and Kashmir National Conference, 1944.

Nehru, Jawaharlal. *Selected Works of Jawaharlal Nehru*. Volume Eleven. New Delhi: Orient Longman, 1978.

——. *Selected Works of Jawaharlal Nehru*. Volume Fourteen. New Delhi: Orient Longman, 1981.

——. *Selected Works of Jawaharlal Nehru*. Volume Fifteen. New Delhi: Orient Longman, 1982.

——. *Selected Works of Jawaharlal Nehru*. Second Series, Volume Three. New Delhi: Oxford University Press, 1985.

——. *Selected Works of Jawaharlal Nehru*. Second Series, Volume Four. New Delhi: Oxford University Press, 1986.

*Raishumari Kyun? Hazrat Sher-i-Kashmir Sheikh Muhammad Abdullah ka Bayan jo 18 February 1958 ko Srinagar aur Dilli se Jari hua*. Srinagar: K.P. Steam Press, 1958.

Rajpori, Ghulam Mohammad Mir and Manohar Nath Kaul. *Conspiracy in Kashmir*. Srinagar: Social & Political Study Group, 1954.

Sarabhai, Mridula, ed. *Sheikh–Sadiq Correspondence [August to October 1956]*. Self-published, undated.

Shamim, Shamim Ahmed. 'National Conference ka Kaccha Chittha' (June 1964). In *Ainanuma* No. 9, edited by Qurrat-ul-Ain, pp. 161–6. Srinagar: Self-published, 2011.

——. 'Sheikh Sahab Kya Kare?' (7 August 1977). In *Ainanuma* No. 8, edited by Qurrat-ul-Ain, pp. 236–41. Srinagar: Self-published, 2009.

*Sheikh Abdullah—Dost ya Dushman? Tarikhi Interview*. Rawalpindi: Faisul Islam Press, 1968.

*Sheikh Mohammad Abdullah*. New Delhi: Lok Sabha Secretariat, 1990.

*Sheikh Mohammad Abdullah's Views Explained: Second Plenary Session, J&K State People's Convention*. Srinagar: New Kashmir Press, 1970.

Singh, Karan. *Heir Apparent: An Autobiography*. Delhi: Oxford University Press, 1982.

Tikoo, M.K. *Resettlement Bill: A Solemn Pledge Redeemed*. Srinagar: Government Press, 1982.

*Trust Deed*. Srinagar: All Jammu Kashmir Muslim Auqaf Trust, 1973.

Wreford, R.G. *Census of India, 1941*, Vol. XXII, *Jammu and Kashmir*. Jammu: Ranbir Government Press, 1943.

Zaidi, Z.H., ed. *Quaid-I-Azam Mohammad Ali Jinnah Papers*. Second Series, Vol. X. Islamabad: Quaid-i-Azam Papers Project, 2004.

## *Private Collections*

Bazaz, Bhushan. New Delhi.

Masoodi, Shabir. Srinagar, Kashmir.

Munshi, Ghulam Hassan. Srinagar, Kashmir.

Puri, Balraj. Jammu City, Jammu.

Taing, Muhammad Yusuf. Jammu City, Jammu.

## *Private Papers*

Gundevia, Y.D. New Delhi: Nehru Memorial Museum and Library.

Jalali, P.N. New Delhi: Nehru Memorial Museum and Library.

Kaul, T.N. New Delhi: Nehru Memorial Museum and Library.

Narayan, J.P. New Delhi: Nehru Memorial Museum and Library.

Nehru, B.K. New Delhi: Nehru Memorial Museum and Library.

Nehru, Jawaharlal, post-1947. New Delhi: Nehru Memorial Museum and Library.

Pandit, Vijayalakshmi. New Delhi: Nehru Memorial Museum and Library.

Rajagopalachari, C. New Delhi: Nehru Memorial Museum and Library.

Sarabhai, Mridula. Microfilm. New Delhi: Nehru Memorial Museum and Library.

## SECONDARY SOURCES

Ahmad, Ghulam. *My Years with Sheikh Abdullah: Kashmir, 1971–1987.* Srinagar: Gulshan Books, 2008.

Akhtar, Kalim. *Sher-i-Kashmir Sheikh Mohammad Abdullah: Tarikh-i-Hurriyat-i-Kashmir ke Aaine Mein.* Lahore: Isteqlal Press, 1963.

Ankit, Rakesh. 'Sheikh Muhammad Abdullah of Kashmir, 1965–1975: From Externment to Enthronement'. *Studies in Indian Politics* 6, 1 (2018): 88–102.

Azad, Sayed Mahmud. *Sher-i-Kashmir Sheikh Mohammad Abdullah: Maazi aur Haal ke Aaine Mein.* Rawalpindi: Zamindar Book Depot, 1964.

Baba, Noor Ahmad. 'Democracy and Governance in Kashmir'. In *The Parchment of Kashmir: History, Society, and Polity,* edited by Nyla Ali Khan, pp. 103–24. New York: Palgrave Macmillan, 2012.

Bandhu, Kashyap. 'A Kashmiri Leader'. *Vitasta Annual Number* XXXIII (1999–2000): 60–1.

——. 'Why I Left National Conference'. *Vitasta Annual Number* XXXIII (1999–2000): 43–7.

Bazaz, Nagin. *Ahead of His Times: Prem Nath Bazaz, His Life & Work.* New Delhi: Sterling Publishers, 1983.

Behera, Navnita Chadha. *Demystifying Kashmir.* Washington, D.C.: Brookings Institution Press, 2006.

Bhatt, Aashiq Hussain. *Sheikh Muhammad Abdullah: Shaksiyat aur Karname.* Srinagar: Watan Publications, 2009.

Bhattacharjea, Ajit. *Sheikh Mohammad Abdullah: Tragic Hero of Kashmir*. Delhi: Roli Books, 2008.

Bose, Sumantra. *Kashmir: Roots of Conflict, Paths to Peace.* Cambridge, MA: Harvard University Press, 2003.

Chattha, Ilyas. 'Escape from Violence: The 1947 Partition of India and the Migration of Kashmiri Muslim Refugees'. In *Refugees and the End of*

*Empire: Imperial Collapse and Forced Migration in the Twentieth Century*, edited by Panikos Panayi and Pippa Virdee, pp. 196–218. New York: Palgrave Macmillan, 2011.

Das, Samir Kumar. *Governing India's Northeast: Essays on Insurgency, Development and the Culture of Peace.* New Delhi: Springer, 2013.

Gaur, Meenu. 'Kashmir on Screen: Region, Religion and Secularism in Hindi Cinema'. School of Oriental and African Studies, London: PhD Dissertation, 2010.

Gilmartin, David. 'Pakistan, Partition, and South Asian History: In Search of a Narrative'. *The Journal of Asian Studies* 57, 4 (November 1998): 1068–95.

Gopal, Sarvepalli. *Jawaharlal Nehru: A Biography*, Volume II, *1947–1956.* Cambridge, MA: Harvard University Press, 1979.

Hussain, Shahla. *Kashmir in the Aftermath of Partition.* New Delhi: Cambridge University Press, 2021.

Jalal, Ayesha. *Self and Sovereignty: Individual and Community in South Asian Islam since 1850.* New York: Routledge, 2000.

——. *The Struggle for Pakistan: A Muslim Homeland and Global Politics.* Cambridge, MA: Belknap Press, 2017.

Kak, R.K. 'Pandit Kashyap Bandhu: Some Reminiscences'. *Vitasta Annual Number* XXXIII (1999–2000): 96–9.

Kanjwal, Hafsa. 'Building a New Kashmir: Bakshi Ghulam Muhammad and the Politics of State-Formation in a Disputed Territory (1953–63)'. University of Michigan: PhD Dissertation, 2017.

Khan, Hafizur Rehman. 'Abdullah's Release and Re-arrest'. *Pakistan Horizon* 11, 2 (June 1958): 99–109.

Khan, Mohammad Ishaq. 'The Significance of the Dargah of Hazratbal in the Socio-Religious and Political Life of Kashmiri Muslims'. In *Muslim Shrines in India*, edited by Christian W. Troll, pp. 172–88. Delhi: Oxford University Press, 1992.

——. 'Evolution of My Identity Vis-à-Vis Islam and Kashmir'. In *The Parchment of Kashmir: History, Society, and Polity*, edited by Nyla Ali Khan, pp. 13–36. New York: Palgrave Macmillan, 2012.

Khan, Nyla Ali. 'Conversation with Suraya Abdullah'. *Kashmir Lit* (Winter 2010). Available at http://www.kashmirlit.org/conversation-with-suraya-abdullah/.

——. *The Life of a Kashmiri Woman: Dialectic of Resistance and Accommodation.* New York: Palgrave Macmillan, 2014.

——, ed. *Sheikh Mohammad Abdullah's Reflections on Kashmir.* New York: Palgrave Macmillan, 2018.

Khan, Sardar Ibrahim. *The Kashmir Saga.* Lahore: Ripon Press, 1965.

Korbel, Josef. 'The National Conference Administration of Kashmir, 1949–54'. *Middle East Journal* 8, 3 (Summer 1954): 283–94.

——. *Danger in Kashmir.* Princeton, N.J.: Princeton University Press, 1966.

Kumar, Rajiv. 'Pandit Kashyap Bandhu: The Karam-Yogi Par Excellence'. *Vitasta Annual Number* XXXIII (1999–2000): 9–11.

Lockwood, D.E. 'Sheikh Abdullah and the Politics of Kashmir'. *Asian Survey* 9, 5 (May 1969): 382–96.

Meister, Daniel R. 'The Biographical Turn and the Case for Historical Biography'. *History Compass* 16, 1 (2018): 1–10.

Mohammad, S. Ghulam. *Hayat-i-Sher-i-Kashmir Sheikh Muhammad Abdullah.* Srinagar: Shaheen Book Stall and Publishers, 1988.

Mullik, B.N. *My Years with Nehru: Kashmir.* New Delhi: Allied Publishers, 1971.

Najar, G.R. *Kashmir Accord (1975): A Political Analysis.* Srinagar: Gulshan Publishers, 1988.

Noorani, A.G. 'The Dixon Plan'. *Frontline.* 25 October 2002. Available at https://frontline.thehindu.com/the-nation/article30246359.ece.

——. *Article 370: A Constitutional History of Jammu and Kashmir.* New Delhi: Oxford University Press, 2011.

——, ed. *The Kashmir Dispute, 1947–2012,* 2 Vols. New Delhi: Tulika Books, 2013.

Para, Altaf Hussain. *The Making of Modern Kashmir: Sheikh Abdullah and the Politics of the State.* London & New York: Routledge, 2019.

Prakash, Gyan. *Emergency Chronicles: Indira Gandhi and Democracy's Turning Point*. Princeton, N.J.: Princeton University Press, 2019.

Qasim, Mir. *My Life and Times*. New Delhi: Allied Publishers, 1992.

Raghavan, Srinath. *War and Peace in Modern India*. New York: Palgrave Macmillan, 2010.

Rehmani, Mohammad Farooq. *Sheikh Abdullah ke Nakush*. Srinagar: Aflaq Publications, 1988.

Saraf, Muhammad Yusuf. *Kashmiris Fight—For Freedom*. Vol. I, *1819–1946*; Vol. II, *1947–1978*. Lahore: Ferozsons Ltd, 1977, 1979.

Saraf, Mulk Raj. *Fifty Years as a Journalist*. Jammu: Raj Mahal Publishers, 1967.

Shah, Ghulam Hassan. *State Politics in India (Sheikh Mohammad Abdullah Voted to Power)*. Delhi: Independent Publishing Company, 1989.

Shah, Muhammad Maroof. 'Revisiting the Life and the Work'. *Greater Kashmir Magazine*, 4 December 2014. Available at http://m.greaterkashmir.com/news/gk-magazine/revisiting-the-life-and-the-work/181699.html.

Singh, Karan. *Heir Apparent: An Autobiography*. New Delhi: Oxford University Press, 1982.

Snedden, Christopher. *The Untold Story of the People of Azad Kashmir*. New York: Columbia University Press, 2012.

Sökefeld, Martin. '"Not Part of Kashmir, but of the Kashmir Dispute": The Political Predicaments of Gilgit-Baltistan'. In *Kashmir: History, Politics, Representation*, edited by Chitralekha Zutshi, pp. 132–49. New Delhi: Cambridge University Press, 2018.

Suri, Surindar. 'Basic Weaknesses'. *Seminar* 58 (June 1964): 16–9.

Tak, Toru. 'The Term *Kashmiriyat*: Kashmiri Nationalism of the 1970s'. *Economic & Political Weekly* XLVIII, 16 (20 April 2013): 28–32.

Taseer, C. Bilquees. *The Kashmir of Sheikh Muhammad Abdullah*. Lahore: Ferozsons Ltd, 1986.

Taseer, Rashid. 'Beg Sahab ki Siyasi Zindagi'. *Shiraza* 24 (September–October 1985): 42–58.

Thakur, D.D. *My Life: Years at the Bar, Bench and in Kashmir Politics.* Gurgaon: LexisNexis, 2017.

Tremblay, Reeta Chowdhari. 'Contested Governance, Competing Nationalisms and Disenchanted Publics: Kashmir beyond Intractability?'. In *Kashmir: History, Politics, Representation,* edited by Chitralekha Zutshi, pp. 220–44. New Delhi: Cambridge University Press, 2018.

Varshney, Ashutosh. 'India, Pakistan, and Kashmir: Antinomies of Nationalism'. *Asian Survey* 31, 11 (November 1991): 997–1019.

Whitehead, Andrew. *A Mission in Kashmir.* New Delhi: Penguin, 2007.

——. 'The People's Militia: Communists and Kashmiri Nationalism in the 1940s'. In *Partition: The Long Shadow,* edited by Urvashi Butalia, pp. 128–54. New Delhi: Zubaan, 2015.

——. *The Lives of Freda: The Political, Spiritual and Personal Journeys of Freda Bedi.* New Delhi: Speaking Tiger, 2019.

——, ed. 'Krishna Misri: 1947, a Year of Change'. Available at https://www.andrewwhitehead.net/krishna-misri-1947-a-year-of-change.html.

——. '"I Shall Paint My Nails with the Blood of Those That Covet Me": Kashmir Women's Militia and Independence-Era Nationalism'. *History Workshop Journal* (2022): 1–30. Available at https://doi.org/10.1093/hwj/dbac004.

Zutshi, Chitralekha. *Languages of Belonging: Islam, Regional Identity, and the Making of Kashmir.* New York: Oxford University Press, 2004.

——. 'Contesting Urban Space: Shrine Culture and the Discourse on Kashmiri Muslim Identities and Protest in the Late Nineteenth and Early Twentieth Centuries'. In *Kashmir: History, Politics, Representation,* edited by Chitralekha Zutshi, pp. 51–69. New Delhi: Cambridge University Press, 2018.

——. *Kashmir: Oxford India Short Introductions.* New Delhi: Oxford University Press, 2019.

# Index


*Aatish-i-Chinar*, xxvi, xxxv, 46, 64, 135, 194, 228, 252–253, 256
Abbas, Chaudhuri Ghulam, 7, 20–22, 25–26, 32–33, 37–38, 50–51, 54–56, 60, 62–63, 67, 79–80, 182–183
Abdullah, Begum/Akbar Jehan, 34–35, 56–57, 75, 86, 95, 146, 157, 197–198, 222–223, 225, 235, 238, 250–251; as Madar-e-Meherbaan, 75
Abdullah, Farooq, xxii–xxiii, 182, 242, 245, 248–251, 257–258; birth of, 57
Abdullah, Omar, xxxvi, 260
Abdullah, Sheikh Muhammad: arrest of, 16, 35, 73, 130, 141, 145, 191; birth of, 3; death of, xxv, 239; detention of, 123, 139–141, 147, 151–154, 164–165, 191–192, 195–196, 214; in Kud, xviii, 139, 141–144, 154, 167; in Kodaikanal, xx, 166, 197–198, 201–202; in Ootacamund (Ooty) 166, 195, 197; dismissal of, xviii, xxvii, xxix, xxxiv, xxxix, 105–139, 141–143, 145–146, 152, 154–155, 162, 169, 172, 204–205, 220, 234, 240, 244; illness of, 238, 250-251; interview(s), 31, 77, 95–96, 108, 142, 154, 190, 207, 210, 241, 246; with Aiwan publications, 1968, 198, 208–210; with BBC, 164, 190; on East Pakistan, 219–220; Karan Singh on, 91, 98, 108, 121–122, 147, 201, 226, 243; as Chief Minister, 231–235, 239–251; as Kashmir's Gandhi, 44, 158; as Prime Minister, 84–91; as revolutionary, 26, 35, 71, 84, 98, 136, 138–151, 143, 162, 166, 193; relationship with Nehru xxvii-xxviii, 49, 56, 67, 69, 74, 78, 80–82, 90, 102–103,111–112, 115, 118–129, 132, 140, 147, 154, 160–161, 167, 175–178, 182, 185; speeches of, xxxv, 46, 59, 102, 122, 131, 138, 140, 149, 155, 157, 216; Suraya on, 198, 209; visit to Pakistan, 161, 180–185

accession (of J&K), to India, xvii, xxxvii, 71, 78, 80–87, 92–93, 102–103, 110–111, 116, 119, 121, 124, 136, 138–139, 141–142, 147, 150–151, 153, 156–157, 159, 164, 177–178, 180–181, 185, 200–201, 204, 217, 220–224, 230, 262
accession (of J&K), to Pakistan, 80, 83–84, 102, 195, 210, 217, 220, 259
Achakzai, Abdul Samad Khan, 66–68
Action Committee (for the Recovery of Moi-e-Muqqadas), xx, 172, 186
Afghanistan, 82, 95, 171
Ahmad, Ghulam, 239–240, 246, 250
Ahmadis [Mirzaies], 15, 30–31, 35-36, 40; movement, 8, 15, 18, 24, 35-36, 40, 45, 272
Ahmadullah, Mirwaiz, 19
Ahrars, 15, 35; Majlis, 24, 272
Akali Dal, 237
*Akhbar-i-Am,* Lahore, 7
Al Fatah, 206
Ali, Asaf, 75
Aligarh, x, xvi, 14–16, 37–38
Aligarh Muslim University (AMU), x, 10, 14, 37, 69, 179
All India Kashmir Committee/ Kashmir Committee, 12, 24–25, 31, 35, 90
All India Kashmiri Muslim Conference, 6
All India Muslim League/Muslim League, xv, xvi, 15, 42, 50, 55–56, 63, 66, 72–73, 78, 82, 87; Lahore Resolution, xvi, 55
All India States' People's Conference (AISPC), xvii, 41, 68, 72, 74–75
Ambedkar, B.R., x, xiii, xxxv
Anand, Mulk Raj, 53
Anantnag, 9–10, 34, 61, 99, 155, 222
Anglo-American bloc, xxx, 92, 116, 133
Anjuman-i-Himayat-ul-Islam, 12–13
Anjuman-i-Islamia, *see also* Youngmen's Muslim Association (YMA), 7
Anjuman-i-Kashmiri Musalman, 12
Anjuman-i-Tabligh-i-Islam, 7
Anjuman Nusrat-ul-Islam, 6
anti-Indian elements/sentiments, 82, 100, 136–137, 157, 163, 199, 202, 204, 215, 220, 237
anti-Muslim campaign/communal elements/overtones, 19, 101, 138–139
anti-national elements, 124, 153
Article 370, 93, 97, 111, 125, 191, 204, 230, 237, 243, 246, 260; *see also,* Constitution of India
Article 35A, 146, 261; *see also,* Constitution of India
*Arya Gazette,* 9
Ashai, Anwar, 227, 271–272, 280, 303, 309
Ashai, Ghulam Ahmad, xxviii, 7–8, 17–18, 21–22, 26, 32, 82, 103, 142, 227, 271; dismissal of, 17
Ashraf, K.M., 50, 62
Auqaf Trust, All Jammu and Kashmir, 57, 59, 69, 244
autonomy, xxx, 78, 94, 97–98, 102–103, 106, 111, 113, 122, 125, 134, 136–137, 152, 176, 198, 201, 204, 211–212, 218, 224, 227, 230, 232–233, 240–241, 243, 261
Autonomy Forum, 211

Awami Action Committee (AAC), xx, 186–188, 196, 211, 214, 233, 301, 313
Ayyangar, Gopalaswami, 92–94, 283–284
Azad, Maulana Abul Kalam, 50, 59, 63, 65, 115, 120, 122, 124–125, 131, 249, 253, 285
Azad Kashmir, 97, 127, 280; *see also*, Pakistan, part of Kashmir
Azad Muslim Party Conference/Azad Party, 1, 35, 37, 274

Bakshi, Ghulam Muhammad, xviii–xx, xxviii, 9, 24, 29–30, 33, 42, 53–54, 65, 68, 72, 74, 76–77, 85, 88, 100, 108, 120–124, 126–129, 131, 135, 150–157, 160–161, 171–174, 186–187, 200–202, 211, 222, 254; regime of, 137, 139–141, 143, 146, 148–150, 152–153, 159–160, 165, 169–170, 179
Bakras (Mirwaiz's supporters), 33, 43, 186, 236, 238
Bakula, Kushak, 115
Bamzai, K.N., 60, 140
Bandhu, Kashyap, xxxiv, 8, 26–27, 38, 53, 59, 62, 73
Banerjee, Albion, Sir, 14; report of, 20
Bangladesh, xxi, 220, 222; war, 230
Baramulla, 23, 61, 82, 84, 202
Bazaz, P.N., xii, xxviii, xxxvi, 6–8, 26, 40–46, 48, 51, 53, 56–60, 62, 69, 80, 168–170, 187, 209, 212, 216–217, 223, 232–233, 236, 238, 254
Bedi, B.P.L., xxviii, 11, 53, 62, 64–66, 70, 84, 86, 88, 96, 152
Bedi, Freda, 53, 62, 64–66, 76, 86, 152
Beg, Mirza Afzal, xii, xix–xxii, xxviii, 9–10, 24, 37–38, 58, 61, 68, 72–73, 85, 88, 97–99, 108, 110, 123, 126–127, 142–143, 149, 157, 167–168, 177, 182, 184, 189, 195, 202–203, 207, 209, 211–214, 217, 223–225, 232–233, 236, 238, 241–242, 254: dismissal of, 241; letters to Munshi Ishaq, 143; Parthasarathy talks with, 203, 225
Beg, Mehboob, 203
Bharatiya Janata Party (BJP), 243, 248, 260–261
Bharatiya Jana Sangh/Jan Sangh, xviii, 105, 113, 118–119, 122, 140,152,174, 189–190, 208, 221–222, 226, 234, 238, 242
Bhasin, Ved, 217
Bhattacharjea, Ajit, xxxix, 128
Bhave, Vinoba, 178, 191, 198
Bhutto, Zulfikar Ali, 181–183, 185, 191, 222, 230
Bogra, Mohammad Ali, 126, 129
Bose, Subhas, xiii, xxxv
Bowles, Chester, 175–176
boycott (*tark-i-mawalat*), xx, 188, 196
British East India Company, 4
Bulganin, Nikolai, 147

Ceasefire Line, 100, 113, 172, 179, 216, 218
Central Intelligence Agency (CIA), xxxvii, 177
centre–state relations, 162, 185, 262
Chadha, Tilak Raj, 90
Chagla, M.C., 177
Chari, V.K.T., 180

Chavan, Y.B., 208, 211
China, xix, 95, 166, 171–172, 180–181, 183, 195, 203, 225; allied with Pakistan, 203; Sino-Indian relations, 190; war, xix, 170
Chou En-Lai, 190, 196
Cold War, xxx, xxxvii, 92, 134
communal: conspiracy, 118; disturbances/violence, 32, 46–48, 52, 68, 117, 119, 202, 217; elements, 66, 101, 119, 186, 205; harmony, 81, 86, 102, 175, 259; organizations, 56, 67, 124, 248
communalism, xxxix, 81, 106, 108, 112, 124, 133, 221
communism, 2, 10, 41, 52, 60, 70, 120; global, 70
Communist Party of India (CPI), xvi, 15, 53, 60–61, 70, 88, 116, 123, 130, 140, 152, 169, 174
Communist Party of India, Marxist (CPI - M), 237
Constituent Assembly of India, xvii–xviii, 93–94, 101, 151, 171
Constituent Assembly of Jammu & Kashmir, xviii–xix, 71, 94, 97–102, 110–113, 119, 138, 146–149, 159; elections to, xviii, 100–101, 110, 113
Constitutional Reforms Commission, 61, 64
Constitution of India, xvii–xix, xxix, 93–94, 99, 111, 119, 133, 146, 149, 151, 162, 171, 195, 202, 212, 217, 221, 230, 260; *see also*, Article 370; *see also*, Article 35A
Constitution of Jammu and Kashmir, xix, xxix, 100–101, 111, 147–151
corruption, xxxi, 6, 61, 96, 99, 106, 117–118, 151, 153, 159, 243–244

Danish, Ehsan, 62
decolonization, xxvi, xxx, 73, 259, 262
Defence of India Rules, 195, 205
Delhi Agreement, xviii, 105–106, 111–113, 118–120, 122, 124–126, 136, 139, 146, 149
demilitarization, 129
democracy/democratic, xi, 52, 58–59, 64, 66, 87–88, 90, 114–116, 125–126, 132, 137, 148, 150, 153, 160, 162, 174, 217–218, 231, 233, 236, 258
Democratic National Conference (DNC), xix, 153
Deoband Theological Seminary, 8
Desai, Morarji, 107, 128, 189, 238
Dhar, D.P., 53, 92, 111, 120, 127, 139, 153, 173
Dixon, Owen, xviii, 96–97, 122
DMK, 237
Dogra, G.L., 88
Dogra, Prem Nath, 113
Dogra regime/Dogras, xv-xvi, xxxi, 3–4, 6, 10–11, 16, 31–32, 38, 45, 75–76, 79, 82, 84, 88–89, 91, 98, 113–114, 130, 144, 253: Muslim subjects of, 5; violence by, 84, 89–90, 281–282
Dutt, Rajani Palme, 75

East Pakistan, xxi, 172, 182, 219, 222; insurgency, 219–220; military attack on, 219; *see also* Bangladesh
economic: exploitation, xxvi–xxvii, xxxiii, 2, 30, 52–53, 252; justice,

xxxix, 14, 69; policies, 99, 113, 165; *see also* Land Reforms; *see also* Naya Kashmir
elections, 131, 150, 178, 214, 216, 218–219, 231, 233–234: 1934, Praja Sabha, xvi, 1-2, 32, 36–37, 40; 1937, provincial, xvi, 47, 49–50; 1946, provincial, xvii, 72; 1947-47, Praja Sabha, 76; 1951, J&K constituent assembly, xviii, 100–101, 110, 113; 1952, Indian general, xviii, 116; 1957, J&K state assembly, xix, 151, 153; 1957, Indian general, xix, 153–154; 1962, Indian general, xix, 169, 172; 1962, J&K state assembly, xix, 169; 1963, Indian bye-, 169; 1967, Indian general, xx, 199, 201; 1967, J&K state assembly, xx, 200–202; 1969, J&K bye- and panchayati, xxi, 213; 1970, Pakistan general, 219; 1971, Indian general, xxi, 219–222; 1972, J&K state assembly, 222–223; 1977, Indian general, xxi, 235; 1977, J&K state assembly, xxi, 235–239, 242, 254; 1980, Indian general, xxii, 244; 1983, J&K state assembly, xxii, 257; 1987, J&K state assembly, xxii, 256, 259; 2008, J&K state assembly, xxxvi; 2014, J&K state assembly, 260
Emergency (1975-77), xxi, 193, 234, 239
Emergency Administration, J&K, xvii, 84–87, 109

Faiz, Faiz Ahmed, 53, 79, 228
Farooq, Mirwaiz Moulvi Muhammad, xx, 172, 186–189, 192, 196–197, 211, 215–216, 224–226, 236, 238
Fauq, Muhammad Din, 14
Federalism/Federal, xxix, 73, 77, 213, 240, 246, 262
Friends of New Kashmir, 152
Fundamental Rights, 94, 149, 171

Gajendragadkar Commission Report, 1968, 243
Gandhi, Indira, xx–xxii, 65, 68, 90, 127, 129, 158, 193, 199–200, 203, 207–208, 219–225, 234–235, 237, 244–248, 250–251, 258; *see also* Kashmir Accord
Gandhi, Mahatma/Gandhian, xxvii–xxix, xxxv, 9, 14–15, 27, 41, 43–44, 46, 66, 75, 78, 86,127, 158–159, 169, 179, 210, 236, 249, 253
Gandhi, Rajiv, xxii, 245, 248, 251
Gandhi, Sanjay, 245
Gandhi, Sonia, 251
Gilgit, xvii, 84
Glancy, B.J., 25
Glancy Commission, 25–27, 32, 43
Golwalkar, M.S., 217, 301
Government of India/Indian government, xi, 88, 90–92, 94–95, 98–99, 102, 104, 107, 110–111, 118, 120, 122–123, 126, 128, 133–135, 137, 140 141, 157, 159–160, 164, 171–173, 175–177, 179, 195, 198, 202–205
Gulmarg, 34, 132, 135
Gundevia, Y.D., xxxvi, 179–180

hajj, xx, 165, 189

Hamadani, Mirwaiz, 11, 19, 21, 29–31, 34,
*Hamdard*, 41, 46–48, 51–52, 61, 63, 80, 216
Hanumanthaiya, K., 208
Haripura Resolution, 47
Hazratbal shrine, xx, xxii, xxv, 33, 57–58, 157, 188, 197, 250; disappearance of holy relic from, 165, 172–173; opening of new, 244; rebuilding of, xxxii, 175, 214–215, 225
Henderson, Loy, 95–96, 116, 120
hijacking, of Indian Airlines flight, 221
Hinduism, 4
Hindu(s), xxxiii, 3–4, 7, 12, 25–26, 37, 39, 43, 45, 51–52, 58–59, 86, 124, 134, 139, 238, 247, 250, 252–253, 261: communalism/majoritarianism/right-wing, xxix, 19, 90, 114, 133, 174, 217, 246, 253, 259–261; interests, 40; of Jammu, 49, 53, 113, 247; of Kashmir, 48, 53, 158, 202 (*see also* Kashmiri Pandits); organizations, 26, 174, 202; politics, 15; refugees, 84, 247; ruler, 78, 134; society, 9
Hindu Mahasabha, 118, 140
Hindustan Socialist Republican Army (HSRA), 15, 28
Husain, Zakir, 207

Ibrahim, Sheikh Muhammad, 3
Iftikharuddin, Mian Muhammad, 50
Income Tax Department raids, 246
India League of America, 199
Indian: Army/forces, xxv, xxvii, xxxvi, 82–83, 96, 103, 120, 161, 246; citizenship, xix, 111, 146, 191, 247; delegation to UN, xvii, 92–93; independence and partition, x, xxxviii, 35, 46–47, 64, 109, 133, 262; Muslims, xv, xxxi, 51, 128, 148, 174, 207, 209, 217; nationalism, xxvi, xxxii, 42, 47, 55, 70, 108, 192, 194, 257, 262; relationship to the US, xxxvii, 170; secularism, xxix, 106, 125, 158, 162, 165, 186, 205, 217, 256; Union, xix, 100, 102, 111–113, 115, 133, 147, 193, 204, 212, 230–232
Indian National Congress/Congress, xv–xvi, xviii–xxii, 9, 15, 43–51, 55–56, 60–61, 63, 66–67, 69, 73–74, 77–79, 81–82, 109–110, 113, 133, 153–154, 162, 165, 168–169, 171–172, 174, 178, 186–189, 192, 199–202, 205, 208, 221–223, 229, 235, 238, 244–246, 249, 257–258, 261
Indo-Pakistan: amity, 166, 183, 217; balance of power, 166; ceasefire, xviii; condominium, 180; dialogue, 141, 186; rapprochement, 162, 166, 184; rapprochement/reconciliation group, xl, 162, 166, 178, 184, 199, 207; relations, 162–163, 177, 179, 183, 185, 191; summit in Karachi, 106; tangle, 94; war, xvii, xx, xxi, 79, 196–197
*Inquilab*, 13
insurgency, Kashmir, xxiii, xxxvi, xxxviii, xl, 225, 256, 259–260

Intelligence Bureau, 121, 128, 130, 156, 161, 171
Iqbal, Muhammad, xxvii–xxviii, 12–14, 20, 24–25, 36–38, 50, 157, 252; death of, 14
Ishaq, Munshi Mohammad, xxxvi, 9, 17, 57, 76, 89, 117, 143–144, 213–214; death of, 214
Islamia College, Lahore, 10, 12, 14
Islamic reform movements, 2
Islamic universalism, 261

Jalali, P.N., 53, 142, 188, 206, 210, 223
Jalaluddin, Mufti, 82, 103
Jamaat-i-Islami Hind, 117
Jamaat-i-Islami Jammu and Kashmir/ Jamaat-i-Islami, xviii, xxiii, 117, 206–207, 217, 222, 233, 245, 248, 299
Jamaat-i-Tulba, 245
Jammu, xii, xv, xviii, xix, xxxiii, xxxvii, 1, 4, 6–8, 18, 20, 24, 48, 50–51, 53, 55–56, 65, 84, 89–91, 97, 99–101, 103, 110, 112, 114, 116, 120–121, 127, 130, 136, 167, 173–175, 204, 211, 217, 220–221, 226, 235, 240, 242–243, 246, 260; agitation (Praja Parishad), 105,113–116, 121, 125, 130; Hindus, 49, 53, 113, 247; Muslims, 4, 7, 20–21, 51, 55–56, 69, 84, 89–90, 216; NC representatives/member, 114, 182, 242
Jammu and Kashmir (J&K): princely state of, x, xv–xviii, xxxi, xxxiii, 4, 10, 13-15, 25, 40, 42, 47–49, 54, 62–63, 67, 69, 71, 73–74, 77–81, 83, 96, 259; accession to India, xvii, xxxvii, 71, 78, 80–87, 92–93, 102–103, 110–111, 116, 119, 121, 124, 136, 138–139, 141–142, 147, 150–151, 153, 156–157, 159, 164, 177–178, 180–181, 185, 200–201, 204, 217, 220–224, 230, 262; Indian state of, x–xi, xviii–xxiii, xxix–xxxiii, xxxviii–xxxix, 70–73, 84, 90, 92–94, 100–101, 103–104, 107–110, 115–116, 119–120, 127, 132–133, 137, 142, 147–149, 151–153, 159, 162, 165, 168, 173–174, 181, 183, 185, 187, 191–193, 197, 201, 210, 212–213, 216, 218–223, 227, 229-233, 237, 239, 246–248, 251, 257–258, 260, 262; government of, xxxvi, 84, 98–99, 111, 120, 122–123, 126, 129–130, 140, 157, 165, 168, 218–219; union territory of, 260–261
Janata Party, xxi–xxii, 235, 237–238, 243, 254
Jeweller, Ghulam Ahmed, 18
Jha, L.K., 235
Jinnah, Muhammad Ali, 55, 63, 67, 79–80, 146, 261; visit to Kashmir, 62–63
Junagadh, 80, 83, 180, 280

Kachru, Dwarkanath, 82
Kak, R.C., 68, 75
Karachi, 106, 129, 170
Karanjia, R.K., 117
Karra, G.M., xviii, 10, 14, 37, 68, 74, 76, 85, 88, 118, 143, 196–197, 223–224, 236, 238; *see also* Kashmir Political Conference (PC)

Kashmir, 2, 4, 6, 41–42, 57, 81, 84, 87, 90, 109, 112, 114, 116: diaspora, xxvii; independence for, 64, 80, 85, 94–95, 104, 106, 116, 118, 122–123, 127–129, 131, 134, 137, 140–141, 150, 159, 195, 219–220; issue/problem, xviii, 83, 91, 93, 95–96, 116, 123, 132–133, 138, 153, 156, 161–162, 165, 168, 170, 174, 176–177, 179, 183, 190, 194–195, 207–208, 210, 217–218, 233; nation/nationalism, xxxii, 41, 55, 73, 75, 86, 108, 119, 136–137, 192, 194, 228, 232, 245; nationalist movement, xxxiii, xxxv, 15, 23, 46, 50, 56, 69–71, 88, 108–109, 145, 150, 165, 172, 182, 188, 213, 220, 227, 244; people of, 75, 79, 84, 126, 129, 136, 153, 159–160, 164, 185, 188, 204, 206–208, 239, 242; policy towards, xxix, 119, 153, 160, 173, 180, 220; relationship with India, xxix, 71, 93, 103, 105–106, 108, 111–112, 121, 124, 126, 131, 137–139, 149, 185, 220, 240, 242, 262; self-determination for, xxvii, xxxi, 77, 109, 124, 135, 137, 139, 142, 156, 158–160, 162, 165–166, 169–170, 184, 186, 189, 198, 207, 215, 217, 226, 228, 230, 236, 245, 256; sovereignty, xxviii–xxix, xxxii, 29, 39, 73, 89, 119, 132, 135, 157, 167, 207, 218, 244; Valley, xx, xxxiii, 2, 4, 6, 41–42, 48, 57, 61, 73, 81, 84, 87, 90, 95, 109, 112, 114, 116, 167, 221, 244

Kashmir Accord, 1975/Indira-Sheikh Accord, xxvii, xxxix, 193, 203, 227, 229–236, 238, 241–242, 246, 252, 258

Kashmir Conspiracy Case, xix-xx, 117, 136, 153, 157, 161, 166–171, 174

Kashmiri Muslim(s), xv–xvi, xxiii, xxxi–xxxiii, xxxvi, 1–2, 6, 8, 11–14, 16–18, 24, 26, 29–30, 32, 35, 37–41, 43, 45, 47, 51, 54–56, 58, 63, 69, 83–84, 90, 103, 106, 109–110, 117–118, 124, 134, 138, 142–143, 146, 162, 165, 172, 175, 181, 183, 186, 190, 194, 196, 199, 206, 227, 236, 258, 260

Kashmiri Pandit(s), xxxiii–xxxiv, 6, 26–27, 43, 47–48, 53, 56, 58, 67, 199, 253

*Kashmiriyat*, 259

*Kashmir ka Gandhi*, Bazaz, 40–41, 44–46, 69, 209

Kashmir Mazdoor Sabha, 53

Kashmir Mazdoor Union, 65

Kashmir Political Conference (PC), xviii, 118, 196, 211, 214

Kashmir Socialist Party, 58

Kashmir Youth Congress, 60

Katju, K.N., 122

Kaul, T.N., xx, xxxvi, 203–205, 223; meeting with Abdullah, 203–205

Kaul, Manohar Nath, 140

Kennedy, John F., 170

Khalil, Sheikh Muhammad, 5

Khan, Ayub, 180–184, 207

Khan, Khan Abdul Ghaffar (Frontier Gandhi), 41, 44, 49, 56, 66–67, 249

Khan, Liaquat Ali, 83

Khan, Mian Ahmad Yar, 72

Khanqah-i-Mualla shrine, 21, 29, 31, 145, 155
Khan, Sardar Ibrahim, xxxviii
Khan, Yahya, 219
Khan, Zafar Ali, 12, 21
Khan, Zafarullah, 92
Khilafat Movement, xv, 8, 15
Khrushchev, Nikita, xix, 147
Khudai Khidmatgar movement, 49; *see also* Khan, Khan Abdul Ghaffar
Khurshid, K.H., 170, 184
Kidwai, Rafi Ahmed, 117, 128, 253
Kitchlew, Saifuddin, 55
Kodaikanal, xx, 166, 197–198, 201–202
Korbel, Josef, 89
Kotla Lane, Delhi, 202–203, 208, 219
Kripalani, J.B., 79, 109
Kud, xviii, 139, 141–144, 154, 167

Ladakh, xxxiii, 4, 97, 103, 113, 115–116, 127, 204, 243, 261; Aksai Chin region of, 170; autonomy for, 115
Lahore, 6–13, 15, 20, 31–32, 34, 38, 49–50, 55, 74, 76, 79
landlordism, abolition of, 64
Land Reforms/Big Landed Estates Abolition Act, 1950, xviii, xxvii, 90, 97–102, 110
Laxman, R.K, cartoon of, 229
Lockwood, D.E., 197

Madhok, Balraj, 113, 217, 243
Mahajan, Mehr Chand, 83
Maharaja of J&K, xv-xvii, 12: Pratap Singh, xv, 10; Hari Singh, xvi–xviii, 13–15, 18, 20–21, 24–25, 30–31, 35–37, 42, 61–64, 71–72, 74–75, 77–80, 82, 89–91, 109, 115, 132, 159; abdication/ removal of, 110, 113
Malhotra, Inder, 184
Malhotra, Jagmohan, 258
Masoodi, Muhammad Sayyed, xxviii, 8, 17, 31, 46, 58, 60, 74, 82, 85, 87, 111, 123, 127, 131, 152, 155, 159, 172, 177, 182–183, 186, 189, 196–197, 201, 211, 222–223, 225, 236–238, 242, 254
Masoodi, Shabir, 183, 201
Mathai, M.O., 140
Matto, Suraya Ali, 197–198, 209, 221
Menon, Krishna, 178
Menon, V.P., 80
Mirpur, 22, 58, 65, 82
Misri, Krishna, 86
Moi-e-Muqqadas agitation, xx, 172–173, 255
Mookerjee, Syama Prasad, xviii, 105, 119, 122–123: arrest of, 105; death of, 105, 122
Mountbatten, Lord Louis, 77, 83: and J&K's accession, 83; visit to Kashmir, 79
Movement, 1931, xvi, 16, 20–24
Muhammad, Z.G., 226–227
Mujahid Manzil, 33, 57, 124, 216, 226
Mukhtar, Omar, 255
Mukti Bahini, 220
Mullik, B.N., 156, 171, 173
Murrow, Edward, 161
Muslim: backwardness, 25–26; communalism, 82, 136; grievances, 11, 26, 45; peasants, 11

Muslim Conference, All Jammu and Kashmir (MC), xvi, 1, 23, 31–33, 35–37, 40, 43, 48–49, 51–54, 56, 58, 61–62, 67–68, 72, 79–80, 86–87, 95, 101, 127, 142
Muslim United Front (MUF), 256, 259
Muzaffarabad, 21, 82, 184

Naidu, Sarojini, 12
Naqshbandi, Khwaja Hassan Shah, 11
Naqshbandi, Khwaja Mubarak Shah, 218
Narayan, J.P. (JP), xii, xxviii, xxxvi, 87, 123, 178, 195–196, 198–202, 212–213, 221–222, 239, 243, 249: Abdullah visit, 201; arrest of, 239
National Conference, All Jammu and Kashmir (NC), xvi, xxx–xxxi, 23, 51, 53–68, 71–74, 76–79, 84–89, 100–101, 105–106, 113–114, 116–117, 124–125, 136, 142–143, 152–153, 165, 187–189, 201, 228, 232–234, 236–239, 241–244, 247–251, 256–257, 259–261: alliance with Congress, 235; regime/government, 84-89, 113; rifts within, 123–124
National Militia, Kashmir, 85, 87
*Nawa-i-Subuh*, 239
Naya Kashmir, xvii, xxxiv, xxxix, 61–68, 72, 78–79, 103, 232
Nedou, Michael Henry, 34
Nehru–Ali Bogra talks, 126, 129, 141
Nehru, B.K., 247–248, 257–258
Nehru, Jawaharlal, x, xii–xiii, xviii–xx, xxvii–xxviii, xxxiv–xxxvii, 41, 46–47, 49–50, 55–56, 67, 69, 74–76, 78–83, 90–91, 94, 96–97, 102–103, 105–107, 109–112, 114–125, 127–135, 140–141, 146–148, 151–152, 154, 160–161, 165–167, 169–179, 181–182, 184–188, 249, 253, 256, 261
Nehru - Kamaraj Plan, 172
Nehru, Motilal, 248–249
New Kashmir Committee, 114
Northwest Frontier Province (NWFP), 44, 49
Nund Rishi's shrine, Chrar, 244

Ootacamund (Ooty), 166, 195, 197
Oriental College, Lahore, 8

Pakistan, x–xi, xvi–xxii, xxvii–xxx, xxxviii, 42, 47–48, 55, 70–71, 78–87, 90–98, 100, 102–104, 106–107, 110, 112, 116, 118–119, 122, 124–129, 132–134, 136–138, 140–141, 146–147, 150–151, 153, 156–157, 159–166, 168-174, 176–187, 190–195, 198–201, 203–220, 222–225, 227, 229–230, 237–238, 247, 256–257, 259–260, 262–263: propaganda, 89, 91, 104, 106, 110, 117, 170, 191, 211; creation of, xvii, 79; delegation to UN, 92–93; part of Kashmir 95, 170–171, 180–182, 184 (*see also*, Azad Kashmir); press, xxxvii, 141, 183
Pandit, Vijayalakshmi, 121
Pandita, K.N., 23
Para, Altaf Hussain, xxxix
Parthasarathy, G. 179–180, 203, 225
Partition of British India, x, xvii, xxvi, xxxviii, 35, 70, 77, 81, 109, 133, 163, 182, 203, 247, 262

pashmina wool, 3, 10
Patel, Sardar Vallabhbhai, 78, 90–91, 94–95, 99, 109–110, 121, 133
Pathar Masjid/Shahi Masjid, 25, 32–33, 54, 57, 85
Patil, R.K., 202
People's Democratic Party (PDP), xxxvi, 260
People's League, 245
plebiscite, xi, xix, 83, 91–93, 95–97, 99, 106, 122, 127, 129, 134, 143, 147–148, 150, 156, 159, 164, 168, 178–181, 183, 186, 195, 212, 214–215, 218, 224, 229, 236, 238: movement, xxvii, 83, 146
Plebiscite Front, All Jammu and Kashmir (PF), xix, xxi, 142–143, 146, 150, 156–157, 165, 168–169, 186, 188–189, 196, 199, 201–202, 205, 210–211, 213–214, 216, 219–223, 231–233
Poonch, xvii, 22, 49, 80, 82, 216; revolt, xvii, 82
Pradesh Congress Committee, 187, 196–197, 221, 231–235, 244–246, 248, 258
Praja Parishad, All Jammu and Kashmir (PP), xvii–xviii, 100–101, 113, 122, 124: agitation/movement, xviii, 105–106, 113–115, 117–119, 124, 130, 138
Praja Sabha, xvi, 1–2, 36, 40
Praja Socialist Party, 136, 139
Princely states, xxvi, xxix, 42, 47, 80: Cabinet Mission on, 73; Congress policy towards, 47, 109; contested, 80, 83; integration into India, 78, 133
prison, x–xi, xvii, xxvii, xxxi–xxxii, xxxv, 19–20, 22, 27–28, 30–31, 45, 74–77, 79–80, 135, 138–139, 142–145, 148, 150–151, 154–155, 157–158, 161, 163, 167–169, 171, 174, 198, 200–201, 226
prisoner(s), xxix, xxxi, 22, 28, 42, 74, 79, 118, 160, 162–163, 167, 195, 198
Progressive Writers' Association, 53
pro-Pakistan: elements, 118, 136–137, 146, 161, 169–170, 179, 199, 206, 212, 216, 224, 237, 257; sentiments/views, 84, 98, 118, 136–137, 199, 206, 212, 220, 224, 227, 237, 257; verdict, 183, 186
Prophet Muhammad, 22, 143, 172, 209
Provisional Azad Government, 82
Pukhtoon tribesmen, 82–83
Punjab, xvii, xxii, 2, 4, 6–9, 11–15, 20, 27, 84, 118, 152, 244, 247, 251: Muslims, 3, 35–36, 55; Muslim organizations/movements, 3, 7, 24, 35–36, 44–45, 48, 272; press/newspapers, xxxvii, 7–8, 12–13, 17, 19, 23, 32
Puri, Balraj, xxxvi, 53, 114, 116, 132, 136–137, 152, 168, 173, 190, 196, 211–212, 216, 223–224, 231, 242–243, 251, 257

Qadir, Abdul, 21
Qasim, Syed Mir, xxi, 34, 187, 199, 223, 231, 233–234, 250, 258
Quit India Movement, xvi, 61, 65
Quit Kashmir Agitation, xvii, 42, 54, 70–76, 78, 85, 88, 109, 143, 150

Quran, 5, 19–23, 32, 48, 58–59, 143, 145, 157–158

Radhakrishnan, Sarvepalli, 173
Radio Kashmir, 123–124, 229
Rai, Lala Lajpat, 12
Raina, N.N., xxxvi, 53, 60, 62, 70, 73, 76, 85
Raina, R.C., 135
Rajagopalachari, C., 129, 152, 178, 195
*Rajatarangini*, by Kalhana, xxvi, 252
Rajiv–Farooq Accord, xxii, 258
Rajpori, Ghulam Mohammad Mir, 140
*Ranbir*, 114–115
Rashid, Abdul, 152
Rashtriya Swayamsevak Sangh (RSS), 113, 118, 248
Rawalpindi, 9, 54, 76, 182–184, 209
Reading, Lord, 11
Reading Room Party, 17–20
Reasi, sub-jail, 76
Rehmani, Farooq, 245
repression, xxxi, 14, 19, 21, 38, 74, 97, 116–118, 139, 146, 148–149, 159–160

Sabir, M.A., 56
Sadarbali, Rahim Punjabi, 144
Sadiq, G.M., xx–xxi, xxviii, 10, 14, 36–38, 53–54, 60–62, 70, 74, 76, 79–80, 85, 88, 108, 116, 123, 130–131, 139, 148–151, 153, 161, 173–174, 187, 191, 199–201, 216, 254
Sagar, Allah Rakha, 51
Sahni, Balraj, 53
Samnani, Syed Nazir Hussain, 188–189
Sanatan Dharma Youngmen's Association, 9, 26
Sarabhai, Mridula, xxviii, xxxvi, 66, 127, 146, 152, 158–159, 222, 249
Saraf, Muhammad Yusuf, xxxviii, 23, 60, 68, 131
Saraf, Mulk Raj, 114–115, 182
Saraf, Om, 53, 182, 185
Saraf, Shyam Lal, 88, 108, 131
Sathu, J.N., 216
Sayeed, Mufti Mohammad, 235
sectarianism/sectarian, xxxii, 10, 21, 44, 58, 67, 108, 172
secular democracy, 88, 115, 125
secularism, xxviii–xxix, xxxiii, xxxix, 48, 69–70, 106, 125, 158–159, 162, 165, 182–183, 186, 205, 216–217, 245, 252, 256, 261, 263
secular nationalism, 194, 259
Security Council, UN, xxx, 92–93, 100, 138, 153, 172
self-determination, xxvii, xxxi, 77, 109, 124, 135, 137, 139, 142, 156, 158–160, 162, 165–166, 169–170, 184, 186, 189, 198, 207, 215, 217, 226, 228, 230, 236, 245, 256
self-rule, 115–116
Sethi, Krishna Dev, 53
Shaal, Saad-ud-Din, 11
Shah, G.M., xxii, 75, 196, 198–199, 217, 223–224, 236, 241–242, 245, 250–251, 257
Shah, Khalida, 75, 250–251
Shah, Mehmooda Ahmed Ali, 108, 116

Shah, Mirwaiz Kashmir Yusuf, 1, 8, 19, 21–22, 29–35, 37–38, 40, 45, 56, 58, 87, 172, 182
Shaida, Mirza Kamaluddin, 215
Shamim, Shamim Ahmed, 187, 222, 235–236, 239, 242
Shamsuddin, xx, 172–173
Shastri, Lal Bahadur, xx, 173–174, 176, 178, 186, 189; death of, xx, 197
shawl, 24, 60: factories, 11; trade, 4, 8; workers/artisans, 3, 5
Shekhar, Chandra, 237
Sher–Bakra schism/divide, 33–34, 236, 238
Sher-i-Kashmir Manzil, 35
Shers (supporters of Abdullah), 43, 186, 236, 238
Shimla Agreement, 222
Shiva Rao, B., 171, 178, 180–181, 195, 213
Sikh(s), xxii; 11–12, 52, 86, 139, 158: community, 101; politics, 15; refugees, 84, 247
Sikri, S.M., 243
Silk Factory in Srinagar, strike of, 11
Singh, Bhagat, 28
Singh, Gulab (Maharaja), 4
Singh, Hari (Maharaja), xvi–xviii, 13–15, 18, 20–21, 24–25, 30–31, 35–37, 42, 61–64, 71–72, 74–75, 77–80, 82, 89–91, 109, 115, 132, 159; abdication/removal of, 110, 113
Singh, J.J., 178, 198–199, 207
Singh, Karan, xviii, xx, 18, 89, 91, 98, 101, 108, 112, 114, 120–123, 132, 135, 139, 147, 171, 201, 211, 220, 226, 243, 247
Singh, Khushwant, xxxvi
Singh, Pratap (Maharaja), xv, 10
Singh, Zail, 251
socialism, 2, 41, 166, 245, 261
Soura, xv, 3, 17, 35, 57, 145, 158, 225, 256
South-East Asia Treaty Organization (SEATO), 147
Srinagar, 3, 6, 8–11, 16–18, 20–21, 24–25, 30–31, 33–34, 53–56, 63, 67, 75–76, 78–79, 82–84, 86–87, 154–155, 202, 215–216, 221–223, 225–226
Srinagar–Muzaffarabad road, 218
Sri Pratap College, Srinagar, 6–8, 10, 53
State People's Convention: 1968, xxi, 212–213; 1970, xxi, 216–219, 221, 225, 232; 1974, xxi, 226
Stevenson, Adlai, 105, 116
Students and Youth League, 206
Subbarayan, P., 148
Suri, Surindar, 185
Swatantra Party, 169

Taing, M.Y., 228, 252
Tamil Nadu, 166, 191
Tamiri, Jai Lal, 87
Taseer, Bilquees, 250, 319
Taseer, M.D., 53, 62, 79, 92, 251
Tashkent Declaration, 197
Thakur, D.D., 88, 242, 320
Thimayya, K.S., Maj. Gen., 96, 120–121
trade unions, 88
Treaty of Amritsar, xv, 4, 42, 73, 75
Trumbull, Robert, 128
Turkman Gate shooting, 239

two-nation theory, xxvii, 90, 119, 161, 256, 261
Tyabji, Badruddin, 179
Tyndale-Biscoe Mission School, Srinagar, 9

Union of Soviet Socialist Republics (USSR)/Russian Republic, xxx, 64, 171, 198: pro-India stance on Kashmir, xix, 116, 134, 147
United Nations (UN), xvii, xxx, 72, 92–93, 96, 100, 181, 195: mediated Ceasefire Agreement, 79, 100; *see also* Security Council
United Nations Commission on India and Pakistan (UNCIP), xvii–xviii, 89, 94–95, 282
United States (US)/America/American, xix, xxx, 92, 95–96, 100, 105–106, 112, 116–117, 123, 127, 133–134, 140, 147, 161, 170–171, 173–175, 178, 180, 197, 199: and Indian relations, xxxvii, 181; and Pakistan relations, xxxvii, 147
Upadhyaya, Deendayal, 208
Urdu biographies, xxxviii

Vaishnavi, Ragho Nath, 217
Vajpayee, Atal Bihari, 190, 217
Vakil, Moulvi Abdullah, 8, 56

Wahhabis, 31
Weil, Margaret Lee, 112
Whitehead, Andrew, 64, 87
Wint, Guy, 190
Women's Self-Defence Corps (WSDC), 86, 108

Youngmen's Muslim Association (YMA), xv, 7, 18, 20
youth, 18, 40, 145–146, 166, 214, 249, 254: Kashmiri Muslim, xxviii, xxxvi, 8, 44, 47, 48, 146, 166, 206, 211, 214, 226, 236, 240, 245–246, 260; protests, xxiii, xxxvi, 10, 243, 260
Yusuf Shah Chak tomb, 234

*Zamindar*, 8, 12–13, 21, 23
Ziauddin, Mufti, 17

# About the Author

**Chitralekha Zutshi** is Class of 1962 Professor of History at William & Mary, Virginia, where she specializes in the history of South Asia and the Indian Ocean World. Her areas of expertise include nationalism, regional and religious identities, and traditions of historical thought and writing, with a particular focus on Kashmir. Her previous books include *Languages of Belonging: Islam, Regional Identity, and the Making of Kashmir* (2003-04); *Kashmir's Contested Pasts: Narratives, Sacred Geographies, and the Historical Imagination* (2014); *Kashmir: History, Politics, Representation* (2018); and *Kashmir: Oxford India Short Introductions* (2019).

# HarperCollins *Publishers* India

At HarperCollins India, we believe in telling the best stories and finding the widest readership for our books in every format possible. We started publishing in 1992; a great deal has changed since then, but what has remained constant is the passion with which our authors write their books, the love with which readers receive them, and the sheer joy and excitement that we as publishers feel in being a part of the publishing process.

Over the years, we've had the pleasure of publishing some of the finest writing from the subcontinent and around the world, including several award-winning titles and some of the biggest bestsellers in India's publishing history. But nothing has meant more to us than the fact that millions of people have read the books we published, and that somewhere, a book of ours might have made a difference.

As we look to the future, we go back to that one word—a word which has been a driving force for us all these years.

Read.